Paganism in the Roman Empire

Paganism in the Roman Empire

RAMSAY MacMULLEN

New Haven and London
Yale University Press

Designed by Nancy Ovedovitz and set in Baskerville type. Printed in the United States
of America by Courier Companies, Inc.

Library of Congress Cataloging in Publication Data

MacMullen, Ramsay, 1928–
  Paganism in the Roman Empire.

  Bibliography: p.
  Includes index.
  1. Rome—Religion. I. Title.
BL802.M32   200'.937   80-54222
ISBN 0-300-02655-2   AACR2
       0-300-02984-5 (pbk.)

10   9   8   7

To friends in libraries:
CML; REB, JG, SS, GV, CHC,
and (in general) SML

Contents

Illustrations

Preface

It was a proper melting pot. If we imagined the British Empire of a hundred years ago all in one piece, all of its parts touching each other, so that one could travel (not very fast, of course, in the days before the automobile) from Rangoon to Belfast without the interposition of any ocean, and if we could thus sense as one whole an almost limitless diversity of tongues, cults, traditions, and levels of education, then the true nature of the Mediterranean world in the two centuries of this study would strike our minds. Then, too, we would acknowledge the inevitability of interchanges to a degree and with historical significance not found earlier. Few corners of that ancient world can have lacked their own quite distinct way of life, as few can have felt no challenge at all to that way of life from others forced on their attention by their conquerors, or by their neighbors no longer sealed off in enmity, or by soldiers, traders, government clerks, or inquisitive tourists and their slaves who knew shorthand.

The tidy mind, abhorring so confused a scene, divides it for better comprehension into several social strata, provinces, language areas, tax districts, and so forth. The Romans themselves treated what they had conquered in this manner; in this manner its historians treat it today. But something is thereby lost, as if one tried to comprehend a good rich Irish stew by eating in succession, no matter with what speed, each one of its ordinary ingredients.

In this book I try to repair that loss. It is on the system as a whole and interchange within it that I focus. The constituent parts, the individual cults and their derivation and internal nature, are not my concern.

I begin by surveying the variety so as to subordinate the lesser to the more important cults. From there I move on to the question, Who cared, and how much, about religion? From that to the categories of written evidence that can be used in answer—themselves so many forms of advertisement for one or another cult. From that to the concourse attracted by cults in their daily routine or at special festivals. And after this group of topics, all having to do with the outer face of religion, I address a second group, dealing first with the inner vitality of paganism as a whole and its roots in urgent human needs, and next with the vitality of certain of its parts and the extent

xi

to which one can discern a dynamic in paganism across the two hundred years chosen for study. It is, after all, change and movement that historians are expected to talk about.

In handling such topics, naturally I aim at broad, clear statements. They are not easy to frame. I have found myself continually having to distinguish, for accuracy's sake, between the views and practices common in one kind of source but not in all or in one class of person but not in some other. The need for accuracy sets me at odds with my own aim of easy generalization. It also sets me at odds with many of my predecessors, including "Franz Cumont, whose unique authority in the field is universally acknowledged."* So far as possible, I have left argument to the endnotes; but some sense of controversy inevitably appears in, and complicates, the text of my discussion.

In the religious history of the Roman Empire, the chief event was of course the triumph of Christianity. It would be good if the pages that follow helped to explain how the one religion could succeed universally across the endless variety of cults surrounding it. It seems fair to infer from that universality, however, some set of broadly shared religious ideas and practices within the boundaries of which Christianity could make its converts in Gaul as in Syria; or to put it in other words, the thing so arrogantly called paganism, being in fact all the many hundreds of the Empire's religions save one, must really have shared certain widespread characteristics. It remains to determine what they were within the spans of time and space that saw the triumph of Christianity. The area may be roughly marked out within the two centuries before Nicaea (or the two centuries of the Apologists, Quadratus up to certain works of Athanasius, let us say), and within the oblong of territory having as its corners Alexandria and Origen, Carthage and Tertullian, Lyon and Irenaeus, and Pontus and Gregory the Wonder-worker (not an Apologist, granted, but a great missionary and saint). These are the names and reasons which set the boundaries around my curiosity.

The epilogue is no more than that. Had I been competent to handle Judaeo-Christian texts, early Church history, art and epigraphy, then I might have attempted something more. In explaining the triumph of Christianity, however, the first need that I see is to sponge out of the picture of paganism those false outlines and colors that have been painted in over

---

*Marcel Simon (himself no mean authority), speaking in praise of Cumont's *Religions orientales*, in *Religious Studies* 9 (1973), 392.

the course of the present century. Thereafter, other hands may complete the picture by adding the Church. But not too fast.

July 1980

The courtesy of the publishers allows me, for the second printing, to add a half-dozen supporting references in my notes, to correct various typo-graphical errors and one of fact, and to make my thought clearer on several pages. I may also mention an essay I have written (appearing in *Vigiliae Christianae* 1982) that shows, more fully than pp. 88f. and 94f., how I would explain conversion to Christianity in the period before Constantine.

September 1982

● Apulum

DACIA

● Tomi

MOESIA

● Abonuteichus

PONTUS

● Comana

THRACE

● Philippi

Samothrace

● Nicomedia

Nicaea ● BITHYNIA

● Ilium

MYSIA

CAPPADOCIA

● Caesarea

● Comana

● Pergamon

Smyrna

Teos ● Hierocaesarea

Chalcis

Claros ● Ephesus

Eleusis

Amyzon ● Aphrodisias

● Apamea

Tyana ●

Doliche ●

Dura ●

CILICIA

Epidaurus

Miletus ● Lagina

PHRYGIA

PISIDIA

Tarsus ●

Aegeai

Hierapolis ●

Troezen

Didyma ● Stratonicea

● Panamara

● Oenoanda

● Perge

● Antioch

Cos

● Rhodes

● Telmessos

● Laodicea

● Emesa

● Palmyra

Labraunda

● Byblos

● Baalbek

● Damascus

● Sidon

● Tyre

AURANITIS

● Tiberias

● Caesarea

● Gerasa

● Ascalon

● Gaza

Alexandria

● Petra

Memphis ●

Paganism in the Roman Empire

I
Perceptible

1. FINDING ORDER IN CHAOS

To move about in the Roman Empire at all, or to make the hastiest survey of its religious variety, brings home the pullulation of beliefs. The standard Roman city, if such a thing could have been discovered within its boundaries, would need room for temples to the Capitoline Triad (Jupiter, Juno, and Minerva), plus Mercury, Isis and Sarapis, Apollo, Liber Pater, Hercules, Mars, Venus, Vulcan, and Ceres. So Vitruvius recommends, the architect writing about 27 B.C. and speaking (*On Architecture* 1.7.1) of Italy in general. But he indicates cities with gymnasia, hence he is including the more Hellenized southern parts of the peninsula. At the other extreme, in the secluded little Val di Non among the Alpine foothills, an even more generous pantheon appears in dedications set up to Jupiter, chief, and Minerva, Apollo, Saturn, Mercury, Mars, Venus, Diana, Luna, Hercules, Mithra, and Isis, with only the one true native, Ducavavius.[1] Inscriptions from Philippi in Macedonia give us a Greco-Roman mix of Jupiter or Zeus, Juno or Hera, Minerva or Athena, the properly Italian Vertumnus and the properly regional Souregethes, Myndrytus or Etepancus, to the number of two dozen or more deities;[2] just as the coins of Nicomedia, farther east, advertise more than forty that receive worship in that city, Sabazius and Isis and Apis and Sarapis, Helios, Cybele and Men (all extraneous), plus dozens of more familiar Greek names.[3] Or we can read the satirist Lucian, in mid-second century imagining a congress in heaven well attended by Bendis (from Thrace), Anubis (Egypt), Mithras (Persia), and Attis and Men from different parts of Asia Minor, not to mention another half-dozen more often seen on Olympus;[4] and Eusebius a few generations later reels off the worship in different provinces of Horus, Isis and Osiris, or Melkart and Ousoros, or Dusaris and Obdos, or Zalmoxis, or Mopsos, depending on whether you found yourself in Arabia, Egypt, or some other place.[5]

That last testimony points to an obvious explanation for so many gods: not that the Thracians and the rest, to say nothing of Greeks and Romans, were especially given to the picturing of new unseen powers about them, but that the political unit here under survey had been assembled out of many peoples, each of which had its own system of faith. In the course of time, conflict had brought into being successively fewer but larger states that drew strength from the absorption of divine, as of human, resources. To rehearse that whole story would be to rehearse the whole of ancient history. The process was now over. Rome's Empire under our gaze was complete, and completely tolerant, in heaven as on earth.

Perhaps not quite completely: Jews off and on, Christians off and on, Druids for good and all, fell under ban, in the first century of the era. So did human sacrifice. In the second century, laws forbade mutilation, even voluntary and for divine service. But humanitarian views were the cause, not bigotry. For laws against soothsayers, the cause was fear of popular unrest, not any hostility to preaching in itself.[6] Even a Christian could declare that everyone's ancestral beliefs were permitted—*ta patria*.[7]

That was only half the story. The other half was a widespread feeling that to slight the gods, plural, was wrong. I leave aside the active persecution of Jews and Christians, except to note that monotheists rated as atheists: to have one's own god counted for nothing if one denied everybody else's.[8] I leave aside also, for later discussion, the existence of real atheism. But there was very little doubt in people's minds that the religious practices of one generation should be cherished without change by the next, whether within one's own community or another's. To be pious in any sense, to be respectable and decent, required the perpetuation of cult, even if one's judges themselves worshiped quite other gods. So the Jews could be excused because they were at least loyal to their own inherited error, as one of them can declare to a pagan audience. He declares, of course, only a reason that he is sure will be acceptable. It duly appears unprompted in the mouths of pagans.[9] Entangled in exactly the same presuppositions, Christians were continually on the defensive as deserters from what was seen to be their true spiritual home, namely Judaism. They replied by appealing to considerations that might weigh against ancestral piety, for example, "philosophy" and "reason" against "superstition" and *ta patria*. Whatever their answer, the debate demonstrated polemically one of the bedrock beliefs of both the Greek- and Latin-speaking halves of the Empire in the second century and on into the fourth, a belief presented, moreover, out in the public arena and intended to win approval from a wide audience.[10] As Eusebius explains it, pagans "have thoroughly persuaded themselves that they act rightly in honoring the deities, and that we are guilty of the greatest impiety in making no account of powers so manifest and so beneficent, but directly break the laws, which require everyone to reverence ancestral custom, *ta patria,* and not to disturb what should be inviolable, but to walk orderly in following the religion of our forefathers, and not to be meddlesome through love of innovation." [11] Less often because less stimulated by opposition, pagans thinking only of other pagans affirm exactly similar views. "Such is the chief fruit of piety," says Porphyry, "to honor the divinity according to one's ancestral custom." [12]

Porphyry indicates one reason anyway for saying what he does: the impious man wrongs his own forebears as well as the deity. [13] Human attachment to parents or grandparents inspires the perpetuation of whatever they held dear. Plutarch's father reveals a little more, through the warmth with which he asserts, "The ancestral, ancient faith suffices in itself, than which no demonstration can be declared or discovered more palpable . . ."; and in Plutarch's own generation, among his circle of friends, various members express very similar and very lovingly espoused opinions about religion. [14] All these passages do no more than testify, however, to what anyone would assume to have existed throughout the Roman world, that is, a strong emotional element in religious conservatism. What is more particular and useful is the hint in the quotation from Eusebius above, that innovation in itself was not only painful but bad. "New" was a term of disapproval, used in that sense both in and beyond the debates between pagans and Christians; [15] "old" was good. In the apologies written by Christians, the reader is struck by the emphasis, through position near the front of the works or through length and frequency of discussion, accorded to proving the religion of the Jews, Moses, and the Pentateuch older than Hellenism, Homer, and the Iliad, or to proving the priority of Jewish ethical positions over Platonic. The writers agreed, then, with Hesiod's mode of reasoning, which Porphyry appeals to: "ancient law is best law." "With you pagans, too," says Tertullian, "it is almost a religion to demand belief on the basis of age." We could add many other statements to the same effect. [16] All that needs to be marked out in them is the common ground occupied by authors of divergent origins or aims and their audiences, providing a ready respect for all cults. Truth as well as venerability had been established through the number of persons approving, whose approval was in turn implied by the long survival of an idea or custom. The result was seen as a sort of community decision formed across time, slowly fixed, and therefore even more slowly to be set aside. On that view, more than any other, rested toleration of beliefs boasting a long past.

"Ancestral" is a term ordinarily applied to deities in inscriptions in one of two ways. In the first, it salutes "him who watches over us here at home," and other adjectives may be added to make the feeling clearer: "guardian," "patron." [17] The individual or the community asserts some special claim and devotion. For whatever reason, such rich language is far easier to find in epigraphy of the eastern provinces than of the western. The second way in which the word "ancestral" is most often attached to a deity is for remembrance's sake and from a sense of being a stranger abroad. A letter of the Tyrians settled in Puteoli, addressed to their original home, uses the term in appealing for financial help to maintain traditional cults.[18] A number of other texts from Italy but more often from less central regions record the lonely and fervent thoughts of strangers turned back to their homes.

The particularly possessive assertion of loyalty to local gods can be noticed in still a third way, though much less frequently: on the occasion of prayer for the imperial family, in the form "to the ancestral god Such-and-Such for the well-being of our emperor."[19] The latter for his part repaid the courtesy, when he visited a city, by offering some cult object in precious metal, a statuette or the like, or simply a prayer to the god of that place. So Hadrian, being in the vicinity, climbed to the sanctuary of Zeus Casius; again, made an offering to Aglibol and Malakbel of Palmyra. Caracalla offered a sacrifice to Asclepius at Pergamon, an act advertised on coins; and Diocletian dedicated an offering to Minerva at Ilium, to Zeus and Leto at Didyma, to the sun god at Comum, to Mithra at Carnuntum, and to Belenus at Aquileia.[20] Evenhanded respect shown by the emperors to the familiar pantheon was shown also to divine figures of only regional fame.

Regional or topical names: Tars giving his name to Tarsus, Kakasbos of Telmessos, Vintius on the northern Rhone.[21] Of such, there is no end and no story. A step up in prominence are those names of localities (really attesting purely local gods) that are tacked on to the better known, like Zeus Thamaneitanos in Lebanon, Artemis of Perge, Mother of Zizima—not the great Mother Cybele.[22] In the eastern provinces it is Zeus around whom, or hyphenated with whom, the richest ferment of devotion gathers—there exist some dozens of local versions in Caria alone, for example—and in the western provinces, Mars.[23] These transformations, substitutions, elisions, conjunctions, impostures, whatever they may be called and of whatever origin or end, produced an approach to a defined pantheon for the whole Empire much closer in titulature than in reality. Labels had been attached to the outside of hundreds of separate worships that were in fact very little changed from their form as it had been before Greek or Roman conquest. We will return to the matter later.

For the moment it is enough to recall those lists of independent and by no means entirely Greco-Roman gods and goddesses cited above, from writers like Vitruvius, Lucian, or Eusebius; to which we can add more, from Minucius Felix—"among the Eleusinians, Ceres; among the Phrygians, the Mother; among the Epidaurians, Aesculapius; among the Chaldaeans,

Ba'al; Astarte, for the Syrians; Diana, for the Taurians; among the Gauls, Mercury"—or from his contemporary and fellow-African, Tertullian. Tertullian has a wider range, taking in Astarte for the Syrians but also Dusares for the Arabians, Belenus in Noricum, Caelestis in Africa.[24] A little later, the lawyer Ulpian offers quite a different selection of deities recognized by the government as entitled to receive bequests. Of the eight, five are to be found in western Asia Minor.[25] He has apparently picked out the more familiar names from some much longer list; or perhaps only more familiar ones stood much chance of gaining grants of money; but in any case he excludes the exotic ones that Apologists for their own faith might choose, for polemical reasons, and he excludes the conservative Italian and long-naturalized ones that Vitruvius must think of when reviewing the likely needs of Roman cities.

The purpose pursued thus far, to find some grip, some orderly way by which the mind can fasten on the shapeless profusion of polytheism, can be advanced a little further through the epigraphic evidence. We have at our disposal a quarter of a million published inscriptions. A sizable share have something to do with religion. Those from the Latin-speaking parts of our field of survey are well indexed (not the Greek inscriptions) so that some impression may be easily gained of what deities appear most often. The bar graph below shows the relative popularity of the fourteen most mentioned, so far as inscriptions can be trusted, and excluding the most popular of all in each district: that is, Jupiter everywhere except Africa. In Africa, Saturn is added to Jupiter to make a more trustworthy total.[26] In the four districts, the number of all inscriptions of all sorts naturally differs; the customs dictating how commonly religion received mention on stone at all may have differed, too; so for each of the four districts the total of the numerically dominant god has been determined and divided into the number of mentions of the other fourteen gods, to yield a percentage. The percentage is what determines the length of the bar for the fourteen.

The results must be discussed again in the second chapter, but they need some qualification immediately. First, a goddess like Nemesis, much favored in the eastern provinces, has little following in the western and by average therefore fails to make the select company of those tabulated;[27] similarly Caelestis in Africa and Belenus in Venetia, though both appear in Tertullian's list. Next, allowance must be made for the gods not being what they appear, as, for instance, Apollo sometimes hiding a Gallic god of oracles, Hercules sometimes hiding a Phoenician or Punic god, and so forth. This produces one distortion in particular: Mercury served as the chief translation into Latin for the dominant Celtic deity Teutates,[28] and one cannot ordinarily be sure when that translation has been made or not.

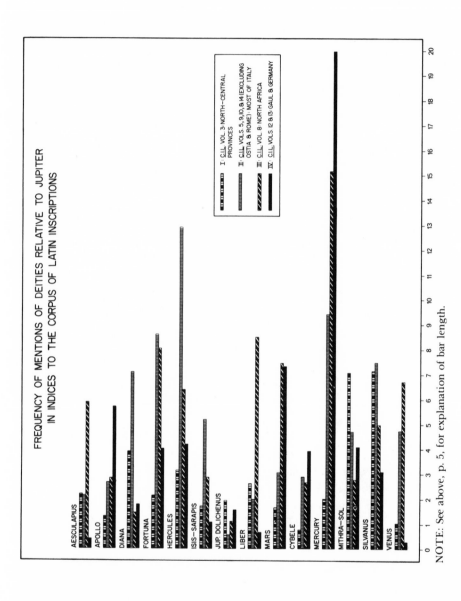

FREQUENCY OF MENTIONS OF DEITIES RELATIVE TO JUPITER
IN INDICES TO THE CORPUS OF LATIN INSCRIPTIONS

NOTE: See above, p. 5, for explanation of bar length.

Finally, certain localities rich in evidence beyond their actual size of population are disproportionately represented, though the gods they favor may not be favored more widely. This inflates the importance of Jupiter Dolichenus especially, in Africa, through the disproportionate number of texts from the military camp and nearby civilian city of Lambaesis. The frontier zone has the same effect again on Dolichenus in the total of texts from Gaul and Germany. And exclusion of Ostia has the reverse effect of deflating certain numbers—of eastern deities like Isis, Cybele, and Mithra-Sol, but also of Venus and Silvanus—in the total from Italy.[29] For what it may be worth, private worship in Pompeii favored Fortuna first, then Vesta, and Bacchus-Liber, Venus, Jupiter, and Mercury in that order. All figure in the group of fourteen-plus-Jupiter used for the bar graph, with the exception of Vesta, who naturally bulks larger than life in domestic worships.[30] The sizable presence of Jupiter, even here, and of course overwhelmingly in public inscriptions, contradicts the view that worship of the supreme deity was mere empty ceremony.

Because of the unlucky way they have been published, to say nothing of their far smaller numbers and arbitrary clustering in particular sites, Greek inscriptions cannot be used to provide even a general impression of the hierarchy of worships in the east. But, in a standard collection for Asia Minor, if one sets aside Zeus, invoked two and a half times as often as any other god, the rest offer no surprises: Apollo, Athena, Dionysus (=Liber), Artemis (=Diana), Hera (=Juno), Aphrodite (=Venus), Asclepius, Tyche (=Fortuna), Hercules, and the Great Mother (=Cybele), in that order.[31] Overlap with the picture in the north and west is striking, but good Greek gods and goddesses, Athena and Hera, more than take the place of the oriental Mithra, Jupiter Dolichenus, Isis, and the rest. Even Cybele enjoys little prominence.

The many gods of the second and third centuries can be arranged in some sort of ranking, then, with ten or fifteen rather easily identifiable ones atop a mass beyond ordering. There is a clear summit to this pyramid, Zeus=Jupiter; there are much less clear planes of cleavage in the pyramid according to regions rather uncertainly defined. But lastly, the gods may be arranged according to the social position of their worshipers.

That the human population of the Empire formed a pyramid like the divine, anyone would guess. Perhaps its strange proportions, however, need to be recalled, with the senators, governors, legionary commanders, and in short almost every single name to be found in the ancient historians lying at the absolute tip, that is, within the upper 1 percent, while a similar figure circumscribes the bare names (lacking anything else we would like to know about them) that appear in municipal senates; so the extreme steepness of that upward slope from the masses to the local leadership is the prime fact to be noted in society of the times.[32] But it is important further to determine if the social fact had anything to do with religious feelings. Where digging unearths the objects offered in sacrifice, as in some of the sanctuaries west or south of Carthage or in eastern Gaul, they vary a lot in cost of manufacture, indicating that rich and poor alike worshiped in the same place and the same way. And in eastern sanctuaries great crowds, plainly of all conditions, gathered in holy days to perform the same rites in honor of the same divinity. Against such evidence, on the other hand, there are to be set, first, more than ample testimony to a gulf separating rich from poor, in contexts having nothing to do with religion but suggesting broad habits of thought; and second, explicit statements that emphasize the gulf. These deserve consideration.

What is likely first to attract notice are the blunt words of contempt and disapproval with which the lettered aristocracy, in talking about religious views, belabor the simple, unthinking, ordinary folk, the unlearned.[33] It is a pagan, but it could almost equally well be a Christian, who deplores any sort of theological speculation by the "crude untaught raw yokels, to whom it is not even granted to understand citizen affairs, let alone to discuss the divine,"[34] just as it is a pagan who tries to place Christianity among the "goatherds and shepherds, led astray by yokel tricks," "the stupid and servile," "wool-workers, cobblers, laundry-workers, the most illiterate and bucolic yokels," only to be answered by a Christian's description of detractors as "the scum of the marketplace, a godless chorus of superstition."[35] Each polemist assumes that his words will strike a sympathetic chord in his audience—readers in both camps, that is, and the more than literate. A public speaker on the other hand must go about it differently. He must not think to offer profound poems on religious subjects "to the crowd and the populace, for they will be thought pretty unpersuasive and ridiculous by the masses."[36]

We may note in passing the categories that are held up for derision: in cities, petty artisans and people of no fixed place of business, the unpropertied; in the countryside, peasants; also, everywhere, slaves, children, and women.[37] What we do not find in anyone is a sense of distance from some particular ethnic enclave, nor even from life in the backcountry. The line of cleavage that counts is a matter not of place, then, but of cultivation, or, we may say, of culture. That line would correspond very considerably with one of class; but among those managing to attain a higher education, there were always some not born to it. Whatever their origin, the educated were exposed to ideas beyond the horizon of the unschooled. Thus they sometimes grew away from the most broadly held beliefs. It is common to find specific distinction made between a theology or point of creed proper for the masses and another reserved for the learned, for initiates, or for believers specially capable of deeper understanding.[38]

Anyone in the Empire who ever picked up a book must have been aware of the two kinds of knowledge, inner and outer, in the philosophic schools, mystery religions, or other pagan or Judaeo-Christian religious circles. It might be treated lightly and with common sense, as a fact of life calling for a simpler and selective presentation of doctrine to the unlearned (so Clement), or it might be treated heavily and with dark exaggeration, to arouse awe of secrets about to be revealed (so in magical papyri). In all its forms, however, it reminds us of something important for the forming of a just acquaintance with ancient polytheism: the testimony that reaches us on paper—papyrus, parchment—comes from witnesses of a particular kind, not only a tiny minority within the whole population but one whose members generally felt themselves to be different from the majority, different in culture, sometimes aggressively so. When they speak to us about religion as they observed it in the rest of their world, their report must be heard critically. When they speak about their own ideas and feelings, though they are much more to be trusted, their report cannot be used as the basis for any generalization about the whole. The point might seem obvious but is sometimes forgotten—with the less reason, given the varieties of countervailing evidence.

In truth, even if we define "literary" evidence very broadly to include fragments of philosophical treatises or collections of laws, it holds disappointingly little on our subject: the essay on the Syrian goddess ascribed to Lucian, the closing chapters of Apuleius's novel, the spiritual diaries of Marcus Aurelius (but that is really philosophy), and Aelius Aristides (and that is hypochondria), all amounting to a couple of hundred pages quite ill suited to the demands of our curiosity. However enlarged by oddments from the satirists or historians, the dark theologists and seers (to whom we must return in the next chapter), this whole body of writings suggests (wrongly, as will appear) that the inhabitants of the Empire were simply not much interested in the variety of worships around them. Had that been true, of course the vitality of interchange would have been correspondingly low, and our subject would bear a very different character.

When one wanted to refer in broad terms to the library of available information about religion, the headings first offered were "poets and philosophers." The pair are a fixture in the Apologists.[39] By "poets" were meant Homer above all but Hesiod also, and others. Their antiquity in itself sanctified them. Moreover, all poesy was divinely inspired, according to its practitioners;[40] and the great ones, at least, were so widely known in the Greek world that reference to them would be understood among all the literate.[41] To be sure, they had no equivalent in the Latin west. Neither did the philosophers. That fact did not deter Latin writers from using both members of the pair as touchstones in debate and verification, for they joined in generally intelligible abbreviation the two main aspects of religious heritage: myth and theology, the irrational and the rational, or however it might be phrased. Philosophy interpreted the poets. The interpretations by Plato and other heads and followers of all the schools circulated not only in works still surviving but in many others unfortunately lost: by the Epicureans Philodemus and Diogenianus, by the Stoics Cornutus and his contemporaries the Elder Seneca and Heraclitus, writing treatises on theology; by the Cynic Oenomaus in the second century who exposed religious frauds, as the Elder Seneca had written on superstition; and by a number of Platonists, notably Numenius and Porphyry in the second and third centuries, the latter in works some of which survive, some of which are known only through quotation.[42] There were special treatises that focused on a single cult,[43] others dealing with particular liturgies and rules of sacrifice.[44] Anyone too lazy to refer to them or in a center too small to supply them might turn to more or less standard handbooks on religion, by Apollodorus in Greek and Varro in Latin.[45]

The object of this rapid survey is the measurement of educated interest in the subject of our study. True, the evidence that can be brought to bear is very little for the span of two centuries in question. It weighs little against the popularity of the sensational—against "the tens of thousands" of essays on oracles that Eusebius mentions, with whatever exaggeration,[46] or against those scenes of worship, marvelous signs, or picturesque rites generally called for in novels and generally supplied.[47] But more intellectual works could still find a public in the west as in the east.

That public was certainly quite small. On the other hand, we can go on to show that it shared its enthusiasms in unexpected ways with a considerably wider community. A traveler to Argos in the 170s found a guide there ready to unfold local myths in poetic version; a novelist or biographer, it is not clear which, has his hero at a temple in Elis encounter the author of a just-finished disquisition on Zeus, which he plans to recite in public the next day; most extraordinary, a citizen from an obscure place inland in Asia Minor obtains permission from the authorities to inscribe on a wall near the city center, in columns six feet high and across a distance of well over fifty yards, it cannot be said how much more, a collection of mainly philosophic, partly theological texts.[48] The inscription would strike the eye of small farmers and peddlers as they came to market. Its author sought to raise their thoughts to a higher plane. With what success, who can say? The substance of the collection of writings is elevated, the language at points obscure, but Diogenes the expositor of the whole must know his fellow citizens better than we and thinks to address them all. He makes clear that he is also in erudite correspondence with students like himself in Athens, Rhodes, Thebes, and other cities. He is not alone, then, in his passionate interest in theosophy. And before he is dismissed as unique, his effort to share it with the general public should be put side by side with something similar at Phlius, where, in the third century, an observer could study "the so-called 'rites of the Great Mother.' There is a portico in it [the city] and in the portico is depicted to this day an outline of all the doctrines expounded. Many things are depicted in that portico that Plutarch discussed, too, in his books *On Empedocles*."[49]

In addition to general public libraries, temple libraries are attested in both the Greek and Latin halves of the Empire.[50] There is no special reason why they should be mentioned at all, so their presence can perhaps be imagined at most large centers. Public lectures presented in temples also crop up casually, at Aigeai and elsewhere (we will return to them); and temples drew people interested in discussion of philosophy and religion—the man Plutarch met at Delphi, perpetual note-taker and intellectual tourist, lately returned from Egypt and points east, or the other stranger back from Britain, all three joining Ammonius the philosopher in the temple of Apollo, for a good talk.[51] Such travelers will reappear later. Temples had resident experts, their theologues, ready to join the discussion.[52] An epitaph from early in our period or a little before praises "the man of many books, guardian of all research, who picks out the ancient page of the poets; lover of wisdom, Gorgos mighty in mind, the servant of the tripod in Apollonian Claros." A wonder of learning![53] But no doubt Claros was atypical: a much bigger and better equipped shrine than most, and as an oracle, for the preparation of responses, specially in need of someone like Gorgos.

Great pains might be expended on determining the things most suitably to be said, offered, or done before a given temple. When a new cult center was established, all this had to be made clear at the very outset and posted where strangers could not help but see the regulations they must follow. Regulations were needed for the worship of a man's son, revealed to be a demigod or hero; they must be specified for worship of a little-known local Jupiter-the-Free in an Italian village[54] or *ad hoc* for relief of particular situations.[55] Some required re-publication through the fresh cutting of an inscription blurred by age.[56] Cult associations bound their members to detailed usages,[57] incidentally offering us a glimpse of what not to do: you were not to vomit up your wine or carve your initials on the walls of the temple's banquet rooms.[58] But entrants in general, at whatever sanctuary, were likely to find notice of what was expected: you were to present yourself suitably clothed, uncontaminated by recent childbirth, by sexual intercourse with woman or dog, by sight or touch of a corpse, or by consuming pork or garlic or milk;[59] you were to offer specified animals in sacrifice to specified deities, or not animals but wine only, or incense only; and at particular shrines you were to respect local conditions, not lighting a fire near the walls, not poaching sacred fish or cutting trees in the sacred grove. Directions might be given on the whole range of daily service, a subject that will recur. And the text might be very long—190 lines, at the shrine of Demeter and Kore in Andania—or very short. At Athens, "by oracle from Hygieia and Asclepius: the celestial serpent of the gods [directs the setting up of?] these statues, where should be offered sacrifices unmixed with wine, on the 5th and 10th of the month at noon. Send a good taste to the good gods!"[60]

"By oracle" was a common way of finding out what the gods wanted. The learned Gorgos would intervene for that purpose, after consulting the proper works of reference. They were, as we have seen, readily available to say what was proper for every sort of divine purpose and why.[61] Neopythagoreans and Neoplatonists were full of information about the effects of diet or sexual regimen on worship, or about the reasons for offering sacrifices on one rather than on some other day of the year. Research in their treatises and the like would lie behind the moment when "the god replied oracularly."[62] Occasionally a god was alleged to have spoken through some person he had chosen as his voice, his commands being duly recorded on stone.[63] Sometimes, again, ancestral customs might be invoked to sanctify the rules of worship because, simply by virtue of their great age, they could only have been learned from the gods themselves.[64]

Whatever the means by which they were communicated, cult practices made up a body of revealed truth rich in content and stimulating to informed piety. Anyone who wanted could read the rules prominently on display. At Oenoanda, home of the eccentric Diogenes, a city wall bore the text of one of the answers given by Apollo of Claros to a certain Theophilus who, in the early third century, inquired about the nature of the divinity. He was told: "Born from himself, innately wise, without mother, unshakeable, abiding no name but many-named, living in fire, that is god. But we are particles of god, his messengers. Whatever persons ask god what he is, he answers, 'Looking upon him, the Aether, the All-seeing god, pray facing east in the morning.'" At Claros, this too on stone: "When someone asked Apollo whether the soul remained after death or was dissolved, he answered, 'The soul, so long as it is subject to its bonds with the destructible body, while being immune to feelings, resembles the pains of that [the body]; but when it finds freedom after the mortal body dies, it is borne entire to the aether, being then forever ageless, and abides entirely untroubled; and this the First-born Divine Providence enjoined.'" Direct glimpses of celestial verities could be had not only through inscriptions scattered about Miletus but collected for easier reference in the Oracle Archive in neighboring Didyma. Before the mid-third century a compilation circulated. Lactantius used it and, much more fully, the pagan theologian Porphyry, in the writing of his *Philosophy Drawn from Oracles.*[65]

Before leaving the subject of religious practices as they were described for contemporaries in epigraphic form, note should be taken of the wide spread of so-called sacred laws given to cult centers. Certainly more often drawn (and better edited in modern dress) from the Greek-speaking provinces, they are known also from Palmyra, Africa, Italy, and Dalmatia.[66] A dedicant C. Domitius Valens puts up a long notice in Salonae to fix the right procedures for sacrifice to Jupiter, and "the other regulations for this altar shall be the same as those assigned to the altar of Diana on the Aventine [in Rome]. By these regulations and within these points, as I have declared, this altar I give, assign and dedicate to you, Jupiter best and greatest, that you may willingly favor me and my colleagues, municipal senators, citizens and residents of the Julian Martian colony of Salonae, and our wives and children."

The text serves as reminder of the particular character borne by the regions within Rome's reach: far more susceptible to cultural challenge than the eastern half of the Empire, where various ways of life were so much better able to maintain their differences; far more directly touched by a civilization, the Roman, that actively favored uniformity and made use of it in the planting of its outposts. From even a cursory reading of Caesarian colonial charters, it is easy to sense that Roman inclination and to infer some corresponding pressure from the center to establish traditional Roman worships in traditional Roman forms wherever settlements were made. If we have only the one *lex sacra* of Diana used for such a purpose, we can at least see it taken as a model in the establishing of practices at two other points, in Italy and Gaul, and with the key phrase, "this temple shall have the same laws as Diana at Rome on the Aventine," all reduced to abbreviations—obviously from being routinely repeated in records now lost to us.

On the larger question, what to make of the chance survival of evidence on stone and the distortions to be feared in the resulting picture, there can of course be no last word. As a working principle, better too much caution than too little. Yet the single inscriptions of Valens, of Diogenes, and of Gorgos each invite generalization outward to whole categories of people and practices. Of all three men, assessment may and should be made by asking oneself, What surrounding and supporting modes of behavior must be assumed to account for their having done, in the face of their whole community, what each of them plainly did do? Students of ancient religion or of society or culture in any of its manifestations must be willing to pause over individual pieces of evidence and make an attendant effort of imagination, in which the only aid that can be expected will come from a survey of analogies. That means footnotes. Apology may as well be entered here as at some other point for all the dense documentation that my purpose seems to call for. In the broadest terms, it is at least clear that a very great deal of religious lore was not only in lively motion among educated people but actively thrust upon their attention from the walls of public buildings in cities east and west.

The *lex sacra* is not the only genre of exposition (or however we might call it) that is hardly known to us save through inscriptions: there is aretalogy as well, the narrating of wondrous powers at work. Thus an inscription from a temple in Stratonicea states "that statues are set up ˙. . . of the aforesaid deities [Zeus of Panamara, Hecate of Lagina, and others—see below] to make known the wondrous deeds, *aretai*, of their power," through further inscriptions no doubt displayed on the bases.[67] Narratives of this sort found an eager audience. Hence professionals, hawking them about— heard agog by the simple but scorned by the wise. Hence, too, a half-dozen texts that survive on stone around the Aegean from as far back as the second or first century B.C. running down to the third century A.D., all in honor of Isis. Their common source one dedicant places in Memphis's Ptah temple: a source already in Greek, however, and in a style that would blend easily into the Greek world. One derived version slips into literature in excerpts; another, into both verse and prose on stone. The most recent version runs like this:

> To Karpokrates, to Sarapis, to the ears of Isis, to Osiris who gives heed, to Hestia who rears from childhood [. . .] I am Karpokrates, son of Sarapis and Isis, of Demeter and Kore and Dionysus and Iacchus [kin?], brother of Sleep and Echo. Every good season am I, providing for every time, discoverer of the

beginning [and end?]. I am the framer. I was the first to construct shrines and palaces for the gods; the modes of weighing and counting [...] I devised. I it was that made Isis' sistrum, and devised the hunting of every sort of beast [...] and I who established forever in cities their magistrates. I directed the children as they were brought up. Hymns and choruses of men and women with the Muses I established. I discovered the mixing of wine and water. Flutes and pipes [...] I forever attend among those in court, so that no injustice may be done. I join in Bacchic revels of men and women, I gave free rein to [...]. I cleansed all the earth, I who live in mountains, seas, and rivers. I spoke from oracular thrones and stars [... I who am] formed as a crescent, and Apollinian, Highway-guard, [Dionysian] Bassareus, [Jovian] Heights-dwelling, [Dionysian] Ind-slayer, brandisher of the thyrsus, Syrian hunter, dream-visitor, vision-sender [...]. I welcome, while dealing justice to unlawful loves. I hate the accursed. To physicians for recovery, every medicine [I give?].

    Titanius of Epidaurus. Greetings, O Chalcis, who bore and raised me.
Liguris

(What the name Liguris signifies at the bottom, and who Titanius is, no one knows.)

Isiac hymns survive in Latin prose of the second century, in first- and third-century papyri, and from the pen of the second-century poet Mesomedes.[68] Apuleius in the second century celebrated Asclepius as he had learned to do in the god's temple at Athens, in both prose and verse, but published in North Africa—"published" both through declamation and circulation as books in Latin.[69] There is a still-surviving Latin hymn to the Mother of the Gods, and in Greek, on papyrus, an author's unfinished verses to Dionysus;[70] and there are favorite old hymns now lost[71] and other favorites even more ancient, recovered now from inscriptions: the Paeans to Asclepius by Ariphron of about 400 B.C. and by Sophocles a generation earlier,[72] plus some otherwise unknown verses to the god by Aelius Aristides.[73] These last are somewhat fragmentary; but it is pleasant to think that in a museum in Turkey a traveler today can read the same stone read by that gifted, boring, tenacious, pitiable, godly sufferer who dedicated years of residence to the healing sanctuary at Pergamon, undergoing a thousand experiences of divine assistance recorded for us in his spiritual diary. It is pleasant to suppose, too, even if we cannot be quite certain, that Sophocles' verses were sung before temples of Asclepius every morning in series unbroken for six hundred years up to (and, as we know, more centuries beyond) the date at which their text in his own city was most recently inscribed on stone.

    That particular inscription is on a monument containing several other similar compositions, not all by very inspired poets. Further epigraphic texts could be added to them in good number, and from as far afield as

Mauretania and Britain.[74] But clearly their ancestry and origin had once been Greek, and in the lands of that language is found the bulk of evidence about what hymns were like, who wrote them, for what purpose, and how they were sung.

So-called Orphic ones survive in a collection perhaps the best known (though there were other collections in use).[75] It contains twenty-eight rather sorry exercises six to forty lines long, sometimes addressed to local deities of Asia Minor (where all the poems were written, most likely in the second or third century), more often to deities like Artemis, Asclepius, Eros, and Hermes. For example, the ninth: twelve lines that string together nothing but thirty-three adjectives, seven adjectival phrases, two imperative verbs, and two nouns ("king" and "maiden"), one of which is very boldly repeated three times. Sophocles did better! But it is not untypical of the genre, in apostrophizing the deity named, describing him or her honorifically as descended in thus-and-such a line, capable of thus-and-such wondrous actions, known in thus-and-such celestial haunts, gracious to petitioners, Hail! Attend! Occasions needing particular celebration in verse outnumbered and exhausted the Muses. There was the initiation of aspirants to a fuller knowledge of some god,[76] plagues or imperial visits to be called to divine attention,[77] festival parades, and daily services.[78] Quality suffered. For hymns, simple shouted phrases might be substituted in the god's honor (for Asclepius at Pergamon, at least sometimes) or the mystic litany, "Bedu, zaps, chthon, plectron, sphinx, cnaxzbich, thuptes, phlegmo, drops!" (for Apollo at Didyma).[79]

Instrumental accompaniment one expected to hear from worshipers of Cybele, Mother of the Gods, both those itinerant and at fixed sanctuaries. Typically, they played pipes made with reeds like oboes or bagpipes, ah! bagpipes of a shrill and carrying note.[80] The cithara belonged especially to Apollo;[81] to Isis, the rattle (*sistrum*), along with other instruments.[82] Censorinus writes, "If it [music] were not welcome to the immortal gods, theater spectacles would not have been instituted to conciliate the gods, the horn-player would not be used in all sacrifices in sacred temples, nor would triumphal parades be conducted with the horn or bass-horn player in honor of Mars, with the cithara for Apollo, with the pipes for the Muses...."[83] The picture Censorinus offers, of accompaniment suited to the god honored, may be too schematic, but in its broad assertion of the habitual place of music in worship it is certainly true to life. It serves further to introduce scenes of worship that are not Greek. In fact, music could be heard at shrines of many —we cannot be sure of all—large regions throughout the Empire.[84] Both at the heart of Greece and in an obscure shrine of Asia, both to the great Apollo and to the unknown Sinuri, hymns were inscribed on their temple's walls with musical notation, presumably to instruct casual worshipers in the most acceptable tune.[85] Hymners who appear to have been specialists and at least semiprofessional were sometimes heard; but they cost more than cities, and obviously more than cult groups, could easily afford; so either the emperor paid for them to serve the imperial cult or they served more than one master.[86]

The word "hymner," *hymnodos,* may also indicate a sort of master of musical ceremonies, semihonorific. Choruses made up of amateurs were the general rule where cult and music were joined, choruses sometimes of men or women of the upper class, sometimes of their daughters, normally of their sons, boys before their voices changed.[87] They sang in groups of twenty-five or thirty, except when they traveled to the oracle of Apollo at Claros near Colophon. Then they usually numbered nine. As many inscriptions from Claros make plain, it was almost obligatory for corporate inquirers, that is, cities as such, to return thanks for answers given them by singing a hymn. In the second century, when the oracle enjoyed great fame, it heard delegations of boys, their trainers, and conductors from many distant places.[88] It is odd to think of little groups of children, of course very strictly chaperoned, traveling a hundred miles or more to the sanctuary "in obedience to the oracle," as the inscriptions declare. After their performance was over, they had their names put up on the walls of the shrine, along with the names of the adults in the party.

From hymnology and aretalogy to my point of departure—general knowledge about religion—I return by way of hymners who were also theologians, or theologians who were in charge of religious music;[89] for in either combination they suggest a close working relation between the two kinds of expert. Moreover, hymners had also to pronounce prose hymns, called "theologies."[90] The third-century professor of eloquence, Menander of Laodicea, wrote a short guide to their composition. They were to dwell "on the naming of a god, or on valedictory, or on the god's nature or story or birth or form, or to invoke or deter, or a mixture"—which sounds exactly like the advice offered by Alexander the Rhetor in the preceding century or like the epigraphic texts discussed some pages past—with the difference that they were not versified. Menander indicates elsewhere the freedom he would allow to speeches of praise—here, however, praising men, not gods: "You should invent dreams and pretend to have heard certain voices and wish to proclaim them to your listeners, or of dreams, for example, that Hermes stood by your bed at night, commanding you to announce who was the best of the magistrates; and, 'Obedient to his commands, I will repeat from the very center of theaters what I heard him say. . . .' " [91] That last boast recalls another passage with the same setting, "when the populace assembles in the theaters and someone enters wrapped in some special robe, carrying a cithara and singing to it (as he says in the hymn of the Great Initiation, without knowing what he says), 'Whether offspring of Kronos, whether blessed of Zeus, whether of great Rhea, hail to thee, mournful message of Rhea, O Attis. The Syrians call you Adonis, thrice-desired, all Egypt calls you Osiris, Greek wisdom calls you the heavenly crescent of the month, Samothracians, venerable Adamna; the people of Haemon, Corybas; and the Phrygians, sometimes Papa, sometimes the corpse, the god, the sterile unharvested, or the goat-herd, the verdant ear of grain gathered in, or the piper whom fruitful Amygdalos brought forth.' " And so he continues, quoting next from a hymn to Attis. [92]

2. ATTRACTING CROWDS

"In the theaters . . ." Alexander and Menander, who made their living by speaking to a general audience and, in their handbooks, by writing for a still wider one, and who must then be supposed to have intended nothing at odds with prevailing views but everything conventional, acceptable, and safe, are the very best witnesses a historian could ask for—that is, if he seeks to define broad cultural phenomena. Of which, first and most obvious to be noticed is the size of audience implied by the need for a theater at all, a theater called into use to hear verse or prose hymns about the gods only because there were very large numbers of people to whom such things were really important.

In the northwestern provinces, the evidence for crowds of worshipers gathering around some cult exposition or spectacle is archaeological, unassisted by the literary; and the prime site is typically rural, not in some city center. Adjoining dozens of more or less isolated temples are cult theaters, sometimes right inside the same sanctuary wall. Functional links between the two kinds of building are clearly indicated by various facts but are actually clinched by those cases where the pair lie along a single axis; so seated spectators could see past the stage (which lacks or breaks the backdrop or *scaenae frons*) to the temple's front, beyond. Just what those spectators witnessed, no one knows—no doubt the acting out of scenes or musical performances illustrative of the beliefs of the local cult. It was not one god but many that received this tribute, in central and northern France and the Moselle and upper Rhine valleys. It can have been offered only at festivals, not daily or weekly, to attract the crowds requiring such accommodations. They numbered many thousands where they can be counted, for example at Sanxay and Grand in southwestern and central France.[1]

In the provinces of North Africa, only one similar site is known, a Hadrianic temple to Liber having a small stepped structure suitable for seating at one end of the sanctuary, but lacking a stage.[2] It turns its back on the temple. Tertullian gives a characteristically high-colored treatment to theatrical presentations in Carthage with religious subjects. We will return to them. But they were offered in secular amphitheaters, connected to shrines only by the inaugural parades that reached them "from temples and altars."[3] Moreover, they only followed Roman practices, brought in with everything else Roman in the course of conquest and settlement. In their land of origin, Italy itself, such practices are too familiar to need description.[4]

The Syrian priest and worshipers of Hadad and Atargatis dedicated a theater on Delos in 108/7 B.C. It lay at one end of a terrace, the other end of which held the temple; and on holy days the seated idol was paraded out of her house, along the terrace, to a marble throne that faced the theater, there to receive offerings at an altar in front of her. What else was shown the spectators is not known. Not quite a century later in the Hawran (Auranitis) at Seeia (Si'), the temple of Ba'al-shamin was equipped with steps that could be sat on along three sides of the main court, shaded by a portico behind them, and with the temple front as the fourth side. The whole can be identified as a theater by an inscription, and compared to closely similar arrangements at two other sites in the region, Sur of the first century B.C. or A.D. and Sahr of a slightly later date, with the difference that in the latter two the steps are actually inside and covered by the portico, and that the temple at Sahr is also flanked by a small proper theater capable of seating several hundred people.[5] Moving north, a mile outside Gerasa lies the sacred pool for the Maioumas festival, connected to the city by a sacred boulevard and flanked by a Severan theater with fourteen rows of seats. From the upper ones there was a clear view through the stage (lacking a backdrop) to the pool.[6] Next, to the obscure sanctuary of Artemis at Amyzon in Caria, with a theater;[7] and so on to Dura on the Euphrates. There, the theater attached to the shrine of Artemis Nanaia was a little smaller (fourteen meters in diameter), ensconced in a closed building, and therefore too dark for anything but dancing or singing; and there were four more tiny theaters in the town tied to shrines of other Syrian deities.[8]

Theaters for the ceremonies of Syrian cults, spread over several centuries and a very wide area, display a good deal of variety, but they have in common the need to accommodate only limited numbers. The most natural explanation for that is the use of the facilities for special doings in which a minority of worshipers participated at any given time. That in turn might be explained by the cult's offering revelations to which all members were exposed only once in their lives, or rarely. Of this, however, nothing can be said for certain; and in any case it is not my purpose to discuss more than the open face and shared aspects of religious practices.

Accordingly, there is no need to do more than mention some of the cult theaters for initiates in the Greek world proper. Of these, Eleusis is best known. Clement of Alexandria, for example, speaks of its rites as still administered in his own day.[9] The telesterion at Samothrace, with wooden benches around three sides and a sign at the door, "Noninitiates stay out," is familiar, too.[10] More to my purpose because of its more significant dimensions is the theater facing the temple front of the god Cabiros, a few miles from Thebes in Boeotia. It had room for one to two thousand spectators.[11] And better still, the great Asclepius shrines at Pergamon and Epidaurus. The former lay some distance out of the city, at the end of a sacred boulevard, and included a 3,500-seat theater adjacent to one corner of the quite immense walled and porticoed sacred enclosure; the latter, Epidaurus, though its shrine lay far off the beaten track, nevertheless required a theater to hold 12,000–15,000. That was for crowds attending the festival every four years.[12] Pausanias in the second century marveled at its proportions.

We cannot assume, however, that the wide and intense interest and enjoyment in the "spectacular" side of worship (using the word in its root sense), here at these locations so spectacularly accommodated, did not also exist where similar facilities do not happen to be demonstrable. People rather made do with available substitutes. They used wooden bleachers which have left no trace for the archaeologist,[13] or, as at Altbachtal near Trier, they placed odd-sized, half-cut stones for seats in a rough half-circle around the slopes of a natural cup of land—facilities very easily overlooked in excavation. Or again, they borrowed the city's central square for a few days[14]—preferably, the city's secular theater or amphitheater. In Italian or Romanized cities, performances with religious themes so offensive to the Apologists inevitably took place where, on the next day, there might be executions or gladiatorial combats. We will touch on those scandalous dramas very shortly. But in the eastern provinces, in what category, secular or holy, should we place the theater in which ended the procession of Artemis's worshipers, in Ephesus, and in which the icon was ceremonially enthroned to oversee, perhaps in its wooden way to enjoy, the musical, dramatic, and athletic events? In what category should we place the gladiatorial troupe hired for exhibits locally by high priests, or (no doubt purely secular) dancers and musicians paid to perform in the city theater all year long, as a gift from the ministrants of Hecate?[15] Above all, there are the shows that took place in the precincts of temples where, as is already clear in shrines of Syria, steps could serve as seats. As much may be assumed of the hundred yards of stairway with its eleven steps that stretch around the enclosure at Lagina in Caria; as much is implied by the like features at Didyma near Miletus and Eleusis near Athens.[16] Direct testimony to the requirements of gatherings largely or wholly religious in purpose is enough, surely, to give some sense of the weight or significance of that purpose in the daily life of the Empire. But indirect testimony, too, carries weight: for every piece of evidence must be measured in terms of the likelihood of its survival. By that measurement, crowds attending in hundreds or thousands must be taken for granted even in settings where their voices have been cut off by the total silence of our sources.

Spectators in the numbers described could hardly have been assembled for a lecture on theosophy. Something else it was that drew them: a varied bill of entertainment, but still all holy. The Maioumas, notorious set of rites at Gerasa, brought women out of town to a sacred pool in the suburbs, there to bathe naked, that is, to be purified and magicked in some way never really described, before the stare of the townsfolk.[17] But it happened only every third year. Annually at Patrai, on the other hand, occurred a sort of roundup of wild animals, a great battue, driving them into a corral dedicated to Artemis, and up a ramp, and so (apparently) right on to a bonfire. Pausanias describes the amazing scene—perhaps duplicated, however, at another city in Pontus.[18] In areas and cities not enjoying an inheritance of customs so dramatic, there were nevertheless very rich entertainments provided to visitors by the generosity of liturgists, hiring professionals. Companies of dancers made their living through sale of their services to many, many shrines. They specialized in the forms traditional to particular cults: the Silens of Dionysus at Pergamon, the *kinaedoi* or wagtails of Oriental cults (most often connected with Egypt), the *ballatores* of Cybele, the *akrobatai* or toe dancers of Artemis, the armed Couretes for the same goddess at Ephesus.[19] What everyone most liked to watch, however, were miming dancers. Those in Egypt added their motions to the reading aloud of holy texts by the priest, producing "danced hymns," as they have been well described. The performers were professionals, men and women popular the length and breadth of the province.[20]

Clement of Alexandria has a great deal to say, none of it good, about the depiction of gods and goddesses acted out in initiatory performances. Perhaps he means plays, not ballets; but his brother Apologists to the west— Cyprian, Minucius Felix, and the other Africans of the second and third

A relief found not far from Rome (Ariccia) shows a religious scene in Egypt, identified by the ibises in the foreground and icons in a row at the back. To the right, on the stairs of a temple, worshipers gesticulate with the music. In the temple court—though C. Picard (1955) 244 would see a cult theater—dancers clack sticks like castanets and whirl and wiggle frenziedly. Some may be female, others male. The latter are nicknamed in Greek "wagtails" after the word for swallows, since the swallow is a bird "qui agite particulièrement la partie inférieure du corps" (so Bernand 2 [1969] 121, discreetly).

centuries—make clear that there was no sharp distinction between actors and dancers. The same word was used for both, and their means of portraying stories were mingled. In the amphitheaters, "your deities dance, supplying themes and stories to the wicked." Performers can "call up your tears with make-believe agonies through the empty movements of hand or head," and Venus leading a troupe of child dancers as Cupids uses her own glances so expressively that she can be said "to leap with her eyes alone."[21] Venus was a popular subject, Hera also, Zeus or Jupiter, all in erotic scenes no doubt presented very suggestively. Tertullian (*Ad nat.* 15) reels off a list of common favorites on the stage: "Anubis Adulterer, Mr. Moon, Diana Flogged, Jove's Last Testament, and as a comedy, Three Hungry Herculeses."

In Italy, too, dancers and actors were more or less interchangeable.[22] They were of course active in the capital, but in lots of towns up and down Latium and Campania as well, playing the same parts as their like in Alexandria or Carthage and just as closely tied to some of the major cults.

They too used the tilt of the head, eyes, eyebrows, hands, and very fingertips to communicate a great range of thoughts and feelings, much like Oriental dancers to this day.[23] Presumably they found a responsive knowledge of sign language among their audience, for much of the repertoire was highly traditional, and symbolic gestures would soon settle into their own conventions.

Tradition went by region. Each had its own. So one writer speaks of rites addressed "to Egyptian deities generally by lament, to the Greek for the most part by choruses, but to the non-Greek by the clangor of cymbalists, drummers and pipe-accompanists"; or to the same effect, another reports that "the Bacchic dance is taken especially seriously in Ionia and Pontus, although it belongs to Satyric drama, and has so taken hold of people there that, in the appointed [i.e., festival] time, they put aside everything else and sit the day through, watching corybants, Satyrs and shepherds; and people of the best lineage and foremost in every city dance, not in the least embarrassed but proud of it."[24] Lucian, the author of this latter passage, also cites a number of other local specialties. "At Delos not even the sacrifices are offered without dancing. . . . Boy choruses assembled and, to the pipe and cithara, some moved about, singing, while the best performed a dance in accompaniment; and hymns written for such choirs are called dances-for-accompaniment."[25] It is likely that, wherever cult dancing is found in the Greek-speaking world, it has something of local color about it.[26]

That takes care of the great public ceremonies on holy days and the religious use of the really large municipal theaters at places like Pergamon; but there are the smaller facilities at Samothrace and elsewhere still to be filled. They served "Mysteries." The word conjures up quite mistaken ideas of secrets about the gods revealed in darkness to a tiny circle of oath-bound devotees. At all periods there were indeed such groups and rituals—elaborate ceremonies reserved for the specially devout (or wealthy), or more often viewed by neighbors with disapproval or alarm (see section 3, n. 29, below). A *mysterion* normally meant something more open and unexciting, essentially a lesson in a cult to be learned, perhaps by very large numbers at a time, as in the Eleusinian rites or in the mystery cult best known in the period of our study, that of Cybele. Its setting might be in cities of Asia Minor, where "the populace assembles in the theaters and someone enters . . ."—but the description has been quoted already.[27] We gather from the context as well as the explicit words that anyone at all could attend, quite unchallenged, exactly as one would gather also from the facts: first, that children and professionals—that is, outsiders—were employed in the choruses to sing the hymns of revelation;[28] second, that theaters for mysteries were designed to hold, not scores, but hundreds or thousands. Lucian, in his recollections of his old teacher *Demonax* (11), reports how that free-thinker was pilloried in Athens as "the only person of all that had never been initiated into the Eleusinian mysteries." No very select company, those votaries! And the same author, in his essay *On Dance* (15), tells us "there are no ancient rites of initiation without dancing," which satisfactorily distributes over a very wide area the conclusions forced on us from other directions: so-called mysteries were in general quite open, come-if-you-wish ceremonies, to which as large an audience as possible was attracted by interpretive dancing, singing and music of all sorts.

"Barbarian" or "non-Greek" rites, notably of Atargatis, Isis, and the Phrygian Cybele, made use of inspired, mad dancing that produced a great impression on observers and was also easily and often seen, since its practitioners wandered about in public in search of an audience. To the sound of rattles, tambours, and shrill pipes, with their heads tipped back or rolling wildly on their shoulders, accompanied by their own howls and yells, they whirled about and worked themselves into a state of frenzy. Then they held out the begging bowl. The scene meets us in poems, novels, and frescoes—all too familiar to need discussion.[29]

The entire range of musical instruments known to the world of the Apologists was called into the service of the gods in one cult or another,[30] along with every conceivable style of dance and song, theatrical show, prose hymn, lecture or tractate philosophizing, popularizing, edifying, and so forth—in sum, the whole of culture, so it would seem. The same conclusion can be expressed negatively. From the arts of those centuries, remove everything that was not largely devoted to religion. The heart of culture then is gone.

But another conclusion emerges: the heart belonged to the cultivated. Hardly a novel insight! —yet very strikingly demonstrable through the foregoing pages. Theaters were built and programs and artists chosen and paid for by the more educated well-to-do, who, themselves, also offered some of the performances. Of anything that could be called popular culture, hardly a trace appears.[31] Naturally, that fact reflects the state of the sources, not of reality. The materials from which ordinary people made their lives were wretchedly impermanent. Ovid gives a glimpse of a simple gathering on the Tiber bank for a feast in honor of Anna Perenna. Of those who attend, some pitch tents, others patch together huts of reeds or blankets. They spend the night there. When the sun rises they begin the holy day's dancing—and drinking. The glimpse is that and no more. Afterward, nothing is left but the trampled grass. What are attested much, much more often are "advanced" manifestations of the religious impulse through specialized skills and settings, that is, through theaters and telesteria, not tents; through trained choruses of aristocratic boys and girls under paid trainers; paid dancers, too, and instrumentalists, not villagers and cottagers doing their best. The structure of religious leadership corresponds in its human shape to that divine hierarchy of frequency-of-mention which we examined earlier. Within it, the many were quite subordinate to the few. They acquiesced in the elaborate tribute of the arts bought by the few for Zeus, for Minerva, Artemis, and Mars. They acquiesced by streaming in to the theaters and festival celebrations; not to the extent of quite forgetting Anna Perenna and her like. There was room for many gods.

Throughout most of the eastern provinces, cities advertised their principal, most characteristic religious beliefs by sending out delegations of heralds or by issuing small change, that is, bronze currency from their own mints and of their own design. They wanted to attract wide attention, inspired by a mixture of sins: pride and avarice. So Ma, better known as Bellona in the west, showed herself on the coins of her home in Pontus, Men on coins of cities in his home Pisidia, the river oracle ΧΡΗCΜΟC on coins of Limyra, Asclepius on those of Pergamon, the Mother of the Gods, all over, and festival presidents on coins of many cities, of Apamea, for example—by their title and prominence indicating what occasion they and all these mintings chiefly served. Visitors not only fed their hosts' self-esteem; they were good business.[32] Nor should it be thought that the phenomenon of the cult festival, advertised to and drawing from the population of a wide region, was not to be found where the imperial government forbade municipal mints. On the contrary, the evidence comes from everywhere, even if not on coins, and so abundantly as almost to match, within the economy, what we have seen cults supplying in higher culture: the very heart. Their economic importance in itself has no claim to discussion here; but the role of festivals in the exchange of ideas as well as goods is very much our business. People assembling for commerce could not avoid exposure to the challenge of others' religious beliefs.

Lyon, for example, had "a festival that was populous with throngs assembled to it from all the provinces," in Marcus Aurelius's reign; under Augustus, in half-deserted Fregellae near Rome, the people of half a dozen surrounding towns "gather in it still to conduct fairs and certain religious rites"; and to these welcome but rare hints from literary sources can be added more from the archaeological, showing us facilities for trade, booths or shops, built into the porticoes of sanctuaries or attested indirectly by quantities of dropped coins in the soil, even by inscriptions recording this or that trader as having his business at this or that temple.[33] To be sure, we do not know if these signs indicate annual gatherings or, more likely, gatherings at closer intervals. They offer their testimony, in any case—the "cafes and gardens," "the sales-tax-free monthly holy days on the fifteenth and thirtieth" of each month—in the east as well as the west. In Syria, the sanctuary wall at Damascus embraced a sacral area twice the size of a football field, constituting at the same time the principal bazaar of that great caravan city.[34] In Greece, the traffic that once nourished Tithorea now, in Pausanias's time, flowed instead to the half-yearly festival-cum-market at the Isis shrine a few miles away. Olympia had the same magnetic force on commerce, earning its meetings the name *mercatus Olympicus*.[35] *That* tells something!

The fullest evidence of all, however, comes from the cities of Asia Minor. In this region, the system of free gifts of money and services provided by the well-to-do to their communities, and a healthy economy during most of our period, combined to produce relative luxury at the holy days of smaller centers and remarkable brilliance at the major ones. The liturgists involved had saved up, sometimes for years, to be able to lavish quite disproportionate sums on the duties of their term of office, magistracy or priesthood. The greater the concourse attracted from round about! Hosts found it a little hard to maintain their smile of welcome.[36] Their guests were, after all, a very mixed crowd, in part unrestrained and unrespectable, in part pitiably gullible, and most giving a good deal of consideration to pursuits entirely secular. Hence, need for the authorities to put extra amounts of money into circulation and give extra care to the policing of the marketplace. In time, the office of festival president could be seen absorbed into that of agora superintendent. Where that happened, it revealed much about the focus of their concern.[37] How mixed the interests, how various the types of person drawn to a festival, can be measured in the scene sketched for us by a contemporary: "some people attending out of curiosity, some for shows and contests . . . , and many bring goods of all sorts for sale, the market folk, that is, some of whom display their crafts and manufactures while others make a show of some special learning—many, of works of tragedy or poetry, many, of prose works."[38]

Developing out of terrain, seasons, plain routes of travel, and human needs of all sorts, some of the smaller religious fairs known in the second and third centuries filled those needs so naturally that, with changes only on the surface, they were still being held in the nineteenth.[39] Some of the grand ones drew worshipers "from remote regions for religion's sake," as Artemis did to Perge or Ephesus, "venerated not only in her own home-city

. . . but by Greeks and barbarians.''[40] Whatever their size or area of attraction, they constituted one of the chief means of introducing someone to a larger world than that in which he was likely to pass his workaday life. Thereby they help to answer the chief question latent in the last several pages: How did the isolated and the uncommitted, people away in their villages or people who had no interest in a given belief, come naturally to a knowledge of it? In the absence of missionaries and mass media, it is not easy to picture the two kinds of individual learning of many gods. Such was certainly not the chief object of (for example) the high and mighty colonels and imperial bailiffs who paid a call on the hot baths of Scaptopara, so handy (as close as two miles) to a rustic cult center and its holy days. Religious learning can have been of no concern at all to those sons of heroes who patronized a company of whores on circuit around Thermopylae as it went from one holy day to another. And the desire to find out about strange gods was certainly not what accounted for the peddler who set up his skin tent near the sanctuary walls or for his customers fresh come from the plow, in Tithorea. Nevertheless, their senses were assaulted by messages directing their attention to religion: shouts and singing in public places, generally in the open air, not in any church, and to an accompaniment as loud as ancient instruments could sound; applause for highly ornate prose paeans before large audiences; enactment of scenes from the gods' stories performed in theaters and amphitheaters by expert actors, singers, and dancers, while the idols looked on from seats of honor; the god-possessed swirl of worshipers coming down the street to the noise of rattles and drums; and all of this without the onlooker's offering a pinch of incense or so much as glancing at a temple. So obtrusive upon the attention of the least interested was the world of the divine.

Holy places only by chance lay where cities grew. Many lay rather at some distance away: the Asclepieion in the suburbs of Pergamon, Didyma twenty-three miles from Miletus, Daphne outside Antioch, Eleusis twelve miles from Athens. There was thus much traveling out to see them. But some deities themselves had to make an annual visit to convenient water. Among them, Isis. Early in the spring her image was taken from its house down to the shore, to set the ships asail, and again in the autumn, to find Osiris. Other images went to water for a bath;[41] many were ritually carried to a secular or cult theater,[42] many simply paid a brief call on their friends and relations. They were borne on carts drawn by a pair of horses, by a deer, by elephants (at least in representation);[43] they were carried on a litter with human bearers (the means of transportation most often shown in reliefs, coins, and frescoes). Or the parade included no icon, but instead people assigned to carry a reed, a tree, a wooden phallus, a box, a jug, the god's ornaments or clothing, a miniature temple or image.[44] They moved along to the sound of hymns and pipes.[45] Many processions were nocturnal, lit by torches. Animals driven to be sacrificed had signs on them proclaiming their donors' names.[46] In Greece and western Asia Minor, specifically attested, regularly recurrent religious parades number in the hundreds, in some towns taking place several times a year on behalf of different cults; but beyond this area, too, and especially as a feature of Oriental cults, they are known, though not so familiarly.[47] The reason for drawing out the evidence on them is the same that required the describing of other public cult activities: the need to make as vivid as possible the degree to which testimonies and teaching about religious beliefs demanded notice, even from the most uncaring observer.

But perhaps the point has been labored, and to the neglect of a more obvious truth: most inhabitants of the world here under inspection were by no means uncaring observers. Had they been that, there would be no explaining their efforts to attend great or little festivals a day's journey from their homes, or a week's journey—in short, there would be no explaining pilgrims. These were a phenomenon distinct by themselves. Like many a visitor of festival times, they spent money when they arrived at their destination; but only to make offerings. That is what Lucian means by saying of the Holy City, "to the great goddess' temple in Hierapolis comes wealth from Phoenicia, Babylonia, Cappadocia, and Cilicia."[48] Wealth, that is, coins, discovered in the excavation of a shrine to the Mother of the Gods, south of Pergamon, similarly shows the origin of visitors to lie in a number of cities fifty, a hundred, or more miles away.[49] They had to be lodged in a special hostel such as has been found in one form or another, and with a few or with dozens of rooms, in many shrines,[50] though most frequently where visitors' business would keep them for a matter of days, even weeks. That could be necessary for the attending of a long festival (Olympia or Panamara), religious study (Jerusalem), consultation of an oracle (Trophonius), treatment by Aesculapius (Pergamon), or a water cure by deities of hot or cold springs in many Celtic shrines beyond the reach of this study. Divine doctors received many calls. Asclepius alone maintained hundreds of offices open for patients throughout the Greek-speaking provinces,[51] of which those at Epidaurus and Pergamon are only the most famous. The size of their adjacent theaters suggests the numbers drawn to them. But memorial inscriptions can also be used to learn the distances traveled by people searching out the obscure springs at Vicarello on Lake Bracciano, all the way from Cadiz; others, to Samothrace from far north; and so forth. Pilgrims were ordinarily men, rarely women.[52]

In Egypt, a land to all of which the Nile served handily as main street, it was customary as nowhere else to pay one's respects to many gods, traveling if need be many miles. Witness to the custom are some two hundred texts on the walls of the Isis sanctuary and the buildings it contained, on the island of Philae. They were inscribed in the period of the Empire, most of them on the pattern, "I, Apollonius son of Theon, came to the Lady Isis [to offer] the prayer for . . ." (relatives—plus date). The prayer may, however, be versified, like this: "When we arrived at the island of Isis, splendid and holy, at Egypt's edge, before Ethiopia, we saw in the river Nile swift boats that bore noteworthy shrines [miniatures, as offerings] from Ethiopia to our land rich in crops and worth the beholding, which all mortal men on earth venerate."[53] When, particularly in the second century but right up to the end of the third, too, we find visitors to the remotest shrines of Egypt coming from Greece and Italy, it is more easily understood why Greek and Latin literature in the same period should be able to show so many readers and writers well informed about Egyptian religion. Of course, the same instruction could be gained secondhand. Every pilgrim who visited some exotic temple then came home. His neighbors would hear all about it the next evening, and for perhaps more evenings thereafter than they would have predicted, until they were fully acquainted with whatever he could tell them. Pilgrims not only learned but taught, too.

To repeat: they were a distinct phenomenon. Their journeys were the physical expression of a faith greater than prevailed generally. But they were not unique in their interest. At sanctuaries they were joined by, and hard to distinguish from, another stream made up of plain tourists. And the two met a third category: local experts. Lucian at the Holy City mentions a hereditary corps of hosts to pilgrims; Aristides at Pergamon like Pausanias in Lydia and at countless sites of Greece encounters and quotes from guides, exegetes; Athenagoras, Lucian, and Plutarch and his friends quote the priests both in Egypt and nearer home.[54] And there were people casually on hand at temples, to be described just as learned or wise men, but of a special religiosity accounting both for their presence and their lore.[55] They would be most drawn to festivals, "a time at which," says Strabo, "it is best for the participants to see and hear about these matters," namely, details of the local cult.

Bookish Plutarch sat down with strangers in the precinct at Delphi, near the temple, to discuss with them the significance of the letter E over the entrance. They were soon joined by a chief priest and other people from the shrine (not further explained, but ministrants of some sort). In the course of their conversation they refer to "the tourist-guide view." The scene is thoroughly believable—confirmed by Pausanias's report of a very similar argument begun by chance at the Asclepieion in Achaea.[56] It could, perhaps, just as well have taken place in a secular setting, in which other conversations about religion arose: a beach at Ostia made famous by Minucius Felix. But that was the scene of a debate no less profound between one of Plutarch's friends and another philosopher.[57] Religion was talked about in a public portico, where two strangers met, one of them in the characteristic cloak of a philosopher. They entered on a debate before a cluster of bystanders. And in the same sort of building but another time and temple, Lucian imagines two philosophers of contrary schools colliding before "a multitude of men, some inside the portico itself, many out in the courtyard, some shouting and straining forward on their seats"—concerning the question, Do the gods exist?[58] The stridency of interest is what counts for our purposes—an interest which is far more easily documented among Christians in the history of their internal debates but which animated non-Christians as well. There even survive a few hints of the two engaging in a dialogue with each other.[59]

Contemporary with some of these moments, a rhetor of the type we have seen elsewhere on display in cult theaters offers us a lecture exactly on the subject of chief concern to us: what were the means by which ideas of the divine came to be shaped. He lists ideas inborn, those derived from the poets, and those derived from decreed cult regulations. So far, familiar sources. He adds a fourth, works of art. He proceeds to an extended discussion of them. They belong of right to his subject. We have seen Plutarch using them as a means of approaching and understanding the divine.[60] Pausanias in his tours of Greece, like Pliny earlier around Italy or Lucian in Gaul and the Danube provinces, comments on the paintings he saw in sanctuaries.[61] He expects to learn what beliefs are held at a given shrine by studying them closely and hearing them interpreted by resident experts. They are evidently to be looked for in any well-maintained sanctuary in Greece or, indeed, in Asia Minor, in the Danube provinces, or in Africa. That much appears in inscriptions boasting of their installation.[62]

Figured frescoes still survive on temple walls from an area even wider.[63] Bas-reliefs were ordinarily painted, as too were architectural details on Greek or Hellenizing temples (the practice is familiar) and on theaters also (as may be learned from the example at Stobi); most wall surfaces not marble would be stuccoed and painted; and, for the famous old cult statues of earlier Greece or Rome, there was a match in the Sarapis of Pergamon, thirty-five feet high even seated, or in the many images everywhere that were gilded. That rhetor of the previous paragraph, Dio Chrysostom, whose ideas on art we can examine quite fully, delivers his address while standing in the neighborhood of the great Zeus image by Pheidias at Olympia, a fact no doubt explaining why he should attach special importance to sculpture compared with painting; but he is surely right in attributing to any true masterpiece a kind of tyranny over every worshiper's subsequent perceptions (*Or.* 12.53)—"by this glorious vision, conquering and uniting Greece first and then others—revealing something so wonderful, so splendid, that thereafter no one who saw it could form a different view."

Depending on the good will and wealth available to freshen the paint, sacred enclosures and their buildings, frescoes, friezes, and statues must be imagined, first, as drawing the eye with a very rich display of color throughout, and second, as rewarding it with scenes and symbols full of meaning for even a stranger. To this striking polychromy, inscriptions contributed their share. They too were ordinarily painted, the letters alone or the background as well, with the obvious intent of providing better advertisement.[64] The importance attached to some of them is manifest in the efforts of the authorities to maintain them in good repair, to show them off properly or otherwise reaffirm them.[65] They constituted the best means by which priests and pious alike could impress their beliefs on the public entering the shrines.

While gods and goddesses resided in every temple and could be seen in secular surroundings, too, at street corners or ensconced in niches in the town hall, nevertheless it was the stone population inside sanctuary circuits but outside temples themselves that contributed most to the total of 30,000 statues of deities estimated to exist in the Empire as a whole; and this population received additions all the time, to the point of needing to be thinned out.[66] Prolific piety commissioned many of these conceptions, even if many others were the offspring merely of convention: "to great Artemis Thermia, this bronze image in obedience to her command and revelation"; "So-and-So the barber, seeing it in a dream, erected an Asclepius to the Nymphs, for his health, and gave thanks"; "the Ionian Polemo, sophist, following his dream, set up a bronze statue of Demosthenes the rhetor in the Asclepieion of Pergamon in Mysia, inscribing on it this epigram. . . ."[67] Only a selection from epigraphic memorials in the provinces east and west suggests that a variety of cult reliefs, fonts for lustration, and whole chapels as well as dedicatory statues were offered by worshipers obedient to the gods' own expressed will. And if worshipers could not give life to the images they set up, they could and did, by the score of texts surviving and the 30,000 lost to us, communicate some of the vitality of their faith to anyone who read on a statue base their affidavits of direct revelation.

No one dared disobey divine commands—or almost no one. Isis of Tithorea wished only certain individuals at her festivals, and let them know by appearing to them in dreams. Worth heeding, in the view of local folk. "They say that someone uninvited entered the shrine and died soon after. . . . I heard the same thing from a Phoenician man," adds Pausanias, speaking of Isis in Coptos.[68] An often-discussed type of inscription from Lydia and Phrygia, belonging to our period, relates how some person went against the will of this or that local deity, Apollo Lairbenos, Artemis Anaitis, the Great Mother Artemis, or Mis (Men, and in that name settled with his worshipers in Attica, too); whereupon the sinner is struck by some punishment to self or kin or property, learns of the trouble "in a dream" or "through command," confesses openly, and concludes his requital at the deity's orders by posting an account of the whole affair on a stone tablet, to advertise the deity's "powers" and "manifestations" (*epiphaneiai*).[69] Too many gods are involved for the practices reflected in these texts to belong to any particular few; rather, to a region; and a fairly wide one.

Moreover, punishment for offenses against right and wrong, for example, theft, is as sharp as for any against the rules of worship. The two kinds of punishment together fall on someone who swears falsely before the altar. Such perjury receives its due at Palmyra, where Iarhibol reigned; and contempt for a deity brought on its penalties in Mysia near Pergamon and at Epidaurus, too, as we can see in the very inscriptions that Pausanias himself saw and reported in about A.D. 170.[70] They recorded from the fourth century B.C. well over a hundred remarkable medical case histories, for example, one in which a man came to the Asclepius shrine suffering from crippled hands, and, "seeing the tablets in the sanctuary" (i.e., of exactly the same kind as these texts themselves), "he disbelieved the cures and somewhat sneered at the inscriptions. But going to sleep, he saw a vision . . . ," etc. Or another man who, "transporting fish to Arcadia, in prayer saying he would give a tenth to Asclepius from the sale of the fish, did not fulfill the prayer. The fish suddenly bit him . . . ," etc. Or a third visitor to Epidaurus, "suffering from an unhealed wound. While he was in Troezen about to be cauterized by the physicians, in his sleep the god stood by him and told him not to be cauterized, but to sleep in the temple at Epidaurus . . . ," etc.[71]

But whether the painted letters on marble stelae told stories five or five hundred years old, anyone like Pausanias whose curiosity led him to enter the Asclepieion at Epidaurus would see them set out where they could not be overlooked. Like the hymns written up on walls with indications of the tunes best suited to accompany them, like the examples of aretalogy already mentioned, in which wondrous deeds were strung together in rapid series, or like the rules of ritual declared to be given by a god through dream, oracle, or vision, the whole of a cult was displayed to the observer in the most accessible fashion possible. Exegetes were at hand to address a stranger and invite his questions. Benches invited him to sit down and talk or think about what he saw before him:[72] the texts, the friezes on the temple, the dedicatory statues with their inscribed bases, and the paintings most often in stoas, where the rain and sun could not spoil them.

In Asclepius's casebook at Epidaurus, an alert editor can find the style of simple folk,[73] the pinning down of highly improbable tales to named persons and places, and other points of presentation likely to win credence. Some of these same qualities Pliny remarked in an out-of-the-way sanctuary deep in the Apennines. There "stands Clitumnus himself, girt in decorated official costume. That he is a present power and prophetic, the oracular responses show. . . . You will read many things written up by many persons on every column and wall, praising that holy spring and the god. You will admire most—but laugh at some." The passage serves as reminder that the same devices of explanation and advertisement found on an elaborate scale in a great center like Epidaurus were to be found also in the most remote nooks of Italy.[74] They were not the monopoly of Asclepius at Cos, Epidaurus, or Pergamon—not a peculiarly Greek possession, that is;[75] for inscribed testimonials to divine cures distinguished shrines also in Italy, North Africa, and Egypt.[76]

The modern student is unhappily aware of the capricious capacity of evidence to survive at one point and perish at another. So much depends on the nature of the materials to which records were originally committed: in the Greek-speaking world, a great variety of topics on stone, and quite fully expressed, but in the Latin west and north, a habit of inscription much, much more shallowly rooted and perfunctory in its style. An ephemeral literature on papyrus once existed to attest to miracles of healing wrought by Asclepius in his Egyptian manifestation and, no doubt more often, by Isis and Sarapis;[77] there were prayers on papyrus once pinned to statues; and almost equally perishable wooden panels once bore painted texts.[78] None of these records still exists today, therefore none of the beliefs and events to which they bore witness can be substantiated. Luck, not truth. To disappear without a trace is of course most likely to be the lot of those simple folk and their faith sensed in the Epidaurian affidavits or smiled at by Pliny the Younger; hence, a specific distortion that is social, added to the regional.

The illiterate worshiper could learn from unwritten wonders perhaps as much as the lettered could learn from the written. He could infer the obvious meaning from a pair of ears carved on an altar as thank offering to a goddess in Bithynia. She had heard the suppliant. The symbols really needed no explanatory text. They could be seen in shrines throughout the area of our study, as reliefs on stelae or on a wall.[79] Their ubiquity is striking. In the major Asclepieia they seem to have been offered as things or places (carved, and with a hole in them?) for a visitor to address, like telephones linked to Olympus. And they expressed silently the character often attributed to the gods in dedications, the character of listening.[80] Without that, prayers would have no reason.

In healing shrines, ears carved in relief occasionally indicate a part of a suppliant made well, i.e., hearing restored. Two- or three-dimensional representations of feet occur,[81] which more often tell of the presence on the spot of whatever person commissioned the carving; but they, too, may signify a healing of that part of the body. There are quantities of other parts and organs represented in stone or terracotta or, in the western provinces, in wood, as is known only through mention in a literary source.[82] So much is lost! There remain only tantalizing lists from earlier centuries, cataloguing objects in some sanctuary: "on the third row, a leg in relief, uninscribed, dedicated in the priesthood of Lysias," something else "hung from the ceiling," or "on the left as you enter," "on the wall," "two tripods, two small masks, two breasts, two phalluses, a snake, a hand."[83] It must be supposed that the contents of temples had not changed by the point in time studied in these pages; for stray objects of the sort one would expect to find in the glass cabinets of an old-fashioned medical school turn up, most improperly, in the excavation of second- and third-century ruins.

3. DISPLAYS AND ACCOMMODATIONS AT TEMPLES

It was customary for men to leave, nailed to the side of some building in a holy place, a lock of their hair cut off to mark the end of their adolescence. Accumulation of gifts could produce a peculiarly furry wall.[1] There were elephant tusks nailed up at two temples in Africa, an elephant skull at a third, in Capua (with a clever poem inscribed below it).[2] There was a pair of sculpted camels on view in a shrine a few miles from that skull, a pair of sculpted lions elsewhere, and live lions, bears, and bulls wandering loose but tame in the enclosure of Atargatis at Baalbek;[3] tame sacred snakes very fittingly at shrines of Asclepius, both the famous one in Epidaurus and at Sicyon also, which visitors fed gingerly;[4] and at Baalbek again, sacred fish in a pond—but Aelian rightly tells his readers that "tame fish which answer to a call and gladly accept food are to be found and kept in many places," for instance, at Labraunda in Caria, where he says they had gold collars around them and gold pendants like earrings on their gills.[5] A number of other ancient authors comment on the sanctity of fish in the cults of Syria. They were one of the things that caused religion to be talked about. As a wonder or a curiosity, they drew people to strange places of worship.

The whole city of Hierapolis served as sanctuary for doves held sacred to Atargatis. The effect can be judged from the scene at Ascalon, in the same region. When Philo arrived there in his travels, he "observed an enormous population of doves in the city-squares and in every house. When I asked the explanation, I was told it was forbidden to catch them . . . , and the creatures, having no cause for fear, had become so domesticated that they not only regularly share one's roof but one's table, too." Similar consequences must be imagined at Aphrodisias, where the governor intervened to protect Aphrodite's holy doves; in Phrygia and Lydia, the gods themselves punished poachers; Achilles, worshiped in South Russia, guarded or was served by "hordes of birds" on a holy island; and the Romans in our period, it must not be forgotten, still put out to bid each year the feeding of the geese on the Capitoline hill.[6]

To complete the picture of religious centers constituting also cultural centers, with zoological parks, aviaries, museums, concerts, art galleries, and public lectures, or the equivalent of all these things provided nowhere else in most cities, we must add botanical gardens: one consecrated to the goddess of the woodlands, seat (says Pliny the Elder) of "a famous tree." And he goes on to tell of the Italian bamboo, "which we commonly see in temples."[7] At Ephesus, the shrine of Artemis had woods around that contained rare trees, and perhaps still the deer parks of earlier times, near the copse in which ran the sacred spring.[8] Cybele shrines in every province owned woods from which annually a pine was cut on the day "the tree enters": *arbor entrat* (March 22).[9] It was in a copse that the Arval Brethren, priests to the Dea Dia in Rome, held their frequent ritual meetings. All over Italy it was immemorial to feel divine presences in such a place. No different the Greeks, or other peoples of the east.[10] Indeed, whether from a feeling of awe before the darkness of thick-clustered trees or to enjoy the refreshment of their shade, the inhabitants throughout the world here studied attached a special value to groves, set them apart and regulated their use. Mentions of these doings and feelings are as many as they are casual, in the literary or epigraphic record—a subject to themselves, in which the careless student could be lost without a trace. Safety for us lies in our having a clear and limited purpose: it is to appreciate the ways by which religion was established close to the center of daily life and therefore forced itself on people's attention. That is easily imagined happening in, for example, the sanctuary of Aphrodite at Cnidus. The space before and around the temple was not paved but agreeably planted with orchards. "Under the most deeply shadowy trees were cheerful picnic places for those who wanted to provide a banquet there; and some of the more well-bred used these, sparingly, but the whole city crowd held festival there, in truly Aphrodisiac fashion." [11]

In this description we encounter a distinctive and ubiquitous feature of cult centers, a place where a number of people could sit down together to eat and drink. It is best understood through our first asking what is known of ordinary social life and the equivalent of parties in the ancient world. To this inquiry, answer is very hard to give. In larger houses, a dining room could be expected to accommodate the usual nine guests. Only a really grand mansion had couches for more. How then could lavish entertainment take place? And for the great majority of people, whose quarters had no dining room at all, where could they play host to their friends? The solution lay in sacred tables, where religious and social life were joined in a common occasion.

The priests of Atargatis have already been seen at a fishy meal by themselves, from which worshipers were excluded. Similarly the Arval Brethren: as might be guessed, being of the nobility and sometimes including the emperor, they dined well. [12] These companies, however, and their like in whatever region for whatever god are too private to serve common sociability. Dedicatory banquets are too rare—by definition, once only. [13] More to the purpose are those regular meetings indicated by the existence in sanctuaries of buildings called kitchens. Let us look first at Italy. There they are supplied, for example, by and to worshipers of Venus. Would guests attend wearing the popular earrings of dangling little Cupids? [14] The gods met one's glance everywhere unexpectedly. In Aquileia, gateway to the Danube lands, there are a number of sanctuaries equipped with kitchens for an equal number of different gods. On the river's bank at Carnuntum was built, and later repaired by an ex-legionary in the early third century, a shrine to the spirits of the woods and crossroads with a monumental entrance, stoa, and banquet area. Throughout the whole region there prevailed a cult of the so-called Rider Gods in which banquets were evidently common, because representations of them in painted stone reliefs are also common, at least in the third century. [15]

St. Paul provides the most familiar evidence for our subject in Greece. He speaks to the Christian community in Corinth about its members, or about people who are at least not devotees of some given pagan deity, joining the real devotees in that deity's temple grounds to share in the eating of sacrificial meat. His rather offhand reference to the scene as something quite everyday fits with the frequent epigraphic mention of dining rooms opening off the stoas that ran around sacral areas.[16] As we would expect, those Greek buildings and the custom they accommodated found a second home in Asia Minor.[17] Also predictably, the best-known example was one built for worshipers at the foremost cult center of all, for Artemis of Ephesus. The benefactor who paid for it was, significantly, also noted for his charities to the poor in the city. That beggars and the homeless found refuge in temples will become clear shortly.

From the many terms used for the facilities that received the diner, it is obvious that they varied in size and shape, some being big enough to hold large crowds of guests, others, to hold only nine; and they might be found only one to a shrine or, more often, judging from excavated remains, in numbers ranging from three to more than twenty-five.

In Syria, even a little rural shrine might have five separate rooms for eating; even a remote center might boast a banquet hall with a portico around it.[18] Two well-excavated sites have supplied evidence on detail. At Dura on the Euphrates, Syrians in small groups equipped their places of worship (the word "temples" perhaps conjures up the wrong picture), each group with its own dining room, eight or ten or twelve persons constituting a cell or cult society (*thiasos,* as the Greeks called it) and their quarters closely following a set model for size and shape—at the Adonis shrine, anyway, and with a single grand exception which, according to its founder, was to enjoy a peristyle and wine cellar. The building up of a congregation of worshipers cell by cell can be seen also at the second site, Palmyra. One whole temple there, though not very large, turned into a banquet hall seating about forty-five. Again, in the long, long effort of constructing porticoes, entrance colonnade, propylaeum, and so forth around the temple of Bel, right through from the earlier first to the early third century, the workmen coalesced into small religious fraternities serving the holy triad that they had ensconced in the temple already finished; and they built and feasted in separate chambers.[19] Throughout the city, where four tribes made up the dominant part of the population and established and maintained various cult centers, there were unknown scores of privately funded sacred dining rooms in which, on just what holy days and how frequently, no one knows, there gathered the guests of the members in response to little

tickets of invitation, for elaborate cocktail parties—so they have been called
—at which there were dishes of hot meat and vegetables, perhaps (or afterward only?) pipe and cithara players to add entertainment; and next, the
guests having departed, the hosts settled down by themselves to serious
eating and still more serious drinking, served by butchers, bakers, chefs,
sommeliers, cupbearers, dancers, and musicians. Good manners obliged
the lolling votaries to toast all their companions but at the same time to
observe the sacred regulations against "whoever vomits up his wine."

People from this corner of the world, wherever they went, took with them
their loyalty to their religious customs. So when a temple was erected in
Dacia "to the ancestral deities Malagbel and Bebelahamon and Benefal and
Manaval," the donor provided it with a kitchen; the same in Rome and
elsewhere.[20] And worshipers of the one god in particular, the divine pro-
prietor of the town Doliche, hence called Jupiter Dolichenus, added (once
at least "at the command of the god") a dining chamber to his temple.[21]

Our circuit of survey comes last to Egypt. From this land spread the cult
of Isis and Sarapis, along with its cult meals, even to Germany. Tertullian
reminds his western audience of sumptuous feasts in Sarapis' honor.[22] At
home, however, Isiacism is far better documented through papyri. Eleven
of these resemble the hundreds of surviving Palmyrene invitations. In
almost unvarying words, as if by strict courtesy or convention, the writers
ask the recipients to meet them "at the couch [or dining room] of the Lord
Sarapis." Not always in his temple: "Dionysius asks you to dine on the 21st
at the couch of Helios, Great Sarapis, at the ninth hour, in the house of his
father"; or in the temple of some other deity. The best suggestion to explain
this is that, on any of the more obvious holy days of the year, the numbers of
people wanting to celebrate with their friends exceeded the capacity of a
single shrine, and some parties had therefore to find space elsewhere.[23]
They could the more easily do so because there would be many gods in
town, and each or most evidently had commodious facilities for private
banquets, either built permanently in stone or less elaborately in the form
of arbors over stone couches. Users would lie on leaves or straw, hence the
name "mattress" given to a banqueting place as a whole; and they would be
shielded from the sun, hence the word "tent" used for the same purpose.

Aelius Aristides, the rhetor, reminds his listeners that "in sacrificing to
this god [Sarapis] alone, men keenly share a vivid feeling of oneness, while
summoning him to their hearth and setting him at their head as guest and
diner. . . . [He is] the fulfilling participant in all cult associations, who
ranks as leader of toasts (*symposiarch*) among them whenever they as-
semble" (*Or.* 8.54, 1, p. 93f. Dindorf.). The passage tells something of the

human feelings at such occasions, and invites speculation about other, similar gatherings when defined, select groups added an express religious element to a meal together. The phenomenon was widespread. "Devotees of Hercules," "the devotees of Jupiter Axoranus," "the association of Aesculapius and Hygia" (all these in the west) assembled at periodic dinners in temples—but then, of course, entirely secular fraternities used, perhaps rented, parts of a convenient temple for their meetings or even inscribed their rules on its walls; and the same customs could be found in the Greek provinces.[24] Observing the latter from a distance, Tertullian remarks that "for the Apaturiae, the Dionysiac or the Attic mysteries, a draft of cooks is proclaimed."[25] From the east to the west, too, there spread the worshipers of Mithras, bringing with them, like worshipers of Jupiter Dolichenus or of Isis and Sarapis, their own religious practices, which included common meals. Wherever they built their cavelike chapels, archaeology uncovers gnawed bones of all sorts of edible animals.[26] And for votaries of every sect or none at all, there were graveside meals in memory of the deceased. Those too are common.[27]

What emotions animated these scenes? The question, because of its intrinsic interest as well as its bearing on the Christian Eucharist, has been often examined. It barely touches our subject proper—fortunately, since material for an answer hardly exists. Two points may nevertheless be made without need of any long discussion.

First, the idea that a god might join worshipers who were eating together was widely diffused, most overtly in celebrations called *lectisternia*, when the icon was brought out of its house and was laid on a couch beside the celebrants; but also in other settings, larger and smaller; and obviously the emotions prevalent in some one setting could not be expected in all. The range would run from moments of great intensity (of hope, love, abasement, peace, and more) to moments, hours, or days of a festival in which religious meaning was all but forgotten. It has been the tendency of recent studies, in my view very persuasively, to deny much scope to the former, the more intense feelings.[28]

Second, many signs prove the grossest indulgence of the appetites at banquets of the sort being considered. At least it indicates their reputation, that a novel could describe an initiation at which the banqueters eat, vomit up, and eat again human flesh, while, in drinking, only the presiding priests exercise any moderation. A wild, revolting fantasy, no doubt; but the vomiting of wine we have seen at Syrian meals.[29] When Christian graveside meals enter the literary record a century later, scandalous drunkenness at them earns rebuke,[30] and it is a fair guess that their patterns of conduct had

been taken from the pagan. When we turn to citywide parties, evidence for
heavy drinking grows. We will consider them shortly. Does all this add up
to something less than the spirit of worship, to shallowness of feeling, a
secular devaluation of once-fervid beliefs? Or can that only be said if some
extraneous standard of behavior, defining what is and is not "truly" religious, were imported into the world of the Apologists? That was the latters'
intent. It need not be ours, at our remove.

Citywide cult celebrations are described, not lovingly, from a Christian
viewpoint. They are said to be staged in the name of false worships, "to
which most men abandon themselves at festival time and holy days; and
they arrange for drinking and parties, and give themselves up wholly to
pipes and flutes and different kinds of music and in every respect abandon
themselves to drunkenness and indulgence."[31] Against this interpretation
of how people usually acted, an apologist, Plutarch (*Moralia* 1102A),
might offer another: "It's not the abundance of wine or the roasting of meat
that makes the joy of festivals, but the good hope and the belief that the god
is present in his kindness and graciously accepts what is offered." The picturing of the scene thus aroused in contemporaries a range of emotions; but
the visible events were clear enough. A good meal was had by all, or many
meals: for thirteen days, free meat with hymns and parades to, from, and in
Apollo's shrine at Didyma; or feasting, dancing, and singing for the twelve
days of Aglibol and Malakbel in Palmyra.[32] We will turn later to more
detail about such long-drawn-out affairs, as it can be recovered from the
inscriptions of Caria; but here it is enough to offer no more than the two
quoted descriptions from the Greek-speaking world. Their like are found
very rarely in the west.[33]

In opening a glimpse upon these festivities, my aim is to place religion at
the heart of social life as surely as it must be placed at the heart of cultural
activities of every sort. For most people, to have a good time with their
friends involved some contact with a god who served as guest of honor, as
master of ceremonies, or as host in the porticoes or flowering, shaded
grounds of his own dwelling. For most people, meat was a thing never
eaten and wine to surfeit never drunk save as some religious setting permitted. There existed—it is no great exaggeration to say it of all but the
fairly rich—no formal social life in the world of the Apologists that was
entirely secular. Small wonder, then, that Jews and Christians, holding
themselves aloof from anything the gods touched, suffered under the reputation of misanthropy!

In rejoinder, they pointed with elaborate repugnance to "the pollution
around the idols, the disgusting smell and smoke of sacrifices, the defiling

gore about the altars and the taint of blood from the offerings."[34] Did they overstate the case? It was a pagan who described "the priest himself [who] stands there all bloody and like an ogre carves and pulls out entrails and extracts the heart and pours the blood about the altar."[35] It is clear that the great bulk of meat (not fish or fowl) eaten in the ancient world had been butchered in temple precincts, most of which, ill-supplied with water, could not be swashed down easily, accumulated ugly piles of offal in corners, and supported not only flies in clouds but stray mongrels as well. There would have to be wood stacked handy to the altars, and provision to store the hides stripped off the carcasses, since at least in some temples they were reserved for the priest. He was entitled, after all, to make his living from the premises.[36] It appears common for him to have received a portion of each victim which went to "the god's table" and which he could then do with as he wanted: give for a feast or sell to retailers. That latter choice would explain Pliny's remark that, as Christians in Bithynia were persecuted, "the temples begin to be crowded and the meat of victims to be for sale everywhere"; but a number of cult regulations specify that the hide, the head, or a set fraction of the whole animal belongs to the god (hostile observers making fun of the mean portion he receives), and such parts are to be sold.[37] As to what worshipers could keep, they consumed it on the spot. Rules might even forbid their taking anything away, since symbolically all had been consecrated. Here served those kitchens, cooks, couches, arbors, and so forth that have been discussed. "Sacrifices were devised by men, I do think, as a pretext for meat meals."[38]

Though most of this detail about the apportioning of sacrifices comes from services in Egypt, Asia, and Greece, enough touches other regions to suggest that practices were broadly similar everywhere within the lands here being examined. The western provinces, however, yield a different kind of evidence of their own in the form of the remains of feasts, bones, skulls, and broken cups. The use of horses as sacrificial victims in Celtic areas seems securely attested but not explained.[39] In the region to the south and inland from Carthage, Punic custom directed worshipers to tophets with altars but no temples (perhaps a small chapel or two), where sacrifice was made and the remains usually consumed in a feast by the party that brought the animal. Unused parts were buried under memorial stelae, often decorated with painted reliefs that help to explain the whole routine. In one such sanctuary dedicated to Tanit, "pêle-mêle with the charred wood was a prodigious quantity of half-calcined bones, among which could be easily distinguished the jaws of oxen and sheep and a large quantity of leg-bones," plus thousands of lamps, hundreds of unguent bottles, and so forth, built up over time to a depth of six feet.[40] The absence of stone couches at shrines of that god who was by far the most widely revered in Carthage's old dominions, namely Saturn, and the Celtic practice of sacrificing horses, together warn against assuming uniformity too readily across all parts of the empire, where explicit evidence is lacking; while, on the other hand, in all parts were many gods, one or another displaying the predominant cult practices—the offering of a sheep that worshipers then shared with family and friends, and the like customs—that we have been surveying. What was not native might thus still be familiar.

At the Pergamon shrine of Asclepius, Aristides dreamt the god appeared to him with instructions to "make an offering to Asclepius . . . and distribute the holy portions to fellow-pilgrims." The latter must be added to the number of possible or likely beneficiaries of sacrifice. They would include persons making long stays for a cure, of months or years. At the shrine favored by Aristides, vast though the whole complex was, its recovered plan does not show clearly just where they lodged; but other Asclepieia offered good accommodations. Some of the buildings have been described above.[41] Against modern stereotyping, Asclepius drew pilgrims also for initiation into the mysteries of his cult at Epidaurus, and Artemis to Ephesus, for healing. Many or most deities attracted seekers of many sorts, it should be remembered.[42] Inscriptions of Asia Minor speak specifically of a category of persons whose existence we could generally assume anyway, the more or less permanent hangers-on and dependents of the whole fat, smoking cluster of buildings and activities that Aristides dwelt among. Who these were, besides paupers and fugitives enjoying asylum, cannot be said.[43] A second category to be taken for granted St. Paul encountered at Ephesus in the person of Demetrius, "a silversmith who made silver shrines of Diana and provided a great deal of employment for the craftsmen"; and the pagan holy man Apollonius met the like in Athens, a wholesaler of statuettes of gods for sale to worshipers.[44] Excavation of shrines in Africa and the European provinces often turns up quantities of objects all nearly alike, which had somehow become conventional offerings to this or that deity and in whose manufacture there was obviously involved a sizable population of artisans. These one would expect to find in or near temple precincts.

4. ROUTINE STAFF AND ADMINISTRATION

With temple servants proper, with priests above all, we return more closely to our intended subject; for, to the extent that they were not purely municipal magistrates of secular character, they took care of dressing the face of religion for its votaries. But it must be remembered how far from purely secular were most elected officials in cities of Greek or Roman derivation. This year to the gods, the next to the city—such was the pattern of service rendered by the local aristocracy. Even within a given office, the two kinds of duties could not always be kept apart: "the strategos assisted at the traditional procession for the great goddess Isis . . . ," "for the visit of the most distinguished prefect . . . , all [statues] in the temple crowned with wreaths . . . , anointing of all the statues in the temple with oil . . . , workmen accompanying the image of the god to go and greet the prefect, wreaths for the image, a rhetor addressing the most distinguished prefect . . ."—so read the entries in the daybook of a magistrate and of a priest regarding quite similar public occasions and, for both of them, quite similar duties in third-century Egypt. It would be the same in any province.[1] As the gods came out to meet officials, so officials visiting a city for some secular purpose paid courtesy calls on the gods;[2] and magistrates made free use of accommodations in the porticoes of sacred enclosures, for their business, in just the same way that votaries as such met freely in civic buildings.[3] So closely were sacred and secular services confused in some settings.

In others, not. From the gallery of faith in the Roman world no picture is better known, because none has been more often painted, than that of the fanatic who, half-naked, whirls about in a mad dance, flails at himself till the blood flows, gashes his arms and legs, even castrates himself in the transports of his faith. From northern Asia Minor originally came the cult of Ma, providing Romans with their first sight of such wild doings; then from Phrygia, the cult of Cybele and her eunuch priests who howled like dogs; then from Syria, the cult of Atargatis, another goddess served by eunuchs; and Isis, whose devotees shaved their heads and twitched about in dance to demonstrate their grief at the death of Osiris, later to rejoice as extravagantly at his recovery.[4] Their long hair was thought to be a sign of divine inspiration, the longer the better,[5] and they and other priests, not only those of Isis and Cybele, wore distinctive costumes.[6] Outside the cults of the four eastern female deities just named, ascetics are indeed attested—extremely rarely; and in Cilicia you could see inspired votaries walk barefoot on hot coals, in trust or tribute to their local goddess, as still today in Macedonia the votaries of St. Constantine walk on coals "at the command of their General," as they say.[7] But the sum of all this evidence for enthusiasm in the literal sense is striking by its narrow limits, all things (all gods) considered.

The essential figure in sacred precincts is no doubt neither the aristocrat nor the fanatic but the priest, ministrant, or caretaker of whatever title.

Often a group of them acted together, answered questions and kept order. Enthusiasm was not the mark of such persons at all. Mentioned by travelers, they remain always nameless, humdrum, and helpful. In the sanctuaries of most gods it was rather the worshipers in whom eccentric behavior appears. So we can gather from scattered small hints, and from a single description that survives of people in a temple enclosure. It was written by Seneca:

> Go to the Capitol and you will be ashamed of the folly there disclosed, and of the duties which a deluded madness has assigned itself. One servant informs Jupiter of the names of his worshippers, another announces the hours; one is his bather, another his anointer, that is, gestures with empty hands to imitate the act of anointing. There are women who are hairdressers for Juno and Minerva; while standing far away from the temple as well as from the image, they move their fingers as if they were dressing the hair, and there are others who hold a mirror. There are men who summon the gods to give bond for them, and some who offer them lawyers' briefs and explain their case. An expert leading actor in the mimes, now a decrepit old man, used to act a mime each day. . . .[8]

Certain elements here we can identify: interpretive cult dancing and the calling of the god to witness and judge suits and oaths. Such customs we have seen before, though not at Rome. One element is obscure: the naming of worshipers. Others will need to be discussed.

For with this passage we approach the center of our subject, the actual idol in its house. Our first—and by anticipation, it may be said, likewise our last—impression is curiously disappointing. Once past that circle of devotees that Seneca describes, we are left to the company of sextons. They have their everyday duties. They can sometimes be made out at daybreak opening the temple doors and singing a hymn to the deity—this for Sarapis, Asclepius, or Dionysus.[9] The altars had to be lit, too, each one to a prayer or acclamation.[10] There followed one or two later junctures for hymns or sacrifices during the day, and then the doors were closed again.[11] But it may be that very few places of worship were regulated according to so nice a timetable. Certainly some temples never opened their doors at all, rather were secluded from their worshipers behind an anterior screen or fence. Others were never closed. Apparently it did not matter. And some admitted worshipers to their interior for services that required permanent seating arrangements or for sacrifices of burnt offerings.[12] Lack of any pattern of practice, almost total lack of mention of gods seen in their own dwellings, suggests that idols played no very active part in the ongoing life of their cult. They represented the pictorialization prevailing in a community at a given moment, caught by an artist, thereafter to serve as a kind of aide-mémoire to the faithful. It was what the faithful did in the precincts around them that counted for much more than what could be seen, or never seen, deep in the inner sanctum.

To both precinct and temple within it, night brought the illumination of lamps dedicated as offerings or of statues holding torches.[13] The effect had something magical about it, a sure sign—part of the evidence deserving discussion later on—that persons in charge of the premises consciously arranged things to arouse certain feelings in observers. The same inference may be drawn more specifically from the revised liturgy of the Arval Brethren, whereby, after the Brethren's cult dance, the statues of the goddesses in the temple were rubbed with perfumed oil, candles were lit all about, and the temple doors were thrown open.[14] The anointing of idols, if not merely mimed, made them gleam in lamplight. It was also a symbolic attention, like the dressing of them in rich clothes. As if they had been great dolls, they were prinked and bejewelled and shown off in processions by specially titled servants: "robe-bearers," "adorners."[15] The same literal piety was seen earlier washing them and stretching them out on couches in the company of their devotees for a feast.

Much of the long-elaborated, colorful sequence of activities that went on about the gods in their daily or yearly calendar has left its trace in sources for Greece and Asia Minor (actually, parts only of these broad areas), but not elsewhere. How is this unevenness of evidence to be handled? The most obvious recourse is simply to indicate what can be found where. But beyond that, it would be good to know if paucity of evidence corresponded to paucity of show in the cults of the province of Africa Proconsularis or Gallia Lugdunensis. It appears certain that Mithraism, Isiacism, and Cybele worship were well known (though not of course known to literally everyone, either in the west or in the east) throughout the Empire. With them they brought a full liturgy, in every sense of the word. It figures in a long list of pagan and Christian Latin authors. Authors, however, by no means tell the whole story. If it were not for the two words written next to figures on the wall of a Roman chapel, in a text all but destroyed, we would never have learned that Mithra was addressed with hymns.[16] They and other features of cult are relatively familiar in the east, not in the west. The chief cause for the difference lies in habits of epigraphy, by which the Greeks set down a large variety of subjects on stone, rather discursively, while the Romans did not. We have confronted the consequences of those customs above. The people they conquered took on their masters' habits. Thus it could be argued that, in Latin lands, the example of liturgy of eastern type and origin was placed before people, therefore no doubt copied, but not reported in the type of source on which we depend in Greek lands, namely inscriptions. On the other hand, had the Romans possessed a native elaboration of cult to match that of their eastern subjects, it seems odd that they should have imported so much from the east into practices of emperor worship. Such borrowing is plain in texts from Gythion and Arsinoe, for example, and the role of the Dionysiac artists is specially revealing. But all that evidence has still to be put together into a single picture, one that does not belong to the gallery that is my concern here.

Perhaps what is of concern, the salience of worship that could not be ignored in daily life, can best be illustrated by the customs of Stratonicea, near the southwest corner of (modern) Turkey, with its two nearby sanctuaries, Hecate's at Lagina and Zeus's at Panamara. The cult of the latter is especially well documented. Indeed, it may be known in fuller detail than any other in ancient times save Judaism. It is, however, quite neglected,[17] perhaps through appearing nowhere in any classical text, only in inscriptions, and through being neither Roman nor Greek. Students who attach much living significance to those latter two words in the world of the Apologists, except as they refer to language itself, have (I would think) a good deal of explaining to do; but that is a separate matter. Enough to say here that the coloration taken on by one of those regional deities with which this chapter began throws useful light on the degree of uniformity that may be looked for in our area of study. It was, as I said at the outset, a proper melting pot.

Panamara was the home of a male divinity whom visitors and conquerors settled on as Zeus, whatever the natives once had called him. The sanctuary occupied the flat top of a hill. The circuit wall enclosed a space about 100 by 85 yards. In and around the space and on the temple itself were more than four hundred inscriptions. They were published in quantity beginning about a century ago. There was also a Hera temple in the sanctuary, receiving new paint and plaster one year, as we are told; a dining hall; "the god's tables" supplied by the gods' share of the sacrifices offered; a building called the Komyrion; and a monumental portico dressed in stucco. Among the votive objects to be seen, perhaps the most precious were four feet made out of gold to commemorate the gods' active manifestations or epiphanies. Around the sanctuary were ox and sheep pens for sacrificial victims and inns nearby for those who were going to eat them. Inside were seating arrangements large and formal enough to be referred to as a theater and room for crowds to sit or lie at meals under tents. Wherever the eye rested, there must have been the inscribed and painted letters of honorific decrees, testimony to miracles, or regulations specifying the music and victims appropriate to this or that act of supplication or thanksgiving.

"Since, by the celebration and veneration at the festival and mysteries we enjoy great benefits from the gods' manifestations . . . ," begins a decree of the Stratonicean senate and citizenry.[18] The pride and piety that speak in the text spoke also in written invitations that went out to senate and people of many cities—some elsewhere in Caria, but also in distant Miletus and Rhodes—and in posters and by heralds to the population of Stratonicea itself, from the priest of Zeus, asking everyone to join his festivals. They were the annual ten-day Panamareia, the one-day biennial Heraia, and the two-day Komyria every fifth year. At the beginning of the Panamareia, the idol was set on horseback and taken along the road, a part of which is still paved, for a sojourn in Stratonicea, during which his priest used the city theater to present dancing, singing and acting by professionals hired for the occasion, and in the public baths distributed free oil to the bathers, men and women in their separate buildings, plus cash to the needy in the marketplace, wine, and take-home meals. At the end of the sojourn, those who accompanied the god to his home received gifts of sweet pastries and wine en route.

For the other two festivals (the Komyria having been instituted only in the first century to solemnize what had been a private rite of adolescence), the amenities were still more lavish: aged wines at banquets with no head table, for the ordinary arranging of guests of course involved worse or less food to *hoi polloi*; no head table, but drinking parties, love and good cheer, *symposia, agape,* and *euphrosyne,* often advertised as part of the "mysteries" which begin to appear in Marcus Aurelius' reign in connection with the Komyria.[19] In a period and sequence not easily fixed but nearly complete by the later second century, men are first (and necessarily ever after) admitted to the Heraia, and women to the Komyria; and persons not of Stratonicea—Roman citizens, country folk, even slaves—are invited, and then feasted; and then new items of increasing luxury and frequency are added, in a great tower of celebration built by competitive generosity among the leading citizens over many decades. In the third century the so-called gymnasiarchy of the high priest, meaning the period during which he supplied anointing oil to the baths and gymnasia in the city, totaled twenty-two days; in the fourth century, thirty-four days.

But that included the Key Procession of Hecate in Lagina, whose shrine, a couple of hours' walk from Stratonicea in another direction than Panamara, also fell under the presidency of the same annually elected priest. He would be expected to improve the facilities there, for example, by commissioning and paying for "three porticoes and monumental gateway and the stoa along the front of the temple toward the food market, and a decorated sideboard for the Table of the Goddess";[20] and such a generous person could expect to be thanked by vote of the senate, citizenry, Elders, and inhabitants of the shrine, who, with the hired entertainers, lived there year-round.

From among the children of those inhabitant families, the priest chose a choir of thirty to sing "the customary hymn to Hecate just as it has come down from the past."[21] This was to be done every day in the municipal senate building, the choristers wreathed in flowers, holding flowers, and accompanied by someone playing the harp. A charming sight, before the lawmakers bent to their labors! Outside, in the portico, since a date near the turn of the second century, stood statues of Zeus, Hecate, Artemis, Asclepius, and Hygieia, statues which wrought miracles. In honor of these, musical performances began to be staged on the spot.[22] Were we to choose one point in space and time that brought to a focus the beliefs and practices described in our first chapter, surely it would be this columned portico on some morning around the year 200.

II
Debatable

1. NEEDS AND ANSWERS

Was every one of these many gods just an invention? And did the whole structure of belief that we have surveyed thus rest at last on pure delusion? A challenge to be taken seriously. As superstition, so-called by some, much of that whole survives today; much (a little changed) receives attention daily in the newspaper, for readers who see stars. Historians, however, moved by some natural persuasion or by the dictates of their craft, pretend a terrible impiety. They must pretend, not that the gods lived and ruled, but that they did not exist—yet served.

The altogether human needs they served give us our starting point in examining the life that lay, not in paganism observed, but in paganism felt and thought out. Those needs are reflected in the activities that went on in any center of worship—activities most of which, however, might have fitted just as well in quite different settings. Entertainment or barter or sociable intercourse need not have been sought of absolute necessity in temple precincts and nowhere else. What really did belong? The answer should lie in whatever remains when everything expendable or extraneous is somehow stripped away. There is no more obvious place to begin the search than in Asclepieia. Those particular shrines were very numerous and, if all other places of resort for healing were counted in as well, drew to themselves more suppliants than any competing category of belief. What could be found there? Dreams and health. The chief business of religion, it might then be said, was to make the sick well.

A simple test can be made through inscriptions. They tell us what was expected of gods, sometimes by attaching epithets to them, for example, in address or hymn to "the Healer," sometimes by specific thanks for a cure. By the former practice, Asclepius alone is "the Savior," without further definition; Isis and Sarapis, too, emerge as specially great healers, workers of endless medical miracles; but many or most gods could heal.[1]

A semifictional biography tells us of sickness caused by a maleficent spirit, who can only be destroyed when a holy man, come to help, calls on the power of some appropriate deity. The anecdote is not particularly representative of beliefs and practices prevailing in its dramatic setting, western Asia Minor in the later first century;[2] but it provides a convenient transition from the curing of the body by Asclepius, Isis, and other gods, to that of the mind. Mental sickness, too, could be and most commonly was explained as possession. Cure lay through casting out the devil. And the same holy man, Apollonius, is seen to be capable of this feat also.[3] Powers such as his were commonly on sale in marketplaces throughout the area of our study—so the rather sparse and casual mentions seem to indicate. Though exorcism provided agreeable shivers to the reading public and fed more serious convictions among evidently unlettered folk, the art itself had no great fame or audience.

Christians, however, had their own views. They stood out as frequent and powerful exorcists, ". . . as you can learn even now from things done for all to see: for many persons possessed by demons, everywhere in the world and in our own city, have been exorcized by many of our Christian men"; "for some people incontestably and truly drive out demons, so that those very persons often become believers, those cleansed of evil spirits"; "let a man be produced right here before your court who, it is clear, is possessed by a demon; and that spirit, commanded to speak by any Christian at all, will as much confess himself a demon in truth as, by lying, he will elsewhere profess himself a god"; and "traces of the Holy Spirit are still preserved among Christians, whereby they conjure away demons and effect many cures."[4] It would be hard to frame more specific assertions than these, from both halves of the Empire and from the mid-second century on to the 230s, joining then with tales of saints in action in the second half of the third century, and so on to the declaration of continuing powers by writers, eastern and western, in the reign of Constantine. Such testimony suggests how helpless people felt before mental illness and how inevitably they turned, therefore, as they did also for the cure of bodily illness, to a source of superhuman aid. It duly met the needs of Christians. But while churches, high in their hierarchy, had designated exorcists, pagans lacked any corresponding deities, lacked temples known as places of recourse for the possessed, on the model of Asclepieia, and had instead to trust to luck or to some not very respectable help bought in the shadows.

Therein appears a point of weakness in paganism, perhaps inexplicable; also a point of division in the spectrum of pagan beliefs: roughly corresponding to our word "religion" was the sum of those things to be sought openly in sacred precincts. Other things—a winning horse, sexual pleasure, revenge, foreknowledge to be used against one's adversary, and a variety of trivial conveniences of the kind the Sorcerer's Apprentice tried to master— all belonged to the realm of magic.[5] For whatever reason, exorcism was included. The point of division was fixed by moral considerations, not exclusively but more than by any others. When Apologists charged that among their persecutors could be found some tolerated pagan who prayed for the death of a fellow being, meaning a gladiator, the reproach proved the rule. Whatever Christians might believe, few pagans thought that gladiatorial combat was immoral, therefore few would have hesitated to send up a gladiator's prayer.[6]

What pagans did pray for—their needs engendering and giving outline to the divinity they thought they could discern above them—was health, first. That is the best and most easily proven domain of supplication. Others can be illustrated out of the very small minority of votive inscriptions that specify why they were set up. There was beauty, close to health: thanks "to Minerva for the restoring of hair"; and prayer for new life, "to Leto, that my wife bear a child"; also "to Zeus Helios the Great Sarapis, savior and giver of wealth"; "to Silvanus, from a vision, for freedom from slavery"; for relief from tax payments; many vows for protection from natural disasters like lightning and earthquakes, or rescue from drowning or (most often) from unspecified "great dangers," for example, on a journey; for protection from one's enemies or the safe return of a squadron from patrol; for safety—and booty; or "for the safe-being of the colony and its senate and people . . . because he [Jupiter Best and Greatest] by his *numen* tore out and rescued the names of the decurions that had been fixed to monuments by the un-speakable crime of that most wicked city slave." Which returns us to magic distinguished from prayer. Some wretched streetsweeper had exercised his right to strike![7]

It is disappointing that habits of inscription should not have produced in our period of study a richer body of material; but the sampling just offered is useful in measuring the reach and variety of prayer; and there remain several categories for mention which, if they indicate nothing un-expected, at least define the center of our subject, human needs. Those were the needs, beyond health, which touched an individual's household, do-mestic animals, and crops. The first member of that trinity occurs in vari-ants of the formula, "for himself and his" (i.e., his or her people or kin or the like).[8] The prayer is so often expressed that, in Latin, it reduces to an abbreviation, a mere four letters. The fact signifies as much as a thousand texts in full form. As to the second member of the trinity of needs, inscriptions speak most often of the essential plow oxen, but of other beasts that may be vital, too.[9] Almost none of the evidence, however, comes from Latin-speaking areas; and, in the Greek-speaking, what survives is very little and disproportionately found in Phrygia. As to the third member, there is no relation between the importance of winning one's food, on the one hand, and, on the other, the likelihood of prayers on that score being recorded epigraphically. A god or goddess of fertility does not preside over every regional pantheon—surprisingly, since agriculture certainly presided over real life. The nearest approach is Dionysus, guardian of the vine that classical myth proclaimed him and addressed in that capacity just often enough to meet our expectations. Perhaps folk closer to the soil, and further from writing, held to faiths totally unrecorded.[10]

Other matches exist explicitly or by implication in prayers to Mercury-Hermes from travelers, traders, and market supervisors; to Silvanus from cowherds and hunters; to Poseidon, from those spared in his shaking of the earth; and to Zeus from those spared by his bolts, the gods being seen in the actions assigned to them by all the handbooks. There are special connections we do not understand between young women and Hygia in her temple near Sicyon, as between children of both sexes and Mars Iovantucarus near Trèves.[11] Of spheres of divine functions, indeed, a great deal more can be sensed than demonstrated. More still was probably left uncertain in the minds of worshipers. Warning has already been given against supposing that Apollo or Isis could not heal so quickly as Asclepius. And Artemis in Cyprus or Perge, "national" deities that reigned alone, must have answered prayers for aid of every sort, not only within the bounds fixed by Greek convention. Jupiter and Zeus could do everything, witness whole lexica of epithets tacked on to their names.

When we survey the full range of human requirements, then, from the most central to the peripheral, looking for a logic that might explain the origin and vitality of religious beliefs, we discover the expected lines of connection quite broken and twisted or, more often, to be drawn only by conjecture. We are to blame the loss of evidence, not the inadequacy of the whole system of cults in themselves. It is not to be supposed that comfort was not somehow afforded to all the various causes of misery in the human condition.

It is easy to sense, and worshipers certainly make no effort to hide, in their relation toward the objects of their worship, a spirit of self-interest, of *do ut des* and contract. That spirit has in the past often drawn reproach. It still does—witness most recently the critic who contrasts "the Isiac cult [which] possessed a moral system purer, more elevated than that of classical Roman religion. Who did not feel his soul shaken with feelings of admiration as he watched those votaries of Isis plunge thrice into the frozen Tiber and, shivering with cold, creep about the temple?'' Reference is offered then to the source of the picture, Juvenal.[12] Juvenal did indeed have strong sentiments about it: he found it all ethically and esthetically repulsive. And to the notion of the Christian Lactantius, that God could not be expected to love worshipers who did not first bring *their* love to *Him,* a pagan might have answered that what mattered was rather the service that the deity could provide, since a god (as Aristotle had long taught) could feel no love in response to that offered. The modern or alien critic of prevailing pagan views, judging the reasons for worship, starts from assumptions that are only his. Their own, pagans found quite comfortable.

Among felt wants, the modern observer expects to find none sharper than the need for life, promised for ever. But, like a deity to insure good harvests, assurances of immortality prove unexpectedly hard to find in the evidence. Even the longing for it is not much attested. What can be gleaned from the several kinds of source has been often discussed. The chief features need only brief review.

People belonging to one or another of a small number of cults, and in small groups, sought further lessons in their beliefs, lessons learned through rites designed to catch the imagination and arouse awe. Impressiveness of presentation could be heightened by rules forbidding the lessons to be talked about with outsiders. Obedient secrecy of course obscured the historical record forever. One group, nevertheless, in the worship of Dionysus, can be faintly discerned through inscriptions, developing more formal ceremonies of instruction, at least in Italy, in the later second and early third century. During the ceremonies, participants may have received promises of afterlife. But evidence for all this is unfortunately very little and very indirect.[13] Similarly with Isiacism: the evidence lies in the concluding chapters of Apuleius's novel, in which his hero Lucius undergoes a lengthy and most expensive course of instruction at the hands of Isis's priests. At the end, he is fully satisfied by her promise, "You shall live in blessedness," *vives beatus*; and when life is over, he may continue to worship her. He is the envy of everyone for being *renatus,* reborn "in a sort of way"—defined as having earned the goddess as his patron and at the cost of no more than temporary bankruptcy. There is, however, no word of his being *renatus in aeternum,* which is what counts.[14]

As to Mithraism, it grew like Syrian cults, cell by cell. At meetings in underground chapels, members dined together, sang hymns, and from time to time participated in rites that brought promotion through a series of titles and roles. One line of a graffito on the walls of the Santa Prisca Mithraeum in Rome, almost illegible, seems to read *rebus renatum dulcibus atque creatum*, "reborn and created for delights"; others tell how "you have saved us (?) by the shedding of eternal blood." "Saved" for what? "Reborn to eternity through secret baptism," answers an inscription—a forgery![15] Nor do Celsus and (a century later) Porphyry serve to clarify the matter much. The one speaks of beliefs in the passage of Mithraists' souls through the seven spheres of the planets, the other, of passage after death into some different living being.[16] Which is not to everyone's taste in immortality, even if it could be reconciled with the few other fragments of belief that survive.

When Sabazius cult by the mid-third century had come into contact with Christian doctrines in Rome, one of its priests depicted his departed wife in a fresco, banqueting among the blessed. There in that scene was immortality clearly portrayed;[17] but only a part of the portrait, probably a very small part, could be considered pagan, to throw light on unaltered eastern ideas. A mile away, across the Tiber, a certain Gaionas, servant of a Syrian shrine there, died, so his epitaph declares, "paid in full to death—Gaionas' little soul."[18] So flippant a farewell ill suits the moment of rebirth into eternal blessings. The inscription cannot be used to support any broad interpretation of afterlife in the minds of the inhabitants at the center of our time and area of study.

Other scraps of evidence survive without adequate context. There are indications of inner circles or more advanced degrees of revelation in a few Greek cults, but what was won by them cannot be discovered. Part of their value lay in their being reserved for special seekers, and their deep secrecy.[19] When Theon of Smyrna, some time in Hadrian's reign, speaks of initiation rites as bestowing "a blessed state of divine grace and companionship with the gods," it is not clear what rites he has in mind; when Plutarch, close to the same decade, speaks of finally joining "the company of the sacred and pure," "the fully liberated and released" as opposed to "the uninitiated, uncleansed mob of the living," he does not explain what he means by "The Great Rites," the ones producing these results, whether they are the Eleusinian or some other; and Tertullian discusses rites of advanced instruction through several different phases or moments, as do the preceding two authors, but in a jumbled paragraph which fails to show what belongs to Mithraists (named), what to various other unspecified *mysteria*. "He both celebrates the offering of bread and introduces a likeness of resurrection," runs one key sentence. The last word may as well mean "of the new man," reborn in his life like Lucius, as "of the man that dies."[20]

From all three authors' pictures of initiation, what seems to emerge in clear outline is a considerable clientele—let us say, many thousands at a given moment, but not tens of thousands, since our glimpses are only of the educated classes—in the Greek-speaking world, among whom prevailed some faith in an agreeable afterlife earned by attention to ritual purity; and in Tertullian's world, perhaps similar views more localized in region and class, reflected also in the epitaph of the departed Julia Benenata: "For I," she declares, from her tomb at Mactar in Numidia, "who always lived in a pious body, inhabit, thanks to divine law, the sweet Elysian Fields of Proserpina, that is the sun whom I have seen on high, with the constellations." Echoes of Vergil? And surely of Christianity, now, in the late third or fourth century? Of Isiacism, too, or Neoplatonism? But the ideas are widely shared commonplaces; whether literary or genuinely religious, it is very hard to say; and (returning us to an eastern setting, possibly Egyptian) there remains the one generalization that survives from our period, inserted casually in a religious tract: "as *hoi polloi* believe, when the soul leaves the body, it turns into an animal." [21]

In all the "Oriental" cults in general, whether of Atargatis, Mithra, Isis, or Cybele, the element of resurrection has received emphatic attention in studies old and new—attention emphatic but not always firmly controlled. It should really not be taken for granted, as it often is assumed, that people who believe a god might rise from death also believed in such a blessing for themselves as well. The conjecture needs support—and finds none. [22] Moreover, in one of these Oriental cults, though the death of Attis is primordial, there is no mention of his resurrection in sources before the end of the second century at the earliest. [23] A second feature of the same cult, ritual cleansing in the blood of a bull, has been taken as a sign of belief in the possibility of life after death. What it was actually thought to grant, however, was an extension of one's earthly existence, in a state of ritual purity, and then only for a limited term of years. [24]

On the views of death most commonly held in the world of the Apologists, there exist one or two statements of quite broad import by contemporaries. They should be brought forward as a sort of summary to the positive evidence assembled in the preceding pages. Justin (to begin with that figure of the mid-second century) declares that pagans do indeed envision some afterlife, witness their belief in magic (he means, practiced at tombs upon the spirits of the deceased) and possession by demons. But, in saying this, he chooses peculiarly roundabout ways of substantiating his point, at least, if the Elysian Fields had been much talked about. He goes on to appeal to statements, unspecified, from the oracles of Amphilochus,

Dodona, Pytho, "and many others." That too is not probative, because of its vagueness.[25] Lactantius can do a little better. He cites not only anonymous philosophers and seers but a particular reply from Apollo at Didyma. "Does the soul survive death?" Yes, says the god, it is borne into the aether, there to exist forever. The passage has been quoted above.[26] It is as interesting for what it does not say as for what it does: it instances no easily recognizable, universal, or at least very familiar deity to name, whose followers all trusted in his power to save them from extinction. Nothing like that existed.

In striking the true balance of the evidence we should return, too, to Plutarch's circle. How pious it was can be sensed from many conversations he records or imagines. One of the most forceful is inspired by the subject of Epicureanism, naturally enough, since that was the chief stronghold of atheists. During the exchange, one of the company wishes to underline the delights and rewards of piety. "No visit," he says (1101E), "gladdens us more than a visit to a shrine, no season, more than a festival, nothing done or said, more than what we see and do in regard to the gods, whether we are present at secret rites, or at dancing, sacrifices or initiations." But if those last had conferred immortality, surely they would not have received so casual a mention, added by afterthought to such agreeable diversions as one might find at a church picnic. Initiations, *teletai*, can have meant nothing more soul-shaking than those big, open spectacles encountered in the first chapter, above, as they unfolded in theaters. Spectators received no special promises.

The pagan Celsus takes Christian ideas of resurrection as being, at best, metempsychosis misunderstood; at worst, ridiculous; and the pagan Caecilius, in Minucius Felix's dialogue, agrees.[27] The pagan Seneca rejects with scorn the whole Greek afterlife, Ixion, Cerberus, and the rest, in favor of the disembodied spirit reserved to a second, Stoic existence within the very heart of light.[28] He represented the cast of mind most often to be found within that class that gave its thought to abstract questions; he represents its strengths, also its weakness. For, with no very significant or prominent exceptions, people of all directions of belief, to the extent they could conceive of life continuing beyond the grave, did so in terms of the divine spark, as we might call it, the disembodied soul. That was very much a philosopher's view, one of those convictions one may hold without always remembering one holds it. No one cared greatly that he might gain eternal life if it were not really he that gained it, rather, some *animula*, some particle ephemerally spun off from the Great Soul, or the like. What was felt to be essential was one's true self, a personality; and, in default of that, Stoicism or similar ideas of immortality had little to do with people's most earnest longings.

Inscriptions here as on other points hold out the best hope for a broad sampling. "Savior" in them, or "salvation," had to do with health or other matters of this earth,[29] not of the soul for life eternal. Or in epitaphs, people so often joke about annihilation that the jokes at last congeal into commonplaces or abbreviations: "I was not, I am not, I care not," boiled down to six letters.[30] Or, last, in rules of cult associations, even those intimate gatherings of the faithful around a table that so instantly recall the Eucharist—but wrongly: the most telling note is struck by the injunction, "do not vomit up your wine." If there is no absolute certainty that banquets were not thought of in times past (as they have been so often by modern interpreters) as conferring immortality, there is no scrap of testimony to such a thing; and the silence itself is quite extraordinary. No, at festal meals, as at teletai of dancing and music, the wine, women, and song satisfied wants more simple and secular.[31] At Panamara, at the two-day Zeus festival, the crowds invited from far and wide to what were officially termed "mysteries," and who there received the wine from the priest at solemn meals, enjoyed a fellowship with the gods among them—that may be assumed, that would be typical of such cult meals—but no life promised forever after.

The aim of the foregoing discussion is the quite elementary one of establishing the degree of correspondence between common emotional wants and the satisfaction supplied by religion. That aim it seems natural to pursue first on the level of the individual, but the individual multiplied by millions. Thereby we should gain some sense of the *vitality* of paganism— key word in this second chapter.

Before resuming examination of individuals' feelings, however, it might be best to consider the satisfaction offered by religion in larger contexts. It was certainly recognized throughout antiquity, at least by people able to look at their world with any detachment, that religion served to strengthen the existing social order. Explicit statements to this effect, and very interesting ones (because the juggling of high principle and selfish advantage always rewards the spectator), can be found across a string of well-known writers, who protest the crucial role of religion among the masses. Public largesses such as were described in the preceding chapter—the enormously expensive distributions of wine, liqueurs, meat, pastries, more wine, and cash—should be made, says Plutarch, "on an occasion affording a graceful, noble pretext, through honor to god that draws everyone to piety; for in *hoi polloi* at the same time a strong belief in, and conviction about, how grand the divinity is, and how august, is engendered when they see those whom

they honor and consider great, themselves so liberally and zealously competing in regard to the divine." [32] Which by no means convicts Plutarch of
hypocrisy. He had his faith and believed in its truth; *hoi polloi* had theirs,
and he believed in its usefulness.

Many gods in one particular region, Phrygia, could be counted on to
avenge themselves upon the wicked. That certainty was encountered earlier
(p. 32), along with similar ones thinly scattered in other quarters as well.
Most characteristically, it was the man forsworn on whom some punishment descended. [33] Most often, in both halves of the Empire, it was the water
of a sacred spring or river that scalded or melted away the flesh of the per-
jurer. But (magic aside, which does not quite belong to this book) the
wretch who disturbs a tomb is threatened, too, in epitaphs sometimes
found in Phrygia. One invokes vengeance from "the gods of the Roman
People," no doubt conceived to be supremely effective. [34] And frequent
abasement in Phrygian sanctuaries before a god whose wrath is feared finds
parallels occasionally elsewhere, both as an individual and as a general or
loose-floating belief. Isis, wherever she was worshiped, was thought to seek
out criminals and strike them blind or paralytic, Sol-Helios saw their every
misdeed, and the pagan Celsus professed faith on behalf of himself and
others that the wicked would be made to suffer. So one is taught, he says, in
undergoing initiation into the mysteries. He means, of course, sufferings
on this earth as distinct from the pains of hell fire. [35]

A second distinction must be kept in mind, too: between misdoings
defined in terms of laws divine or human. In terms of the former, offense lies
against ritual purity or the sacredness of a god's own dwelling. Perjurers
will be caught only if they sin in the very face of the god, the virgin-not-a-
virgin, only if she immerses herself in sacred waters. When people expect
divine vengeance, it is usually in circumstances of this sort, not through
supposing that the human and divine sense of right and wrong will be
identically offended and that retribution will thereupon reach out to catch
the criminal wherever he may be. Of such a grander faith there are very few
signs indeed, at least in cults untouched by Judaism. Phrygia provides an
exceptional inscription; Lydia and Lycaonia a few more, nearby; and there
are further scraps and hints in Hermetism and Mithraism. [36] What emerges,
however, are glimpses of an expectation of punishment—that is, guilt—
attached to no one cult in any significant manner, rather little talked about
or counted on, and generally felt in regard only to basic tabus: parricide, for
instance, and incest. With these conclusions we may return to look a second
time at Plutarch's views. They represent the end of a string of statements on
the social usefulness of religious faith, going back to the fifth century B.C.

Perhaps not chance but change of perception and diminishing detachment accounts for their being almost the last. And Plutarch does not, after all, say exactly what his predecessors had said (that religion keeps the masses down, or honest); rather, that the masses' faith should be stimulated so as to direct their thoughts upward in reverence for nobility: to be found among the gods, found likewise among the local—nobility.

Naturally, he could also see the practical value in having as many people as possible discern a sort of harmony and mutual respect between the gods and the city magnates. We have earlier heard an orator inventing and publishing in a theater certain wonderful visitations from above, in favor of this or that sitting magistrate.[37] Cicero told the Roman Assembly that Pompey deserved a high command, being born to it by divine plan, *divino quodam consilio natus esse videatur.* He made the proposition incontestable with his favorite clausula[38]—not that he himself believed a word of it. We might accuse him, and his brother orators in the east, of empty compliments to which not even the most credulous audience could have attached much meaning, were it not for the evidence of private supplications on the people's behalf—that is, by a citizen for his village, city, or neighborhood. It is hard to see what gave rise to these other than a perfectly sincere conviction, a certainty that the gods did care about the whole unit which offered them its cult.[39] More proof of this sincerity appears in plague times, when city senates tried to enlist the direct help, or at least the advice, of some god in their salvation.[40] Again, we ourselves may be skeptical. In desperation, any measure might be tried, however little credited. Yet some of our inscriptions, to say nothing of Aristides' report on his private efforts, declare after the event that salvation had been really won by prayer: plagues or earthquakes had been ended, unspecified benefits bestowed, the Goths scattered.[41] That partnership, mutually respectful, between the powers above and the leadership below, was seen actually to work.

But how, precisely, did it do this? By what means could any contact be established with the beings of another world?

From testimonies to a living faith (which we are not done with yet) we must turn briefly to its quite mechanical functioning. Aside from rare and rarefied speculation on sympathetic magic, inhabitants of the Apologists' world thought first to touch the gods through images, because that was where the gods lived; or at least, to images they could be brought by entreaty, there to listen and to act. Whether or not they fitted exactly, whether they looked like their portraits in stone or wood, they were to be found inside. Christian observers, who had no reason not to be accurate, report this as the generally prevailing idea.[42] Moreover, three Greek pagans attribute miracles to statues of men who lived in their own, the second, century. One statue fell over and killed a man and then, being punished by drowning, got itself fetched up again from the sea. A second provided cures to suppliants. A third and fourth respectively provided cures and oracles. And a statue of Antinous in the city renamed for him wrought unspecified miracles, as even a Christian could concede. So ready were people to attribute powers to images even of mortals, so ready to see the divine even in their fellows![43] A final glimpse takes us to Palestine in the fourth century, there to find women consulting the image of Aphrodite on their choice of husband, or the sick cured by the weeds that grew at the base of a certain bronze statue. Local inhabitants, questioned by a touring bishop, regretted they could not identify it. They suggested, however, that it looked very much like Jesus.[44]

There was a second means by which contact could be made with the gods, beyond their images. That lay through sleep. In antiquity, dreams as such constitute a very large subject, studied for centuries by learned men — their handbooks published, passed on to the next generation, and so fattened into miracles of sound scholarship under the names of Artemidorus, and others. But that is all by the way. So too are the interpreters that served Isis or Asclepius and their customers in dormitories, another large subject in which specially figures the name of Aelius Aristides. More to the purpose are the sheer numbers of testimonies to the appearance of divine figures before the minds of sleepers.[45] They introduce an extraordinary variety of gods and goddesses spread broadcast over all provinces, acknowledged typically in the form, "To Such-and-Such, from having seen," or "having been advised" or "commanded," or "by order" or "in a dream." The formulas occur also in literary sources that describe nocturnal revelations.[46] When a man died, he might somehow earn promotion to demigod and, as "hero," could appear to worshipers in their dreams. So could the Genius of a given legion. The two examples convey how quickly and carelessly the practice of consulting deities through sleep might spread, even to the most newly invented inhabitants of the heavens.[47] Corporate bodies might act on dreams as well, presumably not vouchsafed on one night to every member of the town council.[48] It was their priest's experience, perhaps, and then interpreted to them? And sailors off the north coast of the Black Sea could count on the hero Achilles to tell them in their sleep just where the best anchorages lay. That was common knowledge; visions of the Dioscuri seen by sailors, also common; but less well known, that Patroclus, too, might be seen in local waters. All this Arrian discovered in his tour of the area during Trajan's reign.[49]

Famous only in their own region, these heroes' visits from above serve to correct the impression that might be gained from Asclepius's visits, famous in every region: it was not only in the latter's hundreds of shrines that people counted on contact with the divine through dreams. Origen, external observer and therefore to be heard with special attention, declares that "it happens to lots of people that a dream reveals to them that they should do something" —instructed by an angel or some other means, he adds. He does not intend pagans alone. Celsus, too, is quoted, "that someone in a certain condition, dreaming or out of his own wish, may have an experience, an illusory vision that carries some message to him, as has happened to tens of thousands." [50] "Out of his own wish"—evidently, then, just as one could have them at Asclepieia (else why venture the journey?), so one could turn them on at will in any temple. "I have come to see a dream that will give a sign to me on the matter about which I am praying," reads an inscription from a shrine in the Greek-speaking world. And from the Latin, the incident in a novel in which a woman is sick: "and for that reason I inquired for a treatment through dreaming; and I was commanded...." [51] While there are scattered indications that experts might be called in to the interpretation, that practice was a local matter and not prevalent. [52] Normally, one helped oneself. *Iussus*, "I was commanded," is so frequently a boast as to be abbreviated in Latin inscriptions, *v(otum) i(ussu) d(ei) f(ecit)*. [53] In Greek inscriptions, equivalents are, if anything, more easily found. And the only deity whose votaries seem to enjoy a detectably greater access to his will (such is the impression gained from inscriptions) is Jupiter Dolichenus, from the east, but probably better known in the west. The peak of his popularity belongs just in the middle of our period of study.

In the world of the Apologists, contact with the gods lay most often through signs and scenes longed for and granted to the suppliant in sleep, thereafter in waking to be interpreted. The process served pagans as prayer served Jews and Christians. It would of course be quite parochial to suppose that, in every land and every age, the plea for help can only follow certain forms or not exist at all.

But a third means of contact, neither through idols nor dreams, joined worshipers to the objects of their worship, namely, oracles. This is the means most familiar. It is characterized by the interposing of a third party (not invariably but almost always needed) between the two that must communicate. A priest, priestess, seer, or spokesman of some sort gives the deity's answer to spoken or written questions. Plutarch wrote a well-known essay on the decline of oracles, meaning in central Greece. Very sensibly, he attributes the change to diminishing wealth and population, though in nearly the same decade the Pseudo-Plutarch declares that "prophecy enjoys honor among all men."[54] Lucian, noting the decline at the center, sets against it the high repute of other oracles to the east, where there are various indications of a readiness to credit them, in other sources, into the third century: Amphilochus in Cilicia, Apollo at Miletus, above all Apollo at Claros.[55] The veracity of oracles, many of whose responses were locked in to past history and so to speak immortalized by Herodotus and later writers, constituted a natural point of debate not only among various philosophic schools—Cynics and Epicureans especially expressed their disbelief—but between pagans and Christians.[56] That debate suggests continuing vigor in the institution and in the credit on which it rested, regardless of the popularity of any particular center. More obviously, however, it brings to the fore an element of dissent within the body of polytheism.

2. THE VITALITY OF PAGANISM

The health of that body we must now begin to examine. It is convenient to look first at the group just mentioned, Epicureans, who represented the furthest extreme of disbelief. But aside from their name's being attached in obloquy to anyone who doubted a local oracle—"Atheist or Christian or Epicurean"—they hardly appear in the sources for our period.[1] It is rather their company that calls for comment: they are close to Christians, and that, in mid-second century Pontus, was not good. They are close to atheists, and that was a great deal worse. In public, as many statements make clear, to deny the reality of the gods was absolutely unacceptable. You would be ostracized for that, even stoned in the streets.[2] There is no need to recall the scenes of persecution in Smyrna, Rome, and Lyon in which the mob rails at Christians as godless.[3] An Apologist acknowledges his opponent's feelings: you "believe that to worship no god at all is impious and unholy." A contemporary, but a pagan, Aelian, condemns the atheist who, with alien "wisdom," disputes whether the gods exist or not,[4] and Lucian, a half-century later, declares that "the great majority of Greeks and all the non-Greeks" (which includes Romans) are believers.[5]

To have the same author, in contradiction of himself, tell us there were no worshipers left to Zeus any more is certainly puzzling; puzzling, that our learned friend the Epicurean of Oenoanda, Diogenes, should have dared instruct his fellow citizens in the freethinking of his sect, spelled out across the most public walls in town (above, pp. 10–11); and puzzling, that the same ardent Romans who burnt the "atheist" Justin should, in Juvenal's day, have laughed at anyone professing faith in an altar or temple. So the poet tells us, anyway.[6] Pompeian walls display dozens of blasphemous graffiti, insults to Venus (patron deity of the town), or, in a tavern, an obscene painting at Isis's expense. We may take their like for granted elsewhere, if there were other sites so well preserved.[7] In Africa, down the coast from Carthage, a rich man commissioned a semipermanent, semi-public bit of humor: a mosaic wall with figures and captions making fun of the gods at their feasting.[8]

This is the kind of mixed bag of facts that renders general statements about religious life so hard to frame or so easily criticized if they are framed too narrowly. What, for instance, can one make of the assertion that oracles, "it is true, enjoyed a recovery in popularity in the second century"—for which a single inscription is cited, recording help sought by a city in Sardinia from Apollo in Claros?[9] Such characterizing of the feelings and thoughts of fifty million people on any day out of thirty-six thousand has something ludicrous about it, as if one were to measure the pulse of the western world on the basis of a single headline in the *St. Albans Sentinel.* Worse than that, perhaps: since religious feelings are not something to talk about in public, in some of their aspects, they must prove all the harder to assess from the outside. The more need for care.

Let us consider a few further contradictions suggested by the important role of inner emotions in religion. Lactantius tells pagans to their face (and there is a sort of reliability in such testimony, out in the open and instantly subject to challenge by contemporary readers) that theirs is "a superstition about those gods of theirs . . . in which, for all I can see, there is no more than worship by the finger-tips . . . , nothing required but the blood of one's flocks, and smoke, and foolish libations." In contrast, Porphyry declares "the one who loves god cannot love pleasure or body; but the latter sort of man will love money and so be unjust, and the unjust man is unholy, both toward god and his ancestors, and a criminal in his conduct toward others. So he may sacrifice hecatombs and adorn the temples with a myriad offerings, but he remains impious and godless and, in true calling, a sacrilegious person."[10]

Or we may turn back from the later Empire to the earlier, there to read, "Vesta, be gracious! To you we now open our lips for worship—if indeed we may join your ceremonies. I was completely absorbed in prayer, I was aware of the divine powers; and the earth, joyful, shone back with a dark red glow." And another's assertion that "all men feel a powerful longing to honor deity and pay cult from close up, drawing near and seizing hold with persuasion, offering sacrifices and crowning with wreaths. Just as tiny children, torn away from father or mother, feel a terrible longing and desire, and often reach out their hands in their very dreams to the absent ones, so to the gods, men who rightly love them for their beneficence and kinship are eager to be and to talk with them by any means."[11]

Moving passages, reminders to their audience, western or eastern, of emotions shared in the innermost heart! But consider for comparison the scene of devotion that Seneca painted (above, p. 44), in which simplicity of feeling and intensity itself are derided as madness. And in other pages too long to quote, leading up to that scene, he dismisses the dancing or howling or bloodied priests of Cybele or Isis or Bellona, all of them as revolting as they are demented—the very manifestations of "true" piety that modern students most often point to![12] Even Porphyry's plea for god and ancestors, almost equating the terms of the two, and sounding a note so exactly in tune with all those praises of one's inheritance that were heard in the first chapter (above, p. 3)—even Porphyry's plea Seneca denies head on: "What of the fact that we even join the gods in marriage, and dishonorable marriage at that, the marriage of brother and sister? We give Bellona in marriage to Mars, Venus to Vulcan, and Salacia to Neptune. But some we leave unwed, as if no match could be arranged, especially since some are widows, such as Populonia, Fulgora and the goddess Rumina. I am not at all surprised that there has been no suitor for these. As for all this obscure throng of gods, assembled through long years of ancient superstition, we shall invoke them, but with the reservation in mind that their worship belongs rather to custom than truth." The repudiation of mythology here is echoed by other writers as well.[13]

Enough of such contradictions—which, useful though they may be to indicate the bounds of the possible, chiefly demand resolution. It cannot be found, however often sought, in the change from one century to another— from "the religious crisis in the Roman world at the end of the Republic and beginning of the Empire" to "the second century with its powerful upsurge in religious life," then the mid-second century to the early fourth, all one "age of anxiety," in its later phases coinciding with "the decline of paganism in the second half of the third century."[14] Conventional and representative of a sort of scholarly consensus regarding successive developments within our subject, that succession of periods must nevertheless be looked at critically. All of its parts are made of, or meant to describe, religiosity, not only the whole nexus of thoughts and feelings about the divine, but their intensity or vitality as well. For the final period of decline, substantiation is sought in the much-diminished epigraphic record, not in what it says but in its very silence. The silence itself is a fact plain and uncontested, though its interpretation is something else again. We will return to that matter, later. But for the other periods, the sources used are almost wholly literary, since "inscriptions seldom tell us much about the underlying personal experience."[15] Here too is a fact uncontested, witness the passages called on in the last few pages to convey a sense of what emotions characterized moments of active worship. They are drawn from a metaphysician, Porphyry; a poet, Ovid; a rhetor, Dio Chrysostom; and still others that display or suggest deep attachments or experiences might be found in a novelist and rhetor, Apuleius, in a natural philosopher, Aelian, or in other poets.[16] Inscriptions provide no match.

There are, however, two objections to be raised against reliance on such authorities. First, they represent only a small group. The fact has been stressed before. Summing up a good deal of discussion, it is stressed again, below (p. 88). Second, even that small group they do not represent accurately.

To examine the latter objection: as is clear in the opposing pairs of quotations that were just presented, the religious feelings most common in the Empire, and those considered suitable or "true," covered a very wide spectrum indeed. Explanation lies in plain human variety, not in place or period. Moreover, the range indicated in the comparisons could be easily extended by the inclusion of prinking and frivolity in sacred processions, erotic or abnormal titillation in cult groups (or in novelistic fantasies about them), exaltation roused by concentrated and emotive word pictures describing the great powers and loving kindness of a god—and so forth. Examples of all such passages in the literature of our two centuries of study have been offered above.[17] Except from a sectarian point of view, then, it would be wrong to pick out one or a few particular dispositions as characteristic of paganism.

Indeed, it is my guess that the variety of feelings satisfied in the practice of religion differs inconsequentially from age to age, however much accepted patterns of behavior to receive those feelings change in shape; for, as Nock wrote, "there are fashions in religion as in everything else."[18] If my guess should be right, religiosity in any society as a whole would likewise differ inconsequentially across time, and the several phases or periods which it is conventional to distinguish in the religious history of the Roman Empire would lose all meaning. Whether one age is "more religious" than another, that is, whether it actually stimulates its inhabitants to significantly different levels of emotion in the service of their god or gods, is a question almost too important to leave alone; but surely even those who choose to offer an answer to it for their own living generation, if they were really pressed, would admit they had no evidence anywhere near adequate in scope or weight to support any opinion. Hope of discovering the truth about a remote and ill-documented period it would be foolish to entertain.

Let us rejoin the circle of writers from whom we turned aside a moment ago. None in the present connection is better known or more certain to be referred to than Marcus Aurelius, the Stoic emperor. His Stoicism, however, stands out in isolation. There are no signs of a similar devotion in the preceding half-century. Suppose that we knew nothing of his meditations, or that another spiritual diary of the same bent but from a half-century later were discovered, would historians have any difficulty in accommodating either possibility? Would either be clearly at odds with its context? Surely not. There is a quite inadequate, and therefore indiscriminately welcoming, texture of evidence across the whole period of this study. Accordingly, the emperor's devotion has human interest but not historical. Even—or perhaps one should say, especially—a careful examination of the man and his time must conclude by admitting that we do not know to what extent he typified his own aristocratic circle.[19] The same admission should guide the student of Plutarch's circle, earlier, or Porphyry's, later.

Marcus Aurelius and the other names most likely to occur in a book about the cults of the Empire are in any case self-selected for the interest they felt in their own spiritual life and things divine. They wrote on those subjects. Not everybody did. Some people are simply more given to belief than others, like Teucrus of Cyzicus, who journeyed to Pergamon in search of relief from epilepsy. There Asclepius "appeared to him, and they struck up a conversation, and he developed a quartan fever, and through it recovered from epilepsy." They "struck up a conversation"— extraordinary! Or D. A. Lazurkina at a congress of the Communist party not many years ago, who reported, "Yesterday I consulted Lenin again . . . and he said to me. . . ."[20]

There is epigraphic confirmation for the point, perhaps. Among vows paid to the more prominent deities, where some very rough statistical tests are possible, and particularly among those vows that depart at all from the bare formulas of dedication, dedicants who identify themselves as servants of the god—priests or the like—are present disproportionately, in comparison to ordinary dedicants. Some of them are quite lowly.[21] The cult of Asclepius at Epidaurus presents a striking case: the sanctuary is filled with scores of altars set up by the priests themselves.[22] Another illustration lies in the cult of Jupiter Dolichenus, whose priests made themselves exceptionally prominent.[23] It was naturally to their advantage to celebrate the deity who fed and sheltered them; no less natural, we should grant them, to feel a genuine faith. That faith prevailed over advantage is suggested by those priests of one deity who offered tribute to another.[24] Taken as a class, they were surely representatives of human nature at its most devout.

It would not be too cynical, but simply wrong, to attribute to the professional servant of the gods real doubt about their existence or efficacy; for most of the most highly admired and educated people in the world about him were quite at one with his convictions—at the top, the emperor Marcus Aurelius, who doubted wonder-workers but credited healing dreams, above all, those sent by Asclepius. Everyone agreed: Marcus's teacher Fronto, for one.[25] But there is no need to call up from earlier pages the proofs of unfeigned belief to be found in virtually every writer of the second and third centuries whose works survive. They all believed; which cannot be expected to mean that they all believed everything. The variety of religious convictions or systems (to which we will return) matches the variety of emotions regarding the divine; but the former can be examined with some hope of understanding them. The latter, as has been said, lie beyond reach of profitable discussion.

What is untypical about the religious views of the highly educated we may identify by following them out beyond the surviving literary corpus. Will that distort those views? Apparently not. Some literary works are known only through copies on stone. Our sources epigraphic and literary join without a seam.[26] But acceptance of the gods is as widespread in inscriptions as is implied, for instance, by Lucian, when he counts listeners to atheism as so few.[27] We would have been misled had we given too much weight to his own scepticism, or Seneca's. Here is one illustration of the danger of relying only on a small selection of writers. For a second illustration: the gods addressed in inscriptions are described only in very broad strokes and simple affirmations, in a shouted phrase, for example—"The One," "Greatest," "Savior"—or in a string of epithets without integration: "swift-running," "dwelling on high."[28] Examples of the style have been offered in the preceding chapter. The resulting picture of the gods is oddly pointillist, as if in acceptance of each one's birth and growth out of the visions of all his votaries, individually, by quite uncontrolled accretion— pointillist and motionless: it is rare that the gods are seen in action in any episode of their story, though a life or biography many of them are indeed known to have possessed.[29] The literary treatment of religion in this respect also matches the epigraphic. After Ovid, back at the turn of the era, and all the way up to Claudian and Nonnus at the edge of another great break in history, writers show little interest in anecdotes from "mythology," as we would call it. So it would be misleading to draw our own impressions too much from certain exceptional passages in Plutarch, let us say.

Literary evidence, at least in Greek, joins closely with one other type, papyrological. There is no sharp break detectable in moving from the style and interests that broadly prevail in one, to the other. Good reason, therefore, to trust to Egypt for some impression of the place of religion in literature—though that province was famed for being particularly addicted to sacred lore and studies. Out of some thousands of papyri, whole or fragments, that are of literary character, only a small number focus directly on religion. Numenius, Ammonius, Plotinus, and Porphyry make no appearance; other philosophers very rarely and for treatises on government or ethics or logic.[30] There is a Hellenistic scrap of Orphism, there are two or three scraps of aretalogy, quite a few hymns and paeans (so far, the same mix found in inscriptions, minus the votive), plus bits and pieces of fiction describing scenes of worship. Throughout this little corpus of texts there is a distinctly regional quality, to which Isis and Osiris especially contribute. Had anyone demanded a larger share of the written word for piety, there was an answer ready to meet him: all the big temples had their own libraries, containing no doubt the same sort of prose and verse in praise of native deities that still survives, but in much, much greater abundance; beyond that, representing Hellenic culture in a broad sense, there was Homer. A majority of all identifiable literary papyri are the two epics, or commentary; and Hesiod is high in popularity, too. Those, it might have been said, were the old and the new testaments of truest Hellenism.

In trying to understand the faith prevailing in the lettered classes, use is commonly made of Gnostic, Hermetic, Chaldaean, Neoplatonic, Orphic, or Neopythagorean texts. With favorite selections drawn from other genres, they constitute the material from which the modern account of religious feeling in our period of study is typically composed. They are, however, given an importance quite out of scale with what contemporaries conceived their faith to be. "The underlying personal experience" (above, p. 65) is indeed far better found, at its very deepest, in Gnostic texts and the like. To call this deepest level "religion" without further qualification misrepresents the subject.

So much for the first objection that must be raised against choosing one's sources to fit one's modern preconceptions—against reliance, that is, on a small group of writers. The choice must rather widen to include experiences by no means intense, but no less a fact; concerns by no means profound, but no less sincerely expressed; and indifference or positive rejection almost as strongly represented as high-wrought religiosity. This said, nothing is subtracted from the subject. It is only taken away from a little, rather peculiar collection of books, and restored to a very much larger circle of real people, some of whom (like any sampling from the *Canterbury Tales, Simplicissimus,* or *War and Peace*) felt religion at the heart always; most, at the fingertips, as Lactantius puts it; and a few, never at all.

The second objection lies against the presenting of religion in our period only through the testimony of writers and readers. How few they were in the entire population has already been emphasized. That they were different remains to be asserted.

Plutarch may stand for a type thoroughly accepted among the well educated and well-to-do. He had a broad range of friends and interests Roman and Greek, even (but not untypically) reaching beyond, to write our only extant essay on Isiacism. He counted as more devout than most. In his collection of antiquarian oddments called *Quaestiones Romanae,* he takes up about a hundred customs having to do with Roman religion. For example: (1) Why do the Romans consider Kronos the father of truth? (Because they suppose Kronos is Chronos, Time, and time discovers truth?) (2) Why do they pay honor to the dead in December? (Because in that month all growing things have done with their lives?) (3)Why may the priest of Jupiter never anoint himself in the open? (Because it is not decent for a son to strip before a father, and Jupiter is the father of all?) (4) Why are slave women barred from the shrine of Matuta? (Because her Greek equivalent, Ino, was jealous of a slave woman on her husband's account?) (5) Why may the King of Sacrifices never address the people? (Because the Romans expelled their kings, and wish to limit his semblance to cult acts?) And (6) Why is Rome's guardian deity never named? (Because that protects him from being conjured away?)[31]

The answers he offers to his questions he arrives at through six characteristic modes of thought. They lie in punning, in symbolic or esthetic appropriateness, in analogy with mortal customs, in echo of myth or a deity's life story, in historical accident, and in suitability for achieving some result, through binding or pleasing a deity. Only that last could be called functional, that is, only in that category of explanation does Plutarch consider the gods and their will as really existing. All the others (the next to last being the most often invoked) assume that cult is wholly man-made. His approach, not only in the first category, is bookish in the extreme, and in a sense also extremely rational.

By contrast, an inscription from third-century Dacia in semiliterate Latin describes how Aurelius Martinus Basus and Aurelius Castor Polydeuces, "standing about, saw the spirit of an eagle come down from a hill upon three snakes. One big viper tangled up the eagle. The aforementioned freed the eagle from danger. They set this up as their vow deserved, willingly," to the sky god Jupiter of Doliche.[32] Somehow they felt the divine had entered their lives, and in a fashion far from bookish and rational, they did what needed to be done.

The differences in religion separating the upper class from the lower (and no middle really existed) can be more easily sensed than brought out explicitly through the evidence. That they existed, at least one of the two well knew, and reminded the other in clear and often scornful terms.[33] They may all be gathered under one alone: "superstition." In turn, however, what we and the ancients, too, indicate by that term is a crudeness of conviction in regard to both the gods' sphere of action and their nature. The two elements in "superstition" now to be examined should be kept distinct so as to grasp the meaning of the word clearly and to understand the chief class differences in religious views.

The wonderful happening in which the two Aurelii participated brought the god of Doliche down from the sky to the very roadside. It was a sign that they could touch—as Timoleon's soldiers could touch the load of parsley on the mule's back, when they passed it on their way. They took it for a portent. Plutarch tells the story (the explanation does not concern us), calling it an instance of superstition.[34] He uses the word to express his disagreement with those who would take a perfectly ordinary event, as he saw it, and ascribe divine dimensions to it. The more a person saw the gods at work in the material world—moving things around, for instance—and the less a person explained in terms of natural causes, the clearer was the presence of superstition.

Over the course of the centuries chosen for examination here, superstition within this meaning certainly increased. The fact is best sensed (to say "measured" would imply a degree of accuracy beyond our reach) in the greater prominence of magic; for magic, after all, is most shortly defined as the art that brings about the intervention of superhuman powers in the material world—"moving things around, for instance." Proof of the practice of the art grows more abundant, most obviously in recipes and handbooks written on papyrus. It is to be found in every province, for example, in leaden curse tablets. And people who should have known better come to credit invocations with an efficacy that, in some previous century, would never have been believed. It means nothing that a late orator attributed an ineffectual speech to hexing by jealous detractors; an early orator, consul in Cicero's day, offered the same excuse; but when the very emperor resorted to wizards to aid him in his wars, times had changed.[35] Perhaps no new ideas are to be discovered, but old ones are found in circles previously immune to them, now ready to acknowledge the direct, visible intervention of super-human powers in the world at human bidding.

With the change, no doubt partly cause and partly effect, philosophy in the old sense fell out of favor. This too is a phenomenon well known. It is often remarked among the upper classes. It shows itself in times of peace and prosperity in the later second century, or at least the symptoms that characterize the developed disease are by that period already discoverable. Its origins therefore cannot lie in the decline of wealth, schools, libraries, endowed chairs of learning, and the like, although all these latter indeed suffered in the third century. Alternatively, to explain the waning of philosophy as a mere fashion, in Nock's term (above, p. 65), provides no serious answer unless the fashion itself can be derived. But contemporaries had their own explanation: "philosophers agree about nothing—one of them even says that silver is black. You can hear more uproar from a household of philosophers than from a household of madmen." [36] And variations on the theme: "I frequented the schools of the philosophers [at Rome] and found nothing but preparation for the overthrow of doctrines; competing and arguing; and tricks of syllogizing and the imagining of premisses"— from all of which the wise man would turn away to more profitable studies.[37] At the end of our period, the emperor himself before a learned gathering could describe "Socrates, elated by his debating powers, making the weaker reasoning appear the stronger, and playing about with mutually contradictory arguments . . . , and Pythagoras as well, while pretending to practise self-control in a special degree, and silence, too, was caught in imposture . . . , and finally Plato, up to a point, was wise, but in other matters he is found to have erred from the truth." [38] They had all been wrong, every one.

Disciplined abstract thought, tested by challenges made sharp in the course of fierce fights over many, many centuries, the challenges themselves not to be handled or even understood by the casual observer, had passed from favor. As in the history of warfare periods emerge in which attack prevails over defense, so in the history of thought a time had come in which the nays had it. Every proposition could be overthrown by ten different arguments. All the arguments were in every student's hands, or handbooks. And the casual observer whose interest counted for most had spent his youth, not in a university, but in some catechetical school or, more likely, in a barracks. Thus the balance of techniques of debate, and then political and economic troubles, and the hastening advancement of people new to wealth and cultural leadership, combined to bring on the moment when Constantine could simply wave philosophy aside without being laughed at.

That was the test: ridicule. Fully to sense the meaning of Constantine's preposterous pontification, he must be imagined speaking at Plutarch's table. There, his views would have produced delighted grins; likewise, no doubt, in the company of Lucian or Apuleius. Lucian knew of opinionated ignoramuses in very high places indeed, followers of the pious fraud Alexander. They were the equal in gullibility of the population of Abonuteichus where Alexander set up shop. Lucian expects his readers to laugh at them, as Apuleius could hope (a little anxiously, in a small town like Oea) to raise a laugh at yokel accusations of magic. He practiced no magic, he insisted in his defense, but scientific experiment in the tradition of Aristotle. Who but a clod could misinterpret that? With his trial, we have passed the mid-second century. We still feel a difference—the difference between "religion" and "superstition"—separating the literate few of Athens, Rome, or Carthage from the people of remote centers like Oea in Tripolitania or Abonuteichus in Pontus. Another hundred years pass, and gullibility is no longer a target for ridicule. In the most educated circles that the Empire has to show, enchantments, trances, and wonder-working raise no laugh; rather, fear and awe. It is rationalism, as we would call it, that now must defend itself; and it is easily put to rout by Constantine. Most of his listeners—not all, for such large changes come about very gradually—no doubt shared his views.[39]

To return, then, to our point of departure, in the contrast between the lettered elite and the broad masses of the population, and between the religion of the one and the superstition of the other: it is clear that the differences were sharper at the beginning of our period than at the end. It follows that a sharper objection must be raised against the use of some member of Plutarch's circle than of Constantine's, to represent the whole world of the Apologists. Elite and masses, in their views about the supernatural at work, had at the end drawn much closer to each other. What divided them still was only a matter of complexity or depth of explanation.

A final sign of their approximation: by piety, that is, by a life lived in accord with divine will and laws, one could draw down upon one's whole community all sorts of blessings—wonderful happenings, or good crops and bread at low prices. "The priestess Alexandra of Demeter Thesmophoros asks"—so begins an inscription of the second century from the oracle of Apollo at Didyma. And her question follows: "Because, since first I assumed the priesthood, the gods as never before have been visible through their attentions—and this, sometimes through the virgins and matrons, sometimes through men and boys—what means such a thing, and toward what destiny?" The answer, though largely lost, can perhaps be reconstructed: the cause of the phenomena she asks about was the devotion of the priestess herself, here, as reported also of others in other inscriptions, at Stratonicea (for a specific miracle vouchsafed) and elsewhere.[40] We can recall, too, a traveler of the period talking with a Greek shepherdess who claimed "the power of prophecy given her by the Mother of the Gods; and all the shepherds in the region and the farmers used her for the fertility and security of their crops and flocks."[41] Or we can compare another tourist at Atargatis's shrine, seeing the pillar saints atop their pillars, "whom *hoi polloi* believe to be up there in the company of the gods, requesting benefits for the whole of Syria."[42]

Intercessors for divine favor thus appear widespread in the eastern provinces—but more easily to be found in the hinterlands and periphery (Olbia, Cyrene, Caria, and the islands) than at the center of things; more venerated, too, by the ignorant and simple. It is not till the third century that the very emperors are acclaimed in open ceremonies as winning bountiful harvests for their farmers and calm seas for their sailors, by their piety.[43] The change is not abrupt, a matter of emphasis rather than of innovation; but it assumes in the gods accessibility to direct and specific appeal, it assumes their willingness to make their favor felt by visible tinkering in the natural world. Earlier, by contrast, when a panegyrist credited Trajan with averting famine, it was not the emperor's prayers that had brought supernatural aid, but his shrewd administration that had mobilized quite human forces.[44]

3. HOW THE DIVINE WORLD WAS ENVISIONED

Almost to see, or actually and with one's own eyes to see, the natural order suspended through the exertion of one's will upon the divine, or a wizard's or holy man's will, constituted only one element in superstition. The other element was accused of misrepresenting the nature rather than the reach, accessibility or sphere of the gods. It attributed to them an unpredictable malice forever to be feared and deflected through seemingly irrational acts. Plutarch wrote an essay on the subject (in Greek, *deisidaemonia*, "demon terror"), which he calls folly because it corresponds to nothing in reality. The gods in fact are kind; there is no cause for dread. Well said, the superstitious man would have rejoined; but he himself had a better understanding of reality; and in that, his own mad actions and panic were actually the height of good sense.[1] Only Clement of Alexandria penetrates into the implications of *deisidaemonia* much further, in supposing that wicked people will invent wicked, savage gods, just as benevolent people invent the reverse. The result, a superstitious dread of gods who should indeed be feared, is logical—"reasonable," as he says. Normally, "superstition" is used by ancient writers simply to indicate religious beliefs they do not share, without their bothering to justify the pejorative term. Justification must be guessed, and usually can be guessed, by drawing in to the judgment quite familiar ethical or esthetic standards: temple prostitution or castration to serve the god better was "superstition," and so was rolling about in the mud or shrieking and dancing in public.

Needless to say, condemnation of actual, existing cult practices arises in the library or school, among observers of a certain education and fastidiousness. They are the same on whose experiences it is common to draw for a picture of religiosity in its various degrees and levels. They appear to have their own forms of engagement, however, and their own forms of detachment, just as the masses demonstrate their own loud blasphemy, contradicted by unconditional zeal.

Of the one, quite tiny, circle, Plutarch is a good member to advance our discussion further. He wrote at the outset of the time span here chosen for examination, and from the geographical center, near Delphi. His connections with the Roman as well as the more obvious Greek population have been noted once before. When we glance through his essays in search of his view on the true nature of divinity, to be contrasted with superstitious views, we find him repeatedly insisting on goodness as its essential characteristic: goodness in the sense of active beneficence as well as inactive virtue. Divinity can never be the cause of ill. We must trust what is "suitable, reasonable, and likely" on this score, not what the poets have written. The gods cannot have engaged in violent quarrels—such opinions are "neither sound nor true"—against each other or against or for men. They cannot have suffered wounds from men, as Homer relates, or dismemberment or other mishaps, as Dionysiacs or Egyptians believe, according to myths both "barbarous and unlawful." They cannot be imagined lowering or diminishing themselves by too direct involvement in human affairs. To suppose otherwise would be "naive and childish," disrespectful to the greatness of divine goodness, *arete*.[2] And Plutarch scatters in his writings a good many normative words, showing that he had very clear ideas about the nature of the divine, even if he does not happen to spell out some of the (to us) most interesting ones. No doubt he supposed they needed no explanation.

His contemporary, Dio Chrysostom, and (born about when these two died) Lucian and his generation, can be used to amplify Plutarch's testimony. The divine, says Dio Chrysostom, is goodness complete and the source of all that is good in our lives: good esthetically, that is, glorious to look at, and glorious ethically, for our contemplation. As such, gods can delight in gifts only from mortals resembling themselves, the just and good, though their delight implies no satisfaction of a need. Divinity of course stands in want of nothing, not even of statues or burnt offerings.[3] Indeed not, Lucian agrees. It is impious to imagine the gods being bought or swayed by men; and yet the contrary view, that they care nought for men, is equally wrong. The key to the dilemma is not to portray them too much like men, as the poets do; by whom they are even lowered to physical ugliness or menial employ, like Hephaestus, all sooty and "always in the fire, by his trade"; crucified, like Prometheus; physically restrained in shackles or wounded in combat; caught up in emotions, in love; or melted down, in idols. In Egypt, they assumed the shape of monkeys, birds, and crocodiles![4] All such pictures of the immortals do them violence, by setting them in postures or acts which would be condemned as weak or wicked if they were human.

Lucian and others do not see the difficulty in applying two standards, one anthropomorphizing, the other, more abstract, whereby the gods must be everything that is best in man—handsome, benevolent, high-minded, and so forth—but also what is best in creatures of some other, higher species altogether. That difficulty arose from the conflation of long-established criticisms by Plato, Xenophanes, and others of the past, whose views could not be made to fit together logically.

Making a cast beyond these obvious authors, for beliefs scattered more sparsely but more widely among others of the second and third centuries, we catch some fragments of the Pseudo-Apuleius, the Pseudo-Aristotle, Iamblichus, Porphyry, and others; also of Apologists. In part, at least, the latter spoke to pagans, therefore intended to anticipate and withstand their criticism. It needs no demonstration, of course, that Christians were wholly of the world around them—of what other can they be supposed?—and drew in its everyday assumptions with their very breath; that those among them who engaged in debate with pagans had had the same schooling, beneath or in step with the catechetical; and that in such debate they could best hope to win by anchoring their assertions to points of common conviction. Hence their free characterizing of beliefs as "absurd," "irrational," "folly," "incredible," "outrageous," and the like, without need of refutation step by step. All parties shared the same preconceptions. Accordingly we have for illustration two men who never saw each other (conveniently, they straddle the midpoint of our period), Celsus and Origen, the former at one point summing up some arguments of Christians in order to answer them, while Origen the Christian quotes that passage itself in order to supply the surrebutter.[5]

It is "not reasonable" to consider idols as gods, when they have been manufactured by men, and, worse, by men of low social status and morals; and the point was long ago made by a pagan Heraclitus (of the first century), so says the pagan Celsus—it was no invention of higher-minded Christians. Celsus is indeed right in bringing out how much derisory or outraged criticism of current cult practices, theology, and mythology could be found in pagan writers. Here it is aimed at implications that gods are the mere creatures of men.

And to continue the survey of divinity as it is portrayed in these less obvious sources: gods or divinity can do no ill, being goodness perfect and complete.[6] That, like all the points now to be summarized, has also been found or implied in Plutarch, Dio Chrysostom, and Lucian. Further, the gods are infinitely remote from the material world, themselves incorporeal and insubstantial.[7] To imagine that they have any need of the world would imply some incompleteness in them; rather, it is of the essence of divinity to have no desire, no wish, no lack or feeling at all.[8]

It follows that the gods cannot change, assume other shapes, grow up or grow old. Assuredly they cannot die and be reborn, like Osiris. They cannot be cut up, wounded, put in chains, tossed out of Olympus, crippled; nor have they appetites. They do not eat or drink, defecate, or fornicate. Of course not. Rejection of such pictures is registered or implied in the writings of Plutarch and Lucian but also of Heraclitus and Celsus.[9] And no one may rightly accuse the gods of adultery, sodomy, theft, perjury, cowardice, murder, or wicked or disgraceful acts of that sort—again, features of belief shocking to pagans and highly convenient to Christians.[10] The gods should never be thought of or portrayed as dependent, servile, or menial. The opposite is the truth.[11] Still less should they ever be described as monsters of any sort, misshapen, abnormal, or even as animals: Egyptian crocodiles and so forth.[12]

From conceptualizations, the higher criticism turned to visible routines of worship to make its point. Idols that were in the first place sawn, glued, nailed, and filed could hardly be divine. The materials of their manufacture were base, and they endured the birds that shit on them and mice that nested in them.[13] It was equally misguided, if the gods were conceived aright, to suppose that they could "taste good strong thick stupefying incense-smoke," or respond—still more wicked folly—to human sacrifice.[14] Of all the dancing, singing, miming, or recitation of prose hymns; of all the anointing, bathing, wreathing, robing, and parading about of images; of all the toasting, holocausts, and cheerful tables; of ivory, gold, sublime skills in painting and carving—really nothing remained that held the faintest interest for

Olympus, if that high realm and all its denizens in fact existed. Probably not.

Certainly not in the sense or shapes that Homer meant, certainly not in the Dionysiac's or Isiac's demented terms—not if the pagan purists were to be believed. The gods really lived; but at a great remove. Cult could not reach them. It might be inoffensive, never persuasive. Mythology, not only as the poets had written it but as the Phrygians embraced Cybele in it, or the Syrians, Atargatis, was folly or insult to the true beings above. The sacred had lost its story when its enlightened critics finished with it.

But who cared? The inappropriateness of common forms of worship, seen through the eyes of Seneca or Porphyry, appears not to have deterred a single soul from the inheritance of his tribe. If anyone listened to Epicureans or Stoics, no signs attest to his conversion. Which is not to deny that conversions may have been made—let us say, *must* have been made—but not in numbers at all detectable. The same limits perhaps circumscribed the Apologists. There is no knowing what effect if any they achieved, when they attacked religious customs of their time—idolatry, for instance, or burnt offerings. Had they managed to find many readers for the kinds of arguments and conclusions that have been summarized in the preceding pages, surely Tertullian, at the outset of his *Soul's Testimony*, need not have deplored the fact that "no one turns to our literature who is not already Christian."

And surely, too, we would expect some sign of the higher criticism to show in the corpus of surviving inscriptions and papyri. It is there—barely: the one oracle issued by Apollo from Claros, speaking of the hereafter and recorded on stone; from Egypt, the one fragment of Pseudo-Plutarch's otherwise lost *Placita philosophorum*. Otherwise, of Plutarch, Philodemus, the Pseudo-Aristotle, Lucian, Sextus Empiricus, Celsus, Porphyry, and all the Apologists from whose collective testimony the foregoing views about the nature of god have been reassembled, there exists not a word, not a scrap of papyrus—against some hundreds for Homer alone.[15] One province, and the survival of evidence by chance (unless chance is rather an element to be desired, in this sort of testing), should not be allowed to stand for all the Empire. But what is there better? And besides, why should anyone expect a broader audience for what we might call analytical theology? No, the literature of religion *par excellence* was hymns, in every century (above, pp. 15f.); and hymns present a world of ideas quite cut off from the higher criticism. Anyone may compare the two and confirm the fact.

In any case, if one were made too uncomfortable by inherited worship and mythology, escape into beliefs less gross and more intellectually satisfying could be had through reinterpretation. Menander the rhetor in the third century, describing how to write prose hymns suitable to whatsoever deity, calls attention to one useful device: the discovery of *ainigmata*, riddles. He means a sort of decoding, whereby the speaker detects, or pretends to detect but actually invents, hidden intents in traditional material. By this trick everything can be spruced up: the older hymns and rites, now outmoded; cult objects at initiations that offend prudery or common sense; local images and lore; stories of deities that tell too much or too little.[16] In the same century, Porphyry takes up a stretch of an Orphic hymn for illustration: Zeus, as commonly portrayed, "is seated, the firm seat of his power being shown through riddle (ἀινιττόμενος), for his upper parts are unclothed because he is visible through his thoughts and in the celestial portions of the universe, but the parts to the fore are covered because he is invisible among the things hidden below." And Menander again interprets Apollo as the Sun, Hera as the air, because of the resemblance of her name to the word in Greek. Rather elementary examples.[17] The stories of Kronos eating his young bewildered and revolted anyone who stopped to think of them; but they could suggest cryptically that mind turns in upon itself. So says Sallust the philosopher. Pausanias worried about them, too, but "grew to hold a more thoughtful view of them. In olden times those Greeks who were considered wise spoke in riddles, not straight out. Accordingly, it is my supposition that these legends about Kronos are a piece of Greek wisdom."[18]

Reinterpretation had a long history before the period of our study. The art found favor among Jews and Christians as well as pagans. Seneca thought it nonsense, Dio Chrysostom scorned its exculpations of Homer; but their respective contemporaries Cornutus and Plutarch made frequent, reverential use of it in defense of existing religion—even Egyptian.[19] The tearing apart of Osiris could be understood in a new and most unobvious light; so also the same fate suffered by Dionysus; and passages in Homer and Hesiod could be enriched with marginal commentary pointing out, for example, the former's confirmation of Empedocles.[20]

Most practitioners of reinterpretation felt or appealed to a loving awe, an automatic veneration for everything in the distant past, feelings that were emphasized earlier. It was too much to throw out one's heritage, *Iliad*, *Theogony*, and all, only because of the parts at odds with a university education. And was the more modern enlightenment itself so sure to be right, after all—or was it not rather to be supposed that, in the old poems, old legends and old rituals, men of yore had hidden Cyclopean verities? Up to the end, however, until Porphyry, interpreters either said explicitly that what was drawn out by unriddling should be kept from ordinary folk; or, Porphyry included, they proposed ideas of a sort that few people could have understood. Everyone venerated antiquity, no doubt; but by no means everybody thought its lore required to be rewritten.

Where enlightenment crossed antiquity, the two could be realigned to fit well enough with each other. That, beyond allegorical interpretation, provided another way of tolerating both one's religious heritage and the ideas most in fashion among intellectuals. By realignment, the old systems of belief were made parallel but subordinate to the new, as intermediaries between man and the "real" god(s).

Plato had seen the possibilities in this, his followers developed his thought, and from Middle Platonism it passed into common currency within that tiny circle who read philosophy at all. They believed in "demon" intermediaries,[21] to which could be attributed everything gross, wicked, bizarre, or irrational. To higher planes could be attributed passionless perfection, sedate entirety, and remoteness above everything material.

According to various thinkers, there were more or fewer planes: of demons alone, beneath the divine, three kinds, so said Plutarch, Apuleius, and Plotinus; two kinds, higher and lower, according to Celsus; several gradations not all called demons by Iamblichus, including "angels" and "rulers"; or spheres above spheres at unimaginable distances from earth, each with its special denizens. Seven was a favored number for such regions; but there might be ten; or, if one thought about it—better, in Dr. Johnson's phrase, "if one *abandoned* one's mind to it"—there might be 365. Encountering Gnostic systems, on the lunatic fringe of such speculation, Irenaeus, Clement, and Hippolytus gave hundreds of pages to their destruction, repeatedly in their attacks characterizing their adversaries as quite mad— Irenaeus at one point hanging on to his own sanity, the reader feels, only by giving way to a choice parody of the wilder flights of Valentinianism.[22] "Mushroom growths," he calls the Gnostic systems elsewhere (1.29.1). They were as sudden in their appearing as they were light, and quite as perishable.

But demons were something else again: very deeply rooted in paganism, western as well as eastern, even if much more easily documented in the latter. First, the word itself. It occupied a place apart from "gods," a little lower, in common usage. But there were passages in what might be called sacred writings, notably in Homer, where the two terms appeared synonymously.[23] Christian writers drew a sharp distinction, reserving the proper

At Dura on the Euphrates in 1920, British troops happened on this and other wall-paintings among the free-standing ruins. In due course, word reached the American Egyptologist James Breasted. He visited the site, took color photographs, and presented them with a lecture to the French Académie des Inscriptions (see its *Comptes rendues* of 1922, p. 240). From this resulted the excavations at Dura in the 1920s and 1930s, by the Académie, Cumont, Rostovtzeff, and Yale University. Courtesy Yale University Art Gallery, Dura-Europos Collection.

title for their own God and the lower rank for everyone else's. Their scorn would have had no sting to it had they not been speaking in well-understood gradations.

In paganism itself, then, there were agreed-upon ranks of supernatural power. But the fact emerges less clearly from the vocabulary in ordinary use than from people's mental picture of the divine order. It is often revealed. By far the most usual outline is a regal one: there is a king god, Zeus, from Homer on; there is a queen, or rather, two at least: Isis and Juno regularly receive that title; and Men, Osiris, Attis, and Helios are occasionally called king, too.[24] These are all eastern, perhaps not by coincidence. From Hellenistic times, epithets common for deities define them as absolute masters, like Hellenistic rulers. In Asia Minor, Men is regularly "despot," *tyrannos.* In Syrian cities, like Hellenistic rulers, gods wear military uniform—a mix

ΘΕΜΗC
MOKIMC
IEPEYC

IVLTERN
TIVSTRIE

As appears in the restored drawing by L. North, the faded painting in the Bel temple shows a Syrian triad of deities to the left, dressed in Roman military costumes and with gold disks (the later Christian aureoles) behind their heads. Below are the patron Fortunes of Palmyra and Dura. To the right, sacrifice is offered by the Palmyrene troop commander Terentius, holding some holy scroll, and by the priest Themes Mocimi, who in A.D. 239 shows up in a duty roster assigned to the troop's chapel (*ad signa,* cf. *Corp. pap. lat.* 331 = *PDura* 89, and below, chap. 2.4 n.70). Courtesy Yale University Art Gallery, Dura-Europos Collection.

of Persian, Greek, and then, in our period, prevailingly Roman styles. The sky god of Doliche, in northernmost Syria, wears the baldric, sword, cuirasse, and tunic of the emperor. Mithra on Tarsian coins has the same costume.[25] It is the early first century in Palmyra when the practice becomes noticeable in reliefs; in eastern coins generally, not till the second half of the second century. In disturbed times and places, the unarmed man was weak; surely also unarmed gods; so they were fitted out for war. That may be the explanation at first. Later, they borrowed from the prestige of the emperor. Portrayal as Roman soldiers touches the images of the Rider Gods in the Danubian provinces and of Saturn's guards, the Dioscuri, in Africa.[26] Inscriptions from Germany refer to Sol as "the unconquerable emperor," Jupiter as "*princeps* of the gods," and in Italy even Christ appears in im-

perial military regalia under the title Christus Imperator, before the mid-
third century.[27]

God is given his Guards by Apologists, in the second, third and fourth
centuries, just as Helios is so defended by his worshipers in a magical
papyrus post–300, or as the philosophers' supreme being is, in the second
and third centuries. The imagery is sometimes drawn out into armies, commanders, prefects, governors, and messengers around the throne.[28] Such
were the agents which had to be assumed in order to bring divinity into
touch with the material world or, more crudely conceived, into control of
countless subjects and responsibilities.

Because the divine could will no evil, theorists supposed that demons
served as instruments of vengeance and punishment; likewise as instruments for the dirty or menial business of magic, and for the mechanical
business of providing signs and oracles. It need not be Apollo in person
who spoke at Delphi.[29] Demons were assigned specific spheres of activity—
oversight of animals, delivery of men's prayers to higher authorities, control over mortal events or natural processes[30]—and specific cities or tribes of
men.[31] The pagan and Christian pictures of divine administration were
identical, however different in origin; both could have accepted what the
emperor Julian later said in his oration against the "Galilaeans" (143A–B),
that "over each nation is a national god, with an angel acting as his agent,
and a demon, and a 'hero,' and a peculiar type of servant-powers and subordinates." The titles he chose would have aroused some disagreement; the
authority of the Psalms and Plato's *Laws* might have been matched against
each other—always supposing that the hierarchy had been worked out at
all in the minds of disputants on either side, even by those (both Christian
and pagan in both eastern and western provinces) to whom the thought of
minor beings in action was quite familiar and in whom their names had
always produced a shiver. Not everyone had taken the time to arrange his
ideas in any logical shape. But there would have been no dispute that such
powers did exist.

"Spirits," or however they might be termed, could be found everywhere.
Evidence is more abundant than might be expected, considering that it
must be found in the realm of the shadowy, the shameful, the illegal, and
the illiterate. Everyone believed. But since belief procured no major benefits
—those lay in the gift of the gods—it attracted no priesthood or other
control. Instead, there was a great deal of free borrowing, extemporizing
and invention by ignorant votaries. The description of the spirit world—
the bottom or base of the pyramid—as "the syncretistic, rotting refuse heap

of the dead and dying religions of the whole ancient world," while no doubt a trifle dramatic, conveys the right impression.[32]

Magic without doctrine; devils without priests; prayers unintelligible; worship homeless; and ignominious realms of rule over a single house, a single field, cow, racehorse, gladiator, rival in love or adversary to one's career or party—all, together, constituted the broad underpart of the world above this one, the part with which mortals felt themselves to be most directly in contact. Further above reigned beings of grander dimensions, still confined, however, in their authority to one village, town, or city; next, a smaller number of what Christian writers call "Great-Demons," all one word, like Apollo or Mars. But did the logic of this structure culminate, as it ought to have done, in one supreme being at the highest, the most remote point, in the universe?

The answer is yes, in the minds of some; almost, for more; no, for the vast majority. It was a question requiring more thought than most people were inclined to give to the relations, not between mortals and immortals, but among the latter by themselves. Moreover, to describe Jupiter as prince of gods or as "saving your ancestral gods from every destruction," in public documents,[33] was to imply a subordination not very flattering to the inferior. To accept it diminished them and denied ancestral worship. How universally such disrespect was condemned has been emphasized in earlier pages (above, pp. 2–3). Perhaps that was the reason, then, why testimonies just now cited, which assume some gods to be subordinate to others, cannot be easily found before the very end of our period. By that time, the Roman Empire here beneath had had some centuries in which to suggest itself as a model for the Empire above. That the human should supply a way of being conceived to the divine has been shown to be quite natural.

In the second century, Apuleius writes with real anger about a character in his novel, a baker's wife, "enemy to faith, foe to modesty, who spurned and kicked aside the divine powers of sure religion, and substituted for a true religion the audacious imagining and invented rites of a god whom she proclaimed the only one"; while, in the earlier third century at Rome, when a worshiper set up an inscription to "One Zeus, Sarapis, Helios, maker of the universe, invincible," someone else came along and substituted the name "Mithra" for "Sarapis"[34]—two indications that too high a claim for one god gave offense to the worshipers of others. That sort of intolerant behavior in paganism was extremely rare.

Indeed, the illustration from Apuleius may be unique; for the second belongs to a phenomenon which only appears to be monotheism. In reality, it is the melding of several gods into one chief: "Zeus Helios the Great All-God Sarapis," this on an altar from second-century Carthage.[35] Zeus is worshiped as Papa and Attis, all at the same time, in Bithynia; he is "Zeus Greatest Helios Olympian, the Savior," in an inscription from Pergamon; "Zeus Sarapis" often on gems and amulets, "Zeus Dionysus" in Phrygia or Rome.[36]

More commonly still, supremacy is concentrated in the sun, natural and visible master of at least the eastern skies. So in Mithraism the sun, in hyphenation with Mithra, is the supreme deity. Inscriptions from the western provinces make that clear. They also call the sun "Helios" more often than "Sol," and the dedications are disproportionately in Greek, not Latin, indicating the god's special favor among people of Greek-speaking origin. In western Asia Minor, the sun enjoys favor as a witness to men's oaths, with his all-seeing eye; but that presents him in no regal role.[37] Better, in Egypt, magical papyri invoke the sun in such terms as "Lord god who grasps the whole, gives life to all, and rules the universe."[38]

In the Levant, the sun is most at home. In Emesa, and among Arabs generally as Aziz, he reigns uncontested; and as a god great but not supreme, like Apollo, he is worshiped in Palmyra, Baalbek, and other towns and cities.[39] A mosaic floor from the area (Tiberias) and from the later third or early fourth century portrays him in a characteristic pose, standing in his chariot (like Apollo), wearing the commander's cloak (the *paludamentum*, like the Roman emperor), holding in his left hand the orb or globe of rule (again, like the emperor), and raising his right hand in the typical gesture of benediction and mastery.[40] What was said earlier about how the heavenly powers were most often and naturally arranged in the mind's eye, to resemble the shape of earthly powers, is well illustrated by this picture. It very much resembles also a well-known depiction of Christ in a mosaic beneath St. Peter's basilica in Rome.

To examine a little further the form in which the divine world was commonly envisioned, Roman imperial coins can be used very helpfully, since they reached and presumably did not conflict with the ideas of an enormous audience. At the beginning of our period they advertise Sun or Sun-of-the-East, Sol Oriens, in quite conventional fashion, to suggest that the region was friendly during Trajan's and Hadrian's wars. The same conventions govern portrayal of Gordian receiving the orb of sovereignty from Sol, toward the mid-third century.[41] Sol as *invictus*, whose invincibility is as specific as the beneficent power of his raised right hand, appears on Antoninus Pius's coins first (and about that time, too, in inscriptions); then on Commodus's coins; and on Septimius Severus's (and at that point the

epithet is first applied to an emperor himself on his coins); then on Gallienus's and with great but not exclusive emphasis on Aurelian's; briefly, on
Probus's; again, in A.D. 305–310, minted by Galerius and (in many issues)
by Maximin Daia, with Sol bearing the special title, "Guardian of the Emperors and Vice-Emperors," *conservator Augustorum et Caesarum,* on
issues of both Maximin Daia and Constantine; and finally, after the Tetrarchs
had all been destroyed (all but Licinius), Constantine and Licinius each
resumed a specially advertised relationship with Sol, Constantine carrying
it forward to a point some years beyond Licinius's death.[42] From all of
which it has been thought that solar monotheism spread out from the east
over the center, west and entirety of the Roman Empire, until in the reign of
Constantine that ruler, convert to the Sun himself, changed faith a second
time and so became a Christian.

What we have tripped on here is a point at which religious and political
history intersect. There is no way to keep the two distinct, despite the obvious fact that coins and dates and individual personalities of emperors ill
suit the style of our discussion so far. At best, those implications of the junc-
ture which have to do with emperor worship can be left aside. Imperial cult
hardly belongs to this study; and no one supposes that the worship of the
ruler himself, even where he plainly wanted to be seen as the embodiment
of a god, constituted monotheism. It is supposed, however, that the subordination of all deities to one, and a kind of personal equation with that
one, was sought and advertised by successive emperors off and on over the
course of the whole third century, until at last an orator could declare,
"Surely, Constantine, you have some secret bond with that divine mind
which, delegating *our* care to the minor deities, thinks fit to show itself to
you alone."[43] The idea that, even over the gods (not "demons," note), a
greater being presided, has been encountered in earlier pages, where the
pyramid of powers was described and where people's perceptions of the
celestial and the terrestrial hierarchy were compared. It may seem only the
last stage of a logical development that finally subordinates the many of
traditional paganism to the one, Sol.

To make this seem more natural, too, there are two earlier nexus of events
to be added to that which ends in Constantine—two very much less important and well known, but still quite often described. In A.D. 218, Elagabalus
had come to the throne. He was hereditary priest of the solar deity at Emesa,
in whose favor he now took every measure he could think of to lower other
deities publicly. The principal image of Caelestis-Tanit from Carthage, for
example, was shipped over to pay homage in Rome. A new temple was
built there for the Sun, new festivals and ceremonies instituted, and every-

thing advertised on coins. "He used to say that all gods were the servants of his own god, while terming some its chamberlains, others, its slaves, others, its servants of various sorts." [44] Words from a doubtful source, the *Augustan History*—but at least the picture they offer of a celestial monarchy is recognizable as perfectly conventional. The whole structure of worship vanished the moment Elagabalus died, in 222, leaving no sign it had ever been conceived.

Its obliteration was no doubt due to the unpopularity of its author, since in the 270s Aurelian renewed the experiment, and under his hand its history can be traced long after his death, in the form of a Sun temple he built in the capital. It honored a Syrian deity, from Emesa or Palmyra (the story is confused); and games and priesthoods were established; and the cult announced on the currency through the most emphatic legend possible, "Sol Master of the Roman Empire." [45]

These reigns and their particular religious focus are often thought to support the view that "if the solar cult had not succumbed to Christianity, . . . it could well have become the permanent religion of the Mediterranean area." [46] The prediction, though of course meant only to indicate the general force and dimensions in the cult, seems very hard to substantiate. It ignores or it overvalues evidence, especially evidence that concerns the efficacy of imperial patronage. We will return to that. For the moment, however, our business is only with the prevalence and depth of monotheism, of which the solar is certainly the most prominent species. And further support for its claims can be sought beyond the actions of Elagabalus, Aurelian and Constantine, in wide if blurry statements that are scattered through the literature of the time.

One of Plutarch's friends refers casually to Apollo, "whether he is the sun, or the Lord of the Sun and Father, and of all else beyond our seeing"— that statement at the opening of our chosen time span; and this second from the other end, in which Firmicus Maternus glorifies "the Sun, Best and Greatest" (Jupiter's usual epithets), "who holds the center of the heavens, the mind of the world, the moderator, chief of all and prince." Between these two speakers, Porphyry's voice is heard, too, in Neoplatonic essays which Firmicus had read.[47] All three writers drew their ideas, though in no very clear or discriminating way, from Platonic and Stoic teachings. Further, Dio Chrysostom reminds his audience that "some people say Apollo, Helios and Dionysus are all one, and so you," the citizens of Rhodes, "believe; and many people combine into one strength and power absolutely all the gods, so that there is no difference in honoring one or the other." Quite true—another commonplace that turns up in Porphyry later, but in Seneca earlier.[48] God is one but his force, *vis* or δύναμις, is many, expressed through the various familiar divine personalities. So a Roman says, it matters not whether you receive help from "Lucius" or "Annaeus" or "Seneca"; and a Greek, Plutarch, in analyzing the riddles hidden beneath the Isiac legend of "Typhon's plot and usurpation, that is, the power of drought," and so on through other tales, checks himself: "These matters, however, resemble the theology of Stoics, for whom the generative, nourishing spirit is Dionysus," etc., etc.[49] It appears thus to be a part of the intellectual heritage of the times that god might be one; all "gods," simply his will at work in various spheres of action; and the interpretive structure, as accommodating of Zeus at its center as of Sol or of any other traditional deity, no matter which.

But that was all quite abstract doctrine, taught in universities. It left few signs in surviving literature—beyond the library and school, only one trace. An unknown Cornelius Labeo, a writer who is perhaps most easily dated in the earlier or mid-third century, sought interpretation of an Orphic verse: "Zeus is One, Hades is One, Helios is One, Dionysus is One." What did the poet mean? "The authority of this line rests on an oracle of the Clarian Apollo, in which another name for the sun, too, is added, who is given among other names, in the same holy lines, that of Iao. For the Clarian Apollo, upon being asked which of the gods was meant by Iao, spoke as follows: 'Initiates must hold their secrets—yet know! Iao is Hades in the winter, Zeus in spring, Helios in summer, and Iao in autumn.' The force of this oracular saying, and the interpretation of the divinity and the name, whereby Father Liber [Dionysus] and Sol are meant by Iao, Cornelius Labeo treats in his book titled *On the Oracle of the Clarian Apollo.*"[50] So, like others before and after him, Labeo had asked the gods to speak for themselves. He had sought truth at the source. And if the result was more Clarian than clarity, at least it did not conflict with the wisdom passed down from the philosophers: many gods were really aspects of a single god. That finding had been brought out of the schools into the open.

But it has been seen in the open already. Dio Chrysostom in a public oration at Rhodes ventured a general statement about the beliefs to be found, or assumed, in his audience. To some, he attributed monotheism. It can only have been mixed Neoplatonism and Stoicism of the sort we have discovered in half a dozen Greek and Latin authors already. That the orator was right to expect it among his listeners, however, even in an attenuated or confused form, can be shown out of a rhetor's handbook compiled by a certain Alexander in the second century. In describing how to eulogize a god, he distinguishes the wiser opinions, largely Platonic, from those of *hoi polloi.* According to the former, "the gods were engendered by the first god—as is also the common opinion. . . . And to some, god seems to be one and the same, and unites in himself the power, δύναμις, of a number of gods, as they say Helios and Apollo are the same and Selene and Artemis and Hecate are the same; and veneration is offered by all peoples or by some. For not all gods are recognized among all, but some by one people, some by another. If, however, the god happens to be universally recognized, that is the greatest praise."[51] And last, because later in the century than Dio Chrysostom or Alexander, this declaration by Maximus of Tyre, rhetorician-philosopher: "Amid all these contests internal and external, amid all controversy [on other questions], you will see throughout the world one uniform rule and doctrine, that there is one god, king and father of all things, and many gods, sons of god and his coregents. The Greek says so, likewise the non-Greek."[52]

These writers are all generalizing; all are in touch with a wide public, too, and two of them are known to have traveled around a good deal. It would be surprising if what they said could not be accommodated to the other kinds of evidence that have been gathered, so as to yield conclusions broadly applicable across the whole scene, and throughout the two centuries, of our survey.

We must first confront the very term "monotheism." Like most big words, and "-isms" worst of all, it is no friend to clear thought. It indicates acknowledgment of one god only. Very good. But it suggests no definition of "god." That, as we have seen in our discussion of demons, was a crucial point of disagreement between the Jews and Christians, on the one hand, and most other people in the Empire, on the other. The two sides were united in perceiving a pyramid of powers above them—real powers capable of suspending the laws of nature. They were united, or at least many of their more intellectual leaders agreed, on the qualities, origin, and distribution of power(s) within the pyramid. Plato had established their common ground. Within the pyramid, however, the "monotheists" of our everyday definition discovered the hatred or enmity of the greatest power toward all others beneath, an enmity based on a moral vision. "Polytheists" perceived no split within the pyramid. They could only distinguish the supreme god from others by the amount of power he possessed. If they gave him all— that is, if they adopted monotheism in its radical sense—they must take away power from every other god, thus denying or obliterating everything in the pyramid save the top. To have done so would have involved the destruction of their whole culture. That, it hardly needs to be said, could not come easily.

Accordingly, pagan "monotheism," though not for the reasons usually put forward, barely existed at all. The schools still taught, as they had taught for many centuries, that all the gods were but the applications of the one, or that they drew their strength only from One. So rarefied a doctrine left the gods in fact quite undisturbed and independent entities, so far as ordinary worship was concerned. It was a way of conceiving things as harmless as it was restricted in the circle of its supporters. Once outside that circle, whether Stoic or Neoplatonic, there remained only the question of what name to put to the top of the pyramid. That there should be a top was, of course, the most familiar of notions universally, reaching back to Homer, to Etruscan Jupiter, to the local ba'al of this or that Syrian city. Adherents of one or another might assert for their favorite a special eminence—not monotheism, this, but megalodemonia (to borrow a neologism from Clement and Eusebius). The Great Spirit would be portrayed in perfectly friendly relations with others not quite so great; would have a special claim but no exclusive right to gestures or titles suited in strict logic only to a single supreme being—"unconquerable" or "highest"; and would defend or accept the veneration of worshipers having each his own, different Great Spirit. "Live and let live"—even among the jealous Tetrarchs, bowing to each other's "supreme deity" with perfect affability.[53]

It may well have been easier to do so in those late days than earlier. Rather than indicating ascendant monotheism, "Sol Invincible" on so many coin issues of Maximin Daia may only have shown the popularity, almost the need for mere politeness's sake, of flattering language, used more and more routinely in addressing anyone of a higher status. The later Empire loved hyperbole. It loved shouted phrases of clarion superlatives: "the very best!" "unique!" "savior!", offered to the mayor or governor as enthusiastically as to the god above.[54] To call Artemis "the greatest," then, so far from indicating a serious view of her supremacy, meant no more in later Ephesus than "great" had meant in St. Paul's days; to serve and acclaim a god named only "Highest" did not rule out the veneration of Sarapis and Apollo; and writers in both Greek and Latin routinely shifted from the singular to the plural of "god" in their theological discussions without the least sense of any consequences implied. Modern readers have a hard time getting used to the practice.[55]

All this discussion of ours starts, it should be recalled, from the need to distinguish between the more organized, explicit theology of "the lettered elite" (p. 72) and that of the masses. In what structure the gods disposed themselves was a matter explained in somewhat different ways at different cultural levels.

One practice hard to understand but very commonly found at all levels is polyonymy. Some triple forms have been noted: Zeus Helios Sarapis, for example. But a local goddess, Perasia in Cilicia, was addressed in inscriptions as "Selene or Artemis," Hecate, Aphrodite or Demeter, all the same to the dedicant, who thinks to magnify her in this fashion.[56] Similarly, the Mother of the Gods, Cybele, borrows or lends characteristic articles she is shown with, so as to be portrayed as Bellona or Astarte or Ma of Phrygia; or her name is simply run together with that of some other female deity. In Apuleius's novel, the hero hesitates whether the goddess who saves him is Artemis or Persephone (Proserpina), the latter called "polyonymous" in inscriptions (and so, sometimes, is Cybele); but he rightly settles on her being Isis. After Zeus, she was the most truly polyonymous of all gods in antiquity[57]—witness what survives from the beginning of our period: hundreds of lines of an address to Isis (the opening and closing of the text being lost), "... ruler of the fleet, of many guises, Aphrodite, ... savior, ruler of all, the greatest," Persephone (Kore), Athena, Hestia, "in Lycia, Leto, ... in Sinope, of many names, ... in Caria, Hecate," and so on, through city after city round the Empire to Italy; "first in the festivals of the gods ... thou, of things moist, dry or cold, from which the whole is created," and a great deal more to the same effect, typical of the genre of extended prose hymn.[58] The editors suppose the author was a priest, a likely conjecture. He evidently enjoyed a congregation patient of long sermons.

That audience must have included, over a lifetime, everybody within a day's walk of the temple who felt the least interest in worship (though no doubt a few did not, even if they avoided giving offense as overt atheists). The priest through hymns thus taught a large class, one rather different from gatherings that heard professional rhetoricians. The latter, whether dependent on Alexander's or Menander's handbook or masters by themselves, like Dio Chrysostom and Aelius Aristides, brought to their theme what higher culture could contribute: pillage from "poets and philosophers." That was the pair to whom Apologists forever had recourse, for support or, more often, for a target (above, pp. 9f.). In discussing monotheism as in discussing the afterlife, rhetoricians and Apologists alike spoke to a tiny minority of listeners who read Plato and commentaries, a larger minority who liked to hear about such deep subjects, but a majority who preferred their Homer uninterpreted. The different preferences and relative proportions of these groups can be sensed distinctly (above, pp. 68f. and 77). All together, however, they made up a number far smaller than those addressed by the priest.

The priest taught a very simple lesson: Isis was great! He wished before his listeners only to magnify her name. Isis was great!—or Zeus or Sarapis, Asclepius or Liber. How did he know? Clearly, because so many people said so, in one city after another all over the world. They worshiped her even under other names. To report and repeat them was a work of magnification, not theologizing.

But it naturally proved more acceptable as the habit of free, peaceful travel settled on the peoples of the Empire. On a smaller scale and in the eastern areas, that had been seen in Hellenistic times; now, more noticeably, in Roman times. Given the pilgrims, traders, tourists and, above all, soldiers and civil servants moved about willy-nilly from province to province, comparison of cults was inevitable; and the conclusions inevitably enriched the praises of this or that deity as being really (so worshipers believed) one and the same beneath a dozen local faces.

The people of Rhodes, inquiring of an oracle, were given a little hymn to sing in which Attis was hailed as Adonis and Dionysus, both; in Africa, it was the new god Antinous, Hadrian's younger friend, who at his death was hailed as Dionysus—more correctly, as Liber and Apollo, too.[59] So pervasive and vital and itself polymorphous was the practice of discovering one god to be another. Accordingly, illustrations have been sought in unwritten evidence as well. All sorts of bas-reliefs, coins, gems, and mosaics have religious subjects. Each deity had his or her characteristic attributes—items of costume, an object held in the hand, a stance or gesture. Hence, the equivalent of polyonymy should be discoverable in art. As might be predicted, the earliest signs show up in the east. Mints of cities like Mylasa and Alexandria, even before our chosen period, jumble Zeus and Poseidon together, or Zeus, Poseidon, Ammon, and Neilus (the Nile river personified)—later followed by more and more inventions and combinations all the time.[60] Cult reliefs in a shrine of Jupiter Dolichenus on the Aventine hill in Rome combine the god with Sarapis, assign him a consort (Juno, naturally) and depict her with certain traits also of Isis.[61] And from the middle Danube region the twin Rider Gods, never named, are shown on plaques crowded with the Dioscuri, Sol, the stars, Epona (Celtic equestrian goddess), Mithraic symbols, the tree of life with the snake coiled around it, and much else. The high point of their popularity falls near the end of the third century.[62] Generally speaking, the phenomenon of tossing together many gods or their symbols falls a little earlier, let us say, in the Severan age; but, if there is no great profusion of examples before that, later times right through the fourth century supply plenty, judged against the proportions of all art surviving.

It is tempting to infer from this body of evidence that the religious ideas herein expressed were of the same sort, promiscuously eclectic, and so to use it all as proof of a loose but powerfully working syncretism. Tempting, but risky. In a period of extreme concentration of power into the hands of a Sun King or the like, European artists best pleased their patrons by frescoes crammed with figures of mythology, heroes and heroines; and to affirm the monarchy of Rome at the height of the Counter-Reformation, Bernini designed St. Peter's chair to show a golden mob of dozens of angels and cherubim aswirl above the throne. Art has its line, cult another. In the Rider-Gods reliefs, symbols appear to have been added just to fill space, bearing no relation to the deities honored; in the Saturn reliefs of Africa, the complex overcrowding is rightly recognized as belonging to art of the period, especially the earlier third century, whether sacred or profane; and contemporary fancy coins, Roman imperial medallions, may be used conveniently to illustrate the style, displaying "a strong tendency to elaborate and to introduce subsidiary figures . . . for scenes of *liberalitas, adventus* or *profectio*, battle scenes, scenes of imperial sacrifice before a temple . . . or historico-allegorical scenes with the emperor standing or seated in the presence of deities or personifications."[63] Nock cites these views in support of the argument that the later Principate was a time of widespread, easy syncretism. The coins, however, are all of secular subjects. Like the evidence for ideas about the afterlife in sarcophagi reliefs (see section 1, n. 13), art seems to introduce more that is problematical or irrelevant than helpful to our understanding.

Discussions of the phenomenon are very likely to include a favorite item, the emperor's chapel. Alexander Severus, we are told, for his private prayers set up the images of ancestors and predecessors, Christ, Abraham, Orpheus, and Apollonius of Tyana.[64] The source for such a tale, the *Augustan History*, would rather tell against it were there not so many and so universally distributed examples of many gods being gathered into a single place of worship. For illustration, take Mithraea, in which are found dedications to or images of Silvanus (Ostia), Sarapis (Rome), Venus (Bologna), Vulcan (Metz), Mercury Cissonius (Strasbourg), and Attis (Strasbourg again)—these and others by luck of preservation: for Mithraea were underground, and their collections more naturally kept together. A rarer accident informs us that Mithraic reliefs were set up in a shrine of Jupiter Dolichenus on the lower Danube; Asclepius was honored in Men's sanctuary at Antioch in Pisidia, along with various other gods; provisions were made for the cult of Artemis, Dionysus, Hecate, Zeus, and Heracles in Apollo's shrine at Claros; and in the same god's complex of buildings at Bulla Regia in Africa stood statues of Saturn, Ceres, and Minerva.[65] An interesting inference may be allowed. None of these intrusions into the sacred space of the host deity can have been made without permission of the priests in charge.

Plutarch's friend Clea, herself priestess at Olympia, was also initiate in the rites of Osiris. She, then, could hardly have objected to the accommodation of a second loyalty; no more the priestess of the Sun at Philippi, initiate into the mysteries of Cybele and of Dionysus. A cult association of Hercules set up a dedication to its own god in the temple of Jupiter Dolichenus in Rome, and "the votaries of Sarapis," another guild, built a meeting room for Isis and Cybele in Rome's port.[66] Examples abound of ministrants of one sort or another erecting an altar or a plaque or themselves signing some honorific inscription, in worship of a god other than the one they served. The practice can be observed without distinction of honorand, whether Roman, traditional Greek, Oriental, or Celtic; without distinction of area; and only circumscribed in time, perhaps. It may be that such actions are more often attested in the period after A.D. 150 than before. But even that is not sure.[67]

These apparent betrayals of one's god were of course not only open, else never known to the present; they were divinely authorized. "By the interpretation of the rites of Sol," a worshiper honors Liber and Libera. Obviously the priest himself had overseen whatever was done; or a village honors "Zeus Galactinos according to Apollo's command"; a "priest of Sol *invictus* saw to the dedication to holy Silvanus, from a vision"; and so on, by direct order from Hercules or Men or Apollo.[68] It can only have been priests who guided these acts, seeing in them no betrayal at all. No one but priests can have permitted the placing in the temple of Dolichenus, in Rome, of a relief that shows the god sitting next to his consort and holding busts of Sarapis and Isis: he had welcomed his friends from Egypt into his house. Priests directed that the feasts of Iarhibol and Aglibol in Palmyra should fall on the same day.[69] The accommodation, fraternal welcome, courteous referral, or punctilious deference shown in one or another part of the surviving testimony seems to an unbeliever merely the interaction of the worshipers and priests. But worshipers and priests naturally saw it as the reflection here below of relations existing in the world above. Tolerance in paganism operated at both levels, until Christianity introduced its own ideas.[70] Only then, from Constantine on, were gods to be found at war with other gods.

Returning to Alexander Severus's chapel where he had assembled various holy images for worship: the collection seems to demonstrate the opposite of what is sometimes concluded from it. Not syncretism but discrete beings were on display. By real, undoubted dissolving of the images of two or twenty gods into a single one in people's minds, and by the repeating of the process twenty or a hundred times, the teeming numbers of primordial paganism, of paganism among tribes and cities prior to the Greek and Roman conquests, had indeed been very much reduced. The solvents that brought about this reduction were still at work in Alexander Severus's day. But they had always worked in the gentlest fashion, without affecting the essential character of polytheism. In its upper reaches, as we have seen, "monarchic" or more abstract pressures of interpretation toward unity of worship did exist. They should not be credited with more than their actual, quite limited force and significance.[71] They did not reduce Christ, Abraham, Apollonius of Tyana, and Orpheus to a single figure in the emperor's chapel (if that ever existed); rather, Christ and Iahveh were drawn into polytheism on the latter's terms, simply as new members in an old assembly. There, awaiting fuller incorporation, for a long time they stood at the edges, in magic and folk belief.

As to emperors of the period like Aurelian or Diocletian, making great show of close relations with Sol or Jove, at the most they asserted for their patrons some relative superiority, not a power sole and unique. Jove had succeeded Sol as Sol had succeeded to the position once occupied by Hercules under Commodus, or Apollo under Augustus. Had Constantine not intervened, why should the series not have been extended further still? Or perhaps there would have been slow change. Change is a sign of vitality.

4. CONVERSION

Yes, but if paganism really had retained its nature in good health throughout our period of study, why at the end were there so many scores and scores of thousands who had left it for the Church?

The question recalls the aim proposed some pages back, to distinguish several broad types of theology characteristic of several types of person: Marcus Aurelius at one extreme—he may be chosen for his very long-drawn-out, choice education and for the strong element of philosophy in his faith, a consciously worked-out system of explanation—and at the other extreme, the nameless peasant giving his penny to the shepherd-cum-seer in the hills behind Olympia (above, p. 73). By drawing the necessary distinctions, some offset can be offered to the appeal felt in the former type, whose intellectuality and moral code speak to our own; whose beliefs, moreover, can be known in some detail because they have been written down and preserved for us across the ages. Marcus Aurelius in our minds stands all too easily for "religion in the Roman Empire." Anything toward the opposite extreme is observed without much sympathy or long attention by Pliny, Pausanias, or modern tourists-through-time. Historians, in contrast, apportion their focus on the past according to the significance of people and events—that is, according to the change these wrought on other people and events around them. As there is no sign and very little likelihood that many were affected by the *Meditations*, the extreme they and their author represent have correspondingly small claim on our notice. Human interest is one thing; historical, another—unless it can be shown that Marcus Aurelius in fact imposed his views on his subjects. To the structure of influence in his world we will return.

Meanwhile, we have moved along the spectrum of theology from Neoplatonism and Stoicism and the higher criticism (pp. 74–77) to the convenient theory of intermediaries, demons, and the like; then to the shape in which all supernatural beings together were thought to arrange themselves; and so to successively wider categories of evidence, hymns, inscriptions, and symbolic representations, in which successively wider categories of person dealt, to express their ideas about the divine order. Whether by plan or good luck, we arrive at last among the masses, in whom can certainly be found the kind of historical significance we are looking for. What was essential in their beliefs?

The answer to that question, likewise the answer to the question why such throngs were attracted to Christianity, is the same. It may be seen in the moment of conversion. Converts sought reality, they sought truth, and the definition of what they sought can be seen in what produced a change in their allegiance. There are plenty of explicit descriptions of the moment.

The heretic Marcus, active in the Rhone valley in Marcus Aurelius's reign, won recruits to his doctrines through turning water into wine, or a little into a lot. Another Marcus, two hundred or more years later, brought water to drought-parched Gaza, where "some of the pagans, seeing what great wonders God had performed for us, now believing, opened the gate and joined our throng, shouting 'Christ only is God, He only has prevailed.'" Or in Caesarea in A.D. 306, a miracle is performed "and all the men and women acknowledge the one and only God of the Christians." Or in another Caesarea, this city in Pontus and a half-century earlier, the very priest of a local cult sees a miracle, and "when this happened, the man believed in the Word, on the very instant, and leaving all, followed" the Christian. Or further back by another half-century and in North Africa: "the witness from your gods, then," says Tertullian of exorcisms, "is what regularly produces Christians." Or when the governor in Egypt questioned the Christian Phileas, "'Was Christ God?' Phileas responded, 'Yes.' Culcianus said, 'What has convinced you that he was God?' Phileas responded, 'He restored sight to the blind and hearing to the deaf, healed lepers and raised the dead to life, made the dumb speak, and cured the infirmities of many. . . .'" [1] All but one of these passages were written by someone living at the same time as the events he described. A great many other witnesses to the same effect could be brought forward, separated from the events described by some generations but not necessarily the less to be trusted for that reason. And many extremely emphatic statements about exorcism by Christians should not be forgotten. Some have been reported, earlier. Their point in common was the simplest: announcement of supernatural powers new in the world it would be quite irrational to credit, without proof of their efficacy before one's own eyes. *That* was what produced converts. Nothing else is attested.

Speaking of the votaries of Pythagoras, Iamblichus says, "they recount these things" (various wonders) "to inspire belief"; and, he adds, since none of them was within the scope of humankind, "clearly it was necessary to accept what was told about him as belonging not to a man but to some higher being." By the same logic Marcus Aurelius was reduced, or raised, to his own faith: "If anyone should ask where have you seen the gods or how have you persuaded yourself of their existence, so that you are so devout, I answer . . . , from the continual proofs of their power I am convinced that they exist, and I revere them." And another governor, this time skeptical not of Phileas's god but of the oracle of Mopsus, submitted the oracle to a telling test; when it was passed, "that governor was overwhelmed and made obeisance and revered Mopsus forever." [2] So pagan sources tell the same kind of stories as the Christian.

The last incident about the oracle is related by Plutarch, who in another passage extends the line of logic a bit further. In weighing the merit of mortals who are accorded temples and worship, as if divine, false claimants can be picked out because "their good fame flourished only a short time, and then, convicted of false glory and imposture, with impiety and unlawfulness, 'of a sudden fate, like smoke arising,' (as Empedocles had said) they flew off." [3] True divinity, in other words, will prove itself by its wide or long-lasting impact on the human scene. Therein lies a further test by which mere magicians and manipulators of minor, dark spirits can be distinguished. The Apologists stress this as much as pagans. And still further: the divine is beneficent, as we have seen; demons alone, not gods, do evil; so if the effects of superhuman acts are bad, or somehow reward the wicked, then they have been produced by demons, whereas if they are good and benefit good men, they are really divine. [4] Finally: the divine has no needs, or different needs, compared with humankind. Its working can be judged, and its prophets known apart from frauds, through their superiority to material things.[5] Asceticism will mark them. At the least they will not make money out of their converts.

To credit the divinity behind a name newly presented to one, a person had to discover the qualities generally thought to belong to a god. Of course. Those qualities were: a constitution and substance somehow different and above material nature; the ability to do things humans could not do; and the applying of this ability in ways helpful and desirable to worshipers, indeed, helpful to everyone. Individual instances of conversion (really reducing to two well known, Lucius in Apuleius's novel and Aelius Aristides) only confirm in greater psychological depth the outline of cause and effect that can be traced in scenes involving hundreds or thousands — scenes which in turn fit exactly with the outline of common views about divinity discussed in earlier pages. The fit is predictable, the process following from the fit, ending in a new belief, likewise predictable. The inhabitants of the Apologists' world were, after all, rational beings. That does not mean only or entirely rational. Conversions might lead on to a feeling of overwhelming awe or deepest thankfulness, as we have seen; to love felt toward a deity; even to love felt *from* a deity — once divinity itself was proven.

But we are now fairly involved with the gaining or losing of believers in one or another cult and with the types of belief that moved great numbers. In pursuing these subjects, perhaps the point to begin with is evangelizing.

Aelius Aristides devotes many pages to describing persons of a certain type known to his audience and only too well known to himself. Like himself, they spoke in public, took the title "philosophers," sought out and consorted with the rich and respectable, asserted their candor and freedom of speech, and claimed to offer their wisdom to a wanting world without fee. Actually, he says, they are abusive, greedy, scheming hypocrites, and atheists into the bargain.[6] They may be put beside the eminently respectable Diogenes of Oenoanda, to suggest the wide variety of preachers on metaphysical matters; but they may also be dismissed; for clearly their relation to paganism is quite tangential, indeed hostile.

More to our purpose is "Julius Eutecnius, native of Laodicea, the admired ornament of Syria. . . . When he addressed the Gauls," so says his epitaph, found at Lyon, "persuasion flowed from his tongue. He circulated among various races, he knew many peoples and afforded training to the soul among them. He entrusted himself constantly to waves and seas, bringing to the Gauls and to the land of the West all the gifts that god

ordered the fruitful land of the East to bear—for god loved mortal man."
And so the text trails off into fragments. It reminds the reader of Saint
Irenaeus. Even the dates fit. But had Eutecnius been a Christian, surely the
inscription would never have been set up in public; and had his like been
found only in Christianity, in that case too he would not have been described
in terms to be confused with them; so we must suppose he was a pagan of a
type unusual but not unknown.[7]

A parallel lies at the opening of a third-century Gnostic text, where a
disciple recounts how he was dispatched by the Spirit to preach about what
he had learned of god's beauty. As he preached, men assembled to hear him
and, when he bade them repent, a part laughed at him, others held back, but
some were persuaded and asked for deeper knowledge.[8] With Gnosticism,
however, we approach the Judaeo-Christian tradition, in which despatch
of emissaries from a central organization, and other formal aspects of
missionary activity, were perfectly at home.[9]

The credos carried by Eutecnius and his like cannot have been within the
reach of very large numbers of listeners. Besides, they lacked the ingredient
seen to be essential to actual conversion: the proclamation of wonders.
That figured prominently, however, in evangelizing of a different sort,
centered in the oracle at Abonuteichus. The fraudulent Alexander who had
settled there sent out his agents everywhere to spread the fame of the responses. It was a conscious campaign.[10] Eusebius, speaking in broad terms
of pagans, describes how, "among them, prophecies and oracles are continually talked of, and cures and healings of all sorts of illness, and punish-
ments of the impious, and of this you might see them spreading the report
and inscribing stelae and crying it up in every corner of the earth."[11] The
picture he paints is of course perfectly accurate. We have surveyed some of
those stelae in the previous chapter. Posted where no one could miss them,
their letters recut and repainted periodically, they testified not only to the
wonderful deeds of their patron deities but to a set practice of the deities'
servants: priests could naturally be expected to present the cult which they
supported, and which in turn supported them, as impressively and attrac-
tively as possible. They are even to be found spreading the word of their
festivals by heralds, at least from the two shrines of Panamara and Lagina.

But such activity represented no system of beliefs; it sought to change no
one's life; and it quite took for granted, and assumed that listeners likewise
took for granted, the true divinity of the god advertised. It focused rather on
the attractions to be had at the shrine: healing, foreknowledge, or a feast.
On the road or in the marketplace, one indeed encountered the representatives of Cybele or some other god—who begged, not preached.[12] Of any

organized or conscious evangelizing in paganism there are very few signs indeed, though it is often alleged; of any god whose cult required or had anything ordinarily to say about evangelizing there is no sign at all.

A priest in one Mithraeum in Ostia set up some cult reliefs in a second, where also he served as priest; a priest of Dionysus erected a cult building "at his own expense, for his dearest homeland," Hierocaesarea; and others encouraged worshipers to adorn their shrine. That encouragement may be generally assumed, rarely proven.[13] A single deity, Jupiter Dolichenus, enjoyed an active and prominent priesthood. It figures in the epigraphy of the cult, in the northern and western provinces, far more often than, for example, that of Mithra in Mithraic inscriptions.[14] Its members throughout Pannonia joined in a common prayer for the emperor and his son apparently at the time of the imperial visit to the region in A.D. 202. Perhaps the prayer acknowledged the imperial funding of a temple built at Gorsium in Pannonia a few months earlier.[15] In Dacia, three priests combined to erect a temple to Jupiter Dolichenus; and one later repaired a temple himself.[16] Perhaps all of them drew on temple funds, not their own, since such funds accumulated in other cults and since (unlike some other cults) that of Jupiter Dolichenus did not draw its ministrants from the aristocracy. Most of them came from the east.[17]

Inscriptions occasionally show Isiac priests abroad being drawn from Egypt: one in Rome, a second in Aquileia, and other doubtful cases. The liturgy at the end of our period still required a knowledge of Egyptian. That could have been learned—or faked.[18] Perhaps Mithraism, too, employed some strange tongue at points in its services; the mother of Dusares was hymned in Arabic at Petra, the divine twins at Samothrace, in Locrian; and to Cybele, even in Italy, it was proper to speak only in Greek.[19] But for the worship of the Sun in Dacia, the congregation of local Palmyrenes imported a priest from Greece.[20] Overall, expatriate cults seem to have lost at least some of their native character within a generation or two.

Which raises the question of control and uniformity. Was there in fact such a thing as Isiacism, without further qualification? Was there *a* Sarapis or *a* Saturn?

Obviously not. Consider first, as a test case, Roman Jupiter. From several considerations, his was a worship most likely to have been the same wherever it was found: at home, closely under the hand of authority and tradition; in its forms abroad, safe from the familiarity that forgets or casually corrupts. Jupiter sat enthroned atop many a hill at the edge or center of cities in Italy, Gaul, Germany, Greece, Pannonia, or Africa, in shrines called Capitolia. Therein, each year began with special prayers taken up immediately after those offered in army camps: *prima in principiis,* as Tertullian says, *secunda in Capitoliis.*[21] In Arsinoe in Egypt, the town council in A.D. 215 picked out one of its members "for oversight of everything that belongs to our ancestral deity Jupiter Capitolinus," according to the instructions of the local bailiff of imperial properties—himself no doubt still feeling the weight of Caracalla's edict of 212. The emperor had written, ". . . I would give thanks to the immortal gods for watching over me in time of the recent unforeseen conspiracy—on which account, thinking that I should, with pious magnificence, be able to do something commensurate with their greatness if I could attract to the sanctuaries of the gods. . . ."[22] But when, a little later, in Stratonicea, we discover one man serving simultaneously as priest of that god and of three others, we must surely doubt whether he, any more than the local nominee at Arsinoe, could have been much of an expert in his duties.[23]

That amounts to no more than negative guessing. Jupiter temples at least bore the right name, even correctly transliterated into Greek. A match for Capitolia can be found in the "Vatican Hill" at Lyon and again at Kastel near Mainz, both named after the Cybele shrine in Rome and suggesting close imitation of the Roman model.[24] The tiny Almo river near Rome, in which the statue of Cybele, taken out from the city, was annually bathed, had its descendant in Milan, just as Isiacs built a Canopus at one place or another or worshipers of Apollo named local springs "Castalian," at Antioch and elsewhere.[25] Duplication of such physical features can only have derived from worshipers' sense of a sort of unitary character in cult. An even clearer proof of that sense appears in the careful duplication of cult statues, sometimes attested in words expressly.[26] Then there are the holy days of Cybele, observed in an unchanging calendar wherever she was recognized.[27] Hymnodes of Sarapis in Rome closely followed the Egyptian calendar, and hymnodes of the emperor in Pergamon closely followed old Roman rituals.[28] Lastly, when the cult of Ma of Comana in southern Cappadocia took root to the north in Pontus, her new home was called Comana, too, and her new services "used the same procedures in sacrifices, divine inspiration and veneration for priests." So Strabo reports (12.3.32), although he wrote a century before the period in which we are interested.

These scattered details are meant to suggest the limits of uniformity, not to exhaust the evidence by any means. The use of identical hymns in shrines spread widely over the Greek-speaking regions can be demonstrated in the survival of the actual texts on stone (above, chap. 1, section 2, nn.79f.). More might be said or very plausibly conjectured about the role of those songs in fixing the character of cult across time. Or we could infer, almost prove, the same changelessness in cults all using the rules of sacrifice in force at Diana shrines in Rome (above, chap. 1, section 1, n.66). The typical attributes with which deities were portrayed—a bushel basket for a crown, a two-headed ax in the hand, wings on the feet, and so forth—remain remarkably consistent and in wide use. Enough, however, on such familiar topics.

Equally diffuse but not so often discussed is the evidence for the lack of uniformity in cults. Again, a sampling suffices to show the outline of the subject. In Cicero's day, as his readers know because he took such pains to tell them, that wretch Clodius defiled himself and jeopardized the very life of Rome in no act more expressly than in attending the rites of the Bona Dea. Men in them violated tabu. But in the provinces, in our period, inscriptions record the names of a number of male votaries. Shocking and inexplicable![29] But no doubt the faithful of Baalbek would have been equally shocked at the alien portrayal of their ba'al in his temple (itself also quite odd) on the Aventine hill in Rome. Isiac ceremonies in the west departed from Alexandrine, though perhaps less than one might have predicted; Dionysiac ceremonies, being not so much out in the daylight, took on a hundred forms; and the sanctuaries of Saturn, recognizably Punic in plan around Carthage at the beginning of the second century, along with recognizably native icons, had taken on an altogether different appearance by the end of the century—partly Roman, now, partly "classical" in a loose sense that included Hellenistic elements as well.[30] The development is not surprising. Though a distinctly regional figure, underneath his Latin name, Saturn had no one great temple serving as center, model and arbiter to his worship. So far as the evidence indicates, no one enjoyed authority more than anyone else over questions of correct liturgy, iconography or temple construction.

A good deal is known about Mithraism, for a final illustration. Its cells of worshipers, like those of Dionysus, arranged themselves under a varying hierarchy; in the reverse of what happened with the Bona Dea, women slipped into a cult usually reserved to men; and the central depiction of the god and his great act, the slaying of the bull, took on a variety of postures, attributes, and connected episodes. The god himself was equated not only with Sol and Apollo but with Mercury, too, and he sheltered a great confusion of other gods in his shrines.[31] Other features could be added which have been found by excavators at one or a few Mithraea but not in others.

"The greater part of the people," said Seneca of common Roman rites, "know not why they do what they do."[32] He could as well have meant Isiacism or Cybele cult, in which all sorts of conflicting episodes and interpretations of the divine story circulated.[33] It was not from neglect that the religious heritage had become, over the centuries, festooned with airy, blowing, trailing tales and customs. Rather the opposite: too much attention. Perhaps no deity had roots into a deeper past than the Maid, Kore, Persephone—whose worshiper Damian, at the very end of the time here chosen for study, still approached an oracle in ignorance of the right term with which to address her in hymns. "Savior," answered Apollo.[34] And Menander the rhetor, speaking of hymns, recommends the composing of some in a fashion consciously loose and inventive, for example, in "shaping some new deity, Envy, attributing to her as her veil, Jealousy, and as her sash, Contention"—this in the third century, too, so the free-changing quality of paganism had lost none of its vitality.[35] Everything mentioned in earlier pages concerning polyonymy should be superadded at this point, everything about the various levels of understanding among believers, and everything implied in the "national" origin of the larger cults. The sum was confusion. No counterforce for order existed.

It is, of course, conventional to talk about "state cults." I cite a few illustrations of that, above (chapter 2, section 3, n.42). Beyond that, modern accounts commonly attribute to one or another emperor the advocating or imposing of one or another cult. If such a phenomenon could really be discerned, it would present us with just the force most logical for the attaining of uniformity in religious beliefs. None, however, can be found. Like any city, Rome had its temples. They were supported by taxes. Local authorities administered them, and administration involved control. All this is too well known to need elaboration. It might perhaps be thought, further, that the gods in the capitol enjoyed a position defined and supported throughout the empire. True, temples were built to house them outside Italy, often involving conscious imitation, as we have seen. But imitation included Cybele in its embrace with Jupiter, and without any help from public funds. Plenty of examples do exist to show state monies spent in the provinces on religion, but for the benefit of local shrines whose spokesmen attracted some single imperial gift.[36] The conviction that a real power lay behind some name—Apollo, let us say—must surely have been strengthened by deference and tribute offered from the emperor himself. In that sense, imperial patronage may well have produced conversions to the worship of Apollo. The patron, however, never intended them and still less meant to define or unify Apollinian teachings.

Hadrian's establishing of a new cult to honor Antinous brought the whole of his authority into play. His success was sharply limited: compliant cities built temples, individuals put up prayers, and honorific games were staged. The games lasted; the name, however, disappeared from people's minds. Hadrian's effort, the most emphatic of several he undertook, had never struck root in the west at all.[37]

His successor, the almost motionless old Antoninus Pius, gave Cybele more place in his coins than had been usual. A special kind of sacrifice known as the *taurobolium* is not attested before his reign on behalf of the throne but is so afterward; and an undated law offers rewards to inhabitants of Rome's port city who, for the emperor, offer a sacrifice which is perhaps the taurobolium, according to instructions from the high priest of the goddess. These data have been assembled to show Pius instituting a formal presidency of the cult and a new rite with subsidies, not only at Rome but elsewhere. Which could all be true—or none of it. The dates necessary to fit the pieces of evidence together into one whole are either unknown or fixed only by arguments from silence. Moreover, the taurobolium for the throne can be found on inscriptions in the western provinces but not in the capital itself. The emperor's rewards seem to have stimulated no new piety.[38]

But, if we pause for a moment to examine the scene without preconceptions, we are bound to ask where the very idea of "official" or "state" cults comes from. Surely they have been attributed to the Roman world by reasoning from alien, generally modern and Christian, times. Search for them therefore proceeds with tell-tale indirection, effort, and paucity of proof. In paganism uninterpreted, at any level lower than the throne, zealots were hard to find. In court and noble circles natural to all the Antonines, they were decidedly "bad form." Why should the emperors depart ex officio from the ordinary rules of behavior?

It was perfectly acceptable to favor one deity more than another. One could speak of "Domitian's god" (most likely Isis), meaning whichever he was known to honor specially or which especially aided him. That recognition throws light on a phenomenon very common but nowhere directly explained, the adding of the epithet "August," that is, "imperial," to a deity.[39] Perhaps the deity so described was envisioned as a face more effectually turned upon men's affairs and therefore worth specifying in one's prayers; perhaps only compliment and loyalty were offered to terrestrial authority. No one from the past has been good enough to tell us what he really thought he was doing when he wrote *any* religious message upon stone. But the entirely spontaneous turning up of "Sarapis Augustus," "Mercury Augustus," or "Diana Augusta" in dedications by private persons throughout the west, obviously without conceding the emperor any monopoly on these gods' attention, suggests that what was most in the dedicant's mind was not the gods' claim to extra veneration but rather their relation to the emperor. As the other side to that same fact, the emperor himself could announce the relation without trying to impose it on others ex officio. He differed from his subjects only in his responsibility to see that the gods received enough thanks and respect to win their favor for the realm. That is more or less what Caracalla said in his edict of A.D. 212 (above, p. 100); and it was in defiance of that that his cousin Elagabalus, the zealot, wrought his own destruction.

Though the whole family of the Severi have been portrayed as "Orientalizers," there is no evidence that any but the mad boy Elagabalus wanted or tried to change anyone's religion.[40] From his reign we pass to others in which Sol and Oriens were advertised or favored. The sequence of events was sketched above (pp. 84–85). Until after 312, however, there is no sign of imperial pressure for uniformity in cult. The independence, not to say license and shapelessness, of paganism had suffered no disturbance from above.

No one contested the government's right, of course, to do whatever it wished in this area. The potential for interference is indicated by a number of odds and ends of administrative action. An ancient committee for oversight of religion, the quindecimvirs in the capital, formally installed the Cybele priest of Lyon in A.D. 160, and his like, too, in Arausio in Gaul and in several Italian cities subsequently. Those were all *coloniae*. Perhaps other centers enjoying that legal status were similarly controlled in other provinces.[41] The priest of Hercules Augustus in Apulum in Dacia was installed by the governor and other priests in Smyrna by the emperor and Roman senate.[42] And government intervened, often by local request, in matters of little concern to us, but vital to temple management: the law regarding rights of inheritance by temples, adjudication of their boundaries, scheduling of their festivals, even building of new facilities.[43] Early in the second century in Bithynia, the younger Pliny planned some urban redevelopment that would have touched a Cybele sanctuary. He inquired locally what rights might exist of record in a *lex dicta templo,* a founding charter; but, he discovered, local customs of consecration were un-Roman. That tells us that Republican formalities were still commonly in force in Italy as the *mos* that Pliny expected to find abroad.[44] At home, when he planned a shrine in Tifernum, he applied to the local senate for the assigning of the land to be consecrated and so got what he needed.

To determine the fixity of beliefs gathered under the name "Isis" or "Dionysus" or "Mercury," the need was seen to determine also if there existed any force in the empire at work in that direction. So our search began, it will be recalled. Thus far it has uncovered almost nothing. Having passed over the obvious areas, in the educated elite and in the imperial administration itself, we have arrived at Tifernum in Italy. Did cities even within their own restricted boundaries seek, or manage, to control local beliefs?

Though the matter has never been studied, clearly town governments in the west controlled the use and allocation of space within some limits, perhaps within the city walls. That accounts for the very common use in religious inscriptions of the abbreviation *l. d. d. d.*, "in space given by decree of the decurions."[45] A fair number of inscriptions show town governments as such, and with town money, erecting a temple, idol, or dedication, most of all in Africa but occasionally in other regions.[46] Pliny mentions how the people of Hispellum in central Italy had set aside funds to build an inn and maintain a hot baths at a shrine outside the town. Money well spent: such facilities were bound to be attractive—at Scaptopara in Thrace, they were to prove dangerously so, later. But it was only hoped that tourists, pilgrims, and the idly curious would contribute a little to local markets.[47]

Civic pride, an ardent wish to put one's town on the map, to advertise and embellish it, was a salient feature of Greco-Roman civilization. Everyone gloried in the god or goddess who watched over him and his fellow citizens, gloried in the size of the shrine, and loyally supported with his pocket or applause the most ruinously generous subsidizing of worship. Such feelings best account for the reward of membership in the Pompeian senate extended to a little six-year-old for his (that is, of course, his father's) rebuilding of the Isis temple after the quake of A.D. 62.[48] In Narbo, the authorities collected money to pay for a particularly expensive kind of offering on behalf of the emperor—the taurobolium, quite often made by cities, not by individuals, in Gaul—and determined the type and calendar for sacrifices for the *numen* of the emperor. The act would be a prime illustration of secular authority controlling worship were it not actually a part of the imperial cult.[49]

In the eastern provinces, a match for Narbo's act, but quite unconnected with emperor worship, can be found in Teos. There, the senate and people laid down the rules for the honoring of "the god presiding over the city, Dionysus, on each day, by the priest and the ephebes," and so forth. The details are spelled out fully, including the matter of who pays (the god, from temple resources).[50] At Ephesus, it was the Society of Elders (*gerousia*) that oversaw most religious concerns; elsewhere, it was usually the same bodies that are found at Teos. Use of sacred buildings for secular, public business, and vice versa; the honoring of sacred officials in secular settings, and vice versa; the prominence of the one or the other at each other's ceremonies; the alternation of offices from sacred to secular in a given man's career; and the confusing of aims and benefits in assemblies for the gods or for civic business—all reflect the closest relations. They were nowhere plainer than in Stratonicea, where we have seen how town senators, deliberating as such, included among their leaders the past and present incumbents of the chief priesthoods.[51] Implicit in such overlap was the potential for interference in religion at the narrowest local level quite as much as any we have seen at the provincial or imperial level; and we may now repeat our challenge: was this control not used to produce uniformity in cult?

The question may sound a little odd. How could there be anything but uniformity in the worship of Zeus of Panamara at his very shrine (or of the like deity in any sanctuary anywhere)? But the matter is not so simple. Even at the absolute roots of faith, paganism tolerated disagreement. It may be discovered up and down Syria, where a triad was worshiped, somewhat like the Capitoline, except that it consisted of a male sky god, a consort, and another male. At one town or sanctuary, however, one member of the triad would bear one name, another at another.[52] At Sidon, Byblos, and Hierapolis, the tourist who inquired within the very walls of the shrine would be told two contradictory stories about one or another myth or feature of worship; the same again in Greek centers. Sometimes dispute lay between versions of the wise and *hoi polloi*. Still, the wise might disagree among themselves.

We have already noticed, too, that rites and beliefs changed over time: among the Arval Brethren in Rome; among Mithraists in Italy, Pannonia, and Syria; among the devout of Cybele in Italy and Gaul, or of Saturn in Carthage and the African backcountry.[53] So long as paganism retained its full life, it went on growing. Even if a part of it had somehow been well unified across all the Roman empire at a given moment—which we have seen to be never the case—we might nevertheless expect the vitality of faith to have produced within that part continual disuse of old practices and introduction of new. Our expectation is met. In a sizable number of cults well enough documented for us to tell true innovations from features that are simply not earlier known to us, a general refreshing can be seen over the course of the second and third centuries. It affected the rituals associated with Demeter at Pergamon, Artemis at Ephesus, Hecate at Lagina, and the hoax at Abonuteichus.[54] All these developed their own "mysteries" because, perhaps, that was the thing to do. It was a fashion, at least in the Greek-speaking cities. Each had to have some religious festival, too, and it would be improved or altered from time to time, at Cos, for instance, or at the relatively well known shrine of Zeus at Panamara. The feast days there, as we have seen, underwent several significant, and perpetual minor, elaborations.[55]

Enough to answer the question, Was there one thing called Mithraism or Isiacism? There was not, at least not in the sense in which one can speak of any major branch of Islam or Christianity. Too much in ancient culture, quite aside from mechanical and administrative difficulties, opposed the control that would have been required to produce any sort of unitary cult.

The changefulness of our subject must strike anyone who browses through the epigraphic evidence. It calls before the mind's eye, over and over again, the most striking pictures of dislocation and decay. Their match are common in a literary account of second-century Greece, too: roofs fallen in, votaries departed, idols missing, the whole sanctuary tumble-down.[56] From a third approach, the archaeological, it can be seen that Olympia enjoyed its last bloom in the first half of the second century, while Epidaurus, after a thin first century, recovered popularity and attention in Hadrian's reign. After that, it slid downhill. Inscriptions from the site come to an end in the later third century. Artemis's shrine at Ephesus in the first century likewise suffered from neglect. Staff had to be reduced, repairs put off, and the second century continued on the same level. Claros, however, enjoyed good times then and to the end of the third century, and Panamara, almost as long.

If the catalogue of sites were extended, as it most easily might be, to dozens of others, the conclusion forced on the observer would be a simple one: the ups and downs in fortune of any cult had nothing to do with missionary activity or (so far as anyone can demonstrate) with properly religious forces.

Among extraneous elements may be mentioned, and set aside, the purely art-historical, in which taste is misunderstood as faith. An instance inspected above is the liking for Dionysiac scenes among the patrons of fancy marble sarcophagi. This developed in Italy in Hadrian's reign, favoring what were then antique motifs issuing from newly popular workshops.[57] At the same time, in the same circles, archaizing in all sorts of things like word choice and daily manners showed itself as well in a fondness for almost forgotten ancient rites and icons and names like Juno Sospita.[58] Needless to say, the vogue could only be cultivated by the upper classes. Finally, they continued in their liking for Egyptian culture, a liking which had been marked for a full half-century and which produced both the Canopus at Hadrian's villa and the Flavians' importation of obelisks to the capital. It produced also the fourteenth century B.C. statue of Atoum with hieroglyphics found in a house in Herculaneum. A rich Pompeian mer-

chant who commissioned Nilotic scenes in his house and Nilotic arrange-
ment of his garden was at the same time a worshiper of Isis. Very natural—
or rather, very affected.[59]

The cultivating of Juno Sospita, Liber-Dionysus, and Isis distinguished
the beau monde of Italy and its admirers but needs to be mentioned only
because of their disproportionate prominence in the surviving evidence.
The ages intervening between the present and the Roman past were of
course bound to preserve the best of literature and art more carefully than
the worst or mediocre. For just the same reasons, students today turn to the
best, first, in trying to reconstruct that Roman past. But in defense of the
resulting distortion, it must be granted that the beau monde, or their
equivalent in confined settings, made people look, conferred prestige, and
gave expression to their private preferences through all that money can
buy. In particular, they financed religion. The contrary to testimonies of
decline that can be read in Latin inscriptions or in Pausanias's Baedeker of
Greece lies in the elaboration of facilities at Lagina, typifying (except in
richness of detail) what can be known or guessed about any sanctuary:
"three porticoes" erected and the record carefully kept on stone—"three
porticoes and monumental gateway and the stoa along the front of the
temple toward the food market," and so forth (above, p. 48). Donors from
the aristocracy of nearby Stratonicea thus preempt our attention; but after
all, they paid for it.

The appearance of ruin that Pausanias mentions—half a wall here, an
unroofed building there—might be offered by a cult center rising in fortune. Expansion or improvement had begun, but money was not flowing
into it at the rate allowing its prompt completion. So at Athens the in-
credibly enormous space and parts of the Zeus temple under Hadrian still
awaited a finishing hand 650 years and more after they had been first conceived by Peisistratus. At Claros, outside of Miletus, the shrine of Apollo on
an almost equal scale likewise had stood for centuries incomplete. It never
did get its roof.[60] It calls to mind half-done or lopsided cathedrals in Europe.
At Damascus, perhaps the biggest shrine in the ancient world still needed
part of its circuit wall done in A.D. 264–265, and work on the interior bazaar
in 286/287, and more work in 339/340; at Dougga in Africa, the Caelestis
temple was given to the city piece by piece through the generosity of the
local Gabinii (the same whose members Aulus Gabinius Datus and his son
Marcus Bassus under Hadrian paid for the complex dedicated to Concord,
Frugifer, and Liber Pater).[61] But the special responsibility assumed by a
clan or family for a shrine, and the repair or expansion or completion of it
as their fortunes allowed over the generations, is familiar from Rome itself

and from a number of examples in the provinces: for Ceres, in Uchi Maius in Africa, by the Pullaeni; for Jupiter, at Iciodurum in Gaul, by the Petronii; above all, in Palmyra for Ba'al-shamin by the bene Ma'zin, for Belhammon by the bene 'Agrud, and so on.

As anyone would guess, sometimes a poor man got together the cash to pay for a religious building. More often the poor, if they were to afford that, had to organize themselves in congregations.[62] On any rich man's land, if it was not he himself who put up a shrine, his permission would have to be sought—his or hers. In the Roman Campagna in the mid-second century, a consul's wife, Pompeia Agrippinilla, headed an association centered in Liber-Dionysus, whose four hundred or so devotees were overwhelmingly of Greek-speaking origin mixed with a substantial minority of Roman citizens. These latter, under Agrippinilla, supplied all the officers in the association and were all of one clan, originating generations earlier in the household of a certain friend of Pompey. Of Pompey, too, the Bacchic high priestess herself, to judge from her name, was a descendant or relative. The arrangements here recall a group encountered earlier at Samothrace, where one rich man carried the costs of worship for his dozens of dependents.[63]

It is equally predictable that by far the greater part of building for cult purposes in cities, too, would be paid for by the rich. Among them, only two special categories need to be noted. One is made up of repeaters: men and occasionally women of wealth whose names recur more than once.[64] There is Marcus Aurelius Decimus, former head of the noncitizen community at Lambaesis and governor of Numidia, honoring "Jove Bazosenus, ancestral god," plus Mithra, Minerva, Mars Pater, Fortuna Redux, Hercules, Mercury, Aesculapius, and Salus, "and all the gods and goddesses." Punctilious polytheist!—outmatching in the same town even the legate's, Cominius Cassianus's, restoration of the Septizonium, vows recorded in the Aesculapius temple, and dedication of the Capitolium, all in his one year of office, A.D. 210/211.[65]

The individuality of faith shows through the broader probabilities: names through classes. Simply by natural inclination, some people felt impelled to render more than conventional service to a god. They constitute our second special category. They might offer themselves as priests (exactly how, we rarely know). Their piety was registered, as we have seen, in the dedication of their lives or in the many testimonies they have left in one or many shrines. And when religion came under attack, it was they—in Smyrna against the Christians, similarly elsewhere for the same cause— who rallied support and directed public opinion.[66] They had their purely secular equivalents, too: persons whose actions cannot be accounted for by position or material circumstances. Two illustrations will be enough. Marcus Valerius Maximianus, native of Pannonia, learned to honor Mithra in Poetovio, perhaps; left a dedication in Apulum in Dacia when he commanded a legion there; and in the same rank in A.D. 183/185 in Numidia recorded the same faith again in the Lambaesis Mithraeum. Second, at Pergamon in the mid-second century, Tiberius Iulius Perseus recorded his vows to Asclepius and a little later built the god a home in Utica in Africa.[67] The type of these two men may be as close as paganism gets to missionizing.

Legates referred to among the instances of religious behavior incidentally draw attention to the links between military command and the advancing of some given belief. The connection extends and completes the subject of centralized evangelizing (above, pp. 103ff.). If there were such a thing as a "state religion," it could be imposed on no group more under the emperor's thumb, no group better suited to be the agent of further propagation, than the army. To anticipate a longer discussion, however, there seems to be no evidence that the government saw the possibilities latent in the army for these uses.

A small unit of Palmyrene troops in a Syrian station in the A.D. 220s had and must certainly have observed a written calendar of festivals. Suppose all units had been issued the same: then we could see to what beliefs these hundreds of thousands of men were bent by imperial management. But, first, there is no saying if there was a single calendar for the whole province, even for a whole station; second, the gods actually honored are just what one would have expected in a Roman-citizen setting two or three hundred years earlier, that is, the Capitoline Triad, Mars and Vesta (!), with a few old Italian or Roman municipal holidays; and third, the Palmyrene troop itself, off duty, worshiped its native gods and paid no attention to these others,[68] which can only have seemed hoary, odd, and meaningless. Question de dieu, cela manque de réalité.

There is record of directions issued by Licinius about A.D. 322 to a post on the lower Danube, ordering anniversary prayers on his behalf to be offered in the camp annually to Sol. The ceremony need not have been prescribed for other camps as well. A couple of years later, Licinius's communication with an angel yielded, so he claimed, a sort of monotheistic prayer which he had his troops join in reciting before battle with Constantine. Though the text refers with exquisite ambiguity to "the highest god," it might fit with Sol worship. On the other hand, Licinius was polytheist in his other policies and statements. What seems to fit the facts best is a far more conscious dictation of worship to the army than had been attempted before, in form recalling Constantine's orders to his army in 312, but in content nothing at odds with the long series of developments over the preceding half-century. From Aurelian's coinage in the 270s until almost the 320s, those developments were traced earlier.[69]

Quite incompatible with any theory of a mission for the army is the very profusion of acts by not quite so high commanders and by smaller assemblies of troops. They make vows or sacrifices in shrines and cities, they build temples and appoint priests within the camps themselves—not, however, to one god or authorized pantheon but to the usual confusion of all powers: Diana and Isis, Silvanus and Mithra, Jupiter *optimus maximus* of true Romans, and Heliopolitanus, of Baalbek.[70] The most random and partial search uncovers dozens of inscriptions from widely scattered points in the western and northern provinces set up in commemoration of some act of religion by officers in charge of a company within a legion, a squadron of horse, or an entire regiment, on up to those commanders who were also entrusted with a province like Numidia, and so to governors of Pannonia or Noricum. Since some of the texts also indicate that the individuals were acting as such, and none indicates action ex officio, there is no reason to think that any of these testimonies represents a centralized policy.

Nothing, indeed, explains where that very idea of "state" or "official" cults originates, so universally assumed in modern accounts. It rather appears that persons enjoying an important rank used it in a personal way. If they were religiously inclined, they expressed their inclinations without regard to their predecessors or successors, certainly without regard to the men under them. Much as a fort commander lines them up to receive some dignitary on a junket and leads them in hoorahs without consulting their real views about their corpulent visitor, so it may be imagined Roman legionary chiefs led the praise for Jupiter or Mars. The next year, another commander would praise another god. That was one of the perquisites of power—as, in a municipal or rural setting, it was a perquisite of wealth. On a grander scale, the emperors behaved in exactly the same way.

Having now examined conversion from several points of view, we can begin to see the shape of the process within pagan terms. It may in the first place be described by a number of negatives. It was not in the hands of missionaries. People best described by the word existed, to be sure, but they were oddities. It was not the charge or intent of secular government, either, though the personnel of government from the very top down certainly felt and freely expressed religious convictions. In sum, modern analogies will not work. The professional staff that served the larger shrines, and the practice of putting proofs of the gods' power prominently on display at even such a small shrine as Pliny described (above, p. 33), reached out to visitors and tried to impress them with a sense of awe, therefore of belief. Periodically, parades brought images of the gods out into the city at large, or bore them for miles around the countryside. But ordinarily initiative lay with the unconverted, to come and look and listen, or to do nothing.

The visible structure of paganism cost money. From the beggars, exiles, and cripples permanently camped in temple grounds, on up to the *archigallus* of Cybele in Rome, all needed to be fed and sheltered. The shape of support naturally followed the lines of wealth distribution in society at large. Holy men and frauds alike hung about rich women;[71] and every brick and block that went to make a proper residence for the deity or proper resort for pilgrims was paid for by some member of the aristocracy—paid for or occasionally voted for, out of municipal funds, or supplied by troops under the donor's command. The aristocracy of course enjoyed control over all the heights of wealth and power.

In signing their names to affidavits about miracles or to the cornerstones of temples they had built, they added their titles: "knight" (like "Bart.") or "Judge" (*praeses*) or "Colonel" (*legatus*). That practice did not indicate obedience to higher or central authority. Almost the reverse: assertion of *self*. It was a far better proof of one's high position to act without orders. Testimonies of faith from great personages, without need of any added weight, naturally made a deep impression. Plutarch, in a passage quoted above (pp. 57–58), gives conscious expression to the pride in persuasion felt among the nobility. Not only could they present their opinions in more attractive, moving, forceful words; not only did they speak with the habit of confidence in public, elevated upon thrones, titles, platforms and inheritances; but the mere fact that they themselves had been won over to belief was a sort of proof of divine efficacy—a miracle. By that, everyone would be persuaded. By that, beyond their wealth and influence and eloquence, the aristocracy made religion in their communities their own.

5. THE DYNAMIC CULTS

This outline of the process of conversion fits well enough in the settled surroundings of a city, village, or rich man's estate. With mention of legions and colonels, however, we have touched on a special aspect of the subject: conversion operating across great distances. In religious history, the more dramatic part, in some ways also the more significant part, is the more dynamic. By what force can we explain the appearance of entirely strange faiths hundreds of miles from their homes, in areas that had not known them, especially if it is true that "initiative lay with the unconverted?"

In attempting an answer to that question, the last in this chapter, it is best to start with large, easy statements. First, paganism in the Greek-speaking provinces underwent no significant changes.[1] Individual cult centers became more crowded, or deserted, or richer or poorer; but no major ones grew up or died. Even the Roman Jupiter made almost no impression on these lands.[2] Second, in the Latin-speaking provinces, by far the most important change was the broad establishing of the worship of Jupiter and, after that, of a fairly straightforward, representative mixture of deities out of Italy such as Cicero might have known: that is, a mixture heavily Hellenized, with many features equally characteristic of great eastern cities like Antioch and Alexandria; for Isis and Cybele (as Bellona) had been thoroughly at home in the peninsula for centuries when our period of study begins. So, too, had Dionysus (as Liber). Only two new names, Jupiter of Doliche and Mithra, appear, not prominently, among the top fifteen (above, the table on p. 6).

In the ascendancy of Jupiter, one reservation was noted (above, p. 5). The African provinces opposed to him their own Saturn. Jupiter alone or in the Capitoline Triad was housed in more, and more splendid, temples; but he received few prayers inscribed on stone, especially where Punic traditions were strong. Moreover, those prayers that did address him came from Roman citizens, town magistrates, officials.[3] The native preference for the native Saturn proved too strong—which does not mean that Jupiter inspired merely formal acknowledgment. In the third century and in Numidia, "Jupiter Best and Greatest, of the Apennines," was invoked, whose home lay at ancient Iguvium in Umbria.

Place names like *Apenninus* attached to a god point to people's lively sense of his roots and individuality. Two other deities identified in that way may be used to suggest the vitality of Italian exports to the provinces: Diana of Tifata is given a temple at Intercisa on the upper Danube in the second half of the second century, by a worshiper whose own origins can be traced back to her neighborhood in Italy, and "Juno the Queen, of Populonia, ancestral goddess," is invoked in Dacia by a legionary legate of the same period.[4] This latter text serves also as reminder of the great tides of alien culture flowing into the lands across the Danube in the early second century. Jupiter or Diana or (we could add) another old Latin god like Silvanus seemed quite as likely to turn up on new frontiers then as in the youth of Roman conquests.[5]

Initially, everyone is agreed, the gods traveled only in the baggage of the strangers settling in those regions where religion had a dynamic history— virtually all of the west, as was said just above. The strangers both established themselves with their own faith and communicated it to others. Those others and their visitors can be divided into a number of obvious categories, and weight must be assigned to the two explanations for the rising of a temple or an altar, whether by act of immigrants or of converted natives. It is in terms of these divisions and considerations that the movement of individual cults great distances around the Empire is normally described. Each cult appealed to certain categories of persons, which it is not our business to describe—the decurions, the lower officer class, the rural poor, and so forth. But a few general traits may be brought out.

Once the familiar picture of traders in motion is considered,[6] it is natural to characterize them as carriers of cults. It must certainly be assumed, and can occasionally be proved, that they held on to their beliefs wherever they went. Take for illustration the pair that identify themselves as Syrian merchants on a votive stone to Jupiter Dolichenus in Dacia. But such a stone explains only itself. It would go beyond both evidence and likelihood to turn the dedicants into missionaries, even though that sort of transformation is very often implicit in modern accounts; sometimes explicit, for example, in explaining the substantial popularity of Isis in Italy. Isiacism was plainly not brought back by soldiers, the means whereby so many other cults had been, and were to be, dispersed. The dates and distribution of the evidence will not fit that possibility. Moreover, in the provinces, soldiers are not much seen in Isiac lists.[7]

But there is a third possibility far more attractive than either traders or troops: immigrants to the peninsula brought in by force, that is, slaves and their descendants. For the sake of focus, we may instance the Isis temple in Pompeii, pre-dating 80 B.C. Who knelt there? But the answer imposes itself from a familiar statistic: at the time, a third of the population in Italy was slaves, of whom in turn the great majority came from eastern conquests and purchases and of whom there was a far higher than average concentration in Campania. Isis had watched over them all at birth and again when they took passage to the west with their captors. Over the years, some got money. Their descendants would be freed, and prosper. Yet even so, Isiacism in the town remained mainly the choice of the servile and freedman elements.[8] In Campania generally, as in Apulia and Etruria, three-quarters of the dedicants in inscriptions to Isis are slave or freed, during the span of the Empire; elsewhere, three-fifths, in Rome or Venetia or Sicily.

The same material that underlies these statistics and conclusions can be approached from another direction—yielding the same results. Isiacs appear in somewhat more than three hundred inscriptions from Italy. Nearly half of their names (43 percent) betray non-Italian origin. As we would predict, there are differences according to locale, the percentage dropping lower in the countryside and where Isis had been longest settled. There, her worshipers included some natives as well as immigrants who passed as natives through marriage or other means. By contrast, newcomers clustered in ports. That explains why, in Latium excluding Rome, 85 percent of the non-Italian Isiacs are found in Ostia; in all of Venetia, more than 70 percent in Aquileia.[9] The true percentages perhaps were higher still, for the reason just mentioned: non-Italian women married to natives, and their descendants, might well appear as natives on the surface and so be wrongly counted, even while holding fast to their ancestral faith. Isis evidently inspired fully as much loyalty as any other god, but nothing suggests that she counted much on new recruits.

Such broad conclusions can only be derived from epigraphic evidence.

Table of Frequency of Latin Inscriptions of the Empire

Number of inscriptions per year

Source: Mrozek (1973) 115.

By use of it, we can go on to distribute over time the inscriptions of free-born Isiacs in Italy, so far as they are datable at all: three in the first century; seventeen in the first and second combined; twenty-four in the second and third combined; and eight in the fourth. And we can determine a high point in the fortunes of Isis in the whole Latin west: under Caracalla. Thereafter, a sharp decline.[10] So it would appear. But the evidence can be pressed too far. In actual fact, inscriptions of every sort in the Roman Empire overall trace exactly the same line. Offset by its rise and fall, the lines of freeborn Isiacs and of the cult's history as a whole flatten out completely.

In the early 1900s, Jules Toutain, the first to make good use of inscriptions for the study of religion in the western and northern Empire, confronted the rising high priest of "Oriental" cults, Franz Cumont. The point at issue between them was the historical proportions of those cults. Isiacism, Cumont had said, "conquered new converts in every province"; whereas Toutain believed that it remained everywhere "an exotic cult, taking no root in provincial soil. It did not perceptibly modify the religious ideas or practices of the vast majority of the inhabitants." As usual, Toutain was right, Cumont wrong.[11] The truth appears in the table above, p. 6; even excluding her great center of Ostia and greater, in Rome, Isis stands tall in Italy as nowhere else. In Africa, she had only two temples. One was erected in the completely Romanized enclave, Lambaesis—the camp and the neighboring civilian settlement. From Lambaesis come all of her inscriptions. In Gaul, though the popularity of "Oriental" cults has been defended recently as well as by Cumont, Isiacism counted for nothing. Her only inscription comes from the chief city, Lyon—where more than a quarter of the people whose names are preserved for us at all are Greek, that is, from the eastern provinces.[12] Once more, we can explain what favor the cult did enjoy by supposing it to have been passed on within families, whose members moved about, rather than communicated to new recruits.

We are very much at the mercy of our data. We know that Isis appealed especially to women, but that women rarely put their names and vows on stone. It is likely that the main part of her worshipers are hidden in silence. Other distortions may be sensed in glancing through *CIL* 13, the volume of the epigraphic corpus that deals with the northwest. Here are 125 dedications to "Oriental" deities by persons whose sex can be known. Of this little group, 44 belong to the cult of Cybele, 81 to Mithra, Isis, and Dolichenus all together. Of the 81, only 1 was a woman; of the 44, a majority (24). But most of the Cybele texts come from the interior of the area (35), most of the 81 from the frontier (70). Cybele is very markedly for civilians, many of them old Italian; the other gods, for soldiers; and Isis (as Toutain said) simply not very popular.[13]

In a totally civilian area, Cisalpine Gaul, if we divide by sex the worshipers of the major fifteen deities, we expect to find large numbers of women addressing Cybele; a few, Isis. But in fact we find only one woman honoring any "Oriental" deity against fifty-five who honor the Greco-Roman. Men favored the exotic a little more (10 percent), except in the largest city, Milan.[14] That is predictable. The data teach us, however, that there were different kinds of civilians according to region.

If we look next at the stretch of provinces from Noricum to the Black Sea, we can confirm these various impressions.[15] Here, women amount to 10 percent or fewer of worshipers of eastern deities. Their names are attached only to Isis and Cybele. We find also a marked overrepresentation of districts in which troops resided. As these latter, in Gaul and Germany, provided close to half of all sorts of inscriptions, or as in the great frontier city of Mainz the epitaphs belong 88 percent to soldiers and another 5.7 percent to their kin and veterans, so in the Danubian army towns the same military types predominate—as do those towns, and their neighborhoods, over the interior. The effect is to present the preferences of the troops as if they were valid for the entire populations. Their weight has been doubly exaggerated.[16]

It hardly needs to be said that, even more than women, another category is underrepresented: that is, natives. Their names, for example, make up about 5 percent of the total in inscriptions of Moesia Superior. Another statistic can be used to draw out the meaning of that: only 4 percent of Gallic inscriptions addressed to native gods are offered by persons with nonnative names.[17] The indigenous population is far more completely hidden from us than are immigrant women, and its own beliefs are apparently barred, or of no interest, to the immigrants of both sexes.

It seems likely that the religious history of the West resembled that of the East in its uneventfulness far more than appears on the surface. Superficially surveyed, the one is sated with experiment, occasionally disturbed only by innovations themselves developing along conventional lines, while the other, the Latin-speaking area, is swept by floods of new belief. In reality, however, the new turns out to be ancestral, *ta patria*—only displaced. Underneath the Isiac in Ostia is a man or woman from Alexandria or Antioch, or from a parent or grandparent originating in those cities. Similarly, underneath the Isiac in Lyon: not a convert but an immigrant. And underneath the worshiper of Mars is a worshiper really of Lenus or

Segomo, changing no more than the name to be cut on stone, or changing not even that, because inscribing prayers belonged to an alien civilization. It should never be forgotten that the habit and the price of an inscription, both, were needed to make a mark on the surviving record; and both were lacking among the great majority of the population. The record on which we depend almost entirely in forming general conclusions is itself sadly partial.

But some conversions there were, undeniably. If the old gods were not quite driven from people's minds, at least they made room for new at the level which our information allows us to look at. And two cults in the west appear to have grown to a good size from nothing—therefore, of course, entirely through conversions—over the stretch of time here chosen for study.

The first is that of Jupiter of Doliche, virtually unknown in the east, first attested in the west in the A.D. 120s, seeming to attain a peak of popularity around 200 and falling off steeply after 220 or so. The number of testimonies of one kind or another (mostly dedications) is large enough to earn a place on the Table of Fifteen and recognition from emperors. But for these signs of prominence there is a common and deceptive cause at work: an intimate association with the army. The Tetrarchs might very well salute a god so greatly venerated by the army; and the student today must make a conscious effort to resist the impression given by the epigraphic evidence. It is clear that Dolichenus, however many thousands or tens of thousands of the loyal he may have commanded in a certain sphere for a certain time, enjoyed favor defined by persons of eastern origin or army calling and did not trace so dramatic a rise as the apparent numbers suggest.[18]

The second cult coterminous with our period is Mithraism. In the east, a single monument of A.D. 77 from Phrygia and an inscription and city coins from Cilicia, much later, are the only traces of a cult thought by contemporaries to be "Persian" (whatever that term meant to them); but early in the second century Plutarch knew of its current existence and prior prevalence in Cilicia. He speaks of it as if it might not be familiar to his audience.[19] It was, in sum, then, a somewhat out-of-the-way religion whose adherents perhaps preferred not to advertise it but which was gaining notice in the second century.

In the west, a poet from Naples, writing early in the A.D. 80s, mentions Mithraism. He seems to have in mind a version of an episode from Mithra's life that was later portrayed differently. About the same time (certainly before the end of the first century) Mithraic monuments show up on the Danube at Carnuntum[20] and, about A.D. 100, lower down the river, and on the Rhine and at Rome.[21] From then on, the signs multiply quite rapidly all over, especially in Rome and Ostia.[22] Representation of Mithraism in inscriptions is numerically similar to that of all inscriptions of every sort, throughout the west. About a third of the Mithraic dedicants are to be found in Italy; but so is nearly a third of the *Corpus*. A bare majority of the Italian come from Rome; but that is just the ratio within the *Corpus* overall. The civilian worshipers in Ostia include many (a half) with Greek names, many (more than a third) with Greek names in Rome; compared to the soldiers, their numbers are about typical in Italy (240 to 8) and in the north and east, from Raetia to the Black Sea (247 to 65)—although, in the north-west, they outnumber soldiers in an unusual way (in Gaul, 25 to 3; in Germany, 61 to 20).[23] In chronological distribution (allowing for Mithraism's late start, so to speak), the inscriptions follow the normal curve; and in social distribution (making the same allowance), Mithraists include an unremarkable assortment of one emperor, maybe; a praetorian prefect, for certain; a good many commandants in camps and their vicinity, and other ranks as well; from civilian settings, the highly Romanized in outlandish places (soldiers and tax collectors) and the lowly un-Romanized in melting pots like Ostia.[24] In excavated Ostia, there were fifteen chapels, all small affairs: they might indicate as few as 300 votaries (out of a population in that space of 25,000), or double or treble that, perhaps. Were impatient larger crowds queuing up at dawn before the still-closed gates of older gods?[25]

The weight of a given cult is quite impossible to guess within close limits. Taking account, however, of a possible undervaluation in the east, where its members may have been too poor to put their prayers on stone, and of overvaluation in Italy and the northern frontier zones, where epigraphic habits certainly favored them very greatly, we should no doubt rank Mithraism among the two or three dozen better-known cults of the Empire.[26] What elevates it above that in interest are two special features: first, that it had no home, and second, that its chapels were of a design ideally suited to archaeological resurrection.

Mithraism's ties with the east amount to so little that they can be denied entirely: it was rather "created at a defined moment by some unknown religious genius," best, in the Danube provinces. So say some scholars.[27] When it is found at Dura on the Euphrates in the third century, its presence there is explained (perhaps rightly—nobody knows) as secondary, brought by soldiers from Palmyra who had learned it in their service with legions from Europe. And so forth. But beneath all such guesswork lies the firm fact that there was a long time in which the cult was never attested anywhere; after

These twenty-four pieces of marble statuary were uncovered by chance in 1962 in Constantza (ancient Tomis). Most or all are works of the Severan period. At some unknown moment, most likely in the 250s or 260s, they were carefully but hurriedly hidden. They represent a cross section of local polytheism: the Fortune of Tomis with her mural crown; several Hecates; two Graces; Asclepius; Isis; Cybele; several statues of the Thracian Rider God; and so forth. Also a snake. See Canarache (1963) 133–135. Courtesy Muzeul de Istorie Nationala si Arheologie Constantza.

The statue of the snake found at Tomis is generally taken to be Glycon. The identification is questioned but seems obvious as no alternative is. If correct, it gives us the portrait of almost the only new god to arise in our period, well known through Lucian's essay on its high priest Alexander. Courtesy Muzeul de Istorie Nationala si Arheologie Constantza and P. MacKendrick.

that, scattered notices of it in the later first century; then, within a couple of generations, full stature as the peer of Sabazios worship, let us say. For a god with no great temple anywhere, without *ta patria* in which to anchor loyalty, without a city or a people to proclaim his wonders, the winning of prominence across a full quarter of the empire was quite remarkable.

The nearest parallel, but a mortal one bounded, or almost bounded, by the life of a single "religious genius," was the oracle of Glycon and his prophet Alexander. By artistic combination of Pythagoreanism, Asclepius myths, superstitious regard for snakes, old hymns, boys' choirs, Homer and Moon worship (or lunacy, our unpersuaded informant Lucian would have said), the religious practices and habits of thought prevailing in the northeast quadrant of the ancient world were formed into a brand new, artificial whole. It even had its own "mysteries." That feature, in several older cults in Greece and Asia Minor, took on broadly similar shapes through mutual imitation (above, chapter 2, section 1, n. 20, and section 4, n. 54). The genius of Alexander of Abonuteichus consisted in sensing this and so much else that was common in paganism across the eastern provinces.

So in the western, veneration for the east (Egypt being good but lands beyond Euphrates better still to lead one to new heights of sacred lore) was widespread. Further, everyone could expect some sort of more or less consciously reverent meal together, whatever the name of the deity presiding. And there should be ranks of leadership—that Mithraism had—and ranks of initiates—which Mithraism had, too. For the more curious seekers, there should be complicated doctrines about the return of the soul to its distant home, perhaps explained in hymns accompanying Mithraic services.[28] The west had its ways, a little different from those of the east—less wordy, less sunny. Mithraism summed them all up with almost commercial intuition.

In the first decades of the second century, it demonstrated an ability to make converts throughout the very mixed Italian (and Italian export) population, in a degree most unusual. The cult (to repeat) had no launching point, no center from which to begin a larger life—as once Bendis or Cybele had begun. The puzzle posed by a dynamic faith that came from nowhere has been often addressed. No solution has won general acceptance. To touch on some of the suggested interpretations serves as a review also of major religious trends, at least as they have been commonly perceived.

The most ambitiously overarching explanations for the success of Mithraism lie in the characterization of religious life in the times at large. By contemporaries, that is rarely attempted.[29] Among modern authorities, the best known, Cumont, begins by sketching the decline and recession of older alternatives to Mithraism. In our period of study, "less and less is that sturdy health of character found that, unable to depart at length from the road, felt no need of a guide and comforter. The spreading sense of decline and frailty could be noted that follows the wanderings of the passions; the same weakness that leads to crime urged the search for absolution . . . ," etc. etc.[30] For none of these thoughts does Cumont, or any adherent of the "Spiritual-Fortitude, Spiritual-Weakening" school of interpretation, offer any serious substantiation. The terms of description themselves are useless as too vague; useless a second time as normative according to prejudices not divulged, perhaps never examined; and useless a third time as applied to a population whose moral attributes and inner thoughts are not only almost entirely hidden from us but not even investigated through such few data as could be used.

But Cumont continues: "In the third century, the misery of the times was the cause of such great suffering . . . that people sought asylum in the expectation of a better life." This argument, making of the "Oriental" cults in general a retreat for desperation, can be expanded backward and forward in time to account for all the manifestations and appeal associated with those cults.[31] Indeed, it must be expanded, if their popularity is rightly reflected in the only promising category of evidence available to us, inscriptions. Such a correspondence is generally assumed. The number of epigraphic testimonies begins its steep rise from the earliest Empire, up to a point a little past A.D. 200. As we have seen, however, the correspondence is illusory and the rise means nothing, because all inscriptions of every sort rise equally.

Beyond that, what sense does it make to assign a single character to so long an era?—as if one were to say, "in Italy, Switzerland, the Low Countries, Britain, France, and Spain between about 1400 and 1600, people were tense and worried." The statement denies the very change and complexity which it is the job of historians to discover, and which indeed they never fail to reveal, wherever their sources allow them to portray events and figures of the past full-scale. As if a century, let alone two or three, could be "an age" —that is, a stretch of time in which just about everybody acted in significantly different ways from other human beings before and after, but with something close to a characteristic uniformity among themselves! It can only be the observer's ignorance that would make all the life of a vast area for so long a span, in the mind's eye, blur, shrink, stop. Such ignorance is the natural condition of the ancient historian, paradoxically inviting him to arrange his few scattered facts into grand patterns—the fewer, the grander. Where the temptations and the hazards are so pressing, perhaps it should be a rule that no one may generalize about ancient history until he has served an old-fashioned, seven-year apprenticeship in the teaching, or at least in the formal study, of modern history![32]

If the misery of the times cannot be used very well to explain the popularity of mystery cults, as an alternative it might be argued that "they provided a theodicy which legitimated the existing order by referring it to another plane of existence, and so were able to reduce perceived discontinuities."[33] Such terminology scholars fall into naturally. It is, alas, only too easy to be hard; equally hard to be easy; and translation of one's ideas into simple words opens them not only to understanding but to question. The ancients themselves (above, chapter 2, section 1, n.32), of course, could sometimes see that religion helped to keep the have-nots quiet. In Mithraism specifically, the allotting of initiates to seven degrees, and the number of initiates whose secular lives carried them through ranks, civil or military, perhaps pointed to parallels that were made attractive in worship and, from that, tolerable on the job. But was that likely to be what people wanted? When soldiers take the day off, do they freely seek out associations just like the ones they left in camp?[34] The attraction of the cult lay rather in a broad range of feelings and experiences: in roasting sacrificial hens and pork ribs on the sidewalk or somewhere above ground, with one's friends; descending into the barrel-vaulted dusk of the chapel, into the very presence of the god, for a long meal with much wine; thereafter (it may be imagined) communal chanting of a prayer, fortifying thoughts, perhaps some special verses or paean pronounced by the priest. When and how often the priest spoke of the god's gifts to men and drew worshipers in to a knowledge of the soul's necessary passage to a higher home, there to abide for all eternity, we do not know. But these were familiar parts of Mithraism.

Most modern observers of the cult who discuss how it was organized assume that it had a rather hierarchical feel to it, because of the seven grades of worshiper. Actually, however, more than seven terms for grades are attested. Individual cells may have had eight or ten. Some may have had only two or three. Whether the number produced a special sense of one's place is unknown. The cult and burial society of Aesculapius and Hygia in Rome (*ILS* 7213) had five grades of membership, receiving portions and handouts of different sizes at their banquets. The practice recalls mention of cult festivities at which there were to be, as a novelty, no distinctions in seating (above, p. 47). A huge Bacchic association in the Campagna at Torre Nova (above, p. 109) had twenty-odd ranks and offices. Entirely non-religious associations, for example, of the builders and carpenters (*fabri*) in Latin-speaking lands, often provided themselves with officers bearing military titles, even the mass of the membership being termed (*ILS* 615) "regular privates,'' *milites caligati*. Odd—but the worshipers of Aesculapius and Hygia had a rank *immunis* borrowed from army speech. Where the variety of evidence points in so many directions and the individual pieces are so small, surely nothing certain can be said about the social or psychological meaning of a cult's organization.

If it was in the promise of immortality that the secret of Mithra's appeal lay, those who had attained it were not thought to be in any hurry to take up their claim. "Hail to the Lions, new years and many to them!" runs the salute for those who had reached one of the higher ranks, admitting them among the full officiants.[35] It is certainly odd, too, that the Apologists make no mention of any hope of eternal life, a hope to be ridiculed and undermined, among Mithraists. Mithraists may have seen eternity in no more sharply defined or enticing an outline than votaries of other gods (above, pp. 54ff.). The evidence, however, is hard to make sense of and very much under debate.

Turning to the second feature that holds particular interest, the subterranean nature of most Mithraic chapels, there the most incontestable facts emerge, quite literally, from the earth: benches on which worshipers sat at services or reclined at meals; paintings that show how their officials waited on them, wearing fantastic animal masks; and various curious features of design. The vault might be decorated with painted stars whose centers held glass, to catch light and sparkle; gilt and jewels were used for the same purpose on parts of cult reliefs to be particularly noticed, with bright paint applied to the rest; a round or many-rayed hole in the vault admitted the sun and thus dramatically illuminated some chosen point or person underneath; striking scenes were portrayed in relief and color on the two sides of a stone slab rotating so as instantly to reveal a second message to viewers; and arrangements allowed the sudden raising of a curtain from in front of such a scene.[36] Altars had cut-out crescents with glass in front, to be lit from behind by lamps or candles; or they had cut-out halos or sun rays over a deity's head, or whole figures of deities cut out—in short, elaborate provisions for unexpected lighting effects, the more certain to impress because of the ordinary darkness of the windowless surroundings.[37] In one German Mithraeum, by good luck not rusted into nothing, excavators found a trick sword consisting of the handle and upper part of the blade, attached to a big loop of metal, ending in the continuation of the blade; so, with the loop around half his chest, an actor would appear to be transfixed by the weapon but still alive.[38] That fits with other mentions or proofs of naked men, blindfolds, helmeted men, swords, graves, and corpses real or resurrected, assembled into what initiatory show, no one can say.

Underground roused powerful associations: of death, necromancy, and a separate world of deities and spirits. The physical fact of darkness around you heightened expectation—and Mithraea could be very gloomy indeed. Tertullian remarks on that; the *Augustan History* reports "it was the custom [in Mithraic services] to do or say something for a show of terror."[39] All speculation concerning the doctrine taught in those services aside, all controversy about cult meals aside, all doubts about the Mithraic view of immortality disregarded, one certain thing remains: the subterranean rites were carefully designed to amaze and terrify.

Of no other cult can quite the same be said. Yet of several it is known that crypts, hidden narrow passageways, gloom, and torchlight were played with to produce in initiates feelings of fear and awe.[40] Lucian describes the jugglery used by Alexander of Abonuteichus, Hippolytus knew a bookful of tricks of the same sort. There is really a lot of talk about religious deceits in writers of the time, Jewish, Christian, and pagan. We should not be surprised to find them employed in a widespread way in Mithrasim. Added to an eclectic base of broadly acceptable cult practices, the advantage that Mithrasim may have enjoyed—or rather, manifestly did enjoy—was showmanship. Which is not to deny sincerity to the priests who decided just where best to cut a nineteen-rayed aperture in the ceiling of their god's house, to let in the light, or who had a fake sword discreetly hammered out on the forge of the local smith. Sincerity and deceits may easily go together. Nor is it to deny that the symbols freely applied to a cult scene or myth scene, a fresco or relief, may have been linked in learned discourse to the astrology of the time, the theosophy, and so forth. Those were a part of the common culture of paganism. Different devices appealed to the clever clerk on the governor's staff and to the barefoot porter in Ostia who carried grain sacks on his back all day.

The question raised on a previous page, "How can the exceptional faith be explained that reaches across a hundred miles, or turns up whole provinces away?" can perhaps best be answered through another question: "What made converts?"—converts of any sort, near or far. To that latter, the answer was seen to lie in the visible show of divinity at work (above, pp. 95–97). Thereafter, to make a richer belief, other thoughts and feelings might take over. So it all was with Mithrasim—whether also of the cult of Jupiter Dolichenus, no one can tell. To repeat: these were the only cults whose power to draw in new recruits on a significant scale, at least for a time, is clearly indicated.

Their success has been taken sometimes as a sign that older gods had lost their hold on people's loyalty. The "Oriental" were demanded by some no-longer-satisfied spiritual appetite. Their title, however, has meaning only for those who think that most of the Levant and Near East, with Egypt and parts of the Middle East tossed in, shared religious beliefs and practices sufficiently similar all to fit better together than any of them might fit with the Greco-Roman—that is, that Mithra was more like Sarapis than like Dionysus, the Syrian triad more like Isis than like the Capitoline Triad. So stated, the unity underlying the notion of "Oriental religion" falls apart.

It is still harder to accept the decades around A.D. 300 as those in which the "Oriental" cults enjoyed their most pronounced ascendancy. Close before those decades, Aurelian proclaimed a special veneration of the sun; close after, both Constantine and Licinius put Sol on their coins to advertise their trust in him. But in between came the Tetrarchs, titled Jovian and Herculian. What could be more evenhandedly, quintessentially, conservatively Greco-Roman than that? Diocletian's coins most favor "the Genius of the Roman People." Nothing could be more old-fashioned. But he also reduced the pantheon of his coins generally. At the end, Jupiter, Hercules, and Mars were left almost alone. Hardly a sign of paganism shrinking. The real explanation is unknown, but Antoninus Pius's coins likewise acknowledged only a small selection of the gods.[41] For that policy of his, too, no explanation is known; from it, no weakness in paganism inferred. About the same time, the coinage of eastern cities was becoming more crowded with a larger selection of deities. Possibly the reason was esthetic.[42] We lack the keys to unlock these puzzling phenomena.

Nevertheless, interpretation still insists that paganism was "pressing on to its doom" (or the like phrase). We are invited to consider the sharply diminishing number of inscriptions attesting to the active worship of Mithra himself, in the third century, to say nothing of Vesta in the capital, Saturn in North Africa, or Dolichenus in Dalmatia and Pannonia. I choose particularly striking examples of deities fading out of our sight within their very homes.[43] The data, however, tell nothing about people's faith. It is not the priest who is stilled but the stonecutter. For the last time, the reader is referred to Mrozek's frequency table (above, p. 115). Religion, like many another aspect of life, rises and falls on the quantity of surviving evidence like a boat on the tide. Highs and lows of attestation, if they only follow the line on the table, indicate no change at all.

The tide itself—the number of pieces of data, especially written data, remaining from any decade in the first four centuries—has been noticed only very rarely and casually. The neglect is surprising, in this present era of statistics. But the dating of the pieces is problematical and the usefulness of all the necessary work not obviously apparent. After all, everybody knew there was some approximate correspondence between the general wealth, peace and "progress" of the Empire, on the one hand, and the richness of documentation, on the other.

Perhaps the matter is not so simple as it seems. The custom of presenting some thought or fact to one's community, living and to come, was generally unnatural, at least unnecessary. It assumed literacy. It had to be displayed to those not familiar with it and imitated; it had to be maintained at some cost by those to whom it was a part of inherited culture. Apparently both categories of person found they could do without it. Its decline in the western provinces was precipitous, as we have seen; in the eastern, perceptible but never measured. In a large section of Syria, some hundreds of inscriptions have been found spread across our period and on through the sixth century. They show a gap almost complete over the years A.D. 250–325.[44] Other kinds of written evidence elsewhere in the east also are less abundant then than fifty years earlier. The explanation that might most naturally offer itself is poverty, during the Empire's Time of Troubles. But if that were right, why, earlier, should the number of inscriptions have continued to rise past Commodus, even past the turn of the second century? By then, as everyone surely is agreed, the Empire's fortunes had long since taken a downward turn.

It is not easy to understand why that section of Syria in the mid-third century, or most of Egypt some decades earlier, or Proconsular Africa for a period beginning in the A.D. 230s and Pannonia in the 220s, and so on all around the Empire—perhaps most puzzling of all, the Arval and Vestal cults, snug in Rome—should clearly start to fade out of the written record as they did, at a time when there appears to be no common factor in control of their fortunes. Not even coinage touched them all in the same way. Imperial currency did not reach into Egypt at all; and small change was imperial in the west; in the east, municipal—at least to a considerable degree. Even where both the deterioration of the currency and the fading of the written record can be noted together, unmistakable signs of prosperity may appear (just as the reverse appears earlier: general prosperity, but specific depressed regions like Greece).[45] I must leave these puzzles unsolved, however, and go on to say what I think can be said.

If the fortunes of the pagan record—the number of testimonies to prayer, invocation, praise, and so forth—run parallel to those of other phenomena —to writing itself, in chief—so that one cannot say those fortunes were in decline, yet nevertheless, when the worst is over and other lines begin to rise, it is not paganism that reemerges. Rather, it is Christianity. That, at least, is true in several places.[46] To which another fact should be connected.

Whatever was needed to produce an inscription was more easily found among Christians than pagans. During the same worst period, the curve of epigraphic data drops down for inscriptions of some sorts more than for others: for economic indicators and economic records of municipal life or of private citizens, or for expenses generally.[47] It would be hard to deny, then, that the publicity attending religion had something to do with money.

The connection seems obvious. It can be confirmed. When the pagan masters of the world set about the destruction of Christianity in a thinking manner, they did so from the top down, evidently taking it for granted that only the Church's leaders counted.[48] Suppose that it was the natural but wrong assumption of the ruling class, to think itself, or its like among Christians, the essence of everything; and suppose therefore that the focus of the persecutions does not prove, in paganism, the key importance of the ruling class—yet there are still other proofs. They arise almost by themselves from the nature of paganism as it was portrayed in the first chapter, above. From that portrait, if the aristocracy and their wealth were to be removed, a very, very great deal would disappear with them. Consider a few of the consequences. It was not universal, but it was the prevalent fact, that the gods were decently housed. If possible, they should be housed magnificently, exhausting the resources of local rich families over generations. Paganism, therefore, for us to recognize it in its familiar forms, required the patrons who paid for its temples. Games, exhibitions, performances, and public feasting likewise cost great sums. To offer certain sacrifices was out of the ordinary man's reach, when five months of his labor were needed to make up the price of an ox.[49] The impression of strain conveyed by these considerations is reinforced by recalling from earlier pages the many glimpses of shrines active but only half-built, or half in ruins.

The more prominent, public features of paganism no doubt did fade out in the third century. That fact, unlike the silence that falls on record keeping of several sorts, allows straightforward explanation: costs of cult had come to seem too high. The sense might be challenged: "What sort of religion is it that takes money?" asked the Apologists in derision (above, pp. 96–97). A fair question—if it is also fair to ask, What is especially good about a religion that costs nothing? Why should the hollow-cheeked St. Anthony stare down the Buddha? Eating and drinking may be a form of worship, and dancing and singing, building and painting, writing and reading. Paganism, as it existed in good times and as it was presented in my first chapter, there was no reason to reject; nor was there any general disposition to diminish pomp—not in the age that saw Rome's rebirth sanctified by the emperor Philip with incredible expenditures, nor in the age of Constantine's basilicas. Only, most people who would formerly have paid the costs of festivals and temples at the local level could now, in bad times, no longer find the money.

To the best-attested fifteen cults, or the best-attested thirty, if their traditions had become too expensive, alternatives emerged here and there. They were drawn from the non-Greek, non-Roman substratum to be found throughout the Mediterranean lands. Its religious expression, so rich and varied, underlay a great many hyphenated names, as has been pointed out: Artemis Pergaea, Mars Segomo. Worship of such deities had continued for many centuries beneath the very feet of Greek and Roman (or even earlier, Celtic or Punic) conquerors in Asia Minor as in North Africa.[50] It constituted the oldest part of living paganism—in a Darwinian sense, the fittest to survive, since it required so little nourishment. "Higher" forms of religious life needed, and might not always find, the kind of bountiful patronage that made brilliant the festivals of Zeus of Panamara and Hecate of Lagina. The "lower" unexpectedly gained somewhat in strength and prominence, over the whole of the third century.

But with cults that are centered in cities or tribes, we return to our starting point, "national" gods. They were the beginning and essence of the whole resilient, living fabric of belief. For the most part, however, they lie below the reach of our inquiry, at a level of the merely local and illiterate. Moreover, they were the ingredients of the Empire's culture least dissolved in the melting pot, therefore least to be described in any general statement about paganism as one whole. When political and economic conditions favorable to them settled in, as was clear by (indeed before) the end of our period of study, the point at which this study ought to end is also clear.

Epilogue

THE MANNER OF DEATH OF PAGANISM

Paganism as one whole is most easily seen as the patterns of thought and action, and their attendant feelings, roused by belief in the existence of superhuman powers; such powers are most easily grouped in the mind as a structure having a narrow summit and a broad base; and such a structure most easily accommodates the known facts about it if it is conceived as changing all the time, therefore alive. The metaphor of the pyramid has been, in earlier pages, employed often enough to make it familiar, both in regard to the superhuman world with its few great and many minor beings, and in regard to its worshipers, among them, the few of the ruling and literate classes and the many of the obscure and illiterate. The organic metaphor likewise is familiar. It underlies phrases like "dying paganism."

Metaphors have their uses, also their deceits. Paganism died, agreed—like the last stegosaurus or like a coral reef?

Having its origins in particular localities, its upper parts generally corresponded with the fortunes of the natives of those localities. Athena and Jupiter were great because they were the deities of conquering peoples; Artemis and Saturn guarded great cities. They inevitably preoccupy our notice. Indeed, the elaboration of their worship becomes, for us, the very canon and definition of paganism. It is, however, in fact only the upper parts that we are looking at, and they are vulnerable to changes in fortune as the lowlier cults of less important peoples are not.

For one thing, if the means by which we know them are lost to us, they themselves will appear to have receded. The appearance may be false, but we cannot easily make correction for it. It is this difficulty that the diminishing of inscriptions creates—of coins, too, and of papyri and written works generally. But most inscriptions, unlike these other media, served no obvious or practical purpose. They arose from someone having something he wanted to communicate to his whole world, from which in turn he expected approval or esteem: approval for piety or achievement—or both, as for example in a text that might read, "So-and-so, high magistrate, erected

this monument to Such-and-Such a god at his own expense, willingly."
Much of the epigraphic record on which we depend for an estimate of
paganism reflects not only what people believed but whether or not their
belief was likely to raise them in others' eyes. For the same reason, then, that
few Christians declared their faith during the third century, few pagans can
have cared to do so, once the emperor, and with him, those who sought his
favor, changed allegiance.

For Constantine ushered in a new age, in which for the first time there
was such a thing as a state cult—moreover, one animated at the center by
that missionary motive unique to Christianity. In a number of his statements and in more still of his actions, he declared his intent to increase the
ranks of the faithful. Contrast with the adherents of other gods needs no
underlining. At the very towering peak of their appalling rage and cruelty
against Christians, pagans had never sought to make converts *to* any cult—
only *away* from atheism, as they saw it. Toleration gone mad, one may say.

Such were those times, cruel and violent. Under the Tetrarchs, Church
leaders in the chief eastern cities were arrested and tortured; even pagan
priests and dignitaries if suspected of fraud.[1] Thereafter, shrines and the
holy things within them were again confiscated or destroyed; leaders exiled;
humble worshipers beaten up. In these incidents, pagans were now the
victims.[2] Occasionally they reacted with their own violence—over the long
run, unavailingly.

They did not suffer at the hands of the governors' guards, as Christians
had done. The army remained in the fourth century predominantly pagan
—so it is safe to say, though just when the balance tipped the other way no
one knows.[3] A. H. M. Jones puzzles over the supine acceptance by the army
of now one faith in its commander, now another, from Constantine through
the 360s. There is no clear explanation; and the behavior of Arbogast's and
Eugenius's soldiers extends the problem almost to the end of the century.
One conclusion, however, imposes itself: soldiers somehow managed to
keep their religion separate from their business, even when their business
appears to us to have lain with religion. That was as true in the 390s, in
Italy and the west, as it had been in the east, in the transition from Julian to
Jovian to Valentinian. It suggests that emperors and commanders dared
not press their views upon those of their servants who bore arms.

Powerful people made their own rules. Those in Italy, even unarmed but
of high station, maintained their loyalty to the old gods quite openly. Their
story has been told a hundred times. Little details add themselves continually, in the form of inscriptions recording the repair of temples or the
holding of priesthoods by private individuals or officials.[4] So long as they

were left alone, they gave more than respectability to their faith. There is no reason to suppose theirs was not the majority party until the fifth century. Because of their family holdings and prescriptive right to governorships in the central African provinces, those latter also yield many indications of paganism respected, open and confident, throughout the fourth century;[5] but there were deep-rooted cults there, too, which needed no support from Italy.[6]

To the north, the restoration of a long-deserted Mithra temple was advertised by an inscription of the period, in Virunum; but this was under Julian the Apostate, therefore perhaps an insincere act. What could be more genuine, what could better testify to the confidence of pagans even under a Christian emperor, than the celebrations at Emona when Theodosius visited the city? There went out to meet him "senators notable in their snow-white dress, the flamens venerable in city-purple, the priests standing out because of their peaked hats."[7] It was officially a pagan reception.

The Danube lands suffered such destruction in the third century from barbarians and so much more, from Christian ardor, in the fourth and fifth, that idols and temples of the late Empire are hard to find in one piece. Outside Pautalia, the sanctuary of Zeus and Hera, enclosing several temples alive and well over the fourth century, at the end received such a smashing that only two simple capitals remained intact. They were of granite.[8] Meanwhile, the inscriptions of the region change under Constantine. Pagan gravestones and ex-votos are no longer set up, while Christian epitaphs and increasingly rich burials come into view. All this is best explained by imagining a takeover of the town senates by new converts, while humbler folk and the countryside remained little affected.

In the east, the continuing prominence of paganism in Athens is well known; of Asclepius's cult, too, at various shrines.[9] In Syria, in its greatest city, Antioch, the masses appear to have been Christians for a long time, by (let us say) A.D. 375; the city senators, mostly Christian; but the peasants over the countryside generally a mixture, possibly half and half.[10] In Egypt of the mid-fourth century, an army commander had plenty of Christians, including priests, who were in courteous correspondence with him; but in his headquarters' chapel an image of the goddess Nemesis presided, and his personal servant took oath by the gods, plural. Perhaps that meant nothing. A deacon of the Church toward the same date "swears by the divine and holy Tyche of our all-conquering Lords," the emperors.[11] Inside people's minds the most contrary beliefs might coexist, at some moment suddenly to be recognized as mutually intolerable. In that same fashion Christians and pagans lived together for generations in the cities of the Empire, in peace disturbed rarely by spasms of frightful violence, both before and after 312.

Gaza, around the end of the century, illustrates how the religious forces might change their balance. Being an out-of-the-way place, it had been hardly touched by Christianity. The emperor Arcadius is imagined saying, "I know very well that the city is full of idols. But it loyally pays its dues and contributes much [to the treasury]. If we suddenly impose a reign of terror, they will flee and we will lose all that tribute. Still, if you wish, we will squeeze them gradually, removing the dignity of their idolatries and other municipal offices." To that, an impatient missionary replied with more direct action, performing miracles in the town. Thereupon "some of the pagans, seeing what great wonders God had performed, now believing . . . , shouted, 'Christ only is God, He only has prevailed!'"[12]

Enough of these disconnected episodes and glimpses, picked up around the whole Empire. Since so much of the raw fact, the archaeological, epigraphic and papyrological material, remains still unevaluated, to say nothing of its being assembled into broad regional surveys, there is little that can be said at this point with any confidence. Just a few broad statements may be hazarded.

First, as Peter Brown has said, "the historian of the later Roman church is in constant danger of taking the end of paganism for granted."[13] His warning gives shape and weight to all the scattering of facts just reviewed— a warning the more needed because what it warns against appears so thoroughly reasonable. We naturally assume that such wonders as were worked at Gaza had long since had their effect in other places. It surprises us, indeed, still to find an almost wholly pagan town in the Holy Land in the fifth century (but there remained others in the sixth!). If wonders had not availed everywhere, it surprises us that laws against sacrifices, seizure of idols by the state, and so back through the crowded chronicles of violence to Constantine's own reign, should not have turned everybody Christian. But pagans survived, unterrified. To the emperor's face they shouted, "The gods save you!" Their priests turned out to welcome him on his journeyings. The higher reaches of his government—not only barbarian generals like Arbogast, but civil functionaries—were predominantly pagan before Julian as after, too—and not in remote regions but in the eastern provinces themselves. The enormous thing called paganism, then, did not one day just topple over dead. No metaphorical description of that sort will apply, even if the process of demise is somehow stretched out over a generation past the great conversion of 312 (and more than a generation, it is not the fashion to suggest: Julian must be a dreamer, doomed, born out of his time, or the like).

Second, distinction must be made between two elements in religion: the perceptible, meaning the activities and all that those activities imply in consequence of a person's being an open participant in some belief; and the debatable, as I have called it, meaning those feelings and thoughts that accompany a person's acknowledgment of a god; and a person may grow up into certain religious activities without ever believing, or come to believe but never participate, so the priority of the one or the other element is not fixed, nor even their occurrence as a pair. It was the perceptible and its pomp and privilege enjoyed by leaders of a congregation that the emperor Arcadius thought to strike at, so as to turn them from their pagan ways; while the missionary who asked for his help aimed *his* efforts at another point.

To force acknowledgment of their God, Christians commanded remarkable means. Tertullian had called the blood of martyrs the seed of the Church. Backhandedly, the emperor Julian had shown later that he attached the same importance to martyrdom, through what he decided not to do even more than through what he did. Surrender of one's life for one's faith was bound to work most powerfully on witnesses. It was quite beyond nature, a wonder. Along with miracles of other kinds and exorcism routinely (above, pp. 95–96 and 50), it goes far to explain how thousands, not mere dozens of the uncommitted, might be induced really to look at another man's god and really to open their minds to a new reality. Indeed, if we relied only on pre-Constantinian sources, we would suppose that such supernatural acts accounted for very much the greater part of all conversions. There should be nothing surprising, then, in the missionary's miracles in Gaza at the turn of the fourth century.

But many students of the ascendancy of the Church (being thus by implication also students of the dying away of paganism) would rather emphasize the importance of the social ethics, status-structure, congeniality, moral challenge, and psychological support offered to those who joined the Church.[14] Perhaps it is all a matter of definition: When does the process of conversion cease and the process of living in a faith begin? Or perhaps the two elements of religion distinguished above cannot be known and separated in enough instances for us to tell which best explains the fading of pagan cults.

Anyway, Arcadius had no doubts; and by his day existed, thanks to his Christian predecessors, many, many laws aimed against the prominent sort of pagans. They could not legally pass on their estates, they could not enter on profitable careers, their sanctuaries had been stripped of land and wealth.[15] As added penalty, in the good gold solidus dispensed by Constantine and his successors to the Church, pagans could recognize the metal confiscated from the treasuries of their gods. They were financing their own destruction.

And this they were made to do in a period that was, for quite secular and impersonal reasons, radically inimical to the pagan "Establishment"— that is, inimical to local urban magnates. Their difficulties had sharpened in the third century. By the fourth, many of them had been driven into the refuge of their villas, or into bankruptcy. In either case, they were not on hand to pay the bills for what, some pages back, were called the upper parts of paganism.

Upon those upper parts our account has naturally focused, because they were the most visible in the surviving record. They were also the most fragile. Like a coral reef, to live and grow further, they required conditions favorable within quite narrow limits. When conditions changed, life and growth must end. The more substantial, older, primitive parts of the pyramid of beliefs, however, lying at a level below the reach of our inquiry, died more slowly—just when, no record declares.

From the triumph of Christianity, it is natural but not certainly right to reason backwards: Christianity in its now familiar outline, Christianity as it was "supposed to be," prevailed because it was intrinsically better. It was freely espoused by people who could see its superiority. But that view should not involve the quite crude error of supposing the now familiar outline to have been already clear in the period of our study. In fact, of course, the Church was undergoing constant change in its early history as in its later. The marked prominence of exorcism in its outer face, and of demonology in the inner, faded rapidly away during the fourth century—to name two areas of development that have received mention above.

Crude error avoided, there remain several further points of doubt. First, is it possible to define, almost a priori, major human wants to which answer must, or can only easily, be made through religion? So, if nothing in all the variety of paganism answered some of those wants, but Christianity did, the rise of the latter could be explained. As one illustration (pp. 53–57—but several others, I think, offer themselves from the preceding pages or have been discussed in other books): no pagan cult held out promise of afterlife for the worshiper as he knew and felt himself to be. Resurrection in the flesh was thus a truth proclaimed to the decisive advantage of the Church. In making any such assertion, however, much care would be needed against attributing to the third century social and spiritual needs that were created rather than answered by Christianity.

Second, is it possible to weigh the impact of two adventitious factors, the destructive political and economic forces at work upon the more prominent parts of paganism after 250 and the constructive dynamic of Constantine's reign in favor of the Church? Together, one might argue, these factors over three-quarters of a century coincided with, and were very nearly enough to account for, the great changes in the Church's fortunes. But the argument must be tested.

Third, from the study and especially from the dating of pagan testimonies post-312, is it possible to determine just how much and how early paganism retreated? The most casual reading in the late Empire suggests that there is plenty of material to reward inquiry on this front.

Those are points that occur even to an inexpert observer. It is curious, when one stops to think about it, that the success of the Church in taking on historic proportions has never been described with much care.[16]

Abbreviations

Citation in the notes is abbreviated to the form "Jones (1967) 100," or, where I cite two works by the same author published in the same year, I add "a" or "b" to the date. The abbreviated citations can, I hope, be expanded without difficulty from the bibliography. A few works of reference receive their standard abbreviations, all of which may be found in the *Oxford Classical Dictionary*. There too, or in the *Greek-English Lexicon* of H. G. Liddell and R. Scott, may be found the usual abbreviations for primary sources, including collections of papyri and inscriptions. The only abbreviation I use which may not be widely familiar is *ANRW*, for the ongoing series of volumes on the *Aufstieg und Niedergang der römischen Welt*, edited by H. Temporini and W. Haase.

Notes

CHAPTER I: PERCEPTIBLE

1. Finding Order in Chaos

1. Degrassi (1962) 995-1004, passim.

2. Collart (1937) chap. 4. Note the absence of the oriental gods Mithra, Sabazius, Jupiter Dolichenus; and compare, almost at random, such another city as Lambaesis and suburbs, LeGlay (1971) 129-141, with epigraphic attestations of Saturn (161 in number), Mercury next with 13 (to be explained, p. 132, by "Mercury" as the interpretation of the local deity of agriculture, esp. oleiculture); Minerva (12); Silvanus (11); Mithra (9); Fortuna (6); dii Mauri (6); and so forth.

3. Bosch (1935) 102-130.

4. Lucian, *Jup. trag.* 8f. and 12; cf. some of the more exotic names again in *Icaromen.* 24 and 27.

5. *De laud. Const.* 13.4f. (*PG* 20.1400)—a list similar to that given by Athenagoras, *Leg.* 14, offering a dozen deities ranging from Transjordan to Sicily and Carthage, the rest Greek. His purpose being to show idiosyncrasies, he offers some very odd ones, as Geffcken (1907) 187 points out.

6. *Pauli Sent.* 5.21.1, prophets being very common, cf. *Dig.* 21.1.1.9f. and other texts in MacMullen (1966a) 142-155; Latte (1960) 328f.; and Parassoglou (1976) 261 and 266.

7. Athenag., *Leg.* 1.

8. Harnack (1905) 9f. and passim; Geffcken (1907) 186.

9. Nicolaus of Damascus, in Jos., *Ant. Jud.* 16.44, to Agrippa in 14 B.C., consonant with the view Cicero indicates about the Jews (*Pro Flacco* 69), *sua cuique civitati religio*, etc. The pagan audience replies, in Claudius's declaration that one "should safeguard traditional customs," Jos., *Ant. Jud.* 19.290, and again, in A.D. 45, Claudius's piety urges "each to offer cult according to τὰ πάτρια;" and so to Celsus the pagan defending the Jews ca. A.D. 178, Orig., *C. Cels.* 5.25, on the grounds of their loyalty to their own native customs, τὰ πάτρια. "It is not pious to dissolve what has been assigned from the beginning to each locality . . . ," cf. again, 5.34.

10. Just., I *Apol.* 12, setting "truth" against "customs"; Celsus, in Orig., *C. Cels.* 5.34, cf. 8.28; Clem. Alex., *Coh. ad gent.* 10.73 and 12.91 (*PG* 8.201 and 237); Tert., *Ad nat.* 2.1, and *Apol.* 6.1, 6.9, and 6.10, where pagans claim to defend customs of *maiores* and *patres*; Min. Fel. 6.1; Origen replying to Celsus, *C. Cels.* 5.35; Porph., in Euseb., *Praep. ev.* 1.2.1; Galerius in Euseb., *H.E.* 8.17.6; Licinius in Euseb., *Vita Const.* 2.5, Constantine τὰ πάτρια παρασπονδήσας, τὴν ἄθεον εἵλετο δόξαν, κτλ,

cf. *Orat. ad Sanctos* 9 (*PG* 20.1253); Euseb., *Praep. ev.* 1.1 (5a–c); and Julian often, e.g., *Ep.* 89a.453B, 89b.302B; *C. Galil.* 238D.

11. *Praep. ev.* 4.1 (130C), trans. Gifford.

12. *Ad Marc.* 18 and similar statements showing veneration for τὰ πάτρια in Sext. Emp., *Adv. dogmaticos* 1.49, and Dio 52.36.

13. *Ad Marc.* 14.

14. Plut., *Moral.* 756B; for his friends, cf. 402E, 416C, and 1125E; good commentary by Andresen (1955) 264 and Dreyer (1970) 50 n.164; and the often-quoted, passionate injunction in *CIG* 5041, lines 4f., "Consider first the ancestral gods, and worship them," etc.

15. *Ep. ad Diognetum* 1.1 and 8.7–9.2; Suet., *Nero* 16.3; *Pauli Sent.* 5.21.2; Euseb., *Praep. ev.* 1.1 (5a); Julian, *C. Galil.* 306A.

16. Porph., *De abst.* 2.18, on Hesiod frg. 5.169; Tert., *Apol.* 19.1f.; also Just., 1 *Apol.* 23, 44, and 59f.; Theoph., *Ad Autol.* 1.14, 2.3, 3.1, etc.; Tat., *Ad Graec.* 29, 31, and 40, and in Euseb., *Praep. ev.* 10.11 (495bf.), cf. 10.9; Min. Fel. 6.3; Orig., *C. Cels.* 1.14, 4.36, and elsewhere; and Eusebius revealing his own reasoning, *H.E.* 5.28.2, "they wished to make it holy, as if it were ancient." For discussion of such texts, see, for example, Andresen (1955) 63f. and 70, and Pépin (1966) 232f. Compare Tac., *Hist.* 5.5, Jewish beliefs *antiquitate defenduntur*, or Sext. Emp., *Adv. math.* 1.203f., using age as the canon to determine the best usages in Greek.

17. On *patrius*, πάτριος, πατρῷος, see as a mere selection *IGR* 3.89 (A.D. 68), to Zeus and Hera, τοῖς πατρίοις θεοῖς καὶ προεστῶσιν τῆς πόλεως at Amastris, the latter term often by itself, e.g., Zeus and Hecate are προεστῶτες θεοί τῆς πόλεως at Panamara, in LeBas-Wadd. 519–520 (ca. A.D. 200—cf. Laumonier [1934] 85), or Dionysus in Teos is termed "the presiding deity of the city," in Robert (1937) 25 n.2 and 30f., as Artemis in Perge is termed ἄνασσα and προεστώσης τῆς πόλεως, cf. Pace (1923) 304; further "ancestral" gods in *IG* 10, 2.199, Thessalonica in the mid-third cent., "to the ancestral god Kabeiros"; Seyrig (1941) 246, Iarhibol is "ancestral" at Palmyra, A.D. 192/3; Rehm (1958) 117, Aphrodite at Didyma; *Forschungen in Ephesos* 2 (1912) 126, "your ancestral deity Artemis" at Ephesus in A.D. 200/205, cf. Xen., *Ephes.* 3.5.5, her priestess calls her "the ancestral" (second cent.); Hatzfeld (1927) 74 and 77, Zeus of Panamara; LeBas-Wadd. 2576, Helios at Palmyra; *BGU* 362 (A.D. 215) p. vi, "our ancestral crocodile god the great Souchos"; Men "the ancestral" in texts of Antioch, Lane (1971–1978) 1.102–110 and 3.64; and *MAMA* 3.56, Helios "ancestral" in Cilicia (with editor's comments). In the west, see *IRT* 289, Hercules and Liber pater concealing Punic deities, like Apollo *patrius* in Merlin (1908) 25, of the second or third cent.; Liber pater, *lar Severi patrius* at Lepcis, in Guey (1953) 341f., on *IRT* 295; *CIL* 8.21486, *dii patrii et Mauri conservatores*; and 8.19121, Baliddiris in Numidia. Possessive epithets like "city-guardian," "god of our people," etc., can be easily found, e.g., in *IGR* 4.1571, Robert (1950) 68, and LeBas-Wadd. 400.

18. *IGR* 1.421=*OGIS* 595, A.D. 174. D'Arms (1972) 258 and 267f., encountering *cultores dei patri* in Puteoli, ca. A.D. 340, struggles with the strange notion that there was only one particular deity termed "ancestral" in Italy. This example cannot be surely identified. For other instances of gods called ancestral by worshipers abroad, see Seyrig (1970) 111, on *IG* 14.962, the Palmyrene Arsou invoked in Rome; *IGR* 1.45 and 46, the same, in A.D. 235; *ILS* 4341 = *CIL* 3.7954, Palmyrene gods invoked by a Palmyrene in Dacia, cf. Birley (1978) 1518, adding other similar texts from Lam-

baesis addressed to eastern gods by an official; *IGR* 1.1293, a Roman commander invokes *dii patrii* in Egypt, 29 B.C.; *IG* 4, 1².417, a priest in Epidaurus invokes Hera of Argos and Zeus of Nemea in A.D. 297; *IGR* 1.387, Gaza invokes its gods to honor Gordian, in Portus; *ILS* 4349 = *CIL* 3.3668, in Pannonia on the Danube, to Arabian deities by Arabians (?), cf. Salač (1956) 168f.; in Augsburg, to Elagabal by a Syrian, cf. Radnoti (1961) 385 and 401; to Egyptian deities by an Egyptian (to judge from his name) in Miletus, cf. Vidman (1969) 147, though Isis and Sarapis, "ancestral" in Cadyanda, are taken as naturalized there, by Dunand (1972-1973) 3.7; to Syrian deities, πάτριοι, Atargatis and others, by a cult group in Rhodes, *IG* 12,3.178; at Intercisa in A.D. 214, to Elagabal by Syrian soldiers, cf. Fitz (1972) 101; to *invictus patrius*, Mithra, by an eastern official in Italy, cf. Pflaum (1960-1961) 899 and 901, on *CIL* 5.5797; and last, Fronto of Cirta, in Rome, praying to *"dii patrii* and Jupiter Ammon, god of Libya," in his *Ep.* ed. Naber 121 (Loeb ed. 2.135).

19. Examples in Robert (1937) 319, at Aphrodisias a priest who "made sacrifice to the ancestral deities while himself offering prayer for the health" of the emperors; Vidman (1969) 164, Hadrianeia (Mysia) in A.D. 206; *IGR* 3.348 (Sagalassus), 664 (Patara), and 4.1497 (an obscure *pagus* in Asia Minor), all under Pius.

20. SHA *Had.* 14.3; Milik (1972) 10f.; Ohlemutz (1940) 130; *IGR* 4.214; Rehm (1938) 78, 80, and (date) 83; and Ianovitz (1972) 37f. Emendations to Rehm's texts by Grégoire (1939) 321 and Wilhelm (1943b) 168 do not affect my use of them. Note also the interesting text in Reinach (1906) 86, where the governor of Asia in the 220s promises offerings "to your ancestral goddess on behalf of the safety and eternal rule of our emperor," at Aphrodisias.

21. *RE* s.v. Tarsos (Ruge 1932) 2415; Robert (1946b) 39; Dufournet (1974) 382f.

22. *IGLS* 2960; Artemis Pergaea widely famed, cf. Robert (1948a) 64 and Onurkan (1969-1970) 289 and 294; on Mothers, cf. Graillot (1912) 383, and, more generally, 381-399 and 435.

23. Laumonier (1958) 714f., and 29 Apollos in the same confined corner of Asia Minor, ibid. 716f.; for Mars, see the Indices to *CIL* 13, 5 (1943) and 12 (1888), listing some dozens of local Mars versions; Süss (1972) 169 n.39; and Hatt (1979) 125-138 passim.

24. Min. Fel. 6.1; Tert., *Apol.* 24.7.

25. Ulp., *Regulae* 22.6 (*FIRA²* 2.285), one each in Italy, Spain, and Africa, and the rest are Minerva in Ilium, the Mother at Mt. Sipylus, Diana in Ephesus, Nemesis in Smyrna, Apollo at Miletus; cf. Marcus Aurelius, *Ep. ad Front.* 3.9 (Naber p. 47), praying to "all the governor-gods of all peoples" and to Aesculapius at Pergamon and Minerva=Athena at Athens.

26. I have had to make three somewhat arbitrary decisions: from the Saturn count I have excluded the 156 inscriptions of 5 Saturn sanctuaries; from the Cybele line I have excluded 55 taurobolia inscriptions from particular shrines; and from the Fortuna line I have not excluded 44 Fortuna-Primigenia inscriptions from Praeneste, the cult center.

27. On Nemesis, whose centers lay in Smyrna, less prominently in Antioch and Alexandria, cf. *RE* s.v. col. 2356; commonly near theaters and amphitheaters in the west, ibid. 2359-2361.

28. Jullian (1908-1926) 6.28f. and Hatt (1965) 90 and 106f., both calling Teutates "le dieu national"; further, Zwicker (1934-1936) 177 and passim.

29. Lambaesis supplies no texts at all for Liber, but all for Dolichenus. All the

Gallo-German Dolichenus inscriptions come from frontier centers like Mainz, Neuss, Bonn, Köln, and Wiesbaden. The one city Portus-Ostia, if included, would raise by 50 percent or more the Italian totals for the five cults specified, of Isis and the rest. On the other hand, one might expect to find Lyon atypical, but its deities are in fact in proportion with the Gallo-German totals, barring a slight exaggeration of Apollo; but note nearly half of the Cybele texts come from Lactora (Aquitania) alone.

30. Penates in combinations, in Boyce (1937) 104—though the numbers are small: for Fortuna, only 13 *lararia*, etc.

31. *IGR* vols. 3–4. How little the data are suited to statistical analysis appears from the totals, 527 inscriptions for all these gods, as opposed to 5,897 Latin texts used for the bar graph. Note also that a quarter of the inscriptions for Hera come from the one site where she presided, Ilium, and more than half of Aphrodite's from Cyprus, where that goddess too had her most famous shrine.

32. MacMullen (1974) 89–97.

33. Tert., *Prax.* 3, *simplices, imprudentes, idiotae*, or ἰδιῶται and ὀλιγομαθεῖς, Iren., *Haer.* 2.26.1, quoted in Lebreton (1923) 483–488, cf. Min. Fel. 2.4, *vulgus superstitiosum*, and 3.1, *imperitiae vulgaris caecitas*, and Tert., *Apol.* 49.4, *caecum hoc vulgus*, etc.; Lucian, *Alex.* 30, ἰδιῶταί τινες οἰκέται; *Hermotimus* 1, "the great mass of folk of no account"; *Dea Syria* 8, 11, 28, etc., and Athenag., *Leg.* 15, Art., *Oneir.* 4 praef., οἱ πολλοί contrasted with persons better informed; Euseb., *Praep. ev.* 4.1 (132b), "the imbecility of critical powers among the masses, οἱ πολλοί, the weakness of reasoning and gullibility of the general populace, τὸ πλῆθος," and similar views expressed by Porphyry, ibid. 3.7.1.

34. Min. Fel. 12.7, with very much the same view and tone in Synes., *Ep.* 105 (*PG* 66.1488A). An egalitarian passage like Plin., *Ep.* 2.3f., is very rare, hardly matched in our period by Dionysius of Alexandria in the 270s, Euseb., *H.E.* 7.25.26: remarking on John's uneducated style, whose errors Dionysius refers to "not in mockery, let no one think it," but solely as *differentia* for analysis. Other, later, passages are discussed in MacMullen (1966b) 110f.; and exception is naturally made by Christians discussing Christ's disciples, e.g., Euseb., *H.E.* 3.20.5 (interesting) and 3.24.3, or *Demonstr. ev.* 3.7 (*PG* 22.241).

35. Celsus, in Orig., *C. Cels.* 1.23; 3.18, 44, 50 and here quoted from Chadwick's translation, 3.55; cf. a similar violent passage in Ps.-Apul., *De deo Socr.* 3.122, or the scorn in Apul., *Apol.* 9.1, 10.6, and 16.10, against *rustici,* or Diog. Oenoand. frg. 1 p. 3 Chilton; violent scorn matched by Clem., *Coh. ad gent.* 10.41 (*PG* 8.209), or similarly Euseb., *Praep. ev.* 13.14 (692b).

36. Menander Rhet., *Epideiktika* 5 p. 337 Spengel, *Rhet. graeci* vol. III; an exactly similar distinction in material to be presented is made by Alex. Rhet., ibid. III p. 4, and put into practice by temple exegetes, Paus. 2.23.6.

37. Plut., *Moral.* 407C and 756C: Lucian, *Amores* 42; Juv. 6.511–591; Clem. Alex., *Paedogogus* 3.4.25 and 27f. (*PG* 9.593 and 596); Min. Fel. 8.4; Athenag., *Leg.* 11; and Tat., *Ad Graec.* 33. Note in Juvenal and Clement the wealth of some of the women depicted and, in Iren., *C. haeres.* 1.13.3 (*PG* 7.581), rich women are the natural target of heresy-mongers.

38. On esoteric believers, see Plut., *Moral.* 352B (Isis priests); Art., *Oneir.* 4 praef.; Philostr., *Vita Apollon.* 8.7.9; Orig., *C. Cels.* 1.18; Plot., *Enn.* 2.9.9 and Eunap., *Vit. soph.* 455; Clem. Alex., *Strom.* 5.9 (*PG* 9.89A-B and 88–95 passim); Porph., *De antro*

3 and *Ad Marc.* 17 and 28; Firm. Matern., *Math.* 7.1.1 and 3; 8.33.2; *Asclepius* 1 and 10; *Corp. herm.* 13.13; *PGM* 4 line 1872; Philo, *Quod deus immut.* 54; *De Abrahamo* 147; Clem. Alex., *Strom.* 5.10.24 (*PG* 9.100); Iren., *C. haeres.* 1.3.1; 1.24.6 (*PG* 7.679); Orig., *C. Cels.* 1.12 and 29; 5.15 and 29; Arnob. 5.32; Synes., *Ep.* 105 (*PG* 66.1488A); Lebreton (1923–1924) 492, 504 and passim, cf. Aul. Gel. 19.10.14, niceties of grammar treated like the Mysteries, for initiates only.

39. Athenag., *Leg.* 5 and 24; Just., I *Apol.* 4, 20, etc.; II *Apol.* 8; Theoph., *Ad Autol.* 2.3, 8, etc.; Tert., *Apol.* 14.4–7; Aristides, *Apol.* 13; Clem. Alex., *Coh. ad gent.* 2.126 and 7.1 (*PG* 8.96 and 180); Lact., *Div. inst.* 1.4, "poets and philosophers which it is usual to use against us."

40. A cliché, of course, cf., e.g., Dio Chrysos., *Or.* 18.3, and earlier texts in Kroll (1924) 24–34; but acknowledged in debate, e.g., by Orig., *C. Cels.* 7.45, or by Euseb., *Ad sanct. coetum* 10.3.

41. For the ranking of "best-seller" writers, the *Iliad* first, and so forth, see Pack (1965) passim, on papryi (-fragments) surviving: of Homer, 688; next most numerous, of Demosthenes, 81; of Euripides, 76; Callimachus, 50; Hesiod, 48; Plato, 43; etc.

42. On Cornutus, see Tate (1929) 40f.; on Seneca, Attridge (1978) 67 n.159, the work being used by Tert., *Apol.* 12, and Aug., *Civ. dei* 6.10f.; on Heraclitus, Tate (1930) 1f., and Buffière (1962) ix and xxxii; on Philodemus, Lesky (1966) 682, with frgs. in Diels, *Stoic. vet. fragmenta*; on Diogenianus, cf. Theod., *Graec. affect. curat.* 6.8 and Euseb., *Praep. ev.* 4.3 (136df.); on Oenomaus, Attridge (1978) 56f. with note. His work *Wizards Exposed* was used by Euseb., *Praep. ev.* 5.22 (213C) and Theod. l.c., the treatise being evidently similar to another used by Hippolyt., *Refut.* 4.34 and (a third?) used by a certain Celsus who is quoted in Lucian, *Alex.* 21. On Porphyry, note his work on *Images* quoted in Euseb., *Praep. ev.* 3.9 and 11 (100af. and 108b), etc.; and his own use of Numenius, in *De antro* 21 and elsewhere.

43. Porph., *De abst.* 2.56 and 4.16 and *De antro* 2 and 21, on second-cent. treatises about Mithraism; put in context by Turcan (1975) 23; on Isiacism, Nymphodorus (?) in Clem. Alex., *Strom.* 1.21 (*PG* 8.832A); on Cybele and Attis, a section of the poet Hermesianax, Paus. 7.17.8f., and the unknown writers Hicesius *On the Mysteries*, in Clem. Alex., *Coh. ad gent.* 5.64.5, and Timotheus and others in Arnob. 5.5.

44. Philostr., *Vita Apollon.* 3.41 and 4.19; Plutarch in much of his commentary on Hesiod's *Works and Days*, the frgs. in the Loeb edition, vol. 15 pp. 135, 197, 217, etc.; Porph., both in parts of his *De abst.*, e.g., 2.56, and his *Philos. ex orac.*, to be found in Euseb., *Praep. ev.* 4.9 (145bf.) along with Apollonius's treatise again, ibid. 4.13 (150b); and Istros of the third cent. B.C., in Porph., *De abst.* 2.56, cf. *RE* s.v. col. 2270.

45. On Apollodorus's use, see Geffcken (1907) xvii and 225, and Lesky (1966) 787; on use of Varro, see, e.g., Clem. Alex., *Coh. ad gent.* 4; Tert., *Ad nat.* 2.1; Lact., *Div. inst.* 1.6; and Cardauns (1978) 88.

46. *Praep. ev.* 4.2 (136b), cf. Porph., *Philos. ex orac.*, passim, and below, p. 13.

47. Besides scenes from the later chaps. of Apul, *Met.*, or Heliodorus, note Xen., *Ephes.*, passim (dated to the second cent., p. xi of the G. Dalmeyda edition, or in Lesky [1966] 864); Lucius of Patras whom Apuleius read, cf. Cumont (1929) 97, dated to the second cent. by Lesky l.c.; or the scenes of religious initiation in the anon. second-cent. text in Hinrichs (1970) 29–31.

48. Paus. 1.13.8; Philostr., *Vita Apollon.* 4.30, a *logos* on Zeus, perhaps like Dio

Chrysostom's *Twelfth Oration*; and on the gigantic inscription, see Chilton (1967). For the location of the text in the city and Diogenes' scattered friends, consult frg. 2, V lines 12f.; frg. 15, II lines 3f. and 10; frg. 16 lines 10f.; frg. 51, III; and Chilton (1971) xxi and xxxiii. On the religious parts, see frgs. 29–31; also Robert (1971a) 597–613; and M. F. Smith (1978) 39, bibliography to which Smith adds esp. frg. 54, and page 54 on Rhodian correspondents, and page 43 on dimensions of the inscription.

49. Hippolyt., *Refut.* 5.20.5.

50. Aug., *Civ. dei* 2.7, library in Cybele temples in Africa; Apul., *Met.* 11.7, Isiac priest, *grammateus*, reads aloud from a prayer book, cf. the Reader for a native Batavian deity, Menon ἀναγιγνώσκ(ων) in a Flavian graffito, Bogaers (1955) 241; and further refs. in Stambaugh (1978) 587. In eastern provinces, Dio 75 (76).13, in A.D. 200, assumes books in almost all the sanctuaries of Egypt; *BGU* 362 I 19 (Arsinoe in A.D. 214); perhaps *POxy* 1382 (second cent.) lines 19f., "the libraries of Mercurius" wherein is registered a miracle tale; and Orig., *C. Cels.* 1.12, the wise men in Egypt learnedly investigate their received religion through many traditional tractates. Aelius Aristides knew of vast collections of Sarapis's *aretai* in unspecified "sacred archives," *Or.* 8.54, I p. 95 Dindorf.

51. Philostr., *Vita Apollon.* 7f., the Asclepius temple at Aigeai is the scene of lectures on asceticism; Plut., *Moral.* 410 and 412D; *logoi* in many cities, apparently temples (here mentioned), Aristides, *Or.* 25.2, cf. public displays of learning at festivals in Philostr., *Vita Apollon.* 8.18, and Dio Chrysos., *Or.* 27.5–6.

52. Theologues by title, attested in *British Museum Inscriptions* 3 p. 138, who "seem to have to do with the celebration of the mysteries," at Smyrna—they are the two sisters, mentioned with *mystae*, *CIG* 3200; *BMInscriptions*, further, 4.481 line 295, at Ephesus in A.D. 104; *IGR* 4.353, at Pergamon; in Bithynian cities, Robert (1943) 184f.; C. Picard (1922) 208 and 249f.; and Plutarch consulting theologues at Delphi, *Moral.* 417f.

53. Schuchhardt (1886) 428.

54. Herrmann and Polatkan (1969) 10, an endowment for a funerary cult, the divine command for which is revealed in dreams to a man in Magnesia ad Sipylum, date (p. 23) in first cent.; *CIL* 9.3513, 58 B.C., *Jupiter liber* in the *vicus Furfo*.

55. E.g., *CIG* 3538=*IGR* 4.360, and Ohlemutz (1940) 61 and 77, where Pergamon is relieved of plague by prescribed sacrifices and hymns, as the Clarian Apollo directs, ca. A.D. 171; or in Kern (1900) 144 no. 228, late second cent., as "the god revealed," cult shall be offered to Hera in a certain way, cf. Ael. Arist., *Or.* 49.39, I p. 498 Dindorf, in A.D. 149, commands from Zeus.

56. Kern (1900) 140 no. 215; Sokolowski (1962) 59 and 67, second cent. examples at Epidaurus and Sparta; Robert (1975) 308 and 325, an inscription from Sardis of ca. A.D. 150 recalling a document of the fourth cent. B.C.

57. Milik (1972) 288, a *lex sacra* for a cult group in Palmyra; another, in Cilicia, Hicks (1891) 234–236, for Sabazius in Augustus's reign; Sokolowski (1955) 52, a "holy doumos" of Men in Maeonia, and ibid. 55, a similar text; idem (1969) 106f., on the Men regulations just referred to.

58. Milik (1972) 287, in Palmyra, and 216, on *CIL* 6.52=*ILS* 4335, in Rome, *ne quis velit . . . triclias inscribere*; cf. Sokolowski (1955) 55, rules for members of the first-cent. B.C. cult group directed against poisons, philtres, abortions, or spells.

59. Rules evidently posted, to be noted by entrants, e.g., at Olympia, Paus. 5.13.3f., or Blinkenberg (1941) 871, a *lex sacra* on a stele "just outside the entrance to the shrine" of Athana Lindia, ca. A.D. 255 = Sokolowski (1962) 159f. Typical prohibitions: worshipers should "not stare around too much," not wear a helmet or shoes or anything of goatskins, etc.; idem (1955) 186f., a text also discussed by Nock (1958b) 415-418, where, in the second- or third-century Dionysus shrine at Smyrna, abstinence is enjoined "from babies' food," i.e., milk, etc.; *IG* 2².1365-6 = Sokolowski (1969) 106f., Oliver (1963) 318, and Lane (1971-1978) 3.7f., all three scholars discussing the Severan Attic inscription that bans garlic, pork, etc. Compare Sext. Emp., *Hypotyposeis* 3.220f., on pork, goat, and other meat sacrifices, suitable or not, and the learned conversation in Plut., *Moral.* 670E; further, *SIG*³ 736, of 91 B.C., addressed to the cult of Demeter and Kore in Andania (Messenia), women to be unshod, their clothing white and not transparent, etc. Pausanias (4.33.4f.) justifies my use of so early a text, since he found the shrine active in his day.

60. Sokolowski (1962) 43, the date being first or second century.

61. Above, n.59. For some good pages on the philosophy of sacrifices etc., see Sodano (1958) xif.

62. As in the directives offered in inscriptions of Magnesia, cf. Kern (1900) 140 and 144, θεὸς ἔχρησεν; Porphyry taking dictation from Apollo, in Euseb., *Praep. ev.* 4.9 (145b-146b) and in *De abst.* 4.18 crediting *leges sacrae* to the gods; Lucian, *Dea Syria* 15, where cult forms are given by Attis; and Soc., *H.E.* 3.23 (*PG* 67.204), where an unnamed oracle dictates Attis liturgy to Rhodes.

63. Sokolowski (1955) 52, "by the gods' command"; ibid. 53, "to Dionysius in a dream"; *IG* 2².1365, cit., "the god choosing him"; Sokolowski (1969) 224, directions by a worshiper at Dardanus, "which he inscribed by the goddess' command," her name lost; and in Africa, Merlin (1916) 263f. = *ILAfr.* 225, *iussu domini Aesculapi . . . , quisque intra podium adscendere volet a muliere, a suilla, a faba, a tonsore, a balineo commune custodiat triduo; cancellos calciatus intrare nolito.*

64. Sokolowski (1962) 203f., a third-cent. text from Ephesus beginning, "Heading of ancestral law." For the government to intervene was only a police measure, seen in Calder (1935) 217, where the proconsul forbids molesting sacred birds at Attouda in A.D. 77.

65. Robert (1968) 568f., 576, 584, 589f.; idem (1971a) 597 and 602-609: the datable oracles are Severan, but thought and wording are in part Hellenistic. Professor Robert's discussion and the work of original discovery by G. E. Bean and others are enough to restore one's faith in scholarship.

66. Milik, above, nn.58f., and Gawlikowski (1973) 57, at the temple of Bel; a ban on entering shod into the Saturn temple, etc., in Charles-Picard (1954) 130f. and 138, cf. other rules in *ILAfr.* 225, cit. above; in Italy, *CIL* 9.3513, cit. above, and 5.4242 (Brescia, to Dolichenus) and 3.3955 (Siscia, to Jupiter Heliopolitanus), both the latter texts banning sacrifice of pigs; and *CIL* 3.1933 = *ILS* 4907, Salonae in A.D. 137, cf. *CIL* 12.4333 II lines 21f. (Narbonne, A.D. 12), "the same laws in other respects for this altar and notices as for Diana on the Aventine," and *CIL* 11.361, at Ariminum, *h(aec) a(edes) S(alutis) A(ugustae) h(abet) l(eges) q(uas) D(ianae) R(omae) in A(ventino)*, the expansion of the abbreviations accepted by Borghesi, Bormann, and Wissowa, in *RE* s.v. Diana col. 333.

67. *CIG* 2.2715 (with the term ἀρεταί) cited by Longo (1969) 1.17, cf. Strabo

17.1.17, "some writers record the *aretai* of the oracular answers" at the Sarapis temple of Canopus. Of the long bibliography on aretalogy, I need cite only Engelmann (1976) 97–108; Grandjean (1975) 8–11 and 102; F. Dunand (1972–1973) 3.83–87; Malaise (1972) 173f.; M. Smith (1971) 175–177; Witt (1971) 101f.; Des Places (1969) 164–168; Vidman (1969) 40f.; Festugière (1949) 209f. and 231–233; Robert and Robert (1946–1947) 343f.; Harder (1944) 8, supplying the text which I translate immediately below, and much else, passim; finally, Cumont (1929) 232f. n.6. Note *POxy.* 1382, a narrative of the *arete* of (Zeus-Helios-) Sarapis in the second century.

68. Apul., *Met.* 11.25, where the hymnic nature is well seen by Tran Tam Tinh (1964) 109 n.3, the passage "crystallizing devout beliefs expressed in aretalogies and hymns," best printed by setting off successive lines, each to begin *tu . . . , te . . . , tibi . . .* ; *Poxy.* 675; *PSI* 844; and Mesomedes, in Powell (1925) 198 and Lesky (1966) 811, the poet being a freedman of Hadrian whose works occur in manuscripts with musical notation.

69. Apul., *Flor.* 18 and *Apol.* 55.

70. Riese (1894) 1.26f., identified by line 15, *merito vocaris Magna tu Mater deum*; Page (1962) 520f. no. 129, third cent.; Powell (1925) 196, Hymn to Fortuna; Heitsch (1961–1964) 2d ed. 1.157, hymn to Cybele, in Hippolyt., *Refut.* 5.9.9; and Mesomedes' *To Helios*, Lesky (1966) 811.

71. Diog. Laert. 5.76, Sarapis hymn, evidently centuries old but still being sung; Lucian, *Demosth.* 27, Isodemus's hymns to Aesculapius; Ael. Arist., *Or.* 47.30, I p. 453 Dindorf, "the ancient hymn beginning, 'I hail Zeus . . .'"; and Laumonier (1958) 402, at Stratonicea "the customary hymn to the goddess" Hecate.

72. *IG* 4², 1.132–134; Maas (1933) 148–155 and 160f., the stone of the late Empire; and various ancient testimonia to the Sophocles text, cited ibid., e.g., Philostr., *Vita Apollon.* 3.17, it is sung (present tense) in Athens to Asclepius; Oliver (1936) 112–114, mentioning also (115–117) another widely diffused but anonymous hymn to Asclepius of the same period, appearing in inscriptions from Roman times and from many locations—Dium in Macedonia, Ptolemais, Athens, etc.

73. Wiegand (1932) 53f.; Ohlemutz (1940) 148f., the date in the late 170s; on the attribution to Aristides, ibid. 149 n.78. Aristides collected his hymns in a lost book. Cf. *Or.* 26.36, I p. 153 Dindorf, where Asclepius tells him to compose hymns for that god himself and Hecate, Pan, and others also. "And there came a dream from Athena, too, containing a hymn to the goddess with this beginning: 'Youths, come to Pergamon . . . ,' and another to Dionysus, of which the chorus was 'Hail, Lord Dionysus, ivy-crowned.'"

74. Many texts too early for my period of study, e.g., Edelstein and Edelstein (1945) 1.328, on *IG* 2².4473, first cent. B.C. or A.D.; but from later times, Edelstein and Edelstein 1.331–334; Kaibel (1878) 433f. no. 1027 (second-third cent.); *IG* 2².4533 (third cent.); *CIG* 2342=*IG* 12, 5.893 (second-third cent., to Apollo); Mitford (1971) 197, second cent., to Antinous; and in the western provinces, the brief verses in *CIG* 6797=*IG* 14.2524, Autun; *RIB* 1791, on Hadrian's Wall, to the *dea Syria* (*pace* Wright, ibid.); and *CIL* 8.9018=Buecheler (1895–1897) 1.121 no. 253, Mauretania in A.D. 246 to Jupiter Ammon, Pluto, and Panthea.

75. Quandt (1962) 44, for origin and date of the collection; cf. Clem. Alex., *Strom.*, 6.4.96 (*PG* 9.253), the Egyptian cantor typically has at hand a hymnal; and note a good deal of excerpts and influence from hymns in magical papyri, cf. Nilsson (1947–1948) 60f. and Heitsch (1961–1964) 2d. ed. 1.171.

76. To discuss the interior face of the Mysteries would carry me beyond my topic, but cf. Hippolyt., *Refut.* 5.9.9, cited again below, n.92, and Firm. Matern., *De errore profan. relig.* 22, cited by many scholars of mystery cults, e.g., Cumont (1929) 226 n.46.

77. *CIG* 3538, on the Zeus temple wall at Pergamon, ca. A.D. 170; *IG* 2².4533, for relief from pestilence, Severan date, at Athens; Dain (1933) 67–69, for a thanksgiving ceremony at Heraclea near Latmos; and the implications in the description of someone as "victorious poet, composer of verse and rhapsode of the divine Hadrian," in Clerc (1885) 125, from Nysa.

78. Parade paeans in, e.g., Sokolowski (1962) 203f., third cent. Ephesus; morning paean to Dionysus, in Robert (1937) 20f., in Teos=LeBas-Wadd. 90; to Asclepius in Athens, DesPlaces (1969) 168, second cent. or Aelian frg. 98 (ed. R. Hercher, 2.233f.); or to Asclepius in Pergamon, Ael. Arist., *Or.* 47.30 (p. 383 Keil).

79. Ael. Arist., *Or.* 48.2 and 50.50, I pp. 465 and 518 Dindorf; Clem. Alex., *Strom.* 5.8.47 (*GCS* 15 p. 359); and in inscriptions, Latte (1931) 134 and Robert (1955) 86 and 89 (also on gems).

80. Ps.-Lucian, *Lucius* 37f.; for Kore in Alexandria, Epiphanius, *Panarion haer.* 51.22.10; for any paean, *RE* s.v. Paian (Blumenthal, 1942) col. 2345.

81. "First-harper and carrier of the flame for Delphinian Apollo," honored in an inscription, Pekary (1965) 122f., comparing also *Inschr. von Didyma* 182.

82. Quasten (1930) 63–65; Malaise (1972) 122f., 147, and 150f.

83. *De die natali* 12.2 (pp. 21f. Hultsch), written in 238. The passage is cited and compared with other contemporary evidence for the use of instruments, in Quasten (1930) 4 and 7f. Note *SIG*³ 589 line 46 (Magnesia on the Maeander), advertisement of a "concert with piper, whistle-player and harpist," at a *lectisternium* in the second cent. B.C.

84. Aside from much scattered evidence for *tibiae* in old Roman worship and for much more music of several sorts in Isiacism in Italy or anywhere else, the lines in Firm. Matern., *Math.* 3.5.33, may speak for the Latin west as a whole in their mention of *hymnologi et qui laudes deorum . . . decantent. A collegium cantatorum* serving Apollo is once attested in Rome, cf. Marchetti Longhi (1943–1945) 81f. Practices in Syria appear in Lucian, *Dea Syria* 44 and 50f., at Hierapolis, cf. hymnodes serving a Syrian deity (though in Athens, *SIG*³ 1111), and, in Palmyra, Milik (1972) 153. In Africa, note the pipe accompaniment to sacrifices honoring Saturn, in LeGlay (1966) 345.

85. Robert (1945) 105, evidence unknown to recent works that deal with the two Delphic inscriptions of the later second cent. B.C.: Pöhlmann (1960) 80 and Neubecker (1977) 149f.

86. *Hymnodoi* in I. Lévy (1895) 247f., at Smyrna and Ephesus, and in Nilsson (1945a) 66, who adds other cities and deities; serving the imperial cult alone, *IGBulg. 666; IGBulg.*² 15ter and 17; *IGR* 4.1608, cf. Mellor (1975) 192; but doubling with another cult, *IG* 14.1804 (A.D. 146, imperial cult plus that of Sarapis, at Rome); subventions to a guild of imperial cult hymnodes, in Keil (1908) 101–104; imperial cult hymnodes at Smyrna shared with the gerousia, ibid. 110 concerning *CIG* 3201 line 5, just like the sharing of hymnodes of Artemis at Ephesus with the city senate and gerousia, C. Picard (1922) 251.

87. For the god Men at Athens, see Oliver (1936) 108, third-cent. evidence; maidens and matrons in second-cent. Olympia, Paus. 6.20.3; ephebes in Ephesus, Keil

(1908) 107 n.17; ephebes singing to Dionysus in Teos, LeBas-Wadd. 90; in Pergamon, to Zeus and other gods, *CIG* 3538 of ca. A.D. 170; Laumonier (1958) 402 gives the evidence for a thirty-boy choir, cf. Keil (1908) 109, a twenty-four hymnode choir; Lucian, *Alex.* 41, boys recruited to a shrine from neighboring cities, and boys at the Pergamene Asclepieion in Ael. Arist., *Or.* 47.30 (p. 383 Keil); for Claros and Panamara, see below, the Clarian choirs being of seven or regularly nine boys, Robert and Robert (1954) 118 and 215. Whenever we find a *hymnodidaskalos* it is likely we are dealing with an amateur choir, e.g., at Pergamon, Festugière (1935) 205.

88. From Tabai, Heraclea, Laodicea, etc., ca. A.D. 120–185: C. Picard (1922) 262 supposes delegations to have hired a choir "trouvé sur place," but Robert and Robert (1954) 115, 203–210, and 215 offer a better view; also Robert (1969) 299–301; and Wiseman (1973) 168 shows consultation from Stobi without a choir used.

89. Clerc (1885) 124, an inscription from Nysa mentioning a "poet, rhapsode and theologue," who contributed books to the guild of hymnodes; *OGIS* 513, Pergamon, with note ad loc. on hymnodes/theologoi in Smyrna and Rome; and C. Picard (1922) 249.

90. Nilsson (1945a) 67, citing *inter alia SIG*³1109 line 115.

91. Menander, *De hymn.* 1f., ed. Spengel, *Rhetores graeci* 3.333, and *Epideiktika* 4, ibid. p. 390; cf. Alex. Rhet., ibid. pp. 4–5, like Menander distinguishing between two accounts to be offered, one for the many, the other for the few, and detailing what characteristics of a god a speaker must cover: derivation, age, identity with other-named manifestations, powers and deeds, etc.

92. Hippolyt., *Refut.* 5.9.8f., where the setting is somewhere in western Asia Minor; for the type of occasion and large audiences, cf. the inscription in Keil (1908) 107 n.17, "the ephebes singing the hymn in the the[ater were graciously] heard" by Hadrian at Ephesus; and Plut., *Moral.* 417F, "the Delphic *theologoi* believe that a serpent there once fought the god over the place of the oracle, and they let poets and other writers [i.e., rhetors] compete in recounting these things in the theaters."

2. Attracting Crowds

1. The best discussion is by Schleiermacher (1966) 205–212; the most recent, Hatt (1979) 131–133; cf. also Ternes (1973) 7f. and 15 n.73. These three concentrate on the Rhine and Moselle area. For Gaul, see G. Picard (1970) 185; C. Picard (1955) 231–234, on Vienne, the interpretation controverted, cf. Vermaseren (1977) 134; and Formigé (1944) 70–72 and 92.

2. Golfetto (1961) 48f., cf. Charles-Picard (1954) 161: "on imagine de véritables drames liturgiques."

3. Tert., *De spect.* 10.2; *Apol.* 15.4.

4. "There were no Roman games, even theatrical ones, that were not in some way religious"—Gagé (1955) 398. Compare Ps.-Cypr., *De spectaculis* 4, *quod enim spectaculum sine idolo, quis ludus sine sacrificio . . . ?* Bardenhewer (1912–1932) 2.494f., ascribes the essay to Novatian.

5. Roussel (1916) 259, referring also in 260 n.6 to Butler (1915) 373, 379, and Fig. 324, concerning Si'; ibid. 429f. and Illustration 371, Sûr, and 442–445, Sahr, the theater dimensions being 20m. in diameter with seven rows of seats. Further, on the Delos theater, see Will (1951) 62, 68f., and 78.

6. McCown (1938) 159–162, 165, and 167; below, p. 21.

7. Robert (1953b) 409, the theater not yet fully excavated.

8. The theater belongs to the first half of the first cent., cf. Cumont (1926) 185 and 202; Frézouls (1952) 83-85, for certain features of design referring to a (noncult) theater in Palmyra, pp. 87-89. Hanson (1959) 66 refers to still another cult theater in Seleucia on the Tigris, unpublished then and still, to my knowledge. He notes, ibid., the names of occupants inscribed on the seats of the Dura theater. Compare the practice also at various Moselle sites, in Ternes (1973) 8, and Schleiermacher (1966) 209, instancing sites at Altbachtal near Trier and Pachten.

9. *Coh. ad gent.* 2.12.2 (*GCS* 1.11 line 20).

10. Lehmann-Hartleben (1939) 135 and 138; Fraser (1960) 117-119; and Sokolowski (1962) 135f. C. Picard (1955) 236 compares similar buildings at a number of sites, and Bookidis (1973) 206 describes a sort of theater for "at least 85 initiates" of Demeter and Kore at Corinth, in active use during the Empire.

11. So I estimate from Heyder and Mallwitz (1978), the stone seats built in the early Empire (pp. 68 and 71), the activities observed by Pausanias (9.25.5-8), and the dimensions to be surmised from p. 27 Abb. 18 and p. 32, plainly for hundreds but probably for up to 2,000 people.

12. The Pergamene theater in Boehringer (1959) Beilage 1 and p. 155 with Abb. 25 (second cent.), and Behr (1968) 27f.; on Epidaurus, Herzog (1931) 63, citing Paus. 2.27.5, and Kötting (1950) 18 and 31.

13. *CIL* 13.1642, at Forum Segusiavorum near Lyon, a priest *theatrum quod Lupus Anthi filius ligneum posuerat de sua pecunia lapideum constituit.*

14. That was the standard practice in Rome well down into Cicero's time. But note *SIG*³ 589 line 46, where, at a *lectisternium* in Magnesia, there is to be "a musical performance, pipe, whistle and harp" in the agora. St. Andrews in Scotland and Siena do the same every year, though no longer does the Church preside. For sacrifices being offered in the agora by private citizens whenever they felt like it, see Ael. Arist., *Or.* 28.39 (I p. 498 Dindorf) and Ps.-Clem., *Homil.* 7.3 (*PG* 2.217); a *symposion* offered for a local god on the town square at Philippi, in Collart (1937) 475.

15. On Ephesus, see Xen., *Ephes.* 1.2, cited in C. Picard (1922) 331f. and 338; on performers, cf. Robert (1940a) 284, using evidence partly for the east (Galen), partly for the west, too: the *senatusconsultum* of 176/177 (*FIRA*² 1.299, which speaks of the *vetus mos et sacer ritus* in Gaul, to stage gladiatorial shows, and how *sacerdotes* of the imperial cult hired the troupes). Laumonier (1958) 383 and 400f. explains the θεατρικοί of Stratonicea, published by Hatzfeld (1920) 89 and 92, and the key text in Diehl and Cousin (1887) 158.

16. Laumonier (1958) 347.

17. Joh. Chrysos., *Homil. in Matth.* 7.6 (*PG* 57.79) and Malal. 284f., and discussion in *RE* s.v. Maiumas (Preisendanz 1928) cols. 610f.

18. Paus. 7.18.11-13, cf. Herbillon (1929) 64-67, on coins of Amasia.

19. *SIG*³ 1115 lines 30f., Silens at the theater at Pergamon; on *kinaidoi*, cf. Bernand (1969) 2.28, second cent. evidence in Egypt, cf. Firm. Matern., *Math.* 7.25.4 and esp. 14 (dancing to Cybele with drum accompaniment), and Robert (1964) 185; on *ballatores*, cf. *CIL* 6.2265 and Isid., *Etymol.* 3.22.11; on ἀκροβάται, C. Picard (1922) 256, at Artemisia in Ephesus and Magnesia, in one corps numbering 20; ibid. 300, on Couretes.

20. "Danced Hymns" in Wild (1963) 51-53 and 107 n.68, with much additional

material, from the reign of Tiberius to Hadrian, on dances (professional) offered to other Egyptian deities at various shrines, accompanied by tambourine and sistrum, ibid. 61f., 72, and 77–82.

21. The quotations come from Tert., *Apol.* 15.4, Min. Fel. 37.2, and Apul., *Met.* 10.30f. (the author African, of course not the scene); Clement's views are in his *Coh. ad gent.* 2.42f. (*PG* 8.76); 2.60 (*PG* 8.77); 4.58.3–4, hymns and masks, both, on the stage; for *histrio*=dancer, cf. Charpin (1930-1931) 579, who also adds some scandalized passages from Cyprian et al., pp. 580f.; and Fronto, *Ep.* ed. Naber 156 (Loeb ed. 2.105), *histriones, quom palliolatim saltant . . .* (again, the author not the setting African). And the same equivalence appears, too, in Arnob. 4.35 (*PL* 5.1071f.), . . . *quid pantomimi vestri, quid histriones, quid illa minorum atque exoleti generis multitudo? . . . Saltatur Venus . . ., saltatur et Magna sacris compta cum infulis Mater,* etc., and Aug., *De doctr. Christ.* 2.25.38 (*PL* 34.54).

22. *Dig.* 38.1.26 praef., the *Pantomimus vel archimimus* is ὀρχηστής ἢ μῖμος, cited by Mommsen (1868) 462 n.2, who goes on to equate the *archimimus promisthota* of an inscription with a *locator scaenicorum*. For a Severan star actor and priest of Apollo, *parasitus et sacerdos Apollinis* and others like him, cf. Müller (1904) 342–346 and Gagé (1955) 401–407. Ammianus (14.6.20) later describes *mimae* as dancers in Rome who "are borne about in flying gyrations while expressing numberless likenesses invented by theatrical fables."

23. Gaur (1963) 322–325, on South Indian temple dancing, the only kind I have seen; but compare well-known Balinese arts, in McPhee (1966) 6, the clubs or guilds of performers, and p. 16, "dancing and acting are so closely interwoven that it is impossible to define where the one ends and the other begins."

24. Ps.-Apul., *De deo Socr.* 14.149; Lucian, *De salt.* 79; cf. the epigraphic mention of Dionysiac priests, χορεύσαντες βουκόλοι, at Pergamon in A.D. 106, cf. Conze and Schuchhardt (1899) 179f., the eds. drawing attention to Lucian. For upper-class enthusiasm for dramatic religious shows (but perhaps only plays, not dances), cf. Tat., *Ad Graec.* 22 and 35 (the audience will own slaves, indicating wealth). Pollux 4.103, perhaps speaking not of the Roman period, distinguishes a number of regional dances, e.g., "Ionic to Artemis, mostly in Sicily."

25. Hyporchemata, in Lucian, *De salt.* 16; cf. dancing at sacrifices in Syrian fashion with cymbals and drums, by priest and women, introduced to Rome, in Herodian 5.5.9.

26. Attested at Ancyra, cf. Franchi de' Cavalieri (1901) 70, the *Mart. S. Theodoti* 14 (women dancing in the procession to Artemis and Athena), cited by Hepding (1903) 133; at Stratonicea, an ὀρχηστής hired along with dance choruses, in Laumonier (1958) 303, and above, n.24.

27. Above, chap. 1.1 n.92. The inquisitive Naassenes are present: παρεδρεύουσιν οὗτοι τοῖς λεγομένοις Μῆτρος μεγάλης μυστηρίοις. Compare the action of the authorities at Delphi which initiates (κατοργιάζουσα) all Greeks of the peninsula, Plut., *Moral.* 418A. The ceremony is in the open and openly described.

28. *SIG*³ 736 (Andania in Messenia) on the administration of mysteries, including the hiring of dance choruses (χοριτεῖαι) and instrumentalists through λειτουργήσαντες; *CIG* 3200, supplying of the ὄρχησις for the mystae (of Demeter? —*CIG* 3 p. 722) at Smyrna; Joh. Chrysos., *In Col. homil.* 12.5 (*PG* 62.387), telling us that in Greek *mysteria* there are dancing and instrumental music, the dancers to be

dismissed as "prostitutes," i.e., professionals; Clem. Alex., *Coh. ad gent.* 2.60 (*PG* 8.77), women act out the mysteries in various cities, surely professional *scaenicae* since decent women could not perform thus—cf. Aug., *Civ. dei* 2.4, Cybele parades through Carthage accompanied *a nequissimis scaenicis*. Notice, too, that Herodian (3.8.10) witnessed in Rome in 204 the shows staged in the theaters "both for offerings and all-night affairs, celebrated just like 'Mysteries.'" He betrays no sense of holy secrets having been parodied or violated.

29. Cybele cult dancing described by Graillot (1912) 302-306, noting (p. 258) professional performers in third-cent. Italian inscriptions. Add *AE* 1940, 131, an Ostian *tympanistria m. d.*; and scenes in frescoes, Spinazzola (1953) 1.223 Fig. 250, and pp. 224-242 and Plate XIV; Vermaseren (1966) 42f.; itinerant priests of *dea Syria*=Atargatis in Apul., *Met.* 8.27, drawing on Ps.-Lucian, *Lucius* 37f.; and Isiac dancing described by Tran Tam Tinh (1964) 27f. and 102 with Plate XXIV and by Paribeni (1919) 107-111 with plate facing p. 106.

30. All instruments used, including the horn and bass horn, cf. Plut., *Moral.* 364F, *CIL* 6.219, Sokolowski (1962) 204, and Quasten (1930) 15 and 22. But not the organ, apparently.

31. There is secular music of the masses at the service of Caesar's soldiers, Suet., *Divus Iulius* 49.4 and 80.2, and at the service of the Church, Philostorgius, *Eccl. hist.* 2.2, cf. *SHA Firmus etc.* 7.4—two references too early or late for our period. Also Ovid, *Fasti* 3.523-542.

32. As an arbitrary sampling from very abundant numismatic material, see, on Ma, Bosch (1935) 122, third cent. from Heraclea, and Price and Trell (1977) 98 no. 176, Comana (the whole book a model for clarity and interest); ibid. no. 265, Men in Antioch, cf. also Lane (1978) 541, third cent. Prostanna; *RE* s.v. Limyra col. 711, under Gordian, cf. Plin., *N.H.* 31.22, and that other oracle also on coins, the Cumaean Sibyl, in Engelmann (1976) 195f., the issues dated to Antoninus Pius's reign; Ohlemutz (1940) 126 and 150; Graillot (1912) 357-360 (notes); Syrian deities, too, e.g., the temple of Jupiter Heliopolitanus on coins of the emperor Philip, cf. Rey-Coquais (1967) 43. For panegyriarchs, see those of the third century at Apamea and elsewhere, in Ramsay (1895-1897) 2.442, cf. *Sylloge numis. Graec. von Aulock, Nachträge* 4 (1968) no. 8348, where the panegyriarch is eponymous, indicating the importance of the office.

33. Euseb., *H.E.* 5.1.47; Strabo 5.3.10; in Britain, at Viroconium, cf. Wilson (1973) 27, shops around the second-cent. temple; and at two other sites, one of them a temple flanked also by a theater, "sufficient to prove the periodic attendance of large crowds," ibid. p. 31; Wheeler and Wheeler (1932) 50f., shops in the shrine of Nodens; in other western provinces, cf. MacMullen (1970) 337, Spain, Switzerland, etc., and Italy also; further, in central Italy, Evans (1939) 41, a *mercatus* at the time of sacrifices to Liber, and Stambaugh (1978) 585, citing inscriptions from Rome, *vestiarius de Dianio*, etc., and also SHA *Aurelian* 48.4, wine sold in *porticibus templi Solis*. Cf. the beer shop in the Sarapis temple at Arsinoe, *PLon.* 1177 (A.D. 113), and the "cafés and gardens" attached to the Adonis sanctuary in Laodicea and rented to entrepreneurs, explained by Haussoullier and Ingholt (1924) 336, the date falling in the third or fourth century.

34. Ibid. 333; *IGR* 3.1020, at Baetocaece, "those who come to worship" buy "slaves, livestock and other living things" every fortnight; at Damascus, similar

arrangements, MacMullen (1970) 337 n.25 and Dussaud (1922) 224–233, the date of construction being ca. A.D. 200? and expansion being commissioned in 339/340 with use of funds "of the Lord God" (Hadad). That makes clear the connection of cult and commerce.

35. On Tithorea, cf. Kahrstedt (1954) 11f., who, however, omits a few vivid details from Pausanias (10.32.15): that "the peddlers make tents of reeds and other materials on the spot, and on the last of the three days hold a fair, selling slaves and livestock of all sorts, clothes, silver and gold." Further examples of the practice and facilities in the third cent. in Just., *Epit. hist.* 13.5.3, and similar texts from Greece cited in MacMullen (1970) 336.

36. Note complaints against governors, procurators, and soldiers in the well-known inscription from Scaptopara (Thrace), *IGBulg.* 2236 = *CIL* 3.12336, recalling the precautions against forced billeting (πάροχη) in *IGR* 3.1020 line 35.

37. On special coin issues for a *panegyris*, see Mattingly (1928) 202; Franke (1968) 28f., on the πανηγυρικὸς ἀγορανόμος, see Robert (1966) 19 and 24f., cf. idem (1968) 573, "panegyriarch, that is, superintendent of the commercial sector of the festival. . . ." Note the indication in *IGR* 4.144 (Cyzicus), where a priestess is thanked for attending to the "merchants and strangers come to the festival and tax-free market from Asia."

38. Dio Chrysos., *Or.* 27.5f; cf. 77.4, a whoremonger circulating with his troupe in central Greece, from one festival to another. In the period of this study, temple prostitution survives only at Byblos (Lucian, *Dea Syria* 6) and at the festival of Zeus Larasios near Tralles every four years, cf. Robert (1937) 406f.

39. Ramsay (1941) 76; cf. *IGR* 3.1020, the fair at Baetocaece at least three, perhaps five, centuries under the same regulations.

40. Polemo on Perge in Foerster, *Scriptores physiognomici graeci et latini* 1 (1893) 282, a Hadrianic source brought to notice by Robert (1948a) 66. The Pergaean festival is noted by Strabo 14.667 also. As to its wide appeal, compare Roussel and de Visscher (1942–1943) 179, an inscription recording the assertion in A.D. 216 that "this Zeus-shrine [of Dmeir in Syria] is famous . . . and certainly visited by absolutely everyone from around, who come here and send processions." On the Ephesian festival, the quotation is from *SIG³* 867, with a similar description of the attendance in Xen., *Ephes.* 1.2.3.

41. Witt (1971) 98 and 162; for bathing of images, see the *Mart. S. Theodoti* 14 (cit. above, n.26); Cybele washed in the Almo river, Ovid, *Fasti* 4.337f., and *RE* s.v. Pompa (F. Bömer, 1952) col. 1950; for Artemis's image taken to the sea off Ephesus, see C. Picard (1922) 314; for Adonis's trip to the sea off Alexandria and Byblos, see Will (1975) 100; and other *lavationes* in Stocks (1937) 6, the *dea Syria* and her pond, and Graillot (1912) 137.

42. Daremberg-Saglio s.v. Circus 1193; *RE* s.v. Pompa col. 1908; above, nn.5 and 15.

43. Hill (1897) 87f., concerning types of cart; Paus. 7.18.12, deer-drawn cart for Artemis at Patrae; elephants, Daremberg-Saglio loc. cit. and Fig. 1528.

44. Diod. Sic. 1.14.3; Plut., *Moral.* 365B; Xen., *Ephes.* 1.2; Robert (1975) 324, on a variety of "-bearers" (-φοροί), in Latin, *c(a)ernophori, cannophori, cistiferi, dendrophori, hastiferi, pastophori, rhabdouchisa* (*IGR* 1.614), and *Anubofori* (*CIL* 12.1919). For a hilarious picture of articles carried in a religious procession, cf. Athen. 201C.

45. Ovid, *Fasti* 4.179-186; *Mart. S. Theodot.* 14; Paus. 2.7.5; *IG* 7.1773 (a competition at Thespiae in the second cent. for the best marching hymn written); Epiphanius, *Panarion haer.* 51.22.10f.; and Xen., *Ephes.* 1.2.3.-1.3.1.

46. Sokolowski (1955) 28 and 30—but both inscriptions pre-date our period.

47. *RE* s.v. Pompa lists over 350 entries, of which about 100 are once-only affairs. Evidence for the great majority of the remainder pre-dates Roman times, but most no doubt went on into the Empire. Patrai (items nos. 46-48 and 131) and Cos (27, 99, 126, 141, 188, and 229f.) are cities of several parades. Plut., *Moral.* 39A, indicates the keen interest in parades, Macrob. 1.23.13 indicates the high status of participants. The same passage shows *pompae* in Syria and Italy, cf. in Rome, *lecticarii* for Jupiter-Dolichenus cult, in Merlat (1951) 186; also Isis parades, often mentioned. For parades in Syria and Phoenicia, see Hill (1911) 61, and Epiphanius loc. cit. (at Petra); for Cybele parades, cf. Aug., *Civ. dei* 2.4, and in Autun, in a text brought to notice by Hepding (1903) 72, the *Vita S. Symphoriani* 3, which is best consulted in Zwicker (1934-1936) 2.163, with a dramatic date in the late second cent.; Sulp. Severus, *Vita S. Martini* 12.2, pagan deities paraded at Tours still in Martin's day; and Isis parades at Vienne implied in *CIL* 12.1919, through the *Anubiforus*.

48. *Dea Syria* 10. Pilgrims were male only, and shaved their heads and eyebrows and prepared for their trip by continence, ibid. 55 and Macrob. 1.23.13.

49. Ohlemutz (1940) 177, the hostel at the site, and 180, the coins from Cyzicus, Sardis, etc., up into the fourth century.

50. In Boeotia, at an oracle, Pausanias describes the hostels (9.39.5) for the suppliant sick at Tralleis; for the sick finding lodging in a village near the shrine, close to Nysa, see Strabo 14.1.44; at Panamara, cf. Laumonier (1958) 227, inns serving the Zeus shrine; at Olympia, cf. Kunze et al. (1958) 33-41 and 55-67, two inns adjoining the sanctuary, one of second-cent. date (p. 59), the other ca. 200 (p. 67); at Jerusalem, an inscription describing full facilities for needy pilgrims, in Safrai et al. (1974) 192, better dated (Augustan?) by Clermont-Ganneau (1920) 193; and lodging for the pregnant and dying at Epidaurus in a special building, Paus. 2.27.7. In the West, see the evidence in Ternes (1973) 8, *hospitalia* at many sites; idem (1965) 415, emending *CIL* 13.4208 of A.D. 232; Agache (1973) 52, sites in France; Weisgerber (1975) 20 and 83 (dates of active use), a hostel at holy springs, twenty miles northeast of Trier; Binsfeld (1969) 247-252 and 266, a healing shrine by springs, active ca. A.D. 150-275, the hostels having rooms with fireplaces; Formigé (1944) 48, very big buildings at Sanxay; and Wheeler and Wheeler (1932) 44-50, a very large building at the healing shrine, active in and after A.D. 250.

51. More than two hundred known Asclepieia, cf. Kötting (1950) 13.

52. On Vicarello, cf. Friedlaender (1912-1923) 1.329f.; on Samothrace, Fraser (1960) 15f. and 47f. (visitors from Beroea) and 58f. (from the Strymon, Thessalonica, Thasos), in second and third centuries; travelers from good distances to other shrines attested in inscriptions, in Capello (1941) 99-137, *IG* 4.953 and 956 (merely illustrative for Epidaurus), and Laumonier (1958) 110, for the Zeus shrine near Mylasa. On women pilgrims, see Paus. 10.4.3 and Plut., *Moral.* 249E, referring to old times, but the shrine at Delphi was still active, witness Plutarch's friend Clea the priestess. Note also an Isiac on pilgrimage from Rome to Alexandria, in Tibullus 1.3.31.

53. The poem in Bernand (1969) 2.128, discussed pp. 135f.; other texts, pp. 7f., most but not all of pilgrims, discussed pp. 23f.; and second-cent. visitors from

Greece and Jordan, also from Alexandria, ibid. 167, 176, and 368; for pilgrims to other shrines in Egypt, see Nock (1934) 58-67; Bataille (1952) 165; Yoyotte (1960) 55f.; and Hohlwein (1940) 262, 264f., and passim.

54. Lucian, *Dea Syria* 55, cf. Dio 36.11 implying guides at Baalbek, "they recount stories and point out . . ."; Ael. Arist., *Or.* 25.2, ὁ περιάγων, cf. Ps.-Lucian, *Amores* 12, the ζάκορος, the text being of the early fourth cent., says Helm in *RE* s.v. Lukianos col. 1730; Paus. 1.13.8; 1.31.5; 1.35.8 (in Lydian temples); 1.41.2 and 4; 2.9.7; 2.23.6; 7.6.5; and 10.28.7; Athenag., *Leg.* 28; priests do the explaining, in Lucian, *Dea Syria* 1 and 4; Plut., *Moral.* 354A and 410B.

55. Ohlemutz (1940) 143 describes Aristides' lecture on the local spring; Strabo 14.1.44, on the inquiries at Nysa; cf. Art., *Oneir.* 1 praef., Artemidorus's search for knowledge on his subject "in Greece at cities and festivals"; on learned visitors, see Lucian, *Heracles* 4 and *Dea Syria* 15, and Paus. 7.23.7; for Cynics loitering at the temple gates, cf. Dio Chrysos., *Or.* 32.9, and the Cynic who appears from nowhere to comment on a trial for irreligion, *Acta S. Apollonii* 33, at Rome.

56. Plut., *Moral.* 385f., cf. 417F, reference to the theologues of the shrine, and Paus. 7.23.7f., already referred to.

57. Min. Fel. 2.3, cf. Favorinus in Aul. Gel. 18.1.2.

58. Justin, *Dial.* 1.1, where the setting is a gymnasium either in Ephesus or Corinth, cf. VanWinden (1971) 21; Lucian, *Jup. trag.* 4 and 16 (in Athens—the passage quoted).

59. Aside from the familiar but fictional *Octavius* of Minucius Felix, one must note Ps.-Clem., *Homil.* 3.29 (*PG* 2.129), the dramatic date under Tiberius, pitting Peter against Simon Magus before a throng, for three days, 3.58 (*PG* 2.148); Euseb., *H.E.* 4.16.1, Justin against Crescens the Cynic before a throng, cf. II *Apol.* 3; Theoph., *Ad Autol.* 2.1; and Scherer (1960) 13.

60. Dio Chrysos., *Or.* 12.44f.; above, chap. 1.1 n.49.

61. Paus. 1.21.4 and 4.31.11f.; Plin., *N.H.* 35.17; and Lucian, *Heracles* 1-3, puzzling over a painting of Hercules depicted in Celtic fashion, and interpreted for him by a native. Idem, *Toxaris* 6, Scythian religious beliefs studied in local paintings.

62. Paus. 5.10.7, at Olympia—the same assumption in Lucian, *Toxaris* 6, and animating a modern viewer, e.g., Laumonier (1958) 349, on the painted reliefs of the Hecate temple at Lagina. Inscriptions: *IGBulg.* 1592=*IGR* 1.743; *IGBulg.* 679 =*IGR* 1.567=Vermaseren (1956-1960) 2.355 no. 2265; *CIL* 2.4085, the restorer of Minerva's temple calls himself *perfector et pictor; CIL* 8.25520=Merlin (1908) 21, Bulla Regia under Diocletian; *CIL* 8.8457=20343, Sitifis in A.D. 288; Flusser (1975) 13, Samaria (third cent.?); and Reinach (1908) 499, Aphrodisias second cent.

63. For frescoes with scenes (leaving aside all walls merely colored, plus all the rich Mithraic material and Dura), as a sampling from abundant remains, see, in Rome, Graeve (1972) 319, temple for Syrian cults; Gauckler (1899) clx, in Carthage; Tran Tam Tinh (1964) 102, in Herculaneum. As to painted reliefs, for a sampling, see P. Girard (1878) 92, the Athenian Asclepieium; Cintas (1947) 58, 73, and 78, stelae of the first cent. in the Hadrumetum tophet; Brommer (1973) 22, in the Vulcan shrine at Alzey; and Kern (1892) cols. 113f., Eleusinian Demeter stele of the second century. For a painted theater, at Stobi, see Wiseman (1971) 402. For a sampling of striking statues, see O. Deubner (1977-1978) 234 and 248, a Hadrianic Sarapis

statue; gilded ones in *CIL* 9.3146, Cybele in Corfinium; Plin., *N.H.* 33.61, Fortuna at Praeneste, and 33.32, Hecate at Ephesus is dazzlingly bright (=gilt?); Goodhue (1975) 36 and 55, a first-cent. Dionysus in Rome; Merlat (1951) 176, Dolichenus has an *inaurator* in Rome and, 183, statues are gilt (or painted?); Reuterswärd (1958–1960) 2.186, in the Pompeian Isis shrine; and Audollent (1901) 379, the Caelestis shrine at Carthage of the early Empire, with gilt-faced goddess. Oenomaus estimated idols at 30,000 in round numbers, to which more were ever added: 120 Nikai and Erotes in the Ephesus theater, cf. Pekary (1978) 727; 29 gold statues to be paraded in the theater, all of Artemis, *OGIS* 480 lines 6–9, cf. *TAM* 3, 1.136, the ἄγαλμα πομπικόν θεᾶς of Termessus dedicated ca. A.D. 203. In Africa, statues of deities were dedicated regularly in thanks for municipal office, e.g., *CIL* 8.858, 1887 (=*ILAlg.* 3066), 2372, 7098, 7983– 84, 15576, *AE* 1968 no. 609, and Leschi (1957) 227. But the practice is known elsewhere, e.g., *ILS* 9416=*IGLS* 2716, a Jupiter statue given for one's *decurionatus* at Baalbek.

64. Paint in letters of inscriptions: Roebuck (1951) 39; Nock (1934) 58; Bernand (1969) 2.192; Rostovtzeff (1937) 204; and Vermaseren (1956–1960) 1.69 no. 53, Dura; Kabbadia (1885) 199 and Herzog (1931) 43, Corinth, with traces of gilding also— these examples from the east; and from the west, Vermaseren (1956–1960) 1.96 no. 148, Lambaesis, and 312 no. 908=*CIL* 13.1771, Lyon, with gilt; Vermaseren (1956–1960) 2.366 no. 2308; Kan (1943) 69, the Hadrianic dedication in the Dolichenus shrine at Carnuntum. These items of evidence (not methodically sought out) for practice of a fragile sort seem to me to indicate that the letters of all inscriptions were routinely painted.

65. Examples of inscriptions reconstructed or refreshed in Hanfmann and Waldbaum (1975) 68, in the Artemis shrine, Severan setting-up of old stelae on antique bases; *IG* 10, 2.255, cf. ibid. p. 540 n.2, a first-cent. recutting of an earlier *testimonium*; Kern (1900) 140 no. 215, decree recut; the same process in Gawlikowski (1973) 71 and Sokolowski (1962) 67, a *lex sacra* at Sparta in the second cent.; compare a cult relief repainted, in Forrer (1915) 69, and an idol renovated, *sigilum renovavit*, Albertini (1931) 198–200 no. 3, A.D. 209–211, in a Sol shrine.

66. On Oenomaus's estimate, quoted by Pekary, see above, n.63; the passage, surviving in Euseb., *Praep. ev.* 5.36.2, goes back to Hesiod, *Works* 252f., who speaks of "daemons" (also quoted by Max. Tyr., *Philos.* 8.8). On pruning out, see Coarelli (1974) 45f., at the Capitolium in Rome.

67. *IG* 12, 2.108; Buckler and Robinson (1932) 97; and, on M. Antonius Polemo's inscription, for which the setting is given in Phrynicus a little later in the second cent., by Phrynichus 395 p. 494 Rutherford, see Ohlemutz (1940) 134. On directions in dreams, see further *AE* 1941 no. 106, near Doliche itself: "the god Jupiter [Dolichenus] commanded" So-and-So who "set up a statue for the god for the emperor's salvation"; *CIL* 6.30998, image of Sarapis at Rome *ex viso*; a city obeys the Clarian oracle to "set up now a Phoebus at the gates, bearing his bow, to avert the plague," in the emended text of Mordtmann (1881b) 261f.; *IGBulg.*² 370=*IGR* 1.767, from Anchialus near the mouth of the Danube in the second cent., the erection of "icons suitable to the deities according to the oracle of our lord the Colophonian Apollo," by municipal decree (in time of plague?); *ILS* 3526, at Tibur, a Sarapis *signum* erected *ex viso*; Plin., *N.H.* 34.19.58, Augustus, being "directed in his sleep," restored a pillaged Apollo statue to Ephesus; similarly,

altars set up by the *imperium* of the god, *vel sim.*, in *ILS* 3534, and 3973, *iussu Proserpinae*; Schwertheim (1978) 2.792, a Cybele statue set up κατ'ἐπιταγήν (the most common Greek formula); ibid. 796, κατ'ὄναρ (that formula too being very common); an aedicula κατ'ὄνειρον, *CIG* 3947; *CIL* 3.990, *ex iussu dei Apollinis fontem Aeterni . . . NN restituit*; a relief showing Zeus with eagle, κατὰ κέλευσιν τοῦ θεοῦ, *MAMA* 5.17; a similar relief κατ'ἐπιταγήν, to Zeus Brontaeus, in Schmidt (1881) 135; reliefs showing two deities, dedicated κατ'ἐπίπνοιαν Διὸς Κιλλαμενηνοῦ, in Schwertheim (1975) 357; a sanctuary of Venus renovated *ex visu*, *CIL* 10.5167; and *ILAlg*. 2132, a temple built *ex praecepto*. On merely conventional erection of statues, most easily documented in Africa, see above, n.63.

68. Paus. 10.32.13, referring to invitations by dream also in another area, the Maeander valley; 10.32.17f., on punishment; and compare the cures in the Sarapis temple, accompanied by threats against any impiety or blasphemy, in Aelian, *De nat. animal.* 11.31 and 33.

69. Conveniently, a few in *MAMA* 4.279-285; earlier, in Ramsay (1889) 218, giving a good summary; idem (1895) 1.147-149; Wright (1895) 72; Keil and Premerstein (1908) 16; Steinleitner (1913) passim; Buckler (1914-1916) 169-177; idem (1933) 7f.; Longo (1969) 1.158-166, citing *inter alia SEG* 4 (1930) 647f.; Robert (1948b) 108; and inscriptions in Attica, Sokolowski (1969) 106f. and Lane (1971- 1978) 1.46 and 3.20-25.

70. Pettazzoni (1939) 198-200 stretches little evidence very far, to find sin/guilt in all Syrian cults; better, Gawlikowski (1973) 57, the fragmentary *lex sacra*, ". . . qu'on ne vole pas et qu'on ne pèche pas . . . il a juré par Yarhibol . . . et prendra son gage"; and Hermann and Polatkan (1969) 58, "Medon made a *crater* for Zeus Trosus and the ministrants ate the [parts] not sacrificed and [Zeus Trosus] struck him dumb for three months and abode with him at his dreams, that he might set up a stele and write on it what had happened to him," etc. At Epidaurus, see Herzog (1931) 37 and passim, pointing out that Pausanias (2.27.3) saw six stelae, and on the three surviving (plus fragments) there are 66 cases, therefore ca. 130 originally. But in Doric, says Pausanias—which the extant are not.

71. Herzog (1931) 8 (cf. another scoffer, p. 10), 27 (cf. another cheater, p. 31), and 28, with comparison drawn (pp. 43f.) to the stele with case history, *IG* 4².126 = *SIG*³ 1170, a few years before Pausanias's visit to Epidaurus, or (p. 45) *IG* 4².127 of A.D. 224, goiters cured in the dormitory, and the inscription dedicated κατ'ὄναρ. Note the case in *IG* 4².956, second cent. (Epidaurus) where the concluding injunction from the god is to publish (or perish, presumably), ἀναγράψαι ταῦτα.

72. For people seated in a sanctuary in the Isiac shrine in Pharos, Rome, or elsewhere, see Tibullus 1.3.27f.; Martial 2.14.7f.; Ovid, *Pont.* 1.51f. and *Amores* 2.13.17; and Tran Tam Tinh (1964) 110; at the Lerna Asclepieion, Paus. 2.4.5; and other texts for the city of Rome in Stambaugh (1978) 580 n.190.

73. Herzog (1931) 59, "volkstümlich," cf. in the Tiber island inscription, "simplicity of style" remarked on by Longo (1969) 1.85.

74. Plin., *Ep.* 8.8.5 and 8.

75. Of course, even from the three great shrines, most is lost; but the fourth, Aigeai, had its cure inscriptions (Liban., *Ep.* 695.2, addressed to the governor of the area in A.D. 362) and its fame (Euseb., *Vita Const.* 3.56 and Soz. 2.4f.).

76. The Tiber island shrine is well known, if not truly Roman. See cure in-

scriptions in, e.g., Weinreich (1909) 30, Longo (1969) 1.84f., and *SIG*³ 1173 = *IGR* 1.41; from Africa, a similar text in Beschaouch (1975) 112, *in somnis monitus, Saturni numine iussus . . . pro comperta fide et pro servata salute votum solvit libens animo*, A.D. 238; and from Egypt, compare, e.g., the stele with many inscriptions on it, therefore a little resembling the big six at Epidaurus, here thanking Sarapis, *SEG* 8.464. Cf. Aelian, *De nat. animal.* 11.31–35 and the next note.

77. *POxy.* 1381 (second cent.), praising Imhotep = Asclepius, esp. lines 90f. and 144f.; *Anthol. Palatina* 6.231, a poem of thanks if the goddess saves the poet from suffering, "in spirit and intent . . . closely similar to inscriptions," as F. Dunand (1972–1973) 3.214 points out; for collections of cures wrought at the Sarapis temple of Canopus, cf. Strabo 17.1.17; and note Tibullus 1.3.27f., "that Isis can heal, many *tabellae* in your temples assert," closely echoed by Juv. 12.26–28.

78. Veyne (1967) 738 n.2, brings to notice Philostr., *Heroikos* p. 141, 19K, ἐπισφραγιζόμενοι τὰς εὐχάς, meaning pieces of papyrus; as to wooden records (as I take them to be), see the πιττάκια in Lane (1971–1978) 3.28, the πίνακες in Strabo 8.374 and Paus. 9.39.14, and the *tabellae* in the preceding note. Note also Roebuck (1951) 39, a dedicatory "inscription," painted, the letters not cut at all.

79. Besset (1901) 326, from Apollonia on the Rhyndacus, "the ears and [= on?] the altar in the shrine" (of Isis?), probably not similar to the inscription (*pace* Besset 326 n.1) found at Epidaurus, *Cutius has auris* (= *aures*) *Gallus tibi voverat olim, Phoebigena, et posuit sanus ab auriculis*, in Weinreich (1912) 64 = *IG* 4².440, who (for no good reason) calls it falsified. The ears indicate the suppliant's organs cured, cf. parallels in Bieber (1910) 5–8. Milik (1972) 104f. cites from Palmyra the inscription thanking Zeus, "for he turned to him his eye and his ear," explaining the symbol on the *cippus*. Charles-Picard (1954) 119 describes Baal Hammon = Saturn being often portrayed holding the lobe of his ear, listening, or the ears shown alone; for the latter at Philippi, see Collart and Ducrey (1975) 179. In Egypt, "artisans manufacture ears and eyes of precious material, offered to the gods of the temple, symbolizing that the god sees and hears all," says Clem. Alex., *Strom.* 5.7.9 (*PG* 9.69). For addresses "to the ears" of a deity, cf. *CIL* 3.986 (Apulum in A.D. 180), to Aesculapius; *CIL* 5.759 (Aquileia), to the Bona Dea; to Isis, in Vidman (1969) 40f., the "Karpokrates" text given above at section 1, n.67; F. Dunand (1972–1973) 3.208 n.2, ears in a relief from Arles and elsewhere; and "ears" = listening posts in Asclepieia, in Wolters (1914) 149 (Epidaurus) and 151 (Pergamon).

80. Ἐπήκοος, a term attached to dozens of deities, see Weinreich (1912) 5–25; for geographical distribution, see occurrences common in Thrace, *IGBulg.* 682, Collart and Ducrey (1975) 245, and Poenaru-Bordea (1964) 103; in Asia Minor, Rehm (1958) 126 no. 137, Keil and Premerstein (1908) 25, Lanckoronski (1890– 1892) 2.220, and Lane (1971–1978) 3.78f.; in Greece, Weinreich (1912) 26 and Baur (1902) 61; in Rome, *IGR* 1.33 and 35–36 and *AE* 1913, 188; of the statue of any deity anywhere, Athenag., *Leg.* 26; and in Latin *exaudiens, exauditor*, in *CIL* 10.4553 and *ILS* 3744 and 3980.

81. Feet made of stone, e.g., *CIL* 6.572, inscribed *deo Sarapi . . . ex visu*, or uninscribed, as at a cluster of shrines in the Dijon area, with other organs, Toutain (1907–1920) 1, 3.383, or at the Ephesian Artemision, cf. Kötting (1950) 49; but feet carved in relief merely as a sign that the inscriber had been present are common, too, and sometimes mean that the deity addressed had been present. For much discus-

sion of the three meanings, see Mordtmann (1881a) 122, Amelung (1905) 159f., Lanckoronski (1890-1892) 2.220 and 232, Hatzfeld (1927) 106, Déonna (1924) 32, Guarducci (1942-1943) 308-315, giving a full collection from all provinces, Yoyotte (1960) 59, and Malaise (1972) 106 n.3.

82. In addition to the works cited in the notes just preceding, on parts of the body, see the inscriptions mentioning them in Robert (1955) 163; *Inscriptiones Creticae*, ed. M. Guarducci I p. 171 no. 24, "I have set up to you, Savior [Asclepius], two [statues of] Dreams for my two eyes, enjoying [again] my sight" (third cent.); and Greg. of Tours, *Liber vitae patrum* 6.2, brought to notice by Kötting (1950) 13 n.46: at a shrine in Cologne, *simulacra . . . membra, secundum quod unumquemque dolor attigesset, sculpebat in ligno.*

83. Girard and Martha (1878) 420-440 passim, e.g., 436; Girard (1881) 16, the inscription from Athens of the earlier third cent. B.C.; *IG* 7.303, Oropus ca. 240 B.C.; and Homolle (1882) 5, the Delian Apollo's inventory of ca. 180 B.C., with extraordinary variety of objects, e.g. (pp. 130f.), weapons, anchors, sports equipment. For a Latin example, see *CIL* 8.12501, inventory of a Caelestis temple.

3. Displays and Accommodations at Temples

1. Paus. 2.32.1, Troezen; Lucian, *Dea Syria* 60, at Hierapolis; at Panamara, Deschamps and Cousin (1887) 390, and Roussel (1927) 126, the locks of hair offered in stone receptacles; and at Paros in the third cent. post-Caracalla, dedication of "the first-cut hair," "the hair of childhood," to Asclepius, *IG* 12, 5.173- 176. The most striking is Hygieia's temple near Sicyon, almost hidden under the offerings of women's hair, says Pausanias (2.11.6).

2. *IRT* 231 and 295 (Oea and Lepcis); Paus. 5.12.3 and *CIL* 10.3796 (Capua, third cent.)=Buecheler (1895-1897) 1.123 no. 256, "I believe that never as a gift before . . . was revealed a head so vast, born amid the shadows of the hills and forests. . . ."

3. R. M. Peterson (1919) 152, at Capua, to the Arabic god Dusares in A.D. 11, "Because he heard them" (the dedicants); Forrer (1915) 41, stone painted lions; and Lucian, *Dea Syria* 41.

4. Paus. 2.11.8 and 2.28.1.

5. Lucian, *Dea Syria* 47; Aelian, *De nat. animal.* 12.30, instancing several locations; and Plut., *Moral.* 170D. On Labraunda, cf. Laumonier (1958) 47 and 96-98, instancing sacred fish at many Greek shrines, e.g., Attica, Paus. 1.38.1 and Smyrna, *SIG*³ 997 = Sokolowski (1955) 49, the *lex sacra* of the first cent. B.C. cursing those who hurt or steal the goddess's fish (of Atargatis). Du Mesnil du Buisson (1943- 1944) 325 and Lambrechts and Noyen (1954) 262f. and 274 discuss Astarte's sacred fish, cf. Athen. 8.346, worshipers "bring her offerings of fish made of silver or gold, but the priests bring to the goddess every day real fish, which they have fancily prepared and served on the table"; also Cornutus, *Theol. graec. compendium* 6, and Clem. Alex., *Coh. ad gent.* 2.238 (*PG* 8.121), fish worship in Syria. Note the survival of the custom till recent times, Glueck (1937) 374 n.4.

6. Lucian, *Dea Syria* 14 and 54, cf. Clem. Alex., loc. cit.; Philo, *De providentia*, in Euseb., *Praep. ev.* 8.14 (*PG* 21.673), cf. Phoenician worship in Africa producing a Tanit= Caelestis to whom doves were sacred, Merlin (1909) ccxxxvii and LeGlay (1966) 352; at Attouda in A.D. 77, note the proconsul's decree, in Calder (1935) 217,

and Robert (1971b) 92-95; further on sacred doves, Buckler (1914- 1916) 169-171, second half of the second cent.; *MAMA* 4.279, Lairbenos, second/third cent., and Cameron (1939) 155-158; the Achilles shrine in Arrian, *Ep. ad Traianum* 32 (p. 398, C. Müller, *Geogr. graeci minores* I); and Plin., *N.H.* 10.51, geese fed in Rome. But Aristides notices the geese wandering untouched (sacred) in the Isis shrine at Smyrna, *Or.* 49.49.

7. Plin., *N.H.* 16.242 and 16.162, cf. Reinach (1906) 107, Aphrodite's palm grove cared for by a second-cent. liturgist at Aphrodisias.

8. Plin., *N.H.* 16.213, and other texts in C. Picard (1922) 62.

9. Graillot (1912) 122, cf. Monsieur Themanakis (1893) 208, "the festival of wood-cutting" for the deity at Cos; Vermaseren (1977) 63, the inscription of A.D. 147 referring to the *collegium dendrophorum* with its *sanctum*, including a "plot of land . . . *ad pinus ponendas;"* a first-cent. *lex sacra* prohibiting cutting in Hera's woods on Samos; and *IGR* 4.48 and Robert and Robert (1958) 298, a copse sanctified to Silvanus by Romans in Mytilene.

10. *CIL* 6.2033, *anno* 21 and passim, the Dea Dia's *lucus;* compare the Greek reverence for groves like those at Dodona and elsewhere, seen for example in Zeus-of-the-Shadows, in Cook (1903) 414, on Paus. 3.10.6. In Egypt, famous holy groves, Orig., *C. Cels.* 3.17; at Palmyra, Caquot (1954-1957) 78 and Milik (1972) 7, on groves with gardens attached. Generally, see the good collection of evidence in *DE* s.v. Lucus (A. Pasqualini, 1975).

11. Ps.-Lucian, *Amores* 12. A matching glimpse from another region and another kind of source: *CIL* 10.6073 = *ILS* 6284, at Formiae, where a benefactor stages some ceremony for Jupiter, "at which dedication he distributed 20 sesterces to each of the city senators dining publicly in the grove."

12. Fish meal, above, n.5; Fratres Arvales in their *cenatoria* and *triclinia*, e.g., in *Acta arv.* A.D. 218 A 1; cf. the delicious meal of the Salii, in Tert., *Apol.* 39.15 and Suet., *Claud.* 33, or the choice wines of the *pontifices*, in Hor., *Od.* 2.14.28. For other priestly meals, cf. Robert (1940b) 13 n.8, Apollonian in Cyrene; *IG* 5, 2.269, Asclepian in Mantinea; Milik (1972) 150f., for priests of local baalim in Palmyra.

13. Examples of dedicatory banquets in Stambaugh (1978) 567; see above, n.11.

14. *CIL* 6.2273, *cocinatorium* at Rome for Venus; *AE* 1975, no. 197, a *culina* at Casinum given by four freedwomen (explicit evidence of women in cult dining rooms being rare in any province; for the Venus shrine at Casinum, cf. also *CIL* 10.5166f.). For Cupids on earrings, cf. E. Lévy (1968) 530, comparing Attis earrings in Vermaseren (1966) 49, and Philostr., *Vita Apollon.* 5.20, Demeter or Dionysus figurines worn as charms. For other *culinae* in Italy, cf. *CIL* 5.781 and 815 (*mensa*) and 6333 (*mensae* IIII); 6.2219; 10.3781; and 14.3543.

15. *CIL* 3.4441, *porticum cum accubito;* Tudor (1969-1976) 2.71 (painted plaques) and 257 (many showing a *mensa tricliniaria*).

16. 1 Cor. 8.10; cf. a similar situation, of Christians dining with pagans at the τραπέζα of δαίμονες, envisaged in the Pseudo-Clementine *Homil.* 9.9. (*PG* 2.248) and 9.15 (*PG* 2.252), dated by Quasten (1950-1960) 1.62 to the early third cent. For Paul's scene, cf. archaeological evidence from Corinth: the dozens of dining rooms found on a terrace of the acropolis in the temenos of Demeter and Kore, in Bookidis (1973) 206; Roebuck (1951) 51, three Hellenistic dining rooms with red painted walls, each with eleven couches, painted red and yellow, repainted, and regularly

used "throughout the Roman period" (p. 55); and equivalent facilities at the Troezen Asclepieion (couches in wood) and elsewhere in Greece (pp. 52 and 54); other examples in inscriptions, cf. Launey (1937) 402, at Thasos, each οἶκος containing seven κλῖναι.

17. Launey loc. cit. citing rooms at Assos and Aphrodisias; further, on the δειπνιστήριον for Aphrodite at Aphrodisias, Reinach (1906) 242; Robert (1945) 1.49f., σκῆναι; Hicks (1891) 232f., a μαγειρεῖον at a Hermes temple in Cilicia; ἀνδρῶνες in the Zeus temple at Labraunda, in Laumonier (1958) 50-55, one of them 22 × 12m., another with built-in couches; at the Ephesian Artemision, a vast ἑστιατήριον, Philostr., *Vit. soph.* 2.23.2 p. 605, a building meant "to be bigger than all others elsewhere combined" (hence, the architectural form common). Similarly in Plut., *Moral.* 146D, though unhistorical: a party, far larger than the usual, sacrifices at the Aphrodite temple and dines in the adjoining *hestiaterion.*

18. Starcky (1949) 62, the rooms filled with sherds of wine cups, and Milik (1972) 141 (Khasr Semrine) and 142 (*IGLS* 584, A.D. 129). Note at the temple of the Baal at Damascus a chief chef, *archimageiros*, in Perdrizet (1900) 441, and a temple south of Tripolis equipped in A.D. 184 with "a shelter and in it a στιβάς," an outdoor dining arbor with portico and cistern. See Rey-Coquais (1972) 87 and 93; and for the Greek term, *SIG*[3] 1109, lines 47 and 70, serving a Thracian cult group.

19. For Dura, notably the temple of Aphlad, see Cumont (1926) 396, thinking participants in group dinners are pilgrims (corrected by Milik [1972] 122). In Starcky (1949) 55-57 and 64f., the ἀρχιθιασιτεύων of the Syrians at Delos justifies the term *thiasos* for the Syrian cell (also called ἑταιρεία) which meets in its ἀνδρῶν or οἶκος. The amphorae sherds found there explain the use of the rooms; cf. also Milik (1972) 134-140. For Palmyra, see Cumont (1929) 256f., using mentions of a symposiarch in LeBas-Wadd. 2606a and *IGR* 3.1045 (the two, however, are the one same inscription; and Cumont has lost a part of the former text) and *IGR* 3.1533, the symposiarch of the priests of Bel, A.D. 203; Starcky (1949) 52-54 and 58-62; Milik (1972) 121 and 157 on the coalescing of workers (likewise at Hatra); 144-148, συμπόσιον=meeting room for the cells consecrated to the deity; 151-154, the serving staff for the rooms; 184f., tesserae of invitation; and 188-192 and 287, conduct of meetings; also, briefly and broadly, Teixidor (1977) 133-135.

20. *CIL* 3.7954=*ILS* 4341, at Sarmizegethusa; at Rome, Milik (1972) 216, citing *CIL* 6.52, a sacred *triclia* guarded *ex imperio Solis*, i.e., by Malakbel, cf. also 6.712 and 31036; Goodhue (1975) 8, on the *deipnokrites* of the Syrian shrine; and perhaps *CIL* 6.8750f., the *archimageirus.* At Philippi, note the inscription of a Syrian cult group in Collart (1937) 475, cf. Starcky (1949) 66 n.6.

21. The three known inscriptions of this cult that mention a *triclinium* (one, *iussu dei*) or *cenatorium* come from Virunum (Noricum), Bononia, and Rome. They are handy in Kan (1943) 113 and 127, with description of the Virunum archaeological remains, p. 77 (one room with hypocaust for winter meetings).

22. At Cologne, *Soli Sarapi cum sua cline*, *ILS* 4394=*CIL* 13.8246; also Tert., *Apol.* 39.15; Vidman (1969) 55, the second- or third-cent. dedication of a *mensa* to Isis at Amphipolis; and Ael. Arist., *Or.* 45.27, addressing an eastern audience, instanced by Milne (1925) 8. This evidence makes me think the Isiac cult meal was widespread outside Egypt, *pace* Vidman (1966) 115, even if direct testimony is thin.

23. Collart (1944) 136-138, updated by Gilliam (1976) 316, who gathers the (second- and early third-cent.) texts and (p. 320) explains the use of non-Sarapis

quarters. The "Dionysius" quotation is from *PYale* 85, to which editors add that the invitations were usually oral, hence few survive. Milne (1925) 9 draws attention to the δειπνητήριον of two local gods at Karanis, in *SEG* 20.652 (A.D. 69/79)=*OGIS* 671=*IGR* 1.1120; also to the beer bar in a Sarapeion, *PLon.* 1177, to the word οἶκος in one of the invitations, and to *PFouad* 76, an invitation to an Isis meal. Note also *POxy.* 2976 (second cent.), mentioning that "I was dining with my friends yesterday in your [the goddess Thoeris's] most fortunate precinct," and Orig., *C. Cels.* 3.17, remarking on "the magnificent tents, σκηναί, around" Egyptian temples. On the word similarly used in an Asian shrine, see Robert (1945) 1.49.

24. *ILS* 7215; *CIL* 6.10234 (=*FIRA*² 3.106), *CIL* 12.2112, and other inscriptions in Waltzing (1895–1900) 1.210f., adding *CIL* 10.6483 (Hadrianic: Axo[ranus?]=of Anxur?) and *CIL* 6.2219, a gift of *porticus cella culina ara* to a city ward, for an unspecified cult. For the Greek equivalent, found rarely, see Poland (1909) 454f. Greek cult groups generally built or owned their own chapels.

25. *Apol.* 39.15; cf. the συμπόσιον and κατάκλησις of the cult dancers at Ephesus, and there, too, the "procession that carried the picnic," δειπνοφοριακὴ πομπή, in Artemis's honor, in C. Picard (1922) 300 and 312f. The dancers met in the prytaneion, on whose columns their names were inscribed each year, in the first cent. to ca. A.D. 200, cf. Keil (1939) 126f.

26. For example, Cumont (1896–1899) 1.68f.; idem (1915) 206, bones including of boars, in Roman and German Mithraea; Vermaseren (1956–1960) 1.185 and 2.79 and 213, bones of birds being most common; and Bull (1978) 79, at Caesarea.

27. To the better-known evidence from the west, *CIL* 8.20780, Pepe (1964) 326, *CIL* 2.266, a tomb equipped *cum munitionibus tricleae*, and Gallavotti (1972) 360, add Negev (1971) 111 and 127–129, the practice accommodated in much of the Levant by tombside stone tables, esp. in Nabataea of the first cent. to ca. A.D. 300.

28. "Recent studies," and good ones, beginning with Nock (1964) 72–76; Gordon (1975) 235f.; Kane (1975) 321 and 332–349 passim; Turcan (1978) 148, declaring "presque tout ce qu'on lit sur ce sujet dans *Les Mystères de Mithra* de F. Cumont est honnêtement purement conjectural"; and Meslin (1978) 296–305 passim.

29. Hinrichs (1970) 29–31 quotes from a novel in a late second-cent. copy, above, chap. 1.1 n.47; compare Dio 71.4, the Boukoloi in Egypt kill Romans "in sacrifice and swear an oath on the entrails"; the cult society of Priapus, worshiping his *genius* in his *sacellum* with its drunken and erotic orgies, *pervigilia*, in Petron., *Sat.* 17 and 21; also Robert (1943) 190, on the festivals typical of villages around Nicomedia, where "il s'agissait essentiellement d'une beuverie." The poor rustics of the east find a match in those that Ovid observed, *Fasti* 3.541f., *senem potum pota trahebat anus*, or in the scene, surely meant to be familiar, of the half-drunk farmer coming from worship with his family (Tibullus 1.10.51; cf. Propertius 4.4.76–8).

30. E. Josi in *Enciclopedia Cattolica* s.v. Refrigerio (1953) 631 and Février (1977) 35, citing fourth- and fifth-cent. texts.

31. *Clementis Recognitiones* 4.13 (third cent.?); a similar scene in Tert., *Apol.* 35.2, connected, however, with emperor worship, which I exclude from this study. For the open-air eating at such occasions, see also *Acta Marcelli* 1, *cum omnes in conviviis epularentur*, at Tingi.

32. Haussoullier (1899) 317, emending and commenting on *CIG* 2883c, which gives many details; cf. Laumonier (1958) 572–576 on the festival in question. Big givers to such occasions might give often. See, e.g., the priest of Aphrodisias hon-

ored "for many λειτουργίας καὶ ἑστιάσεις," in Reinach (1906) 115. In Palmyra and Syria in general, see cult feasting in Milik (1972) 156f.; Teixidor (1977) 114, A.D. 114 in Palmyra; and Lucian, *Dea Syria* 49, the carcasses to be eaten being hung in readiness from the trees in the Hierapolis shrine.

33. For secular or semisecular (that is, imperial cult) purposes, citywide parties are very amply attested in the west. For a cult feast as an exception that proves the rule, see *ILS* 6328, Misenum in A.D. 169, a feast offered to the city senate on the occasion of "the all-night celebration for the ancestral god." Both the practice of the παννυχίς and, probably, the deity are eastern.

34. Greg. Nyss., *Vita Greg. Thaumaturg.*, *PG* 46.944. The Apologists offer many scattered phrases similar to this passage, but in bits and pieces.

35. Lucian, *De sacrificiis* 13.

36. Firm. Matern., *Math.* 3.10.6, 4.10.8, and 4.14.5, constitutes a very good source to prove the substantial profits normally to be expected from serving in a temple, not only as priest but in other capacities. A. H. M. Jones (1940) 228 and Magie (1950) 545 and 1404 provide good discussion of sale of priesthoods and revenues therefrom, some very large. Add *PTeb*. 298 (A.D. 107/8) lines 32–46; Herzog (1931) 31 no. C55 and 34 no. D68, grateful patients must give a gift to Asclepius; and Roebuck (1951) 28, describing the offertory box to receive the gift, here and at other shrines (this one found filled with coins of the second cent. B.C.). All of this finds confirmation in the accusation by Christians that Asclepius's cures had to be bought, cf., e.g., *Acta Iohanni*, in *Acta Apostolorum Apocrypha* 2 (1898) 206, eds. R. A. Lipsius and M. Bonnet. For the west, note Tert., *Ad nat.* 1.10.24, more compendiously in *Apol.* 13.6, "you [pagans] exact a profit for a place at the temple, for access to the rites ...," and more to the same effect, 42.8, speaking in broad terms; a narrow example in *CIL* 9.3513, the priesthood to be sold, the hides to go to the temple of Jupiter at *vicus Furfo*, by rules posted in 58 B.C.

37. Plin., *Ep.* 96.10, condensed; hides reserved, cf. the preceding note and the very fragmentary second-cent. Phanagorian *lex sacra*, Sokolowski (1969) 176f., with the late second cent. Attic inscriptions, in Lane (1971–1978) 3.8 and 12f. = *IG* 2².1365f. = *SIG*³ 1041 = Sokolowski (1969) 106f. = Oliver (1963) 318, defining the date; other portions of victims specified in the (undated and unpublished) Didyma *lex sacra* in Robert (1945) 1.49, also specifying "sale of the whole by weight ... the cooks shall sell the heads of the animals ..."; Sokolowski (1962) 203f., containing the third-cent. Ephesian regulations. For ridicule of the gods' scraps, see Clem. Alex., *Strom.* 7.6.89f. (*PG* 9.441) and Tert., *Apol.* 14.1. For mention of "the god's table," see 1 Cor. 21; Ps.-Clem., *Homil.* 9.15 (*PG* 2.252), the text of the early third cent.; *IGBulg*. 1592 = *IGR* 1.743, Beroe; Lane (1971–1978) 3.13, Antioch in Pisidia; and the *mensae* above, nn.14f. The most specific information lies in *CIL* 6.820 (Rome), a fragmentary price list of fees for wreaths, hot water, various sacrificial animals in parts or whole, etc.

38. No part of sacrificial victims to leave the precinct: Paus. 2.27.1 and 10.32.14 and Sokolowski (1969) 106. My quotation is Clem. Alex., *Strom.* 7.6.105 (*PG* 9.445). Compare Lact., *De mort. persecut.* 11.1, Galerius's mother "used to offer sacrifices with almost daily sacrificial feasts, and gave banquets to her fellow villagers"; also Dio 51.1.2, "sacred" games are so-called as having distributions of meat.

39. Sacrificial horses in Koethe (1933) 18, without comment, speaking of Germany, and in Dell (1893) 185, at the Carnuntum Dolichenus shrine, also without

comment (though note that Scythians=Celts were known to sacrifice donkeys, cf. Clem. Alex., *Coh. ad gent.* 2.29.4). At the Pompeian Isis temple, bones of fowl predominate, cf. Tran Tam Tinh (1964) 37. On Mithraea, above, n.26. But all of this represents a small and poorly informed sampling from much evidence.

40. Carton (1908) 28, and details in 112–116, the period of activity going down to the late third cent.; concerning painted stelae, temenos arrangements, etc., at other sites, cf. Merlin (1910) 8, 19 and 36f. ("repas sacrés"); Toutain (1892) 4, 13, 17 and 22 (A.D. 182, cf. other dated stelae at pp. 38f.); sacrifices *capite ordinato*, p. 22, on *CIL* 8.16749=*ILAlg.* 2977, different from *capite viso*, where it is the god's head referred to, cf. LeGlay (1966) 339, also *AE* 1942–1943, no. 31, *genio Amsige ex viso capitis*. Further, on stelae and their scenes, see Cintas (1947) 58, 73, and 77; and Foucher (1964) 36–39; but cf. LeGlay (1966) 305 and 345–349, holocausts for Saturn, worshipers eating nothing.

41. Ael. Arist., *Or.* 48.27 (I p. 472 Dindorf); long stays, Kötting (1950) 25 and Herzog (1931) 33 no. C64 (four months). For accommodations, see above, chap. 1.2 nn.49f. and, on the lack at Pergamon, Behr (1968) 30. Pausanias says "people live round about [the Sicyonian Asclepieion], mostly suppliants of the god" (1.21.4).

42. Philostr., *Vita Apollon.* 4.18; Xen., *Ephes.* 1.5.6 and 9.

43. The term is οἱ κατοικοῦντες, at the shrine of Hecate at Lagina, Hatzfeld (1920) 75, where they have some corporate existence and speak as a body (like the Isiacs at Pompeii?—who support this or that candidate for office with their votes, cf. Castren [1975] 115); also at the sanctuary of Pluto and Kore at Nysa, cf. Radet (1890) 233, and of Apollo at Didyma, *CIG* 2879, in Haussoullier (1902) 282 n.1, with whole villages embraced in the circuit of the temenos. Note at Panamara and Lagina the distributions "to the poor," below, chap. 1.4 n.20, and the reference to "the thief, brigand, kidnapper, and every sort of criminal and sacrilegious person" to be found in the Ephesian Artemision, Philostr., *Epp. Apollonii* 65 (1.363). For crowds of fugitives at temples throughout the Greek East, see Tac., *Ann.* 3.60–63 and 4.14.

44. Acts 19.24; Philostr., *Vita Apollon.* 5.20; cf. the *plumbarius* at Hierapolis discussed by Rey-Coquais (1967) 57; the μυρεψός at Philae, discussed by Bernand (1969) 2.97; in Africa, the third- or fourth-cent. maker of lamps who inscribed on his product, "Buy lamps, sieves (?), statuettes," *CIL* 8.22642, 6; perhaps the "merchants" in the agora at Andania (*SIG*³ 736, but cf. above, chap. 1.2 nn.32 and 37, on temple markets defined by priests but overseen by secular officials); and a great deal of indirect evidence of mass-produced, stereotyped objects to be dedicated, e.g., in Merlin (1909) ccxxxvii (figures of Tanit plus dove), or Bessou (1978) 204–206, terracotta Venuses.

4. Routine Staff and Administration

1. Wilcken (1912) 1, 2.65, A.D. 232 at Elephantine; idem (1885) 436, A.D. 215 at Arsinoe; cf. Constantine received at Autun in A.D. 310, where a spokesman says, "we decorated the streets leading to the palace with . . . the images of all our gods," *Paneg. vet.* 8(5).8.4.

2. The external justiciars to cities of the Lycian koinon registered their names in the temenos of Zeus Osogos, LeBas-Wadd. 352–358; cf. emperors' calls on local deities above, section 1, n.20.

3. Suet., *Aug.* 72.5, the emperor *persaepe* presided over trials in a temple at

Tibur; at Miletus, "the senate-house was officially dedicated to the Didymaean Apollo," cf. Laumonier (1958) 557, just as at Ephesus a cult group held its symposia in the prytaneion, cf. Keil (1939) 127, and the prytaneion of Elis was built right inside Zeus's sacred grove, Paus. 5.15.8; and note at Cosa north of Rome, a Mithraeum "constructed in the cellar of the curia in the late 2nd century and continued in use through the 4th," cf. Collins-Clinton (1977) 23 n.43. In Dardanos, the goddess's parade started from the prytaneion, cf. Sokolowski (1969) 224, and a similar role for the prytaneion at Stratonicea, below, n.22.

4. Priests or devotees of Ma=Bellona in, e.g. Tibullus 1.6.43 and Tert., *Apol.* 9, and Lact., *Div. inst.* 1.21; of Cybele, cf. e.g. Ps.-Lucian, *Lucius* 37f., and, on howling, Graillot (1912) 124 n.6; of Atargatis, Lucian, *Dea Syria* 50f.; of Isis, Plut., *Moral.* 364Ef., and Firm. Matern., *De errore profan. relig.* 2.3.

5. Ibid. 4.1f., Aug., *Civ. dei* 7.26, and *ILS* 4168, in Cybele cult; compare Clem. Alex., *Coh. ad gent.* 10.74, on Isiacs "with dirty long hair, disgraceful in unwashed, tattered clothing, knowing nothing at all of a bath, like wild animals in the length of their claws, and many castrated . . ."; Lucian, *Alex.* 13, long hair for a new faith; and often in plastic depiction of holy or inspired men.

6. Tert., *De idol.* 18.1 is the most general statement; on the other two cults, cf. Vermaseren (1977) 97 and Cumont (1929) 241 n.78, with idem (1975) 183 n.174.

7. *IGLS* 2928, in a temple ten miles from Baalbek, *Hocmaea virgo dei Hadaranis, qui annis* xx *panem non edidit* (!) *iussu ipsius dei* (second half of the second cent.), comparing Hier., *Adv. Iovinianum* 2.17 (*PL* 23.316), fasting Isiacs, and idem, *Ep.* 107.10 (*PL* 22.875f.), Isiacs and Cybele votaries, with *IGLS* 2929, showing that *Hocmaea virgo deae Syriae* lived 100 years. For a second example, see Audollent (1890) 534, *Saturninus sacerdos. Si quis possit observare vinum non bibere annos triginta octo, menses septem, ipse possit sacerdos esse.* On fire-walking, see Strabo 12.2.7 p. 537, with Magie (1950) 1151 concerning the location and Dupont-Sommer and Robert (1964) 62 on the rite. They compare Iambl., *De myst.* 3.4. In Macedonia: *New York Times*, June 1, 1956, with photo.

8. Sen., *De superstit.*, in Aug., *Civ. dei* 6.10, trans. Loeb ed. The date when the work was composed is uncertain: A.D. 31 up to the 60s, cf. Attridge (1978) 67 n.159.

9. On Sarapis cult, see Apul., *Met.* 11.20, Porph., *De abst.* 4.9, and Arnob. 7.32; on Asclepius's cult, cf. Aelian frg. 98 and Ael. Arist., pp. 378, 453, and 458 Dindorf, in Pergamon, with Nilsson (1945a) 67f. and Latte (1931) 133; ibid. 134 on Dionysus cult in Teos.

10. LeBas-Wadd. 90, Teos; *IG* 4, 1² pp. 173f. on Epidaurus; and *pyrphoros* is an official found in many cults.

11. Sokolowski (1962) 60f.=*IG* 4, 1².742 add., hymns to Asclepius; Tibullus 1.3.30, to Isis.

12. Corbett (1970) 150f., temples always closed (and others always open, cf. also Stambaugh [1978] 571); Ps.-Lucian, *Amores* 12 and 16, the Aphrodite temple freely entered in daytime but closed at night; Min. Fel. 22.8; Rebuffat (1975) 501, benches inside the Mars temple southeast of Lepcis; sacrifices inside temples in Greece, Corbett (1970) 150; lattice-work barricades around temples shown in Price and Trell (1977) nos. 8, 165, and 262-266, cf. Salviat (1963) 260f., on pre-Empire barriers.

13. Dedicatory lamps common, e.g., in Africa, cf. Toutain (1892) 17 and idem (1907-1920) 1, 3.64; *DE* s.v. Lucerna (M. Manni 1975) 1953; in Rome, *CIL* 6.368 (a

bronze lamp), Goodhue (1975) 28, and Vermaseren (1956) 1.192 no. 473; in Greece, Latte (1931) 134 and Nilsson (1950) 105. For statues with torches, cf. *IGLS* 2716 = *ILS* 9416, and Rey-Coquais (1967) 52 and n.3; Robert (1964) 155 and 157.

14. Piganiol (1946) 250, pointing further, p. 251, to the effect intended by the rite, to "développer aux yeux du peuple des tableaux frappants."

15. Even legionary eagles were anointed on feast days, Plin., *N.H.* 13.23; for *kosmophoroi* and the like, see C. Picard (1922) 242 and Cumont (1929) 89.

16. *Reddite cantu*, in Vermaseren (1956–1960) 1.99 no. 484; cf. Vermaseren and van Essen (1965) 187–232, esp. 223, hymns composed by a priest?

17. Not mentioned by Ferguson (1970), Wissowa (1912), or Latte (1960); in Nilsson (1941–1955) 2.216, mention only of the miracle of ?40 B.C., the cult otherwise dismissed in a few lines (1.127): "der Kult is nicht griechisch."

18. Ἐνεργείαι, in Hatzfeld (1927) 62, the text partly restored. It would be needlessly cumbersome to document every point of description separately. Laumonier provides full, clear treatment of Stratonicea; very briefly, on Panamara alone, Cook (1914–1940) 1.18–24. I also draw on Roussel (1931) 85, a text praising Zeus "since [he has shown us many great and wonderful manifestations] for the salvation of the city, from of ancient times . . . ," the date (pp. 90–92) lying in the late first cent. B.C.; and a similar text in Hatzfeld (1927) 63, "since the greatest and most wonderful Zeus of Panamara saves the city . . . ," (the date, p. 64, lying in the late first cent. A.D.). For more on the shrine, I draw also on Hatzfeld (1927) 69 (remains evidently of a *lex sacra*) -109; Deschamps and Cousin (1887) 373–378; idem (1891) 209; Cousin (1904) 26 (*theoriae*); and Roussel (1927) 124, "the theater which is the ἱερόν itself of Panamara."

19. On the Panamaran "mysteries" see Roussel (1927) 126 and 132–134; Laumonier (1958) 247, 255–259, and 323–329; and Kane (1975) 331f.; on the Lagina-mysteries of Hecate, see Deschamps and Cousin (1891) 174 and Cousin (1904) 241.

20. Laumonier (1958) 365; on Lagina, further, pp. 370–382 and 392–401; Diehl and Cousin (1887) 158; Hatzfeld (1920) 75–77 and Laumonier (1958) 346, actions taken jointly by *boule, demos, gerousia,* and οἱ ἐν τῷ ἱερῷ (or τῷ περιπολίῳ) κατοικούντες; assistance to the poor, pp. 74 and 89, cf. at Panamara, Laumonier (1958) 267.

21. Laumonier (1958) 402, on *CIG* 2715a-b = LeBas-Wadd. 519–520.

22. Above, chap. 1.1 n.67; Laumonier (1934) 85 and idem (1958) 276 and 388 on LeBas-Wadd. 519f.; cf. Laumonier (1958) 275, the not-fully-explained Zeus-wrought miracle whereby (as the inscription records) "the ox in piety toward the priest, during the parade, of its own accord leads the priest to the senate-house and then, after the sacrifice, went off right away."

CHAPTER II: DEBATABLE

1. Needs and Answers

1. For σωτήρ as Asclepius's most frequent characterization, see Bieler (1935–1936) 1.121; examples in Herrmann and Polatkan (1969) 46f., near Pergamon; Weinreich (1909) 30, at Rome; Robert (1973) 161f., at Messina; *IG* 4, 1².127 (A.D. 224) and 415 (A.D. 258), at Epidaurus; no. 417, the god addressed without name, simply as

"savior," as also in Crete, above, chap. 1.2 n.82; his function implied in all the testimonies of suppliants "saved," σωθείς, σωθεῖσα, at Insula Tiberina, Longo (1969) 1.84, or at Pergamon, *IGR* 4.279 and Ohlemutz (1940) 155 and 158. For healing by Isis and Sarapis, cf. Strabo 17.1.17, Aelian, *Hist. animal.* 11.35 (with a welcome pun), *SEG* 8.464, and Vidman (1969) 133 and 159. For other gods also healing, cf. for example Syrian ones in LeBas-Wadd. 2343 and Gawlikowski (1973) 94; Apollo, *CIG* 6797=*IG* 14.2524, at Autun; Sol, *CIL* 3.5862, at Augsburg; and Hestia and other deities at Ephesus, in Robert (1955) 100.

2. Philostr., *Vita Apollon.* 4.10 and 8.7.9, invoking Hercules Apotropaios, cf. Tat., *Ad Graec.* 16 (*PG* 6.811B), demons cause disease, and the same view held by superstitious people, Plut., *Moral.*, 168Bf., and by Gnostics, according to Plot., *Enn.* 2.9.14.

3. Philostr., *Vita Apollon.* 4.20, cf. exorcism practiced on sick animals, ibid. 6.43 and Veget., *Mulomedicina* 3.12; exorcism also in Lucian, *Philops.* 16, the reference to the specific exorcist judged historical if not identifiable by Betz (1961) 12; other nameless practitioners in Firm. Matern., *Math.* 3.4.27 and 3.8.9, and in Orig., *C. Cels.* 1.68. As a youth, Marcus Aurelius was taught skepticism about pagan exorcists, *Medit.* 1.6, but Tatian, *Ad Graec.* 18, had no doubts, nor the purchasers of home remedies, such as Cyranides 1.3.10, 13.25 de Mely.

4. Just., II *Apol.* 6. Cf. *Dial.* 76.6, and various contemporary Apologist passages cited by Archambault (1909) ad loc.; Iren., *Adv. haer.* 2.32.4 (*PG* 7.829A), comparing the Jewish exorcists at 2.6.2 (*PG* 7.724f.); Tert., *Apol.* 23.4 (*quid hac probatione fidelius?*)—27.7; idem, *De spect.* 26; and Orig., *C. Cels.* 1.46, cf. 1.6; also Theoph., *Ad Autol.* 2.8, "up to the present day the possessed are sometimes exorcized"; Cypr., *Ad Donat.* 5; Tatian, loc. cit.; *Acta Petri et Pauli* 33, p. 193 Lipsius, written in Asia before A.D. 200, says James (1924) 300 and 304f. Later sources include Greg. Nyss., *Vita S. Greg. Thaumaturg.*, *PG* 46.916 and 944f., for the mid-third cent.; Athanas., *Vita S. Anton.* 40, 63, 64, and 80; *Or. de incarnat. verbi* 19, 31, and 48 (*PG* 25.129, 149, and 181); Euseb., *Demon. ev.* 3.6 (*PG* 22.233-236); *C. Hierocl.* 4 (in the Loeb ed., with the *Hist. eccl.*, vol. 2 p. 493); Arnob. 1.43-45; Lact., *De mort. persecut.* 10.2f. and *Div. inst.* 2.15(16) and 4.27.1; and Firm. Matern., *De errore prof. relig.* 13.5f. Exorcism was to Christians "a deliberate and official activity and not . . . a private trade pursued for profit," as Nock (1933) 104 sees.

5. Epigraphic equivalent of *defixiones* is very rare. An apparent exception may prove the rule: *IGR* 4.93, fragmentary, the curse likely invoked on some criminal.

6. Lact., *Div. inst.* 5.20, with an echo in Tert., *De spect.* 25.102. Lactantius emphasizes his case by joining a brigand to the gladiator, and a poisoner, etc. But such criminals could only invoke demons, as he well knew. Similarly, Tertullian rebukes the admiration of *scaenici*, *De spect.* 22.101; but open inquiry of Apollo may be made by an acrobat about his upcoming performance, cf. Vidman (1969) 147, or Philostr., *Gym.* p. 283 Kayser (=Jüthner 41), where a nameless god sends a vision that saves a wrestler's career.

7. Baldness, *ILS* 3135; fertility, Hall (1977) 193, but probably before our period of study; Zeus πλουτοδότης, Vidman (1969) 196, under Caracalla, and on coins of Nysa under Nero, *BMC Lydia* p. 175, and Men with the same epithet in Lane (1971-1978) 1.91; to Silvanus, *ob libertatem*, *CIL* 6.663; to Mars, *ob immunitatem* of a cult guild, *RIB* 309, A.D. 152; to Isis, *ob remissa exacta inlicita populo a maximis im-*

peratoribus (Severus and Caracalla), *CIL* 11.1585, Florentia; lightning, in Robert (1949) 31 and Taus and Berardi (1972) 86–88; to Poseidon for safety during an earthquake, Perdrizet (1900) 431, at Gerasa and Byblos; drowning, *CIG* 2716=LeBas-Wadd. 516, *IG* 14.997 and 10, 2.67, cf. *BGU* 423 (second cent., to Sarapis) and Arrian, *Ep. ad Traianum* 34, ed. C. Müller, *Geographici graeci minores* 1.399; unspecified "dangers" in *IGR* 1.107=*IG* 14.1030, *CIG* 3669 (Cyzicus, second cent.), and other texts in Robert (1945) 1.21 and 24, curiously formulaic; life saved, in Gawlikowski (1973) 64 and *ILS* 3160, *Marti Augusto conservatori corporis sui*; danger on a journey (the stele showing a trotting horse in relief), LeBas-Wadd. 515, Stratonicea, and DeRicci (1934) 257–259 (Severan, in Egypt); safe return from danger, to Hera, for the dedicant's sons, *Inscr. Ital.* 10, 3.115, and for troops, Milik (1972) 197f. (A.D. 316, correcting *ILS* 8882, Coptos), Rebuffat (1975) 504 n.28=*IRT* 920 plus another, clearer inscription; Winnett (1957) 1f. (dates) and, e.g., nos. 911f. and 714f. (safety) and 253 and 700 (booty); for the municipal slave, cf. *CIL* 11.4639, Tuder. These thirty-odd examples of inscriptions which name the cause of thanks, excluding the Safaitic, could no doubt be doubled—but not quadrupled, it is my impression. A small corpus to work with.

8. A sampling in *MAMA* 7.243; Lane (1971–1978) 1.60f., children, that word alone, or "of his own" or (1971–1978) 4.18f., "wife, children and slaves"; *IGR* 1.44, "of wife and children"; "of his own [kin]," in Rey-Coquais (1972) 87; "of my masters, self, and all that are mine," *CIG* 3792, in Robert (1955) 32, with other prayers for "masters," pp. 29–31, or "men" and "possessions," idem (1939) 203; prayers for "all who are his" *vel sim.*, in Drew-Bear (1978) 43 and 47; "for his son," in Kalinka (1933) Beibl. col. 62 and Engelmann (1976) 108 no. 42; "for wife, children and kin," *IGLS* 2728; Merlat (1951) 142; and Rostovtzeff (1937) 204, at Dura in the Atargatis temple. In the west, cf. Merlat (1951) 35 and 249, *CIL* 12.403, 8.2625, and a variety indicated by the abbreviation *p(ro) s(alute) s(ua) s(uorumque)*, 3.1133, cf. 7505.

9. "For the stock," ὑπὲρ τῶν ζῴων, in Schwertheim (1978) 793, "to the god Prietos"; *pro armento*, in *CIL* 12.4102, to Silvanus, cf. Cato, *De agr.* 83, how to offer sacrifices *pro bubus, uti valeant*, to Mars and Silvanus; for a mule, LeBas-Wadd. 686, to Men; for the oxen, LeBas-Wadd. 1192 (Pisidia, A.D. 163); Hasluck (1904) 23, from Thrace; in Phrygia, Drew-Bear (1978) 48f. and Robert (1939) 204, citing many of the texts in *MAMA* 5 (add no. 50 of that vol., an anepigraphic relief); for hunting-dogs, see Robert (1955) 29 with Arr., *Cyneg.* 33, where one prays to Artemis for a good dog. For prayers for crops in Phrygia, cf. ὑπὲρ καρπῶν or εὐθενείας, in *MAMA* 5.79 and pp. xliii, and Drew-Bear (1978) 38; in Bithynia, Sahin (1978) 775; in Pisidia, ibid. 780; in Pamphylia, Robert (1955) 240, "to Zeus Galactino according to Apollo's command"; in Bithynia, "for the vines," Hasluck (1904) 23 and *IGR* 3.36 (A.D. 161), and in Thrace, *IGBulg.*[2] 374; in Phrygia, *MAMA* 5 p. 42, the editor referring also to 1.8 (Phrygia) and Dionysus's epithets "of good harvest," *vel sim.* For conscious discussion of the gods' role in providing good harvests, cf. Paus. 2.25.10, *RE* s.v. Zeus, I:Epiklesen (H. Schwabl, 1972) col. 344, Iambl., *De myst.* 5.6, and Max. Daia in Euseb., *H.E.* 9.7.8.

10. No fertility deity—in our period (whatever may have been the origins and scope of deities in darker centuries). On Dionysus in that role, texts are not numerous, but they are roughly in proportion with the total of those that link any deity

with any sphere of activity. See examples in the preceding note, plus *CIL* 5.5543, to Jupiter and Liber *vinarum conservator*, and 8.24520, to Liber from *oenopolae cum meraris omnibus* (= *tabernarii?*) of Carthage; but be warned by Firm. Matern., *De errore profan. relig.* 3, showing that Attis cult serves the fertility of the fields; and *POxy.* 2782 (second/third cent.) showing sacrifices to Demeter (here = Isis?) for good crops and weather is the kind of text that should be common and is not. The more familiar spheres of deities may not be the real or chief ones—as indeed of Liber pater himself, cf. above, chap. 1.1 n.17.

11. For Mercury = Hermes guarding peddlers, cf. Finke (1927) 7, *Mercurius peregrinorum*; Barkoczi et al. (1954–1957) 1.326, *Mercurio lucrorum potenti, NN negotias*(!); and Robert (1966) 25, Hermes statues often preside over weights and scales in the market; for Silvanus, guardian of beasts in the woods, cf. preceding note and Tourtain (1907–1920) 1, 1.265, dedications by *ursarii vel sim.*; Tert., *De idol.* 10.2, the schoolmaster thanks Minerva; Poseidon, earthshaker, in the preceding note and in Philostr., *Vita Apollon.* 6.41; and generally on the appropriateness of deities, the discussion in Plut., *Moral.* 757C–758E. For deities of women and children, above, chap. 1.3 n.1 and Hatt (1979) 131, in the period A.D. 150–225.

12. Tran Tam Tinh (1964) 117, referring to Juv. 6.522; cf. Juv. 6.531f. and passim, Min. Fel. 22.8, the disapproval and ridicule that pagans *nudi crude hieme discurrunt*, and Bickerman (1973) 11, on Lactantius's views and a pagan's probable response. For explicit examples of *do ut des*, as easily found in Greek as in Latin inscriptions, cf. Keil (1939) 119, in Ephesus, the wish that Hestia and Artemis may serve as the dedicant's advocate since *she* had spent *her* wealth freely on *them* (date, under Marcus Aurelius). This may be compared with the broad, self-comfortable statement about worship in Art., *Oneir.* 2.33. In the west, see *Inscr. Ital.* 10, 2.194, *ex voto quot* (!) *a dea petit consecutus*; *CIL* 5.6505, *Mercuri* ... , *ut facias hilares semper tua templa colamus*; *CIL* 5.3221, *quot* (!) *se precibus compotem fecisset* (scil. Deus Aeternus), cf. 5.3321, or the same thought so much a cliché that it is abbreviated *voti c(ompos) d(at)*, *CIL* 6.47, and Cagnat (1898) 440, *v.c.l.m.* For more examples of the cliché, see LeGlay (1971) 130.

13. Dubois (1902) 27, on "a renascence of Dionysiac mysteries in Italy." But the evidence does not exist: Dio 76.16 (no word of mysteries), cult colleges at Ostia (*CIL* 14.4, the date too early by nearly a century) and at Rome (*CIL* 6.641, no word of mysteries). Charles-Picard (1954) 203–205 detects the same renascence, based on sarcophagi reliefs, the symbolism of which may show the promise of immortality. The inference seems quite subjective, at least not well supported. See Nock (1946) 140, critical of the inference in its best-known version, Cumont's, and further, Andreae (1963) 81 n.445, supporting Nock and citing F. Matz to the same end. On the question whether Dionysus cult could insure immortality, Bruhl (1953) 309 professes to lean on Cumont (1942), a work in which I can find nothing solid, and (cf. Bruhl 314 n.20) also Cumont (1949) 256f., again not useful. Bruhl himself (p. 312) offers a number of assertions while admitting scanty evidence beyond the sarcophagi: *CIL* 6.30122, which provides no support, and Plut., *Moral.* 611E, depicting the soul as undergoing modified metempsychosis, and without individuality. Plutarch tells us that he relies on teachings partly ancestral, partly Dionysiac; but they appear rather Neoplatonic.

14. The "mysteries" are new features within the period of the Empire, cf. F.

Dunand (1972–1973) 3.244f. and 253. The evidence lies in Plut., *Moral.* 351Ff. and 364E, Heliodorus, *Ethiop.* 9.9, and Hippolyt., *Refut.* 5.7. The arguments of Merkelbach (1962) 12 and passim, that initiatory rites can be found hidden in Apul., *Met.* 4.33f., seem quite unsubstantial and can be set aside in the light of Williams (1978) 194 and Kane (1975) 342. In Apul., *Met.*, note esp. 11.6, *vives beatus*, life may even be prolonged a bit; but then, *ad inferos*; 11.16, *ter beatus* for winning Isis's *patrocinium, ut renatus quodam modo*—meaning, for Lucius, *spes futura beneficiis praesentibus pignerata* . . . ; 11.24, *beneficio pigneratus*; and 11.30, Lucius earns money *liberali deum providentia.* The real benefits are earthly.

15. *Pie* (?) *rebus renatum*, etc., in Gordon (1975) 236, a far less full text in Vermaseren (1956–1960) 1.199f. no. 485 (A.D. 202); idem, (1969) 254, offering a new version. Franz Cumont, after more confident statements in the past, finally confessed in 1947 to "our well-nigh total ignorance of the mysteries," in *Mithraic Studies* (1975) 198. For the third text, *CIL* 6.736 (A.D. 391), *arcanis perfusionibus* (not *profusionibus*) *in aeternum renatus*, cf. Meslin (1978) esp. 303–305, apparently unaware that it is a forgery (thus omitted from Vermaseren's *Corpus* and specified as false by Duthoy [1969] 66). The date and the echoes of Christianity and of non-Mithraic *taurobolia*, cf. below, n.23, would in any case deprive the text of value for our purposes. Finally, we have *CIL* 3.686 (third cent., Philippi)=Vermaseren (1956–1960) 2.382 no. 2343, in part reading, *sic placitum est divis aeterna vivere forma qui bene de supero lumine sit meritus*, "gifts promised to you in your pure course of life by the natural innocence once commanded by the god." The verse epitaph is pretty poetry, no more. It portrays afterlife "as a Satyr" summoned to Bacchus, or to the Naiads. It has no reference to Mithraism. As to the "dead" man shown in Mithraic frescoes, recalled by SHA *Commod.* 9, that need not be the initiate, about to be resurrected; *pace* Meslin 306, that item in the rites may have many meanings unrelated to resurrection.

16. Orig., *C. Cels.* 6.22, with bibliog. ad loc., H. Chadwick (1965) 334; Porph., *De abst.* 4.16, but these "statements . . . about metempsychosis are not reliable," says Gordon (1972) 115 n.26. He gives no reason for saying this, but Porph., *De antro* 6, is compatible with Celsus—still more so, the statement ibid. 29, if that passage were tied by Porphyry to Mithraism (it is not).

17. Nilsson (1949) 765f. on the fresco called by Kane (1975) 343 "the most convincing instance known to me of an earthly banquet foreshadowing the blessed feast of the future life"; but even here (Nilsson, p. 764), the inscription next to the dedicant contains common and quite opposed pagan sentiments of the sort, "eat, drink and be merry, for tomorrow you die."

18. *CIL* 6.32316, date, A.D. 180, says Goodhue (1975) 9. Cumont (1917) 280–282 and others thought this text was proof of belief in immortality; but (Goodhue 111–114) still others disagree. Cumont (1917) 282 n.2, in his efforts to support his view, offers three perfectly useless citations, to Diog. Laertes (speaking only of Pythagoras), Mnaseas (nearly five centuries too early), and *SIG*[2] 584 (not mentioning immortality). The inscription, in its tone, seems to grin at death, in the use of the diminutive of "soul," *animula*, and in the sentiment, τῷ θανάτῳ μηδὲν ὀφειλόμενος.

19. On two kinds of initiation at Samothrace, see Fraser (1960) 91, where, of twenty-nine people initiated on a single day in A.D. 19, only three received the more

advanced *epopteia*. One was the person heading the whole group. "Schinas paid the bill for all his party," says K. Lehmann, ibid. The circumstances seem to contradict Lehmann (1954) 93, that selection for *epopteia* "was conditioned neither by financial nor by social status." Of the Eleusinian mysteries (the Great—the Lesser being at Agrae), Otto (1955) 23–30 offers a powerful vision; but it must be set against the icy sarcasm of Hippolyt., *Ref.* 5.8.39 (*PG* 16.3150B), specifically speaking of the Great Epoptikon (therefore including the more advanced, if there were several grades). I do not agree with Kerenyi (1955) 34 n.7 that Great rites at Cyzicus (known only in one inscription, *BCH* [1890] 537) necessarily imply Lesser. Nor does the seating in the show-theater of Demeter's shrine at Pergamon seem to me adequate evidence of two levels of initiation—*contra*, Ohlemutz (1940) 211.

20. Theon Smyrn., *Math.* p. 23 Dupuis, an interesting look at a generalized initiatory experience, suggesting that the same procedures were found in a number of rites. For the date, see Lesky (1966) 879, or *OCD* s.v. Similarly, Plutarch in Stobaeus 4.52.49 (Loeb ed., vol. 15 pp. 316–318) may offer a generalized description. He calls them only τελεταὶ μεγάλαι; cf. *Moral.* 1105B, asserting that "lots of people," πάνυ πολλοί, feel no fear of death, believing that the initiatory rites will assure them a delightful hereafter, described just as in the preceding fragment. Tertullian, *De praescr. haer.* 40.1–5, receives most recent comment from Gordon (1975) 234–236. The punctuation of the passage is controverted, but I agree with Gordon that *diabolus* rules all verbs save *signat* (my disagreement on 40.1.5 alone is irrelevant). Echoes of word choice recall idem, *De baptismo* 5, *per lavacrum initiantur* in both Isiacism and Mithraism. But the meaning of the rite may lie (5.1) in the Apollinian and Pelusian Games, "where people are anointed, *tinguntur*, and believe by this they are born afresh and unpunished for oath-breaking" (*regeneratio* to *impunitas periuriorum*, best explained by chap. 1.2 nn.69f., above, and n.34, below).

21. Charles-Picard (1954) 146 n.2; Festugière (1945) 123, *Corp. Herm.* X, 20.

22. Meslin (1974) 290 is only the latest in a long series of scholars to make the assumption. He speaks of worshipers of "the Oriental cults," undefined, as identifying themselves with the suffering and death of their god and his resurrection. But of course Jupiter Dolichenus, Sabazius and Mithra are Oriental but never suffered; and resurrection in divine stories more often calls to mind fertility (planting and growing) than immortality, e.g., in the story of Attis, cf. Firm. Matern., *De errore profan. relig.* 3, or of Kore or Osiris.

23. As pointed out by Lambrechts (1952) 163.

24. Cf. Duthoy (1969) passim, esp. 106 and 110. Meslin (1974) 310 thinks that in *CIL* 6.510 (A.D. 376)=*ILS* 4152, *renatus in aeternum* through *taurobolium*, "Christian influence is here manifest." For the duration of the effect of the rite, usually twenty years, cf. *Carmen contra paganos* 62, and note *CIL* 13.511 and 520, in which the emperor's *salus* is sought by the *ordo* of the city through *taurobolium*—hardly his *eternal* life.

25. Just., I *Apol.* 18. He adds reff. to Pythagoras, Plato, Homer, all remote and literary. Cf. also the view meant to be representative (and negative) in Min. Fel. 8.5.

26. Lact., *Div. inst.* 5.19 and 7.13.5. For the collection of such oracles, cf. above, chap. 1.1 n.65.

27. Orig., *C. Cels.* 7.32; Min. Fel. 11.2–4. Apologists in many passages indicate a defensiveness about the idea of resurrection in the flesh.

28. *Ad Lucilium* 24.18 and 36.10, cf. Min. Fel. 11.9.

29. LeBas-Wadd. 2343, "saved by the savior-gods from illnesses," *CIG* 3827 add. q (Rome), "Hecate savior" (hardly of souls!), or Harper (1972) 225, "for the preservation, σωτηρία, of the priest NN, to Men," are typical of usages too common to need further parallels. Cf. above, n.1, or, in literary sources, Firm. Matern., *De errore profan. relig.* 22, "take heart, initiates, the god is saved; there is salvation for you, out of your pains," or *Orph. hymn.* 67 line 8, Quandt² p. 47, Asclepius hailed as "savior, bestowing a good end to life" (i.e., only a good death).

30. Lattimore (1942) 74–86, esp. 84f.; Cagnat (1898) 262, *n(on) f(ui), n(on) s(um), n(on) c(uro)*, copying the equivalent in Greek, ibid. 262 n.4.

31. For the (still continuing) "old" view of mystic hopes in banquets, cf. the representative conjectures of Collins-Clinton (1977) 19: "those [Bacchic] meals would also have been considered an earthly anticipation of the continuing joyful banquets of the blessed afterlife in which only the initiates could share." By contrast, cf. the writers cited above, chap. 1.3 n.28, adding Laumonier (1958) 322f. and 329, on Bacchic and Panamaran cult meals.

32. *Moral.* 822B; for similar statements that religion deserves support or was invented because it helps to control otherwise antisocial behavior, cf. Critias, *Sisyphos, ad init.* (A. Nauck, *Tragicorum graecorum fragmenta*, p. 771); Polyb. 16.12.9f.; Poseidonius reflected in Diod. 34/35.2.47; Diodorus's own views, 1.2.2; Cic., *Rep.* 2.2.4 and *Leg.* 2.7.15f.; Plin., *N.H.* 2.26; Athenag., *Leg.* 1.2, saying all cults are lawful "in order that men may forbear from wrongdoing through their fear of the divine"; and *Hermeneumata pseudodositheana* p. 39 Goetz (later second/earlier third cent.), Aesopic fables promote moral behavior.

33. Paus. 8.15.2, in Arcadia, "most of the citizens of Pheneus take oath by the Petroma [a sort of betyl] in the most major affairs"; Philostr., *Vita Apollon.* 1.6, near Tyana a spring of Zeus god of Oaths, where perjurers are scalded or touched by a wasting disease, etc.; Achilles Tatius 8.11–14, testing by the sacred spring at Ephesus; Plin., *N.H.* 31.22, in Bithynia, the river Alcas. In the west, Juv. 13.34f., with both believers and doubters at Rome; Paneg. vet. 7(6).21.7, Apollo's spring (at Grand and elsewhere); and testing "at the memorial to the saints" in Milan, presumably derived from pagan beliefs, Aug., *Ep.* 78.3 (*PL* 33.269).

34. *IGR* 4.1376; further, in Phrygia, Ramsay (1895–1897) 2.656, the violator "will have angered the gods in heaven and beneath the earth"; 700, "the subterranean demons"; Robert (1960a) 430 (Jewish); and *IG* 9,2.1201, Thessaly.

35. On the deity insuring justice in Isiacism, see the "Karpokrates" hymn quoted in chap. 1, above; Ovid. *Ex Pont.* 1.1.52f.; and the late third cent. B.C. *IG* 11.1299 lines 26–83; on Helios, see Cumont (1923) 65f., from Rome but in Greek; Arrian on interesting practices in Nicomedia, cited ibid. 67 (the passage cited from Vett. Valens seems to prove little), and 69, citing Aurel. Vict. 39.13; Celsus, in Orig., *C. Cels.* 8.48 (and less clearly at 3.16 and 4.10); the Ps. Plutarchan (but early second cent.) *Amatoriae narrationes*, where divine vengeance enlivens fiction, *Moral.* 774D and 775B and E; and background in Nestle (1948) 568–596 passim. The material in Judaism and Christianity is obviously abundant—a sampling in MacMullen (1968) 90 n.29.

36. Robert (1958b) 112–122 passim, on The Just Divinity embodying "conceptions religieuses plus épurées que les paganismes classiques de la Grèce ou de

l'Anatolie." In Mithraism, Cumont expatiated beyond measure on two fragments of evidence, namely a Dura graffito, cf. Cumont (1975) 204 and the inscription in Vermaseren (1959-1960) 1.49 no. 18. Gordon (1975) 231 n.64 seems a little harsh in calling the latter text "the *only* evidence yet published that Mithras was conceived as *just* in the Graeco-Roman world," and further depreciates even that evidence. But his dismissal of Cumont is not far off the mark. Note Cumont's main statement, (1929) 147, that Mithra presides as judge against the evil—a statement supported (282 n.68) by reference to p. 83 (on Sarapis—irrelevant) and to p. 92 (on Egypt—irrelevant) and to Cumont (1942) 89f., where is offered a dualistic picture of Mithraism, but nothing on Mithra as judge. Here, Cumont also refers to Philo, *De praemiis et poenis* 6, but the passage, contrasting heaven and Tartarus, has no relevance to Mithraism. Tertullian, *De praescr. haer.* 40.2f., refers to the initiate's sins (in an unspecified cult), *expositionem delictorum de lavacro repromittit*, which might perfectly well be violations of ritual, not ethics. Porphyry, *De antro* 15, does not decide the ambiguity, though explicitly on Mithraism. He is cited for other ends by Gordon (1972) 114 n.24. The passage in Orig., *C. Cels.* 3.36, evidently regarding Isiacism, describes oracular or healing gods that also punish people for sins against "some rule about impure food, or touching a corpse"; similarly, Juv. 6.520f. and 535 on Isiacism show that only ritual purity (i.e., regarding sexual taboos or the like) are in question, for expiation; so likewise Plut., *Moral.* 168D, transgressions of diet or, against promptings of one's guardian spirit (*daemonion*), taking the wrong fork in the road; but *Corp. herm.* 10.19-21, ed. A.-J. Festugière (1945) 122f., specifies purity through "not doing wrong to any man." The text is late for our purpose, fourth century.

37. Above, chap. 1.1 at n.91; cf. *ILS* 4326, priests praise a priest/magistrate *iussu Iovis*, and Seyrig (1941) 246, third-cent. inscriptions testifying to Iarhibol's approval or support of this or that local magistrate.

38. *De lege Manilia* 14.42. Such statements are naturally easy to find in emperor worship or anything close to it, e.g., Plin., *Paneg.* 1.4f.

39. A village in Asia Minor is the beneficiary of prayers "on behalf of the *demos*," in Lane (1971-1978) 1.69; villages pray for themselves, cf. Sahin (1978) 775; Buckler et al. (1926) 88, "in obedience to an oracle"; Drew-Bear (1978) 38; Robert (1955) 240; and Hasluck (1904) 22, Bithynia, and 23, Cyprus. In the west, cf. *CIL* 5.8208=*ILS* 3980, *pro salute sua et suorum omnium et viciniae*. Addresses to a deity by a city corporately lie in LeBas-Wadd. 2627=*CIG* 4500 (A.D. 114), at Palmyra; other examples in Hatzfeld (1927) 63f., Stratonicea, and *IGR* 1.568, Nicopolis ad Istrum, "by command from a dream." Cf. above, chap. 1.1 n.17.

40. *CIG* 3538=*IGR* 4.360, Pergamon, cited by Wiseman (1973) 178; ibid. 179 on *IGR* 4.1498, Trocetta; but Keil and Premerstein (1908) 10, doubt the connection with A.D. 166; further, Wiseman (1973) 180-182, possibly Stobi; Robert (1973) 162, possibly Messina; above, chap. 1.2 n.67, further instances; Philostr., *Vita Apollon.* 6.41, earthquakes in Asia under Domitian; and consultation of Apollo's oracle by Caracalla (?), in Birley (1974) 511f., by Diocletian, in Lact., *De mort. persecut.* 11.7, and by Asian cities on a regular basis, above, chap. 1.1 n.88.

41. Ael. Arist., *Or.* 28.39, 1 p. 498 Dindorf; *SEG* 4, 1 (1929) 467, cf. *Prosopography of the Later Rom. Emp.* s.v. Festus 4; compare Ambrose, *Ep.* 15.5-7 (*PL* 16.956), thanks to S. Acholius's prayers, *saevienti lue et ardenti perstilentia perturbati Gothi ac territi sunt*, at Thessalonica in A.D. 380.

42. Athenag., *Leg.* 23; Origen in Rufinus, *PG* 12.789B; Ps.-Clem., *Homil.* 9.14; Firm. Matern., *De errore profan. relig.* 13.4; *Acta Xanthippae et Polyxenae* 2 (mid-third cent., says the ed. M. R. James), the idols in a Spanish town tremble at the sound of Jesus's name; Euseb., *Praep. ev.* 5.2 (182C); Basil, *Comment. in Isaiam* 10.236 (*PG* 30.532C); the same among pagan sources, Ps.-Apul., *Asclepius* 37; Schermann (1909) 12; on statues moving, winking, etc., see for background Weinreich (1909) 145f., and examples of such miracles in *POxy.* 1242 III 51f., Dio Chrysos., *Or.* 31.95, and Euseb., *Praep. ev.* 5.34.6f., on the statue of Theagenes in Thasos; also Athenag., *Leg.* 26, on Nerullinus in Tralles and Peregrinus at Parium, and Paus. 4.32.2, on Aithidas in Messenia. For pious kisses and touches perhaps wearing away parts of statues, cf. Jucker (1960) 91, credible but inconclusive.

43. To the refs. in the preceding note, add testimonies to the worship accorded to Plotinus, in Eunap., *Vit. soph.* 455, with Porph., *Vita Plot.* 22, where Apollo in an oracle declares Plotinus after death to be a *"daemon,* though yesterday a mortal" (lines 11f. of the hymn). On Antinous, "his" miracles after his death can only mean "through his statue," Orig., *C. Cels.* 3.36, Origen attributing the deeds to mere magic. For the worship of a deceased person as "hero," cf. *CIG* 3936 (early second cent.) and Ramsay (1895–1897) 2.603, a text of A.D. 245; ibid. 566, a text much improved and discussed by Robert (1937) 132f., regarding a priestess heroized who prophesies from her tomb.

44. Marc. Diac., *Vita Porph.* 60f., the Aphrodite statue at Gaza inhabited by a demon; Euseb., *H.E.* 7.18.2f., at Caesarea.

45. The bulk of the evidence is epigraphic. I withhold most that I have gathered. It seems to prove nothing. But there are useful discussions in Robert (1940a) 72, Weinreich (1909) 7, Gaertringen (1935) 369f., and Nock (1925) 95f., all these on Greek usages; on Latin, cf. *ILS* 3006–3847 passim (apparently nothing of value in secondary literature). I have tried to scatter illustrations generously through the notes to the first chapter.

46. Art., *Oneir.* 4.2, "after seeing [=in a dream], make sacrifice and offer thanks"; Achilles Tatius 4.1.5f., κατ'ὄναρ or ἐνύπνιον; Marc. Diac., *Vita Porph.* 60, κατὰ κέλευσιν; *ex monitu deorum,* Ulp., *De off. procons.* 7.6, *FIRA*² 2.580; *imperiis deum,* Apul., *Met.* 11.29; *ex imperio,* Sen., *Ep.* 108.7 and *De vita beata* 26.8. In the Levant, oddities: ἐξ ἐνκελεύσεως in Gaza, *IGR* 1.387 (the stone in Rome); "directed in a dream," in Aramaic, Milik (1972) 388.

47. Herrmann and Polatkan (1969) 10, first cent., and, on "heroes," above, n.42; and *AE* 1971 no. 208, *Genio leg. VII Gem. fel. . . . ex iussu Genii votum,* second cent.

48. *IGR* 1.568, . . . κατὰ ἐπιταγὴν ὀνείρου, ἡ βουλή . . . ; 1.387; and other examples to be sought in or through n.39, above.

49. *Ep. ad Traianum* 34, C. Müller, *Geographici graeci minores* 1.398f.

50. Orig., *C. Cels.* 1.66 and 2.60.

51. Bernand (1972) 133; Petron., *Sat.* 17.

52. Examples in Strabo 14.1.44; Gsell (1931) 254 and 257, on a third-cent. African inscription and its parallels throughout various western cults; and *AE* 1975 no. 722, a Dacian inscription (restored) in which a debt to Liber is discharged: *secundum interpretationem sacrorum Solis in tabulam scribendum curavit.*

53. Collart and Ducrey (1975) 239, comparing *CIL* 3.11137, *i.d.f.*

54. *Moral.* 414A, cf. Juv. 6.555, at Delphi, *oracula cessant;* and *Moral.* 574E.

55. Lucian, *Conc. deor.* 12, where, as Betz (1961) 58 says, Momus "complains

about a sort of oracle-inflation" (and n.5, refs. to other Lucianic passages on oracles; note esp. *Alex.* 29). For Amphilochus, cf. Lucian, *Alex.* 29 and *Philops.* 38, Dio 73.7.1 (indicating that "it foretells through dreams," an unusual method), and Paus. 1.34.3, praising its veracity. For Claros, note esp. Porph., *Ep. ad Anebonem* 2.2d, Sodano pp. 9f., "far-famed and inspired" in his day, and below, p. 63. Euseb., *Demonstr. ev.* 5 *praef.* (*PG* 22.337), in declaring the oracles, indiscriminately, to have been "quenched," is simply wrong. So too is Cumont (1929) 285, for "the scepticism regarding oracles" in the early Empire. He cites Strabo (who speaks *obiter* and obscurely of his own views), Livy (skeptical of portents two or three generations earlier), and Lucan 5.111 (who actually *laments* the silence of Delphic wisdom and justice). Dodds (1965) 57 likewise errs in speaking of "the increasing demand for oracles" in the second half of the third century. He adduces oracles quoted by Porphyry (but these predate the crisis, cf. above, chap. 1.1 n.65) and *POxy.* 1477 (but that also is not relevant, cf. *POxy.* 2832f. and *RE* s.v. Astrampsachus col. 1797).

56. Euseb., *Praep. ev.* 4.2 (136a-b), 4.3 (136bf.), and 5.22 (213c), esp. citing Oenomaus's view that all oracles were human impostures, "the deceits and sleights of wizard-men." Against the challenge that paganism was authenticated in its oracles (e.g., Celsus, in Orig., *C. Cels.* 8.45), Christians could thus draw on a rich skeptical literature. The Christian arguments appear compendiously in *Passio SS. Carpi, Papyli et Agathonicae* 17f. (H. Musurillo, *Acts of the Christian Martyrs* p. 24), also often in the Apologists, e.g., Lact., *Div. inst.* 2.17.

2. The Vitality of Paganism

1. Lucian, *Alex.* 38—and 44, where one of the school appears as active challenger. Chilton (1971) xxivf. finds Epicureans on the rise in the century, but Drachman (1922) 121 finds that "an essentially anti-religious school like that of the Epicureans actually dies out at this time," the first half of the second century. The evidence, either way, is scant.

2. The charge of atheism against the Christians was extremely serious, and seriously repulsed. The evidence, e.g., Just., I *Apol.* 5f., or Athenag., *Leg.* 1, has been often discussed. Harnack (1905) 11 shrewdly notes the counterattack made by Apologists Greek and Latin through the pagan atheist Diagoras, as reproach against all pagans. For atheism being allegedly illegal, cf. Dio Chrysos., *Or.* 43.11 and 75.5 (obscure)—most likely a matter of public scandal but not actual crime, as also in Athens (Lucian, *Demonax* 11, with danger of stoning).

3. Euseb., *H.E.* 4.15.6; 4.16.3; and 5.1.9.

4. Athenag., *Leg.* 1; Aelian, *Varia hist.* 2.31—"like Euhemerus or Diogenes or Epicurus."

5. Lucian, *Jup. trag.* 53, "a few men" accept atheistical arguments.

6. Lucian, *Timon* 4; above, chap. 1.1 n.48; and Juv. 13.34f.

7. Tran Tam Tinh (1964) 108 and 115 n.2.

8. G. Picard (1954) 420–422.

9. Cumont (1929) 285, quoting Taramelli. Taramelli in fact ventures no indication of date for the inscription, and it is actually not of the second century. Cumont goes on to claim, here adducing no facts at all, that oracles "in the 3rd century fell under complete disbelief."

10. Lact., *Div. inst.* 5.19; Porph., *Ad Marc.* 14, with more to the same, high moral effect, ibid. 15f., 18, and 23.

11. Ovid, *Fasti* 6.249-252, stressed by Wagenvoort (1966) 965f., a scene to which one may compare Plut., *Moral.* 270D, "just as today, still, men who have offered their prayers and made their obeisances in shrines are accustomed to linger and sit about," or Tibullus 1.3.27f. The second quoted passage is from Dio Chrysos., *Or.* 12.60f. It is noteworthy that Mars Lenus, who should be a god of war, saved a worshiper by his love: *servatus Tychicus divino Martis amore, IG* 14.2562 = Buecheler (1895-1897) 2.394 no. 850—explained by Drexel (1922) 25: the deity locally is a healing one. In *POxy.* 528 a man prays for his wife to "Thoeris who loves you."

12. Sen., *De superstit.*, in Aug., *Civ. dei* 6.10 passim. But, for a later audience, also one meant to be more general, an Apologist presents identical views, ridiculing winter acts of expiation (borrowed from Juvenal? above, chap. 2.1 n.12) and the fanatic who slashes his arms and body, and thus *vulneribus suis supplicat*, Min. Fel. 22.9, cf. Sen., l.c., *vulneribus suis ac sanguine supplicant*; compare Min. Fel. 23.1, ridiculing Isiac lamentation for Osiris, with Juv. 6.534, presenting the priest *derisor* of the *plangens populus*.

13. Most methodically, mythology is destroyed by Heraclitus, *De incredibilibus* (first cent.?), in *Mythographi graeci* 3, 2 (1902) 80-82, indebted to Palaephatus of the fourth cent. B.C., e.g., ibid. p. 6 echoed by Heraclitus, *De incred.* 2; on Pausanias, see Casson (1974) 293; on Lucian, Drachmann (1922) 125; in the Latin tradition, cf. Cic., *De nat. deor.* 2.5 and Plin., *N.H.* 2.14-27.

14. Phrases quoted from Tran Tam Tinh (1964) 116 (whose references, Bayet and Beaujeu, offer no footnotes); Bieler (1935-1936) 1.2 (whose references lead to literary sources only) with Drachmann (1922) 121 offering identical views on second cent. religiosity; Dodds (1965) 9, actually seeing "a wave of pessimism sweeping over the West" (p. 18) in a period of much broader boundaries—for criticism, cf. MacMullen (1976) 14-16 and notes; and Nock (1937) 112, referring to "the anxious questing mood of the time" when he evidently means the second to later fourth centuries (in the context, adducing a second-cent. inscription, Artemidorus, Heliodorus, Julian and the SHA); finally, Geffcken (1920) 20.

15. Dodds (1965) 3, a statement challenged by Gordon (1972) 94.

16. Apul., *Met. ad fin.*, well-known chapters; Aelian, frg. 89, in R. Hercher, *Aeliani opera* 2.230f., a highly colored little tale, pro-Asclepius, anti-Epicurus, very closely recalling the sort of *aretai* that Pausanias read at Sicyon (above, chap. 1.2 at n.70), and full of conviction.

17. Chap. 1.2 n.44 (Xenophon), chap. 1.3 n.29, and chap. 1.2 n.72.

18. Nock (1933) 112.

19. Liebeschuetz (1979) 214.

20. Oribasius 45.30.11-14; *Report of the XXII Congress* (1962) quoted by Bickerman (1973) 5 n.2. Lazurkina had known Lenin personally. Lenin spoke against Stalin, on this occasion. She explained to my friend V. Rudich that she often communicated with Lenin in dreams.

21. In all regions: *CIL* 10.1560, *servitor deorum ex viso; ILS* 3513, *publicus . . . pontificum*, his sight restored; *CIL* 9.3146, *ministra; aeditui* in *CIL* 12.2215 and *AE* 1971, 31; a ζάκορος φίλιος of the god, *IG* 2².4514; ἱερεύς the normal office, e.g., *IGR* 1.106, κατὰ κέλευσιν, or in M. Dunand (1939) 562; also νεωκόρος, *IGR* 1.107 = *IG*

14.1030; in Latin, normally *sacerdotes*, e.g., *ILS* 3831, *ex responso*; Albertini (1943) 377–380; LeGlay (1971) 126; *CIL* 3.7728 and 6.659.

22. *IG* 4², 1.380–430 (notice 386 and 415, "by dreams," "by command," A.D. 148 and 258).

23. *CIL* 6.31181, late Antonine, according to Speidel (1978) 18; *CIL* 3.7760, priests plural, "by command of the god," in Merlat (1951) 20, A.D. 202; and, in general, I. Toth (1971) 24.

24. Below, chap. 2.3 nn.65–67.

25. Marcus Aurelius, *Medit.* 1.6 but cf. 1.17.20; Art., *Oneir.* 4.22, p. 257 Pack, on Fronto; Max. Tyr., *Philos.* 9.7; the often-cited example of Galen, in his *Subfig. empirica* 10, K. Deichgräber, *Die griechische Empirikerschule²* (1965) 78f.; also in *De libris propriis* 2, I. Mueller, *Galeni scripta minora* 2.99, and *In Hippocr. de humor.* p. 222 Kühn; compare another famous physician acknowledging his debt to Asclepius, in Robert (1973) 184. For belief in divine healing, see further Cic., *Ad fam.* 14.7.1, crediting Apollo or Asclepius; Just., I *Apol.* 54.10, cf. Athenag., *Leg.* 23 (but it is really demons, he says, not a god); distinguished devotees of Asclepius, like the rhetors Antiochus, in Philostr., *Vit. Soph.* 568, and Polemo, ibid. 535 and *AE* 1933, 275, or the consul of A.D. 147, cf. Habicht (1959–1960) 112; cf. also notable votaries of the fraudulent Alexander of Abonuteichus, in Stein (1925) 259f.

26. Above, chap. 2.1 nn.45 and 71; in chap. 1.1 nn.48, 65, 67, and 72.

27. Above, n.5.

28. In Palestine, the inscription, "Isis the true!" in *AE* 1948 no. 145, or Robert (1955) 88, at Ephesus, the inscription consisting solely of the words, "Great is the name of the god! Great is the Holy! Great is the Good! Obedient to a dream." Cf. *POxy.* 1382 (second cent.), "as you stand there [in the Sarapis temple], say, 'One is Zeus Sarapis,'" discussed by E. Peterson (1926) 217f.; Marc. Diac., *Vita Porph.* 31: struck by a miracle, bystanders cry out, "Great is the god of the Christians! Great is the priest Porphyry!"; above, chap. 1.1 nn.70–72, 75, and 79; chap. 1.4 n.10; and below, chap. 2.3 n.54.

29. *IG* 4, 1².131 col. II (Epidaurus, third cent.) is the only instance I can recall from inscriptions, of a story being told, however briefly: ". . . to the Mother of the Gods: Maidens of memory, come down from heaven and, with me, hymn the Mother of the Gods. As she came wandering through the mountains . . ." (Zeus spied her, etc.).

30. In Pack (1965) nos. 455, Favorinus, *On Exile*; 1325, Musonius Rufus on infanticide; 2583, anon. second cent. frg. of only a dozen words containing some speculation about the gods (surely not to be asserted as a treatise On the Gods); a few scraps of aretalogy, some (as Pack indicates) perhaps rather from romances (add now West [1971] 96, on no. 2468); a third cent. B.C. Orphic text, no. 2464; some hymns, nos. 1933–1936 and 2481; thus in total, from over 3,000 items, we have the items just cited plus a scattering generally in nos. 2466–2494. For the popularity of individual authors, see above, chap. 1.1 n.41.

31. *Moral.* 263E–291C, 113 customs, the vast majority concerning religion: first, 266F (or 271F, etc.); second, 272D (or 275A, etc.); third, 274Af. (or 266C, etc.); fourth, 267D (or 271D, etc.); fifth, 279Cf. (or 281D, etc.); and sixth, 278Ff. (or 287B, etc.)— two or more examples for each mode of argument. The essay on Isiacism uses the same categories. For the first, cf. *Moral.* 356D or 359B; second, 357F, cf. also 675F–

676B, favorite line of argument for Plutarch; third, 375A; fourth, 358D; fifth, 362Af.; and sixth, 362Ef. In the first century, Cornutus, *Theol. gr. compendium*, makes abundant use of the first and second devices, e.g., in chapters 5, 6, 28, and 30.

32. A difficult text. I hope I present it correctly. See Merlat (1951) 383 on *CIL* 3.7756, with suggestions by von Domaszewski and Hirschfeld as well.

33. Above, chap. 1.1 nn.32-37.

34. *Timoleon* 26.1f; similar incidents similarly described, *Pericles* 6.1 and *Sertorius* 11.7-12.1, examples cited by Erbse (1952) 297; cf. Koets (1929) 59 on superstition and a solar eclipse, *Nicias* 23; ibid. 74 on *Cleomenes* 39; ibid. 32, the word superstition in a bad sense "explained by the everwidening chasm that separated the educated élite from the masses." In Lucian also, *Philops.* 9; but Latin illustrations are hard to find in our period. Otto (1909) 532-544 is superficial and looks only at earlier authors.

35. For a survey of testimonies to magic, see MacMullen (1966a) 100-108. The increase in superstition is generally sensed by modern students. P.R.L. Brown (1972) 122 doubts it. "Thus it is far from certain that there was any absolute increase in fear of sorcery or in sorcery practices in the Late Roman period"—but he offers nothing in support of his "thus." Further, Brown (1971) 82 dismisses the older, and "too often" the modern, view that the increase arose from the "democratization" of culture and "dilution of the ideas of an enlightened minority . . . intrusion into the upper classes" of lower class ideas. "To take issue with such a view would involve rewriting the social and religious history of the Roman world." This, he does not attempt. For the moment, we must be content with conventionally documented interpretations. For lead *defixiones*, besides the standard but old corpus of Audollent (1904), see more recently examples in Mouterde (1930-1931) 110f. and 118, from Beirut and Damascus; Wortmann (1968) 60, from Oxyrhynchus; Elderkin (1937) 384, from Athens; and D. M. Robinson (1953) 172, from Macedonia and Pisidian Antioch. For orators hexed, see Cic., *Brut.* 60.217, the consul of 76 B.C., and Liban., *Or.* 36, in Festugière (1959) 102 and 453f. Emperors resort to sorcery, MacMullen (1966a) 104 and further exploration in idem (1968) 82-95.

36. The summary of an unpublished text, *POxy.* 3008, in *POxy.* vol. 42 (1973) 30 n.1. Inquiry of one of the editors of the series, for more information, went unanswered. For the onset of the decline, one may choose (of course, somewhat arbitrarily) Sextus Empiricus, cf. MacMullen (1966a) 109-111 and idem (1972) 12-15; for the course of the decline, briefly, Nock (1926) xxiiif.

37. Ps.-Clem., *Homil.* 1.3 (*PG* 2.57), the fourth cent. edition of a third cent. document; dramatic date under Tiberius, 1.6 (*PG* 2.61); cf. the similar picture in Rufinus, *Vita S. Eugeniae* 3 (*PL* 22.1108f.), the supposed date being Severan; Tert., *Apol.* 47.5-7 (all schools invalidate each other) and 47.9, condemning mere cleverness, *ingenia*, cf. the contemporary texts in Min. Fel. 5.3 and Parassoglou (1976) 269, "dangerous περιεργία" banned by the emperor in A.D. 199. Foreshadowings of the mutual destruction of the schools are seen in passages of Plutarch, cf. Cherniss (1976) 371; and the condemnation of abstract thought—*curiositas*—by Christians can be traced from Tertullian on, in Labhardt (1960) 216-218. Add *CT* 9.16.4 (A.D. 357).

38. Const., *Or. ad sanctos* 9 (*PG* 20.1253 Bf. and 1256Af.). It is only for brevity's sake that I call these words Constantine's, without a question mark. They represent

in any case what could be asserted in the period with unembarrassed confidence. For a good discussion of the integrity of the source, see Baynes (1931) 48–54. For similar passages a couple of generations earlier, see MacMullen (1972) 13; later, many more.

39. The change in the status of philosophy and rational thought was so gradual, it had still to prevail universally as late as Julian's reign. Liban., *Or.* 16.47, comparing Plato and Pythagoras with the (Christian) wisdom of women and menials, and doing this before an open audience, proposes views that could have been written by Celsus, nearly two centuries earlier. Cf. Orig., *C. Cels.* 3.44. And there are figures like Synesius still to come.

40. Rehm (1958) 299–301 no. 496, discussed by Robert (1960a) 544f., the fragmentary reply indicating it was right cult that induced favor; at Stratonicea, Laumonier (1958) 275; at Cyrene, Robert (1940b) 11f., the indicative epithet for the priest being καλλιέτης, "who brought a good year"; idem (1946) 142f., the same epithet at Olbia and Rhodes and Lindos, that last yielding an inscription that Blinkenberg (1941) 882 dates to the second cent., Robert to the third.

41. Dio Chrysos., *Or.* 1.54, near Olympia.

42. Lucian, *Dea Syria* 28.

43. MacMullen (1976) 27 nn.14f.

44. Plin., *Paneg.* 31f.; cf. 80.4, Jupiter rules the world, barely condescending to lower his eyes to it.

3. How the Divine World Was Envisioned

1. Plut., *Moral.* 165C, 168A–C, 170E, cf. (in other essays) 26B and 1101D, offering (166Df.) the "true" view of the benevolent gods; and *deisidaemonia* can be avoided by an approach through philosophy (355C, in the essay on Isiacism). For modern assessment of these views of Plutarch, cf. Wey (1957) 141 n.444 and Koets (1929) 58f. and 68–80. For the connection between fear (of angry gods) and superstition in other authors, cf. Lucian, *Pro imag.* 7; Clem. Alex., *Strom.* 2.8.61 (*PG* 8.976) and 7.1.4 (*PG* 9.408A) and *Coh. ad gent.* 3.78 (*PG* 8.129), the rationalizing explanation (quoted in the text) lying in *Strom.* 7.4.20–25 (*PG* 9.429); similarly, in *Ep. ad Diognetum* 1.494B. Among Latin authors, clearly drawing on Greek, cf. Cic., *De nat. deor.* 1.117; Varro, in Aug., *Civ. dei* 6.9; Sen., *Ep.* 123.6; Lucr. 5.1161f. and other poets, in Heuten (1937) 3–5 and Dionigi (1976) 120. On *superstitio* in later (second-fourth cent.) texts, cf. Martroye (1915) 287–290; idem (1916) 106f.; and Momigliano (1977) 144–147.

2. References in order of citation: *Moral.* 369Af. and 417C, god is good; 23D; 24B; 20E–F; 996C and 355B (cf. 358E); 414E and 418E (cf. 381E), god must maintain remoteness. Terms like τὸ πρόσφορον (374E) and τὰ πρέποντα (383A) are opposed to τὸ βαρβαρικώτερον (418E, 358F), in describing divinity.

3. God is goodness, Dio Chrysos., *Or.* 32.15, cf. Paus. 8.36.5; beautiful, 12.59, cf. Celsus in Orig., *C. Cels.* 6.75, and Porph., *De abst.* 2.38, in Euseb., *Praep. ev.* 4.22 (172a); the allied reasoning, a form beautiful must be divine, a cliché, in, e.g., Lucian, *Alex.* 3 and Xen., *Ephes.* 1.2.7; gods delight in gifts from the good, Dio Chrysos., *Or.* 1.16 and 3.52; but need no statues or sacrifices, 31.15.

4. *De sacr.* 1f. and 4 (the poets misrepresent the gods as bribable), *Demonax* 11 and *Jup. conf.* 7; remoteness of deity, Max. Tyr. in Merlan (1967) 81, opposed by

Marc. Aurel. 2.11; for Lucian as hostile to anthropomorphizing in general, see Betz (1961) 27, and compare Hephaestus in *Jup. conf.* 8; ibid. on manacles, Prometheus, wounds, shackles, and idols melted, cf. *Prometheus* 1—these various indignities followed out in many dialogues, e.g., *Icaromenippus* or *Jup. trag.* Indignities to idols, *Jup. trag.* 7f. and *Gall.* 24; Egyptian animal gods, in *Concil. deor.* 10f. and *De sacr.* 14f.

5. Orig., *C. Cels.* 1.5: it is μὴ εὔλογον ... , says Celsus; the same word common in this work, and others like it, e.g., 1.32, εὔλογον, εὐλογώτερον; ἠλιθιώτατον and ἐμβροντήτον (5.39), ἄτοπον (8.49); in Justin, ἄλογον (1 *Apol.* 9); in Theoph., *Ad Autol.* 3.7, δεινὸν καὶ ἀθέμιτον; in Athenagoras, λῆρον καὶ γέλωτα (*Leg.* 21) or ἀπίθανον (20); in Aristides' *Apology*, γελοῖα καὶ μωρὰ καὶ ἀσεβῆ (8.4) or ἀνοία (9.5); in *Acta S. Apollonii* (ca. A.D. 185) 17, τίς ὁ λῆρος τῆς ἀπαιδευσίας; and pagans accuse Christians of μωρία, ἀπονοία, *insania*, *Acta S. Cononi* 4.6, *Acta SS. Agapae, Eirenae et Chionae* 6.2, and *Passio S. Irenaei* 3.4. For Christian writers drawing on pagan critics of paganism, for use against pagans, see chap. 2.1 n.56 and chap. 2.2 n.12; and below, n.9. Koets (1929) 39, use of Menander and Bion by Clem. and Theodoret (also Justin, cf. I *Apol.* 20); *Apol.* 12.6, using Seneca; Lact., *Div. inst.* 4.28, using Cic., *De nat. deor.* 2.28; for Xenophanes apparently underlying various writers, cf. Raabe (1893) in his notes passim, and Cardauns (1958) 53; for Plato used, too, cf. ibid. and Euseb., *Praep. ev.* 2.8 (76cf.); the debt to philosophers, e.g., to Plato, is stressed by Geffcken (1907) xvii and Chadwick (1965) xf. For the date of Heraclitus, see Buffière (1962) ix.

6. Philo, *De plant.* 130; Iren., *C. haer.* 3.25.3 (*PG* 7.968); Iambl., *De myst.* 1.5; Porphyry in Procl., *In Tim.* p. 208 Diehl; Apul., *De Plat.* 12, *nec ullius mali causa deo poterit adscribi*, the text accepted as genuine by Witt (1979) 384; Plot., *Enn.* 2.9.1; and τὸ δαιμόνιον "most benevolent," in Dexip. frg. 23, *FHG* 3.680 (note the setting).

7. Ps.-Apul., *De deo Socr.* 3.123 and 7.137; *De mundo* 397b and 398a-b; Apul., *De Plat.* 1, *ultramondanus, incorporeus*; Iambl., *De myst.* 1.5 and 1.20, even above rational knowledge, cf. Celsus in Merlan (1967) 81 and Andresen (1955) 159-162; Sext. Emp., *Adv. dogm.* 3.33, "all men have the same assumption in common about god, that he is a being blessed, indestructible and complete in happiness"; and, broadly, Geffcken (1907) 171 with refs. For the view that god takes thought only about himself, as the Stoics say, see Theoph., *Ad Autol.* 2.3, strongly opposed by Just., I *Apol.* 28 and Marc. Aurel. 2.11.

8. Ps.-Apul., *De deo Socr.* 12.145f.; Porph., *De abst.* 2.60; Philostr., *Ep. Apollon.* 26, the gods need no sacrifices, cf. other passages in Windisch (1920) 310f., Des Places (1969) 343, and Andresen (1955) 63; Sext. Emp., *Pyrr. hyp.* 162, ἀπαθὲς εἶναι τὸ θεῖον; Clem. Alex., *Excerpta Theodoti* 30f., and *Strom.* 2.18 (*PG* 8.1020B), ἀνενδεὲς ... τὸ θεῖον καὶ ἀπαθές; and Diog. Laert. 1.5 in the third cent., indignant at the idea of attributing to the gods πᾶν τὸ ἀνθρώπειον πάθος (early third cent.).

9. Shocked by Homer's tales, Plut., *Moral.* 20E, and Dio Chrysos., *Or.* 11.19, with more texts and discussion in Dreyer (1970) 45-47; the gods change, Arist., *Apol.* pp. 8f. Raabe, and Tat., *Ad Graec.* 21; but should not change, Ps.-Apul., *De deo Socr.* 12.146; for the fleshly indignities in which the gods are involved, see Heraclitus, *Quaest. homericae* 26.1; 30.1; and 69.1; Celsus in Orig., *C. Cels.* 5.14; Philodemus, *Piet.* 18.13f., 47.14, with other passages from that author in Geffcken (1907) xviiif., or, more thoroughly, pp. 11, 16-19, 39f., 46-48, 52f., 62-64, and 132 ed.

Gomperz, Philodemus being a writer of the first century B.C.; Varro, in Cardauns (1958) 53f. = Aug., *Civ. dei* 6.5; and Sext. Emp., *Adv. dogm.* 3.147. It is even seen as beneath their dignity that the gods should marry, cf. Seneca, above, chap. 1.1 at n.67, and Plin., *N.H.* 2.5.17. All of these notions being in common circulation, the Apologists make great capital of them, e.g. Athenagoras, *Leg.* 21f.; Theoph., *Ad Autol.* 1.9 and 3.8; Arist., *Apol.* 8.4, 9.5, and 10f.; Iren., *C. haer.* 1.4.4 (*PG* 7.485A-B) and 3.52.4; Clem. Alex., *Coh. ad gent.* 2.164 (*PG* 8.105); Tat., *Ad Graec.* 8; and among later writers, Min. Fel. 23.5; Lact., *Div. inst.* 1.16; Firm. Matern., *De errore profan. relig.* 2.1; Athanas., *C. gent.* 11f.; and Geffcken (1907) 204.

10. Isoc., *Busiris* 38, much pillaged by later writers; Sext. Emp., *Pyrr. hyp.* 159, and *Adv. dogm.* 3.193 (drawing on Xenophanes); Calcidius, *Comment.* 128; and Philostr., *Vita Apollon.* 5.14. Among Christian writers, see Clem. Alex., *Coh. ad gent.* 4.58.3 and 4.60.1f.; Theoph., *Ad Autol.* 1.9 and 2.8; Athenag., *Leg.* 20 and 30; Athanas., *C. gent.* 12 and 15; among Latin Apologists, Tert., *Apol.* 11.12, Min. Fel. 25.2f., and Lact., *Div. inst.* 1.9–11.

11. On divine grandeur: Sen., *Ep.* 41.4f., to be added to many similar texts in Bieler (1935–1936) 1.11 and passim. On menial roles *vel sim.*, Philodemus, *Piet.* 34; Sext. Emp., *Pyrr. hyp.* 157; Cic., *De nat. deor.* 1.38; Porph., *Philos. ex orac.*, in Euseb., *Praep. ev.* 5.9 (196bf.) and *Ep. ad Anebo.* 28 in Euseb., *Praep. ev.* 5.10 (197df.); Ps.-Aristot., *De mundo* 6. Among Christians, note Just., I *Apol.* 9; Arist., *Apol.* 10 p. 270 Raabe; Clem. Alex., *Coh. ad gent.* 2.199 (*PG* 8.113); Lact., *Div. inst.* 1.9; and Tert., *Apol.* 14.4.

12. Gods misshapen or freaks, hermaphrodite: Sen., in Aug., *Civ. dei* 6.10; Min. Fel. 23.5, cf. Athanas., *C. gent.* 22; Athenag., *Leg.* 20f., on deities with many breasts, one hundred hands, four eyes, etc.; as animals, in anti-Cleopatran passages of Horace, Propertius and Vergil, e.g., *Aen.* 8.698; Stat., *Silv.* 3.2.113; Juv. 15.1–8; and Apologists *de rigueur*.

13. Hdt. 2.172 underlies *Acta S. Apollonii* 17, perhaps Just. I *Apol.* 9, ἀτιμῶν σκευῶν, and Min. Fel. 22.4. For pagan ideas about idols of *materia vilissima*, cf. Sen., in Aug., *Civ. dei* 6.10; Varro, ibid. 4.31; Oenomaus, in Euseb., *Praep. ev.* 5.36; mice and birds at work on idols, Geffcken (1907) xx and Iren., *C. haer.* 3.52.4. For many other passages, see *Ep. ad Diognetum* 2.3f. and n. ad loc., in the edition of H. I. Marrou (Sources chrétiennes 33, 1951) 106 n.2.

14. Marrou 110 gives relevant passages from the Apologists; cf. Lucian, *De sacr.* 9; on human sacrifice, Tert., *Apol.* 9.2 and Euseb., *Praep. ev.* 4.17 (164c-d). A. Alföldi (1963) 33 n.7 cites many passages supporting his view that the practice was a fact in early Rome. SHA *Aurelian* 20.7, *cuiuslibet gentis captos*, must indicate human sacrifice in late Rome, in the view of the source.

15. The oracle, above, chap. 1.1 n.65; in Pack (1965) I count the Homer-papyri (not commentaries) dated second cent., third, third/fourth (but not first/second), in total over 330. In the Apologists, it is easier to find harsh scorn of Greek philosophers ("Constantinian" by anticipation, e.g., Tat., *Ad Graec.* 2f., or Theoph., *Ad Autol.* 2.4f.) than respect for them; or the competence of the audience in philosophy is self-consciously emphasized, by Just., I *Apol.* 14f., repeated address to ἐρασταὶ παιδείας and "philosophers," or Athenag., *Leg.* praef. This is not to call the Apologists philosophers themselves. Cf. Bardy (1948) 11 and 22f. on Theophilus's ignorance and ineptitude.

16. Menander, *De hymn.* 2 and 5, in Spengel, *Rhet. graeci* 3.333 and 337; hymns in Porph., *De imag.*, in Euseb., *Praep. ev.* 3.9 (100a-d)=Stob., *Ecl.* 1.2.23, which I quote in the text; Orig., *C. Cels.* 1.18; initiations reinterpreted, the Mithraic, according to Pallas, in Porph., *De abst.* 4.16; initiations in general, Proclus, *In Plat. Rempubl.* ed. Kroll 2.108, quoted by Pépin (1966) 262, and Plut., *De Daed. Plataeensibus*, in Euseb., *Praep. ev.* 3.1 (83cf.); Phrygian and others, in Hippolyt., *Ref.* 5.2-4, interpreted by the Naassenes; statues, Plut., *Moral.* 381Df.; rites, ibid. 368D.

17. Menander 5 p. 336 Spengel. On Hera=air, cf. Porph., *De imag.*, in Euseb., *Praep. ev.* 3.11 (108b), with more of the same for Demeter or other gods, 109f., e.g. (113b), "Cerberus has three heads because the upper positions of the sun are three—rising, noon and setting"; Heraclitus, *Quaest. Homericae* 15.3, Hera=air; similar equivalences in Philodemus, *Piet.* 11-22, in Bücheler (1865) 530f.

18. Sallust, *De diis et mundo* 4; Paus. 8.8.3.

19. I leave aside allegorical interpretation in Philo, Clement, Origen, and others; a large subject. Within paganism, it had its roots deepest in Stoicism, cf. Decharme (1904) 305-353 passim; Tate (1929) 40-43 and (1930) 1-7; Buffière xxxviiif.; and some applications of the methods are touched on above, chap. 2.2 n.31. On the division of theology into three strands of development, cf. Strabo 10.3.23 and Porph., in Euseb., *Praep. ev.* 4.1 (130a-d); and, in the Latin tradition, Tert., *Ad nat.* 2.1, going back to Varro, cf. Aug., *Civ. dei* 4.27 (and 6.5), in turn pointing to Scaevola, cos. 95 B.C., cf. Cardauns (1958) 36-39. On rejection of the art, cf. Sen., *De benef.* 1.3.9f., making harsh fun of it; also Dio Chrys., *Or.* 11.17f., and Philo of Byblos, his contemporary, who expressed suspicion of recent intemperate innovating through allegorizing in initiatory mysteries. Cf. Troiani (1974) 47f., on frg. I, 26; ibid. 13 and Barr (1974) 16, on Philo's dates; and compare Plut., *Moral.* 19Ef. *Contra*, in support of allegorizing, cf. Cornutus, *Theol. gr. compendium*, passim, Dreyer (1970) 67, and Plut., *Moral.* 355Bf., 366E, 368D, 374E, 381, 996C; his commentary on Hesiod, *Moral.*, Loeb ed. vol. 15, e.g., pp. 115 and 119; the art of allegorizing employed by Egyptian hierophants or theologues, cf. Merkelbach (1962) 57f.; Orig., *C. Cels.* 1.12; *Corp. herm.* 13.1; perhaps Ps.-Clem., *Homil.* 6.2.1, where the spokesman for Hellenism shows familiarity with the uses of allegory to hide great truths "from the unworthy and careless," cf. 4.24 (*PG* 2.173). Lucian, *Conc. deor.* 11, shows Zeus defending Egyptian monster-gods as allegories. On the chief practitioner of the art, Porphyry, cf. Bidez (1913) 32 and Pépin (1966) 261f., where Porphyry's aside, concerning allegorizing for the masses, is stressed (*De antro* 3 p. 56, cf. 36 p. 81).

20. Heraclitus, *Quaest. Homericae* 69.8.

21. Plato's demons: Arnim (1921) 62-67; Andresen (1955) 99; Wey (1957) 144; Chadwick (1965) xviif.; Merlan (1967) 34f.; Chadwick (1967) 165; and Den Boeft (1977) 3-15, 42, and 56.

22. Merlan (1967) 35 (Plotinus), 60 (Plutarch), and 72 (Apuleius); Brenk (1973) 2-8, on Plutarch, with such passages as *Moral.* 361Af., 415Af., and 944Cf. (and Stoic views in 277A); Apul., *De Plat.* 11; Celsus's views in Andresen (1955) 62, 99, and 103; those of the Ps.-Plut., *De fato=Moral.* 572f., of the early second cent., cf. DeLacy and Einarson in the Loeb edition (1959) vol. 7 pp. 303f.; Artemidorus's views in *Oneir.* 2.34, distinguishing the ethereal powers above the planetary, who are above the powers resident on earth, in oceans, etc., each of the three types divisible into νοητοί or αἰσθητοί; for Iamblichus's views, see *De myst.* 1.3-9, closely similar to the fore-

going, and at 2.3 distinguishing angels, archangels, demons, rulers, and spirits; at 5.14, also distinguishing the "material" from the "nonmaterial" gods. Less ordered is Porph., *De abst.* 2.37, and still less (with casual indication of *the* God, and beneath, gods plural, and then demons) the author of *Corp. herm.* 16.17. Euseb., *Praep. ev.* 4.5 (141b), summarizes paganism in general, ἡ Ἑλληνικὴ θεολογία: topmost, Divinity; next, gods; next, demons; next, heroes; next, evil demons, with Dio Chrys., *Or.* 3.54, closely approaching this schema of beings. For the seven spheres of Mithraism, alleged, see Cumont (1915b) 163f. or Gordon (1972) 97, comparing St. Paul, 2 Cor. 12.2, and Valentinianism. On the latter, cf. Sagnard (1948) 12 and 25-28 (on the Demiurge in the Seventh Heaven, the Savior in the Eighth, ibid. 27); Clem. Alex., *Excerpta Theodoti* 14 and passim, and *Strom.* 5.6. (*PG* 9.61Bf.) and 7.10 (*PG* 9.481A); Iren., *Demonstration of Apostolic Prediction* 9, trans. L. M. Froidevaux (1959) 44, seven heavens, but ten according to Marcus, Valentinus's disciple, or 365 according to Basilides, cf. idem, *C. haer.* 1.5.2 (*PG* 7.493B), 1.7 and 1.24.5 (*PG* 7.637A and 678B). For a parody, cf. ibid. 1.11.4 (*PG* 7.567 = Epiphanius, *Panarion* 32.6.7).

23. Homer: see the usage through any index verborum, but also Plut., *Moral.* 415A; usage in a specific literary genre, hymns, e.g., *Orphei hymni* 2 and passim, cf. the Index in Quandt's edition of the hymns; Heitsch (1963) 1.166 and 172, third cent. hymns to Sarapis and Tyche; Paus. 1.2.5; Celsus in Orig., *C. Cels.* 7.68; perhaps Dio Chrys., *Or.* 33.4, emended by Emperius; but pagans sometimes sharply distinguished between gods and demons, e.g., Plut., *Moral.* 418E, and Clem. Alex., *Coh. ad gent.* 2.38 (*PG* 8.121). The distinction is normal in the Apologists and other Christian writers, cf. the refs. in MacMullen (1968) 93 n.42, though concession is made through a special rank of Great Demons (or one word, μεγαλοδαίμονες, not in LSJ, but in Stephanus) in Clem. Alex., *Coh. ad gent.* 2.41.2 (*PG* 8.124, Apollo, even "Zeus himself"), and Euseb., *De laud. Const.* 9.4 (*PG* 20.1364B, Apollo, etc.).

24. Dio Chrysos., *Or.* 1.39-40 and 12.22, for illustration of Zeus *basileus*; of queens, cf., e.g., *AE* 1943, 243 (Isis) and *IGLS* 2964 (Juno); compare Hadrian's epigram to accompany a dedication to Zeus Casius, κοίρανος ἀνθρώπων κοιράνῳ ἀθανάτων, in Suidas s.v. Κάσιον ὄρος; Steinleitner (1913) 77, for Men (and Rhea Cybele as queen); Plut., *Moral.* 353B and 354F, Osiris *basileus*; Attis, in Chadwick (1952) 90-92, second cent.; Helios, in Ramsay (1895-1897) 1.308, A.D. 174/5. I omit the king of quite a separate realm, Pluto (e.g., *Plutoni regi magno* in *ILS* 4454).

25. Nock (1925) 97, in part drawing on Cumont (1920) 183f. (better, 185); but Cumont erred in supposing the Romans are imitated. The practice begins much earlier, and with other models. Cf. Seyrig (1970) 77f. and 83, offering the general danger of real life as the reason for arming gods who had nothing military about them—unarmed was weak. Further, idem (1971a) 88 and 95, cuirassed Palmyrene gods. For the Doliche relief, cf. Merlat (1951) 8f. For a broad discussion, cf. Kantorowicz (1961) 369-390, e.g., 379 (Mithra), 382 (coin styles generally), and 384 (Christ).

26. Tudor (1969-1976) 2.81 (date, post-A.D. 150), 111 (reliefs show uniforms), and 126 (gods with dragon-banners); at Siliana, Saturn and the Dioscuri, in Charles-Picard (1943-1945) 378, and idem (1954) 120f. and Fig. 11.

27. *CIL* 13.7399 and 8523f., *Sol invictus imp.*; 13.7571a, [*im*]*p. noster*; cf. 7815, *deo invict. regi* (all these from Germany); and so to Julian, *Or.* 4 to King Helios, e.g., 132f.; *CIL* 8.18219, *Iovi . . . deorum principi gubernatori omnium terrarumque*

rectori, Lambaesis in Tetrarchic times, cf. *Prosop. of the Later Rom. Empire* s.v. Flavius no. 21.

28. Iren., *C. haer.* 1.2.6 (*PG* 7.465) and 2.7.4 (*PG* 7.730A); cf. Tert., *Apol.* 24.4, on the *procurantes et praefecti et praesides* of God, and the Orphic verses cited by Clement, "around your flaming throne stand the angels, rendering much service, who see to it that all is performed for mortals," the passage brought to notice by Cumont (1915b) 173; Ael. Arist., *Or.* 43.18, quoted in Chadwick (1965) xix, and Celsus, in Orig., *C. Cels.* 8.35, divine "satraps and ministers" (cf. also 8.28); Euseb., *De laud. Const.* 1.2 (*PG* 20.1320A) and 3.6 (*PG* 20.1332A), God as King, so hailed by Constantine's troops; cf. Melito, *De bapt.* frg. 4, ed. O. Perler (1966) 232; *PGM* no. 3 lines 555f.; by Origen (not the Christian) in Porph., *Vita Plot.* 3.33, the treatise titled "The King Alone is Creator"; Plot., *Enn.* 3.56; and the Ps.-Arist., *De mundo* 398af., with date A.D. 100, in Lesky (1966) 574, and discussion of the hierarchy of powers in Maguire (1939) 150 and 155f.

29. Demons used for vengeance, in Plut., *Moral.* 277A, and Iambl., *De myst.* 2.7, cf. Origen agreeing, *C. Cels.* 8.3; used for magic, *PGM* passim, or Hopfner (1922) 243; used for presages and oracles, Apul., *De deo Socr.* 4.128 and 6.132; Schermann (1909) 12, magical papyri; and Plut., *Moral.* 418Df.

30. Ps.-Plut., *De fato*=*Moral.* 573A; Apul., *De deo Socr.* 6.13.2; cf. deities' oversight of specific functions in Plut., *Moral.* 377A and 758A.

31. Manilius, *Astr.* 4.696-700, each *gens* assigned by god to its own star. Note also Clem. Alex., *Strom.* 6.17.82f. (*PG* 9.389) and 7.2.52f. (*PG* 9.409) and *Coh. ad gent.* 2 (*PG* 8.121Bf.), saying that each people has its own angel but also its own pagan demon, the closeness of the pagan and Christian views emerging likewise in Orig., *C. Cels.* 1.24 and 5.25, where Origen and Celsus both believe a special supernatural being (and both use the word *demon*) is in charge of each people; again, in Min. Fel. 6, *dei municipes* and *ritus gentiles*, according to the pagan spokesman; each god hears us best in some certain place, according to Marcus Aurelius, and he addresses "all the *dei praesides* of all *populi*," *Ep. ad Front.* p. 47 Naber; Iambl., *De myst.* 5.25; and Symm., *Rel.* 3.8.

32. Barb (1963) 104, speaking of belief in spirits and demons of the period from Domitian to Ammianus (103), which in the fourth century "grew to mountainous height." He uses more highly colored wording, p. 108. For the abundant evidence of magic and superstition (let us call it that, loosely) in the same period, cf. MacMullen (1966a) chap. 3. As a specially relevant example of free borrowing by magic from regular cults, notice "liturgical acclamations as magical formulae," like "One is Zeus Sarapis," in E. Peterson (1926) 232.

33. Above, n.27; Maximin Daia's letter to Antioch, in Euseb., *H.E.* 9.7.7, Zeus credited as τοὺς πατρῴους ὑμῶν θεοὺς ... ῥυόμενος. Cf. Celsus, in Orig., *C. Cels.* 8.66 (perhaps only for the sake of argument?), imagining a great god, μέγας θεός, set over Helios or Athena; or compare Aoth, "before whom every god does obeisance and every demon shudders," a late text (A.D. 300-350), *PGM* 12 lines 115f.

34. Apul., *Met.* 9.14; for the inscription in which the erasure was detected by Cumont, see Vidman (1965) 391; cf. *Acta Pionii* 19.11, Zeus maker of all creation.

35. *CIL* 8.12493; cf. *IGR* 1.144=*IG* 14.1084, A.D. 146, from Rome, the same triad, and again in Robert (1958) 32 in the second cent. and at Stratonicea in the third cent., Laumonier (1958) 289; in Latin, examples in Malaise (1972) 195 n.13; and a

general collection in Vidman (1965) 390, the earliest known being of A.D. 142.

36. Arrian, speaking of broad practices of religion in the province, in *FGr.H.* 156F22; Ohlemutz (1940) 83, an inscription of the second cent. with far earlier antecedents; E. Peterson (1926) 228-231, amulet-inscriptions, the formula itself going back (p. 236) to Flavian times; *MAMA* 6.360 and Malaise (1972) 196.

37. Cumont (1923a) 67-69, citing Arrian on Bithynia, a Phrygian inscription, and an incident in Aurel. Vict. 39.13; also two inscriptions from Rome, p. 66. Cf. Helios Apollo in a Milesian inscription, Rehm (1958) no. 504, Tetrarchic, and the identification Heliodorus draws at the end of the *Aethiopica* (late Severan?) between Helios and Apollo.

38. For example, *PGM* 7 lines 529f. (third cent.); 4 lines 481f., Helios Mithras the Great; lines 640f., "O Sun, Lord of the sky and earth, god of gods" (but, lines 987f., Horos Harpocrates is addressed in closely similar terms); lines 1181f., "Helios, father of the Cosmos," etc., cf. 1997f.; 12 lines 115f. (A.D. 300-350), "the fiery god" is "master of the whole cosmos."

39. Cumont's long-popular interpretations are disposed of by Seyrig (1971b) 338-366. One of the latter's main points is the distinction between Sol simply being worshiped (e.g., p. 365), and being worshiped as Zeus (or as some king-god). On Aziz, see further Hanslik (1954) 180, the god identified with Apollo and put on coins of Gallus, A.D. 252.

40. Dothan (1968) 99-103; the gesture is often discussed, as for example by L'Orange (1935) 89. It appears on coins from Sept. Severus on, as characteristic of Sol, taken up simultaneously by the emperors (p. 95) along with the *globus* in the left hand (p. 97); but Brilliant (1963) 109 Fig. 3.13 and p. 110 shows the gesture earlier (Trajan), cf. also 149 and Fig. 3.111 (Commodus) and 209 (Sarapis in 216)— so Sol has no monopoly.

41. Kantorowicz (1963) 117-126; Fears (1977) 241, Trajanic and Hadrianic aurei; 257 and 267, Gordianic; and the same symbolism with Aurelian, ibid. 285, and with Licinius and Maximin Daia in A.D. 308, cf. Seston (1956) 185. Against Kantorowicz, I think Oriens means "the eastern regions" (sometimes personified as a woman, cf. *RIC* 5,1.290), not "on the rise" or "rising-ness." Against Fears, I think Sol giving the *globus* even to Jupiter indicates friendliness, not superiority, and is therefore not "a numismatic statement of solar monotheism" (p. 285f., cf. Saturn giving Jove his thunderbolt, p. 287—not Saturnian monotheism).

42. Sol *invictus* on second cent. coins, Kantorowicz (1963) 128; the survey carried into the third cent. by Storch (1968) 200-203; the epithet is applied also to Persephone, below, n.53. It is attached to Commodus and Severus on coins and to Caracalla and emperors thereafter in coins and inscriptions, L'Orange (1935) 97; first epigraphic appearance in A.D. 158, Seyrig (1971b) 366; Sol *invictus* on Gallienus's coins, in De Blois (1976) 115, that emperor being the first to wear Sol's jeweled diadem instead of the rayed crown, cf. Arnheim (1972) 25; Aurelian also wore the diadem, ibid. 26, cf. Aur. Vict., *Epit.* 35.3; and his coins proclaimed Sol *dominus imperi Romani*, cf. A. Alföldi (1967) 376=*CAH* 12 (1939) 193, and Redo (1973) 68. Notice, however, that (except for a period in the Serdica mint) Sol does not crowd out Mars and Jupiter from Aurelian's coinage (*RIC* passim). On Sol as *conservator Augusti* under Probus, see Fears (1977) 293. For Sol *invictus* on Tetrarchic coins, see M. R. Alföldi (1963) 197-199, there being one gold issue by Galerius, twelve by

Maximin Daia, and two by Constantine in A.D. 305-309; thereafter, fifteen by Constantine or his sons; cf. Fears (1977) 302, the last Sol-issues dating to 324 or 325, with A. Alföldi (1948) 55f. and Lafaurie (1966) 803. Seston (1956) 185 notes Licinius's coins honoring Sol in 308 and 317 (and see further, below n.53). The best-known Constantinian *Sol-Comes* issue is closely derived from an issue of Probus, cf. M. R. Alföldi (1963) 51. The cult offered by Constantine is termed, by L'Orange (1935) 101 and 107, a *Staatsreligion, staatlichen Sonnenkult*. Compare Merkelbach, below, n.46, or Latte (1960) 365, where Aurelian and others from the mid-third century are seen trying to establish a "Reichsreligion" through Solar cult, very much as Swoboda (1964) 72 can say that "Sol as *invictus* from Aurelian on stood at the center of the state cult." But no such descriptions seem justifiable.

43. *Paneg. vet.* 9(12).2.5, on the *dii minores*, the orator ending, 9(12).26.1, with an invocation to "the supreme creator of things, *summus rerum sator*, whose names are as many as the tongues of peoples."

44. SHA *Elagabalus* 7.4; for the coins, cf. *CAH* 12 (1939) 54 n.2; the main sources are Herodian 5.5.6-5.6.8 and Dio 80.11-13, Dio expressing outrage at the subordination of Zeus himself. Ephemeral traces of Elagabalus's efforts are canvassed by Dupont-Sommer and Robert (1964) 79f.

45. Zos. 1.61 and SHA *Aurelian* 25.4 and 31.7-9 seem in conflict. Homo (1904) 184-189 refers to the Roman temple attested in the Regionaries, etc., and the *pontifices dei Solis* in *CIL* 6.2151, etc. For a short and more sober account, see Mattingly in *CAH* 12 (1939) 309. On the building at Palmyra, cf. Seyrig (1971) 110f.: Belus is actually Bel, not a solar deity at all. Note *CIL* 11.6308 (Pisaurum), *Herculi Aug. consorti d. n. Aureliani*, at odds with any picture of solar monotheism.

46. Grant (1968) 173 speaks of the moment around A.D. 309. Cf. Merkelbach (1962) 234: "The last stage of ancient paganism is the syncretistic Helios cult. In the 3rd cent. it was for long periods the official religion of the Roman state; all other religions were to be subsumed in that of Helios." The statement is in accord with the importance most scholars attribute to the cult.

47. Plut., *Moral.* 413C; Firm. Matern., *Math.* 1.10.14, writing in the 330s, quoting almost verbatim from Cic., *Rep.* 6.17; and Porphyry, *Isagoge* p. 181 and in Servius, *ad Ecl.* 5.66, "according to Porphyry's book that he called *The Sun*, the *potestas* of Apollo is triple, and it is the same being that is the Sun among the gods, Liber [Dionysus] on earth, Apollo in the lower regions" (quoted again, more or less, in Macrob. 1.17.5f.). Some of these passages are adduced by Cumont (1913) 452, 453 n.1, and 461f. n.3. I am not clear about the meaning of Pantheus (*CIL* 8.12493, Zeus Helios Pantheus Sarapis; 9.3145, Liber Pantheus; etc.). Cf. Latte (1960) 334.

48. Dio Chrysos., *Or.* 31.11, cf. the preceding note, for Porphyry, and Seneca, *De benef.* 4.8.1-3 and *Nat. quaest.* 2.45, and Varro earlier still, in the synopsis of Aug., *Civ. dei* 4.11: *Si omnes dii deaeque sit unus Jupiter, sive sint, ut quidam volunt, omnia ista partes eius sive virtutes eius, sicut eis videtur quibus eum placet esse mundi animum*, etc. Compare the Ps.-Aristot., *De mundo* 401a, "Being One, you [god] are of many names, being called by all the conditions, πάθεσιν, which you have created"—Zeus, with many epithets, etc. etc., in a long, hymnlike section. Strohm (1952) 169 notices the literary connections.

49. Sen., *De benef.* 4.8.3, concluding, *omnia eiusdem dei nomina sunt varie utentis sua potestate*; and Plut., *Moral.* 366C, αὐχμοῦ δύναμις . . . ἀινίτεττai, and

367C, on Dionysus, Hercules, Ammon, Demeter, etc. His use of *dynamis* as "god" in the Stoic sense is common, cf. 375B or Nock (1926) liif. and n.62. On *ainigmata* as a means of reading deeper truths into myths, see above, nn.16–19.

50. Macrob. 1.18.18–20; for the date of Labeo, quite uncertain, see Bardon (1956) 264. On the oracle's philosophizing, see above, chap. 1.1 at nn.53 and 62–65.

51. Alex. Rhet. in L. Spengel, *Rhet. graeci* 3 pp. 4f.=C. Walz 9 pp. 337f., the form of praise—"worshipped in all lands," *vel sim.*—a cliché, e.g. in *SIG*³ 867. Cf. Sext. Emp., *Pyrr. hyp.* 3.219, "in actuality," i.e., among οἱ κατὰ τὸν βίον, "some people say there is one god, some, many gods that differ also in shape."

52. *Philos.* 17(1).5=11.5. Eusebius, *De laud. Const.* 1.3 (*PG* 20.1321) says the same, just as emphatically; but from him, the accuracy of the statement is very suspect.

53. Above, n.41 *ad fin.*; on Sol's gesture, n.40; on *invictus* applied to Persephone, see Flusser (1975) 13f., apparently Tetrarchic. Notice also Mars, Mercury, and Sarapis, all *invictus*, in *RIC* 5, 1, p. 305, *CIL* 9.425 and *AE* 1968 no. 232, and Μᾶ ἀνείκητος (Cybele) in Pergamon, Ohlemutz (1940) 185. On *aeternus*, see Cumont (1888) 185, arguing that, because 10 of 21 known uses of the epithet are post-100, all must be (!)—repeated, idem in *RE* s.v. Aeternus (1894) col. 696 and idem (1929) 268, cf. further *DE* s.v. Aeternus (1895) 320: the adjective is restricted to sky deities, Diana (*CIL* 3.6161), Caelus, etc. For *dominus*, see above, n.42—in Greek, κύριος, e.g., "Zeus, Lord" being "widespread" in the later Empire, Robert (1950) 67f., speaking of inscriptions; likewise in papyri, e.g., *POxy.* 1678 (third cent.), prayers to "the Lord God," the editors comparing 1680 and 1773 (both Tetrarchic), and 2984, "Lord Sarapis" (Severan). For local supreme gods, see Ammon among Egyptians, Plut., *Moral.* 354D, "who they think is the whole"; Men in Lydia, "the one god in the heavens, great *dynamis* of the undying god," "the one and only," in Herrmann and Polatkan (1969) 51f., second half of the third cent.; and a variety of hyperbolic phrases in magical papyri or invocations in *PGM* passim; Schermann (1909) 6f., 9 and passim; Keil (1939) 119, "thou, Artemis, greatest name among the gods!" (Ephesus); and Nilsson (1963) 112f. For deities called ὕψιστος, "highest," cf. Poland (1909) 179 on Zeus and his guild in Miletus and Sabazius in Thrace; Robert (1968) 594 on the Milesian guild (but Robert is cautious about a Judaizing element, here, and notes the god's priest also worships Sarapis and Apollo); Simon (1972) 376 showing Zeus the usual recipient of the title "highest," which (384) is translated *summus* in the prayer of Licinius's troops; but (376) Attis also is "highest," cf. Cumont (1929) 59 and 227 n.57 (A.D. 370); other gods also, *MAMA* 5.211=*IGR* 4.542 (Phrygia) and E. Peterson (1926) 211. And finally, among the Tetrarchs, Sol can be "Guardian" of Galerius (above, n.42) without challenging the tenets of the Jovian dynasty.

54. MacMullen (1962) 379f.; but one could add a great deal from Greek inscriptions, as can be sensed from refs. in the preceding note. On acclamations, see chap. 2.2, n.28, or E. Peterson (1926) passim, e.g., 205, 241, and 254 (and among the several hundred inscriptions he gathers, barely a handful pre-date A.D. 300, unless they are also Christian).

55. Noticed by Rose (1924) 61, in Plutarch "as with so many Greek writers," the indiscriminate use of "the divine" or "gods"; cf. also Beaujeu (1955) 1.335; and add two significant texts: *CIG* 5041 (Nubia, second cent.), "venerate divinity, sacrifice to

all the gods!" (line 2); and Max. Tyr., *Philos.* 4(34).6, "Zeus and the gods, fathers and makers of land and sea . . ." (note the plurals, compared to n.52, above). For usage in Latin, see Perret (1949) 799 and Cardauns (1958) 60.

56. *IGR* 3.903, cf. *IG* 4, 1².499, Artemis Hecate (second cent.), or the triple Mother Atemis Anaitis, taken as Ephesian Artemis and Persian Anahita by Anderson (1913) 272, but Buckler (1914-1916) 177 gives it as Atemis; for Ma = Artemis or Ma = Cybele, cf. *RE* s.v. Ma (A. Hartmann, 1928) col. 89; Cybele = Anaitis on coins in Robert (1967) 74f.; Fishwick (1967) 145 on *CIL* 9.3146, showing "the cult image of Bellona actually stood in the temple of Magna Mater" at Corfinium; and, at Baalbek, Cybele portrayed as Atargatis, in Graillot (1912) 190. So Cybele is rightly called πολυώνυ-μος Μήτηρ sometimes, cf. *Orph. hymn.* 27 line 4 or Vermaseren (1977) 81.

57. Apul., *Met.* 11.2, cf. 11.5 where the goddess calls herself by an endless number of names, Proserpina, Cybele, Venus, etc.; Proserpina called "polyonymous" and "the all-regal goddess," *CIG* 2415. Again, note the late *defixio* in Wünsch (1909) 42, dated ca. A.D. 400, p. 45; Cybele "polyonymous," see the preceding note, and Prothyraia, too, *Orph. hymn.* 2; Isis polyonymous in fact or by name (or μυριώνυμος) in *CIL* 3.4017; Plut., *Moral.* 372E; Jerphanion and Jalabert (1908) 472; Vidman (1969) 14, 166, 177, 235, and 280; Witt (1971) 112 and 121; *POxy.* 675; and Bernand (1969) 2.150, 167 and elsewhere. Compare Selene "polyonymous" in *IG* 4,1².422, or the third cent. hymn to Tyche in Heitsch (1961-1964) 2nd ed., vol. 1, beginning, "O goddess of many colors, of changing shapes, winged of foot . . . , whether we call you Clotho the Dark or Necessity," etc. On Zeus polyonymous, cf. Cook (1914-1940) 3,1.945; above, n.48; and Celsus in Orig., *C. Cels.* 5.41 and 45, "it makes no difference whether we call Zeus the Most High or Zen or Adonaios or Sabaoth or, as the Egyptians, Ammon, or the Scythians, Papios."

58. *POxy.* 1380 lines 20f., 72f., 78f., 96f., 113, and Rome and Italy in lines 83 and 109; attributes and deeds, e.g., lines 181-184; similar long lists of titles or qualities in Hermes hailed by Poimandres, cf. Schermann (1909) 6f.; Cybele's titles or qualities in *Orph. hymn.* 14 and 27, or more loosely in Graillot (1912) 196-208; and above, chap. 1.1 nn.63-75.

59. Soc., *H.E.* 3.23 (*PG* 67.204); Caputo (1977) 119, Lepcis, cf. Eros = Liber/Apollo, *IRT* 299.

60. Imhoof-Blumer (1911) 18 (Alexandrian coins of Domitian's reign), 15 (of Severus's reign), 13 (the coins almost all belong to the second/third cent.); and examples, 13-23 passim.

61. Merlat (1951) 166.

62. Mocsy (1974) 254, speaking of several hundred examples known, peaking late, "a pantheistic synthesis of the gods most worshiped toward the middle of the 3rd cent."; and Tudor (1969-1976) 2.81 and 111, dated to after A.D. 150; random, irrelevant symbols added by artists, p. 155. For other kinds of document, which I know only casually, see Levi (1944) 271-313, esp. 306, and Nilsson (1945b) 1-6, on wildly complicated Aion/Kronos symbolism; Charles-Picard (1954) 120-124 and LeGlay (1966) 47 on Saturn reliefs in Africa, the latter speaking of "surcharge décorative . . . décoration somptueuse . . . typique de l'époque sévérienne"; and Eitrem (1939) 59 on magical gem reliefs.

63. Toynbee (1944) 153, cited by Nock (1946) 150 n.42. He cites also Jahn, who draws on undated sarcophagi but, before and after, speaks of Pompeian painting; so

clearly Jahn means sarcophagi of the Empire in general; also Küster cited, *Die Schlange* . . . (1913) 83, who shows that he is speaking of "the Hellenistic-Roman period" (whatever *that* means); also Bonner cited, where the artist being described is said not to understand his own symbols, but belongs to the late fourth/early fifth cent.; also Nock cited by Nock himself, the earlier (1929) article referring to a single coin of 87 B.C. All five of Nock's references, spread over 600 years, or irrelevant, thus prove nothing. He goes on to say, (1946) 151, "analogies from the Middle Ages may be misleading. In the Middle Ages elaboration was individual. . . ." *All* art from *all* Europe over a *millennium*!!

64. SHA *Alex. Sev.* 29.2—highly doubtful. Dodds (1965) 107 cites it without question (and as "Lampridius"!) and it is offered as illustration of syncretism by older writers like Eitrem (1939) 58 or more recent like Frédouille (1972) 339.

65. Vermaseren (1956–1960) 1.333 no. 276; Witt (1975) 486; Brommer (1973) 34f.; Hatt (1978) 284, with instances of other Gallic deities; Forrer (1915) 48; Vučković-Todorović (1964–1965) 179 and 182, at Egeta, Severan; Lane (1971–1978) 4.62; C. Picard (1922) 49; and Merlin (1908) 13f. and 23. Further examples in G. C. Picard (1972) 48f.; Vermaseren (1977) 37; Collins-Clinton (1977) 38f.; Ohlemutz (1940) 83; and LeGlay (1976) 367f. Compare the altars to Hermes, Helios, Asclepius, Heracles, and Zeus in the Demeter sanctuary at Pergamon, Ohlemutz (1940) 218f. And examples could be multiplied further.

66. Plut., *Moral.* 364E; *CIL* 3.686=Vermaseren (1956–1960) 2.382 no. 2343; Merlat (1951) 155 and 157f.; *CIL* 14.123; similar instances of private individuals honoring one deity through another, e.g. *CIG* 3159 or Fontrier (1883) 505. Compare the instances of persons who are priests of more than one god: Laumonier (1958) 278 (late Severan, Caria), *IGR* 4.739 (post-A.D. 200, Phrygia); *AE* 1969/1970 no. 116 (A.D. 330s, Formiae); *CIL* 9.6099 (Brundisium); *CIL* 14.429 (second cent., Ostia); 9.1153 (late first cent., Aeclanum); other examples in F. Dunand (1972–1973) 3.185 n.2, all in Greece and the isles. Or compare dedications to one god by priests of another, e.g., Merlat (1951) 200, to Sol by a Dolichenus priest; *CIL* 6.31181 (later second cent., Rome); 14.375f. (mid-second cent., Ostia); 12.2215 (Grenoble); 3.973 (Apulum) and 78681; 8.24522; and Robert (1955) 100 (third cent., Ephesus).

67. Vermaseren (1977) 36; *IG* 4, 1². p. xxxviii, A.D. 296; *CIL* 8.24519; above, the preceding note, and chap. 1.1 n.73 and chap. 1.2 n.67.

68. *AE* 1975 no. 722, *Liberi et Liberae secundum interpr[etati]onem s[acr?]orum So[lis?] in tabula[m scriben]dum curavit*; Robert (1955) 240; *CIL* 6.659; Schwertheim (1975) 357; *ILS* 3831, A.D. 261, Mauretania; *CIG* 3538, A.D. 170; and above, n.59, Rhodes.

69. Vidman (1965) 393, on the miniature icons as guests, to which compare parallels in Cybele cult, Graillot (1912) 204 n.10 (though his source, Mionnet, is not very clear). On the feast calendar, see Teixidor (1977) 135.

70. MacMullen (1968) 81–96, esp. 86.

71. Nock (1958a) 294, rightly sees the presence of visitor gods in another's temple as no sign of syncretism, but the reverse: the visitors retain their individuality; and Robert (1969) 290 rightly characterizes W. M. Ramsay's views as "hautement fantaisiste," where Ramsay attempts to "syncretize" all gods into each other by endless equivalences. Both Robert and Nock (and I) would not accept some of the views of Toutain (1907–1920) 1, 2.230–236.

4. Conversion

1. Iren., *C. haer.* 1.13.1 and 7 (*PG* 7.577 and 592), Marcus "possesses the greatest *dynamis*"; Marc. Diac., *Vita Porph.* 21, A.D. 396, cf. 31 for a similar cause and effect; Euseb., *Mart. Pal.* 4.15 (long recension. ed. G. Bardy, Sources chrétiennes no. 55 p. 136); Greg. Nyss., *Vita S. Gregorii* (*PG* 46.918); Tert., *Apol.* 23.18; and *Acta Phileae* 4.3, p. 349 Musurillo. Musurillo (1972) xlvii assigns the Greek text to a date "not long after the actual martyrdom" of A.D. 306, i.e. (p. lxxi) 320–350, and Emmett and Pickering (1975) 99f. defend its historicity. The Greek text, p. 335 Musurillo, shows Phileas assuming the governor will accept the logic of belief based on miracles. For passages showing similar reasoning—because miracles have been wrought, therefore people did believe, or one should believe—see, e.g., Acts 8.16; *Acta Petri et Pauli* 32–34 pp. 193f. Lipsius, dated in the second cent. by James (1924) 304f.; Orig., *C. Cels.* 1.46, converts would not have been made without miracles, cf. 1.2, 2.52, 3.3, and 8.45; Iren., *C. haer.* 2.30.7 (*PG* 7.820A) and 2.31.2 (*PG* 7.824); Hippol., *Ref.* 4.42; Theoph., *Ad Autol.* 1.13; Just., I *Apol.* 19 and *Dial.* 7.3, 11.4, and 69.6; Hierocles in Euseb., *Treatise on the Life of Apollonius* 2; Lact., *De mort. persecut.* 2.5; Euseb., *H.E.* 1.13.1; 2.1.7; 2.1.11; 2.2.2; 2.14.5; 5.15.17; 6.5.6; and 9.1.9; *Demonstr. ev.* 3.7 (*PG* 22.244), 3.5 (22.221) and 3.7 (22.244); Ps.-Clem., *Homil.* 2.25 (*PG* 2.93); and on exorcism, above, pp. 50f.

2. Iambl., *Vita Pythag.*, 28.143; Marcus Aurelius, *Med.* 12.28; and Plut., *Moral.* 434D-F. Compare the inscription from the early Empire in Robert (1939) 201, to Augustus "demi-god, manifest through his efficacy," ἐπιφανεῖ ἥρῳ ἀπὸ τῆς ἐρ-γασίας; the inscription from the late Empire, *CIL* 3.13132 (A.D. 312, Arycanda), "the gods revealed in deeds"; Philostr., *Heroikos* passim, as Eitrem (1929) 10 points out; or Eunap., *Vit. soph.* 458, where Iamblichus's disciples see "the manifest proofs . . . and believed everything."

3. *Moral.* 360C; cf. 1126C-E; and among Christian writers, the *Ep. ad Diog.* 7.8f.; Clem. Alex., *Strom.* 6.18.22f. (*PG* 9.400f.); Orig., *C. Cels.* 1.67; *Acta S. Pionii* 13.4f.; Euseb., *H.E.* 10.4.16f. and *De laud. Const.* 16.9 and 11 (*PG* 20.1427f.).

4. Apul., *Met.* 11.15, the *irreligiosi* will now be convinced they are wrong, see-ing Lucius relieved of his sufferings; Celsus, in Orig., *C. Cels.* 2.20 (particularly explicit); Maximin Daia, in Euseb., *H.E.* 9.7.4, Tyre is happy because the gods dwell there; pagans as reported ibid. 9.1.8; Symm., *Rel.* 3.8; and Christians like Origen, *C. Cels.* 1.68, cf. 2.48, or Eusebius, *Praep. ev.* 4.16 (162c) and *H.E.* 9.8.14.

5. Philostr., *Vita Apollon.* 6.10; Porph., *Ad Marc.* 14, love of the flesh leads to love of money, and so to injustice, but love of god leads away from the flesh; Tat. 21.1–6=Euseb., *H.E.* 4.16.8, the false philosopher is a glutton; Iren., *C. haer.* 1.24.2 (*PG* 7.675), followers of Saturninus eat no meat, "by pretended abstinence of this sort leading many astray"; and the debate in Euseb., *Treatise on the Life of Apol-lonius* 5 and 29, no real prophet takes money, cf. above, chap. 1.3 n.36 and Euseb., *Demonstr. ev.* 3.6 (*PG* 22.224A), with the allied and more common reasoning that a true philosopher or prophet lives simply, e.g., in Clem. Alex., *Strom.* 3.5.35f. (*PG* 8.1148), Hippol., *Ref.* 9.7, and Irenaeus and Apollonius (not of Tyana) in Euseb., *H.E.* 5.7.5 and 5.18.4.

6. Ael. Arist., *Or.* 46, II pp. 399–406 Dindorf. As consensus settled on these persons not being Christians, the passage dropped out of notice. It is last seen, so to

speak, in Boulanger (1923) 249–265, esp. 256f. On the type of itinerant and street-corner philosopher, see MacMullen (1966a) 59f. and notes.

7. Reynaud et al. (1975) 57f., the text dated (p. 61) to the second half of the second cent., the deceased a "professeur ou philosophe," possibly (?) crypto-Christian (pp. 72 and 74). But Christianity I think never presented itself as a *regional* faith.

8. *Poimandres, Corp. Herm.* 1.27f.

9. For Jewish missionaries, cf. Val. Max. 1.3.3, ". . . who attempted to infect Roman ways with the worship of Jupiter Sabazios" in 140 B.C.; and Just., *Dial.* 17 = Euseb., *H.E.* 4.18.6.

10. Lucian, *Alex.* 10, 15, and esp. 24 and 36.

11. Euseb., *Praep. ev.* 4.2 (133b), speaking of that aspect of religion he calls *politikon*, including both city centers and their territories (130b); cf. the votary of Bes (who had a famous oracle), in a casual inscription at Abydos, claiming that the god is "testified to in all the civilized world," in Cumont (1929) 233 n.9; for that phrase, a cliché, chap. 2.3 n.51; and advertising on stelae, chap. 1.1 n.67, and chap. 1.2 nn.32, 64f., and 69–72.

12. Graillot (1912) 312f. gathers the refs. on Cybele beggars; Tert., *Apol.* 13.6, says that (pagan) "religion goes the rounds of the cafés, begging"; Val. Max. 7.3.8 describes an Isiac beggar in Italy and Greece; and Fossey (1897) 60 reports an odd inscription set up by a "servant of the Syrian Goddess," "sent by his Mistress Atargatis" to Hierapolis and back twenty times, "filling his satchel"; but there is nothing to show that he begged *for* her, i.e., that he undertook "quêtes faites au profit de la déesse" (p. 61). Other allegations of evangelizing are easy to find but unsupported, e.g., in Cumont (1929) 81, Festugière (1949) 231, Mocsy (1974) 255, or Krill (1978) 40.

13. The multiple priest in Becatti (1954) 67 and Vermaseren (1956–1960) 1.127 and 131, nos. 255 (A.D. 162) and 269; the Hierocaesarean priest in Robert (1948b) 53; a temple to Apollo Belenus built *ex responso antistis* in Prieur (1968) 174; and perhaps *ILS* 3332, to Ops "by order of the priests"—of whose cult, however, is not specified. So that last inscription perhaps belongs in the category illustrated in chap. 2.2 at n.24.

14. I. Toth (1971) 24: Dolichenus priests in 60+ out of 400 texts, cf. for Mithra, 40 out of 2000.

15. Merlat (1951) 72f. and others before him date the inscription to the Tetrarchy; but I am better persuaded by Fitz (1959) 241, on *CIL* 3.3342f., and Mocsy (1974) 394 n.187. The Dolichenus priests were esp. active in imperial cult and prayers for the throne, cf. I. Toth (1971) 27 and Angyal (1971) 17.

16. *CIL* 3.14445 and 7760.

17. On temple funds, cf. above, chap. 1.2 n.34; also *IG* 4, 1².612, "the holy city of Epidaurus" erects a statue of the emperor "from the god's monies." Eastern origin of "the great majority" of priests: I. Toth (1971) 25; but arguments ibid. that they came actually from around Doliche itself seem to me weak.

18. Malaise (1972) 73f.; Porph., *De abst.* 4.9—but cf. fake Egyptian (hieroglyphic) inscriptions on statues in Rome, Italy and elsewhere in the West, in Tran Tam Tinh (1971) 7.

19. Lucian, *Conc. deor.* 9, Mithra "not speaking Greek" (=Persian? Latin? merely a comic touch?); Epiphanius, *Panarion haer.* 51.22.11; Fraser (1960) 65,

Locrian "as a ritual language," cf. Merkelbach (1973) 49f. on *IG* 10, 2.255, a testimonium to the god's powers from the Sarapeum in Thessalonica in Locrian; and Serv., *ad Georg.* 2.394, Greeks and Romans may use their own language for hymns, e.g., to Liber=Dionysus; but not to Cybele.

20. *CIL* 3.7728, *sacerdos creatus a Palmyrenis, domo Macedonia et adventor huius templi.*

21. At year's start: Tert., *De corona* 12. At Lambaesis, the two kinds of vow were next door to each other, cf. the Capitolium there attested, in LeGlay (1971) 125. Capitolia resembled that at Rome, cf. Wissowa (1912) 41. To the list of Capitolia in Toutain (1907-1920) 1,1.184f. or *DE* s.v. Capitolium 93-95, other examples could now be adduced from archaeology or epigraphy, e.g., Jobst (1976) 33-52 passim or *AE* 1925 no. 30 and 1926 no. 26.

22. *BGU* 362 section V. Wilcken (1885) 462 suggested that "ancestral" described Jupiter for Egyptians post-212; further, Jouguet (1911) 402f. For Caracalla's edict, see *PGiess.* 40 lines 309f. as restored (not with certainty) by Oliver (1978) 405.

23. Laumonier (1958) 278.

24. *CIL* 13.7281, A.D. 236, restoration of the Mons Vaticanus by the local *hastiferi*; 13.1751 and 7281, Lyon.

25. Ambros., *Ep. primae classis* 18.30 (*PL* 16.980), *simulato Almonis in flumine lavat Cybele*; C. Picard (1922) 58, Castalia at Antioch and Claros, as at Delphi; cf. the possible imitating at Lyon of the triangular temenos of the Ostian Phrygianum, Vermaseren (1977) 61. On *canopus* as a generic term, cf. Malaise (1972) 107, on *CIL* 9.1685; on a Sarapis-statue at Rome "like that in the Canopus-temple," *IG* 14.1030.

26. Robert (1965) 124 shows copies of old, famous icons planted in Marseilles, etc. (see Strabo 4.1.4); and Malaise (1972) 110 notes Isiac icons in Portus, on true Egyptian models.

27. *CIL* 13.7317; Graillot (1912) 123 n.5 on *CIL* 14.324; cf. *IG* 14.1084, decree of hymners of Sarapis dated by both Roman and Egyptian calendar, "no doubt exactly as if in an Egyptian temple," says Weber (1911) 16.

28. Robert (1960b) 342 points out that, at one time, 32 of 36 hymnodes are Roman citizens.

29. Toutain (1907-1920) 1, 1.249f.; on the Syrian shrine on the Janiculum, cf. Graeve (1972) 322-331 on the building and 334 on the image, and Goodhue (1975) 65f. pointing out eccentricities in the plan, Roman mixed with Syrian.

30. Malaise (1972) 133, 136, and 139 on Isiacism; Bruhl (1953) 276, 285, and 288f. (somewhat confused discussion, and basing too much on *IGR* 1.637); on Saturn, Merlin (1910) 38, noting the assimilation of a local ba'al to Saturn by the second cent.; further, Charles-Picard (1954) 163; Bénabou (1976) 373; and LeGlay (1966) 70, 73, 86, and 89. These scholars also note regional variations, not only chronological, in the susceptibility of Saturn worship to external influences. For other variations regionally, see Edelstein and Edelstein (1945) 2.189 on cult rules of Asclepius, and 75f. on variations in Asclepius's story. For another instance of cult practices changing over time, see Duthoy (1969) 88, 93 n.6, 96 n.7, and 102f. n.7, on the clearly marked phases of Cybele worship.

31. The variations are most compendiously surveyed by Beskow (1978) 9-12; further, Francis, in Cumont (1975) 154f.; Cumont (1975) 199-203, giving forced arguments on behalf of the seven grades; Porph., *De abst.* 4.16, on women Mith-

raists, with *CIL* 14.69; 10.1591, if it is Mithraic itself, as assumed by Vermaseren (1956–1960) 1.104 no. 177; *CIL* 13.7958 = Vermaseren (1956–1960) 2.54 no. 1034; further examples of women votaries Procrusteanly rejected, idem (1956–1960) 1.254 no. 696 and 1.256 no. 705, with nos. 1463 and 1952 (perhaps not Mithraic): idem (1956–1960) 2.310 no. 2065; Toutain (1907–1920) 1,2.122f. and Schwertheim (1979) 35, on cult-relief variation, and 26, on Mithra Mercurius; chap. 2.3 n.65 on Mithra's *synnaoi.*

32. In Aug., *Civ. dei* 6.11; cf. Firm. Matern., *De errore profan. relig.* 16.1, reporting confusions in Minerva or Liber cult.

33. Plut., *Moral.* 352A, 355F, and 356Af.; cf. Lucian, *Dea Syria* 7, and Firm. Matern., *De errore profan. relig.* 1.2, on Osiris's various meanings; on Cybele, the contradictions reviewed by Vermaseren (1977) 88–92 and 111f.

34. Rehm (1958) 301.

35. Menander Rhet., *Epideictica* 8 p. 342 Spengel, *Rhet. graeci.* Compare the wording in Firm. Matern., *Math.* 1.1.4, speaking evidently of writers on religion generally, irresponsibly inventive; and note the sense of uncontrolled profusion of beliefs in Alex. Rhet., in Walz, *Rhet.* vol. 9 p. 337, on Heracles legends, etc.

36. Imperial monies to temples or cults, e.g., at Teos by Hadrian, in Robert (1946b) 89; at Didyma by Trajan, in Haussoullier (1902) 154f. and 281; at Aezani by Hadrian, in *CIL* 3.355 = *OGIS*² 502; at Pergamon by the same emperor, but to hymnodes of the imperial cult, *CIG* 3148 lines 33f., in Keil (1908) 104 n.9; at Baalbek by Trajan and Caracalla, in Rey-Coquais (1967) 38; at Magliano, Tuscany, by Hadrian, *AE* 1946 no. 222; at Puteoli by Pius, in Franciscis (1954) 285, and at Lambaesis by the same, *ILS* 3282; at Kourion, Cyprus, by Trajan, Mitford (1971) 208 no. 108; at Carnuntum by the Tetrarchs, in A.D. 308, *CIL* 3.4413; and dedications or gifts of statues by emperors, at Pergamon, in Ohlemutz (1940) 150 and elsewhere, above, chap. 1.1 n.20. I omit temples built by emperors in Rome itself, e.g., by Caligula to Isis (rebuilt by Domitian after fire) or by Severus to Liber, *ILS* 3361 = Palmer (1978) 1088f. On the Pompeian Isis temple, see Tran Tam Tinh (1964) 24f.—though Henzen and Huelsen, whom he cites (at *CIL* 1, 2 p. 334), do not support him. The two categories, Roman civic cults and extra-Roman, overlap (as with Jupiter, the most obvious example); or they seem to overlap (as with Vesta—cf. Nock [1930] 257–260, surely exaggerating the reach of her cult very greatly).

37. The whole of Antinous's cult is called "artificial and fragile" by Beaujeu (1955) 256, in summing up pp. 249–252; further traces of the cult in *IRT* 279, *Antinoo deo frugifero Lepcitani publice,* and chap. 2.3 n.59. Hadrian's encouragement of the cult of Disciplina is traced by Beaujeu (1955) 164, and of Urbs Roma, by Fink et al. (1940) 103 and 110f.

38. Graillot (1912) 153 on *Frg. Vat.* 148 (= *FIRA*² 2.496); Beaujeu (1955) 314f., who rejects a Claudian date for the new law; and Lambrechts (1952) 151f. and 157f. (noting changes within the cult's calendar, p. 144), which Duthoy (1969) 116f. gingerly accepts.

39. On Domitian's Isiacism, cf. the priests at his dinner table, Plin., *Paneg.* 49.8; on the emperor's favorites, cf. *IRT* 295, *lar Severi patrius.* I withhold dozens of examples of all sorts of male and female deities, eastern, western, or whatever, labeled "August" in inscriptions from Augustus on. Nock (1925) 92 offers some

speculation on the usage and Fishwick (1978) carries it further, but with results still, I think, a little blurry and imprecise.

40. On Elagabalus, see above, pp. 85f.; against the Severi as "Orientalizers," cf. Mundle (1961) 228–237, methodical and persuasive.

41. The inscriptions are given by Graillot (1912) 228 and Tran Tam Tinh (1972) 119. The supporting guilds of *cannophori* etc. had also to be licensed, cf. Graillot (1912) 143—but that was true of guilds of other sorts, too, secular included.

42. *CIL* 3.7751, of the A.D. 170s; *IGR* 4.1431, cf. *BGU* 176 (Hadrian) showing the governor interfering in the staffing of temples (but the text is very fragmentary).

43. Ulpian, *Regulae* 22.6 (*FIRA*[2] 2.285—cf. above, chap. 1.1 n.25); *AE* 1933 no. 123; *SIG*[3] 867; *CIL* 10.7946; and Ivanov (1974) 63.

44. Plin., *Ep.* 10.49; on Republican practices controlling temple construction, see Cic., *De domo* 49.127; Livy 9.46.7, in *RE* s.v. Consecratio (Wissowa, 1901) col. 898; *CIL* 6.360 = *ILS* 366, showing that the *curatores aedium sacrarum* must authorize use of space in Rome for worship, cf. *Dig.* 1.8.9.1 and *CIL* 6.31128, the latter cited by Stambaugh (1978) 559, with *Dig.* 1.8.6.3 and Plin., *Ep.* 10.8.2 (A.D. 99); and see also above, chap. 1.1 n.66.

45. A sampling of much evidence: *CIL* 3.1100 (Cybele); 5.484 and 8225 (Isis), 6351 and 6353 (Hercules); 11.696 (Dolichenus); 13.1738 (Isis); and Fishwick (1967) 146, locations for Bellona; Toutain (1907–1920) 1,2.59 points out the lack of any such texts for Syrian deities, which is interesting. In Africa, the abbreviation seems to be simply *dec. dec.* (the curia approved the dedicant's act), cf. *ILS* 3181 and *AE* 1933 no. 233; but cf. the same bare *d. d.* (no *locus* mentioned) in *AE* 1975 no. 267 (Paestum) or *CIL* 9.5177, *decreto ordinis* (Asculum).

46. In Africa: *CIL* 8.26241 (temple for Saturn); *AE* 1899 no. 111 (dedication to Caelestis); *AE* 1957 no. 63 (temple for Cybele); *ILAfr.* 551 (temple to Saturn); Merlin (1908) 21, temple decorations (now = *CIL* 8.25520); Merlin (1910) 23, to local ba'al and Tanit; and LeGlay (1966) 405. In other provinces and Italy, see Plin., *Ep.* 8.6; *IGR.* 1.420; *CIL* 11.1545; 9.981; Tran Tam Tinh (1964) 33 n.1; *CIL* 13.8701 (Mars in Ger. Inf.); *ILS* 3191 = *AE* 1969/1970 no. 441 (Mercury in Ger. Inf.); and *AE* 1960 no. 355 = Parvan (1913) 386 (temple for Nemesis).

47. On Scaptopara, cf. above, chap. 1.2 n.36; on religious fairs, above, pp. 25f.

48. *CIL* 10.846.

49. Duthoy (1969) 86 and *ILS* 419, etc.; *CIL* 12.4333 (A.D. 11–13).

50. Robert (1937) 30 improves the text.

51. "Senate and people" active in religious oversight at Attaleia, in Dupont-Sommer and Robert (1964) 80; at Laodicea, *CIG* 3936; at Stratonicea, above, chap. 1.4 n.18; the *gerousia* at Ephesus, in C. Picard (1922) 95, though note the role of the *demos* in *SIG*[3] 867; Lydian villages honor Men in A.D. 161/2 and Sabazius in 101, in Schwertheim (1975) 357 and Robert (1948b) 112f.; on other secular/sacred connections, compare the sanctification as "hero," e.g., *CIG* 3936 or above, chap. 2.1 n.42, with the gods applauding magistrates, allegedly, above, chap. 2.1 n.37; or on nonprofessional priests, the sharing of facilities, etc., above, chap. 1.4 nn.1–3.

52. On the Syrian triad, cf. Prentice (1922) 184; cf. also the confusions of cult in Lucian, *Dea Syria* 4 (Sidon), 6f. (Byblos), 11f., 28 and 33. In Greece, notice, e.g., Paus. 2.23.6; 7.6.5; and 7.17.10.

53. Above, chap. 1.4 n.14 and chap. 2.4 nn.30f.

54. On Artemis, cf. *Forsch. in Ephesos* 3 (1923) 144, the priestess of the early third cent. who "renewed all the mysteries of the goddess and established them in their ancient form"—though notice the collapse of other Artemis mysteries in the same city a generation or so earlier, in C. Picard (1922) 290f.; on Demeter in Pergamon, see Ohlemutz (1940) 221f.; on Lagina, Laumonier (1958) 255 and 257, first mention under Marcus Aurelius, and note the invention of the Komyria in the first cent., ibid. 247; on Abonuteichus, see Lucian, *Alex.* 38f.; and there are the otherwise unknown Asclepius mysteries in Athens, in Philostr., *Vita Apollon.* 4.18, evidently a variant on the Eleusinian. Festugière (1935) 202 draws out a few more signs from inscriptions of Magnesia, etc., suggesting mutual imitation and stereotyping among mystery ceremonies.

55. On the *panegyris* at Cos, cf. Themanakis (1893) 208, second cent.; cf. the priest praised as "having renewed the *panegyris* of Zeus Protomysius" (near Prusa, second/third cent.), in Robert (1949) 35; and above, chap. 1.4 n.19.

56. In inscriptions, the phrase is common, *vetustate conlapsum*, e.g., in *CIL* 3.1790, 3342, 4540, and 11676; 8.25520; and 13.7281; *Inscr. Ital.* 10, 1.585; *ILS* 3741; Milik (1972) 197; *AE* 1974 no. 574; esp. *CIL* 3.4796, a Mithraic "temple in ruins, deserted for over 50 years." In Greece, cf. Paus. 1.44.3; 2.15.2; 2.24.3; 2.34.10; 5.27.11; 6.24.10; 8.14.4; 8.15.5; 8.30.6; 8.32.3; 8.42.12f. (roof fallen in, three generations ago, but worship continues); and 10.8.6. In Africa, note the unexplained decline of the Tanit shrine at Hadrumetum from the end of the first cent., in Cintas (1947) 79f.—worshipers few and poor. On other shrines, see Kunze et al. (1958) 59 (Olympia); C. Picard (1922) xxviii and 86f. (Ephesus) and 122f. (Claros); Robert (1953a) 20, the second century was "la grande époque" for Claros; further on Claros, above, chap. 2.1 nn.54f.; Latte (1931) 129 and 134 (Epidaurus); and Kötting (1950) 32 (Epidaurus).

57. Matz (1940) 502f.; above, chap. 2.1 n.13.

58. Beaujeu (1966) 4.

59. Crema (1959) 472; Tran Tam Tinh (1971) 7f., speaking of "l'amour du 'mystérieux' . . . , le goût exotique . . . , égyptomanie ou amour d'Isis?"; idem (1964) 50f.; Vidman (1966) 116, "a temporary fashion which did not affect hearts and souls very deeply."

60. Strabo 14.1.5, compared by C. Picard (1922) 46 to the never-finished shrine of Apollo at Claros.

61. Dussaud (1922) 232f., the Damascus temple possibly begun in Severan times; Golfeto (1961) 42 and 48. For other shrines constructed as family projects, see Merlin and Poinssot (1908) 113f., at Uchi Maius; G. C. Picard (1977) 101, at Yzeures = Iciodurum, in Severan times; *Inscr. Ital.* 10, 1.640 (Ruginium); *CIL* 5.308f. (Histria) with *PIR* s.v. Vibius 404, late Republic; Prentice (1908) 104–123, esp. 122f., an interesting story in a Syrian shrine stretching through the first and second centuries; and above all, in Palmyra, the activities of the four main clans, in Gawlikowski (1973) 38f. and 48f. In Pompei, note the special connection of the very distinguished Popidii with Isiacism, in Tran Tam Tinh (1964) 41f., modified by Castren (1975) 207.

62. Merely as illustrations, note the individual slaves as builders in *CIL* 5.8237 and *IG* 3.74 = *SIG*³ 1042, dated by Oliver (1963) 318 and Sokolowski (1969) 106f. For building by cult groups, see *CIL* 3.1547; 6.647; 7.11; and 8.18810 and 8457 = 20343,

the *religiosi* of Cybele in A.D. 288; *AE* 1948 nos. 26f., late second cent. in Ostia to Bellona, with discussion by Fishwick (1967) 146.

63. Builders of shrines on their own estates: Süss (1972) 169–173, A.D. 180 through the third century in Friedberg; Hatt (1978) 285, Mithra and a local god in Mackwiller housed by an *eques*; a second-cent. imperial bailiff in Galatia builds a temple, in Anderson (1937) 19f. and Macpherson (1972) 219; a late Severan *eques* and decurion of Aquincum establishes a cult on family lands at the request of the villagers, in Balla (1971) 55; and an imperial slave builds to Liber, probably on *praedia Augustorum, Inscr. Ital.* 10, 1.585 (Pola). On the Torre Nova Bacchic group, see Vogliano (1933) 216f., where more than three-fourths of the members are Greek (pp. 227–231) but by now probably libertine. For the Samothrace comparison, cf. above, chap. 2.1 n.19.

64. Casual attention, no special search, produces *AE* 1919 no. 26, M. Aur. Decimus of the later third cent. in Lambaesis, to a minor ba'al; 1973 no. 631 = *CIL* 8.2678a add.; Marcillet-Jaubert (1974) 250f.; and Birley (1978) 1523 n.9, altars by the same man to I.O.M., Juno, Minerva, Sol Mithras, etc.; a Severan centurion restoring a Mithraeum and setting up a Dolichenus altar, in Vermaseren (1956–1960) 1.69; ibid. 102 no. 171, the individual offers a dedication to Mithra and to Mercury in Italy; the Severan tribune in Pannonia who restored/built temples to Diana Tifatina and Sol Elagabalus, in Fülep (1954) 247 and 322, Fitz (1959) 240, and idem (1972) 90; Tib. Cl. Thermadon setting up buildings/statues to Sol Mithra and Fortuna Primigenia in Italy, *CIL* 6.3723 = 11.2684 (and p. 424: Bolsena) and 14.2853 (Praeneste); the aedile of Vulcan and Ostian magnate who restores the temple of Castor and Pollux, Fortuna and Venus and Ceres, mid-second cent., *CIL* 14.373–376; the senator Antoninus building temples and amenities at several shrines at and near Epidaurus, in Paus. 2.27.6f.; the wealthy Cornelia Baebia building to Poseidon and another deity under Commodus, in Scranton (1944) 344–348; the senator Rutilianus serving several deities in Rome and Tibur, in Stein (1925) 260, in the A.D. 160s; a *praef. coh.* from Africa honoring I.O.M. and Liber in two Dacian cities, *CIL* 3.6257 and *AE* 1975 no. 722; and P. Ael. Euphorus building for Mithra in one city (*AE* 1971 no. 384) and honoring Silvanus in another (*CIL* 3.1363) in Dacia.

65. Leschi (1957) 177f.

66. Above, pp. 66f.; Malaise (1972) 111, Isiac priests' gifts; cf. *Mart. S. Pionii* 3.1 and 7.1, in Smyrna (Euseb., *H.E.* 4.15.46), the *neocoros* is leader, and *Mart. S. Cononis* 2, at Magydos the *neocoros* leads accusations.

67. LeGlay (1954) 273–276 and Daniels (1975) 254; Habicht (1969) 63.

68. The Feriale Duranum meticulously edited by Fink et al. (1940). The editors assume extreme centralization: the calendar was not only drafted in Rome but Ulpian "doubtless had a hand in the composition of the *Feriale*" (p. 37). No evidence supports this; and Ulpian is not so good a candidate for the conjecture as Comazon, cf. Syme (1972) 407f. The holidays are all old-Roman or old-Italian, e.g., the Neptunalia (Fink et al. [1940] 148).

69. Seston (1956) 184–186 on *ILS* 8940, set in Salsovia in Scythia. For Licinius's loyalty to gods, plural, though by Christian writers called "demons," cf. Euseb., *H.E.* 10.8.4; *Vita Const.* 1.54 and 2.5, with emphasis on the reliability of the latter text by A. H. M. Jones (1962) 113. For the prayer to *summus deus* of A.D. 324, cf. Lact., *De mort. persecut.* 46.6; on Sol worship earlier, see above, pp. 84f.

70. Corporate, troop-unit dedications or offerings or construction: for Diana Tifatina, in Fülep (1954) 322 and Fitz (1972) 179; to Sol Elagabalus, ibid. 178 (*AE* 1910, 141); to Jupiter Heliopolitanus, *CIL* 6.421; to Silvanus in Lambaesis, LeGlay (1971) 131; to Silvanus in Aquincum, Lörincz (1978) 307; to Jupiter Dolichenus, Vučković-Todorović (1964–1965) 176; to Jupiter Optimus Maximus, a number of examples, e.g., *ILS* 3061 or Birley (1978) 1510; to Liber, *ILS* 3381 = *CIL* 3.1790; to Mars, *ILS* 3154; to Hercules and Silvanus, *ILS* 3740; to Isis, *CIL* 5.4041 and *AE* 1948 no. 145 (with Sarapis); to an unknown deity in A.D. 190, Leonhard (1914) 46; and many from outside our region of study, e.g., Birrens (*RIB* 2092-3-7, 2100-4-7) or Maryport (see Wenham's study cited in *RIB* p. 271, and nos. 815-7, 830-1-7-8 and 842-3). For dedications inside a camp, cf. Schwertheim (1979) 26, for Mithra. And note the Severan *s(acerdos) I(ovis) D(olicheni) ad leg(ionem)* in Angyal (1971) 17 = *AE* 1965 no. 30. There are governors directing temple construction or dedications, e.g., *ILS* 3957, to Tellus; to Fortuna in Oescus, with the town bearing the cost, Ivanov (1974) 63; to Diana Plestrensis, Velkov (1974) 152; and n.65, above. Legionary commanders offer dedications often (I withhold many inscriptions by lower officers, tribunes, centurions, and prefects), sometimes clearly not ex officio—e.g., with their wives, in *ILS* 3085–3087 or 3092 (or wife and daughter, *CIL* 8.2630), or from a vision, *ILS* 3229; cf. *CIL* 3.5862, dated to late third cent. by Schwertheim (1974) 221. Other texts do not indicate whether or not the governor appears ex officio (presumably not): *CIL* 3.1111, 1118, 4796, and 5862; 13.6754; in Africa, a third of all named dedications to Mithra are by consular governors or legionary commanders, in Vermaseren (1956–1960) 2.92–98. Citing several of these texts, LeGlay (1954) 277 infers "the official character of this cult in the military capital of Roman Africa." The inference is gratuitous.

71. Above, chap. 1.1 n.37; Lucian, *Alex.* 35.

5. *The Dynamic Cults*

1. In the east, religious movements include Manichaeism—too late for this book. Also, new but not major cults for Antinous and Glykon, cf. above, chap. 2.4 nn.10 and 37 and MacMullen (1966a) 115–119.

2. In *IGR*, Jupiter is the most often cited western god—with a mere seven mentions. Mithra is unknown, Dolichenus almost so.

3. Toutain (1907–1920) 1,1.188f., 191, and 198, accepted and a little expanded by Frend (1952) 78–81; Charles-Picard (1954) 162f.; LeGlay (1966) 71, 73, and 86 on the long-delayed Romanization of Saturn cult, which is also little seen in the interior of Proconsularis; 402f., worshipers are of the lower classes; Bénabou (1976) 373 on the success of Saturn in taking on a broad spectrum of needs, on the model of Jupiter; and Fentress (1978) 508f. Compare *I.O.M.* apparently quite accepted by the local aristocracy around Aquincum, but not by other classes, in Alföldy (1961) 106. On *Jupiter opt. max. Apennininus conservator,* see *ILS* 3074 (Rusicade).

4. For the Dacian inscription, see *ILS* 3086 = *CIL* 3.1075 (Apulum). On M. Campanius Marcellus who built the Diana temple at Intercisa, see Fitz (1968) 318 and 323 and idem (1972) 90f. and 200, where I cannot accept the idea of Diana being "Orientalized." On her Campanian roots, cf. *ILS* 1398 (Capua). That the "official Diana-cult experienced a new upswing in the 3rd century" is the view of Fitz (1972) 261, who refers to *RAC* s.v. Diana (A. Michels, 1957) 966f. Michels rather singles out

the age of the Antonines for this *Aufschwung*, in turn relying on Aymard (1951) 155f.; and Aymard simply speaks of the Antonine age as "the Golden Age of hunting" (throughout the whole Empire, one must suppose), basing himself entirely on a small number of coins. Other local Italian Dianas are easy to find, e.g., Nemorensis, *CIL* 3.1773 in Dalmatia; cf. Fortuna of Praeneste invoked in Sarmizegetusa, *CIL* 3.1421.

5. On Silvanus in Dacia, though not solely the Italian deity, see S. Toth (1967) 78.

6. *Negotiatores* may identify themselves as such when they make dedications, e.g., in *CIL* 3.7761 (Apulum, *Suri* to Dolichenus) or 11812 (Mainz, to Dolichenus); but the practice is far too rare to produce usable statistics. The clustering of Mercury inscriptions on commercial points and routes produces a striking pattern in the Dijon-Langres area, cf. Renardet (1973) 122, patterns which could no doubt be found elsewhere, too. L. Toth (1974) 346, 352, and map on p. 357, finds it in Pannonia, for Isis inscriptions; Malaise (1972) 350, too, for Isiacism in Italy. He infers traders spread the cult.

7. Vidman (1966) 113 points that, aside from a single example in Lambaesis and another in Britain, there are no Isiac temples in military contexts anywhere in the west (in the east, the picture changes slightly, e.g., *CIL* 3.1342, to the goddess by an ala I Hisp. Campagonum, and see following note).

8. The Isis temple (VIII 7, 28 on the map) was never large, though eventually ornate. On the slave population in Italy (or a fair guess), see Hopkins (1978) 9; on the class of Isis's congregation, cf. Castren (1975) 115 n.8 and 207. Note also Malaise (1972) 76f. for Italy broadly, with *ingenui* totaling three in the first cent., seventeen in the first/second, and twenty-four in the second/third (p. 77 n.2). Compare Zotovic (1968) 63, finding Isiacs in Dalmatia and Pannonia (esp. Pann. Sup.) to be largely slaves, and of Greek descent.

9. Malaise (1972) 71–73. Malaise, esp. in pp. 26–37, 70–74, and 103, offers very valuable remarks on method.

10. Malaise (1972) 77 n.2; Vidman (1965) 389, first dating the high point of Isiacism in the west merely to the third century, and citing only Cumont (1929) 11 — who himself, without specifying Isiacism or offering any substantiation, speaks of the apogee of the "Oriental" cults in that period. But Vidman then turns to "base himself above all on inscriptions," finding their apogee under Caracalla and (p. 394) thereafter a sharp decline. On their chronological distribution, see Mrozek (1973) 114–116, in an article of exceptional value. Mrozek 115 n.2 gently points out how his results invalidate certain findings in Roman religious history. His findings received confirmation in the same year he offered them. Lassère (1973) 133–151 offered approximate dates for pagan epitaphs from a number of major sites in Africa Proconsularis and Numidia. The great bulk of his examples, roughly 4,000 texts, can be arranged into centuries (his own categories, such as "end of the Republic to Trajan," "second/third century," do not lend themselves to a table or graph): they are in the proportions 1:3:2 for the periods A.D. 1–100, 101–200, and 201–"mid-third cent." ("milieu du IIIe siècle," meaning evidently not exactly A.D. 250 but, let us say, 240–260). The high point is Severan (texts dated "end of second or third century," "end of second/beginning of third century," and "Severan" total ca. 1250). After "mid-third century" there are only seven out of the whole 4,000!

11. Toutain (1907–1920) 1,2.34, colliding with a statement handiest in Cumont (1929) 81. Toutain's work seems to me admirable. In all my reading, however, I recall seeing it cited only by Frend (1952)—himself the best of judges. Cumont's work, on the other hand, entirely dominates the study of religion in Roman antiquity. I have offered elsewhere (above, chap. 1.3 nn.19 and 28; in chap. 2.1 nn.15, 18, 36, and 55; in chap. 2.2 n.9; in chap. 2.3 n.39; below, nn.19, 24, and 26) a sampling of points which suggest how little trust should, in my opinion, be placed in Cumont's statements. The collision between him and Toutain was renewed: Toutain (1907–1920) 1,3.5 and 10 against Cumont (1912) 127, regarding the acceptance of Isiacism in North Africa. Charles-Picard (1954) 225 attempted to correct Toutain: there *is* evidence for the cult in Africa. True—but nothing to invalidate Toutain's method, heavily relying on inscriptions as opposed to literary texts; and even in 1954, there was not enough new material seriously to modify conclusions based on the data available in 1920. The indices of *CIL* 8 yield only two inscriptions (excluding, as I do from this book, Mauretania).

12. Hatt (1978) 277 defends the importance of "Oriental" cults in Gaul, but means mostly Cybele and Mithra. On Lyon, see LeGlay (1972) 13: out of 1,150 texts, 306 are of Greek-speaking origin, all texts being almost exclusively of the second and third centuries. In *CIL* 13, in Gaul, I count seven Isiac texts, of which one comes from Lyon, the rest from Belgica and Germany.

13. For distribution of inscriptions according to sex, notice those of the Mainz area which give the age of the deceased: 186 men to 15 women, in Szilagyi (1961) 128f. In *CIL* 13, in compiling the figures offered in the text, I count under Mithra the dedications to Cautes, Sol, and Invictus; under Isis, also Sarapis; under Cybele, also Mater Deum, Magna Mater, and Attis. In the same volume, nos. 1–5192 and 11000–11600 are from the interior; 5193–8860 and 11601–12085 are from the *limes*, somewhat arbitrarily defined (the omitted nos. are milestones, graffiti, and on ceramic material). Of all, 40 percent or more are from the frontier. To show that Cybele worshipers were "old-Italian," observe that in the western and southern peninsula, where there was the least moving in and out of population, this cult shows its largest share among the several "Oriental"—Malaise (1972) 460 lists 37 inscriptions for Isis, 8 for Dolichenus, 17 for Mithra, but 80 for Cybele. Quite different in Venetia: the same four cults produce figures of 44, 5, 25, and 20. The same contrast appears in Dalmatia and Pannonia: Cybele-worshipers are much more likely to be Roman citizens than worshipers of other "Oriental" cults. See Zotovic (1968) 62.

14. In *CIL* 5, where I add Jupiter to the deities listed in the table (above, p. 6), and where I count Dolichenus, Cybele, Isis, and Mithra as "Oriental," the numbers (out of 500 all told) are 394 men honoring Greco-Roman names as against 55 women; 50 men honoring "Oriental" gods as against 1 woman (her memorial coming from Milan, where the men's ratio is 15:8, Greco-Roman and "Oriental," i.e. 60 percent of the men favor "exotic" deities, not 10 percent as in the area overall).

15. For example, in Merlat (1951) passim, 123 inscriptions attest Jupiter Dolichenus: 113 male (35 being soldiers or veterans) with 10 women (6 of them as wives). In Dacia, *CIL* 3.787–1627 and 7624–8060 yield 69 dedications in which the sex of the dedicant is clear and in which the deities are "Oriental" (Mithra, Isis, Cybele, Dolichenus, Dea Syria, and Malagbel). Of these 69, 64 are men (42 for Mithra alone). The women worship Isis and Cybele. The percentages arrived at by L. W. Jones

(1929) 298, comparing men's and women's attachment to "Oriental" or "Italian" deities, are perhaps credible for men, but I suspect that the sampling for women skews the truth through being too small. It shows a positive preference for the "Oriental," 36.6 percent to 31.7 percent.

16. On Mainz, see above, n.13, and Clauss (1973) 399, who compares distribution among epitaphs also in other towns (ibid.): 73.4 percent of all that give age at death are of soldiers and kin in Carnuntum, 60 percent in Viminacium, etc. At Singidunum, city and territory, half of some 62 inscriptions are of soldiers and veterans, cf. Mirković and Dusanić (1976) 39. Mocsy (1970) 167 estimates troops in Moesia Superior, including veterans, at less than 5 percent of the total population but they account for 25 percent of the inscriptions (13–60 percent in different districts). How such maldistribution might affect our picture of a cult may be guessed from comparing these figures with others, for Dolichenus, in chap. 1.1 n.29, above. Note, too (Mocsy [1970] p. 208) that 92 percent of all inscriptions come from 20 percent of the area of the province (or 80 percent come from 8 percent of the area!).

17. Mocsy (1970) 193; Toutain (1907–1920) 1,3.445, on 24 out of 520 votive texts from Gaul; cf. Drexel (1922) 25 describing the Roman and Celtic element in Rhaetia as "the very thinnest crust," covering native deities not one of whose names we know from inscriptions; and (p. 24) we are similarly in the dark about religion in the Rhine provinces. Etienne et al. (1976) 98 offer a revealing figure: at Conimbriga, in Latin inscriptions on stone, one-third of the cognomina are native; but once one turns to those inscribed on clay, the figure rises to three-fourths.

18. For the dates outlining the Dolichenus cult, cf. Merlat (1951) passim; I. Toth (1971) 23; Malaise (1972) 461; and Speidel (1978) 4, 9f., and 73. Fitz (1959) 259 more than once speaks of the cult as being "offizielle," thanks to Sept. Severus. The view and terminology, though conventional, are mistaken. See above pp. 103f. and chap. 2.4 n.70.

19. Cumont (1939) 69 = Vermaseren (1956–1960) 1.51 no. 23, which Gordon (1975) 229 and 231 n.64 oddly dates to 78 B.C.; Gough (1952) 131, an inscription which I judge to be no earlier than A.D. 175; ibid. for the Tarsian coins of A.D. 238, surely indicating the special celebrity of Mithraism in the city; and Plut., *Pomp.* 24. Cf. also the Hadrianic essayists on the cult referred to by Porph., *De abst.* 2.56. Gordon (1975) 237f. persuades me that Dio Chrys., *Or.* 36.39f., shows no knowledge of Mithraism. But the cult is better known ca. A.D. 160, when Justin assumes that an eastern audience will have heard of its cult meals, *Dial.* 70 and I *Apol.* 66. Cumont's views on the connections between Mithraism and Persia, and hence the meaning of "Persian" applied to the cult, are in process of dissolution. See, e.g., Wikander (1950) 6–9, 14, 19, and 36; Hinnells (1975) 303f.; or Beskow (1978) 7f.

20. Stat., *Thebaid* 1.717; Swoboda (1964) 193; Vorbeck and Beckel (1973) 14 and 29.

21. Vermaseren (1956–1960) 2.356 no. 2269 (Moesia), dated in Beskow (1978) 12; Schwertheim (1979) 27 (Heddernheim); and *CIL* 6.718 = Cumont (1896–1899) 1.245, cf. *PIR*² s.v. Tib. Iul. Cl. Livianus (Rome).

22. Becatti (1954) 35f.; Vermaseren (1956–1960) vol. 1 nos. 216, 285f. and 362.

23. For ratios of inscriptions, the Mithraic compared to the whole corpus, I exclude *CIL* 4 (graffiti), producing Italy minus Rome, about 38,000; Rome, about 40,000; the rest, about 70,000. Among Mithraic inscriptions, I give numbers where

Gordon (1972) 103 gives percentages (except on p. 109, where he discusses Greek names at Ostia and Rome). We differ inconsequentially. I count, in Vermaseren (1956–1960) vols. 1 and 2, every person connected with the cult, whether or not doubtful, except where the names occur in inscribed lists of dedicants (of which lists there are two in Italy and one to the north), or where the text has lacunae that might have contained indications of military status, active or retired. I accept questionable texts in the collection, including "Sol" texts, some of which are possibly, some certainly, not Mithraic. In Africa, Mithra is as unknown as in the east, save for the Lambaesis area, as Charles-Picard (1954) 222 pointed out. On the high proportion of soldiers in the epigraphy of the frontier, see above, nn.13 and 16. Bivar (1975) 281 is right to say that Mithraism is conventionally viewed as specially appealing to the military; but the view itself is unfounded.

24. SHA *Commod.* 9—a wild paragraph in an unreliable author. Cumont (1929) 139 offers no substantiation for saying "the conversion [!] caused an immense stir." The phrase was repeated verbatim from Cumont (1896–1899) 1.277 and a third time in Cumont (1902) 70. So truth becomes established, cf., e.g., Ferguson (1970) 48, Commodus's initiation "led to the first great period of the cult." For the prefect mentioned, L. Flavius Aper in *CIL* 3.15156, see Hoffiller and Saria (1938) 1.146f. and 149; and proportions of high officers, etc., are noted by Gordon (1972) 103f.

25. Packer (1967) 86 offers ca. 27,000 as the max. pop. for Ostia (including unexcavated parts; earlier estimates are double that); but density estimates in Packer 86 n.55 are to be modified upward by Frier (1977) 28f. The Mithraea were generally small, mean structures, holding less than twenty up to a maximum of forty, cf. Meiggs (1960) 372. Not all fifteen were certainly in use at any one time. Schwertheim (1979) 57 mentions an average capacity of 20–30, counting larger examples in Rome. For crowds at temple gates, no more than a suggestive picture, cf. Herondas, *Mimiambi* 4.54, cited in Edelstein and Edelstein (1945) 1.273.

26. Cumont (1929) 130 calls Mithraism a more and more pressing presence in the second century, "remaining until the end of the 4th century the most important cult in paganism." His view might still receive general support. Discouraging.

27. M. P. Nilsson's suggestion is quoted as a fact by Nock (1958a) 292—with which Wikander (1950) 44 more or less agrees. Cumont (1975) 205 pictures Mithraism "finally coming under the control of the State and the emperors," so that he can explain the wide dispersal of the cult, e.g., to the Dura chapel, without having to admit a native eastern branch; but cf. above, on "state" cults. I withhold my own inexpert ideas about pre–100 Mithraism, not to add to inconclusive debate.

28. Above, at chap. 1.4 n.16; cf. the ὑμνητρία in the Demeter mysteries, Ohlemutz (1940) 221.

29. Paus. 8.2.5, complaining of evil days as the reason why no new gods come into being from men. The passage happens to coincide with, and contradict, *CIG* 5980=*IG* 14.966=*SIG²* 807, which reports a miracle in Rome, bystanders rejoicing "because the powers were living then in the reign of our emperor Antoninus." Porphyry in Euseb., *Praep. ev.* 5.1 (179df.) speaks of the declining presence of the gods, but in a polemical setting.

30. Cumont (1929) 38—a sort of rephrasing of the "failure-of-nerve" interpretation. Gordon (1972) 93f. rightly puts the latter interpretation aside, speaking of Dodds (but there are others behind Dodds, e.g., Gilbert Murray). For similar gener-

alizing about spiritual sturdiness, compare A. H. M. Jones (1963) 19: "the peasant masses, who were made of tougher stuff than the townsmen," clung to Christianity under the Tetrarchs.

31. Cumont (1929) 39f., above, p. 64, and similarly in Laurin (1954) 8.

32. In works demonstrating the most admirable scholarship and powers in philology, one may find statements that no historian would dream of making. Drawing from major authorities, throughout this chapter's notes, I have scattered examples which it would be invidious to recall at this point.

33. Gordon (1972) 94.

34. Gordon (1972) assumes Mithraism's exclusion of women, special connection with soldiers, moral dualism and notions of sin, derivation from Iran and many other features contrary to my understanding of the facts or wholly unsubstantiated; but, in addition, I cannot accept his main point, that "the departmental boss," slave owners, "various superiors," "senior officers" (pp. 107f. and 112)—in short, the ruling class—encouraged the cult as a "self-conscious piece of opportunism" through "conscious realization" of its usefulness (pp. 110 and 112). That implies a manipulative conspiracy among upper-class worshipers supported by no evidence and, I would say, by no likelihood.

35. Vermaseren and van Essen (1965) 232.

36. Vermaseren (1971) 3, starry vault; Cumont (1975) 167f., gilt and jewels, and curtain; Vermaseren (1956–1960) 2.24 no. 230, ocular in vault; rayed hole, in Bull (1978) 78; pivoted relief, Turcan (1978) 153 and Schwertheim (1979) 27 Abb. 32f.; use of paint or gilt on idols and reliefs, Vermaseren (1965–1960) 1.128 no. 258; 239 no. 641; etc.

37. Altars, in Becatti (1954) 13; Vermaseren (1956–1960) 1.126 no. 253 and 170 no. 392; Wortmann (1969) 411–421, full discussion of lighting tricks; and Schwertheim (1979) 34 Abb. 49.

38. Schwertheim (1979) 29 Abb. 38f. and p. 73; on apparent victims in initiatory shows, combined with literary texts, cf. Vermaseren (1971) 26–29, and above, chap. 2.1 n.24. E. D. Francis, adding a note to Cumont (1975) 206 n.312, supports the view that the rites were dumb show, not recitations of doctrine.

39. Tert., *De corona* 15; SHA *Commod.* 9.6; and compare the use in Dionysiac initiations of "spooks and horrors," Orig., *C. Cels.* 4.10.

40. Note, for example, the elaborate underground facilities for miming and initiation at Eleusis, or at Claros, Robert (1953a) 16–20. As L. Deubner (1932) 86 puts it, "Zauberritus and Götterritus steht im Kulte sehr häufig nebeneinander." On Hippolytus's passage on theatrical effects in cult rites, see *Refut.* 4.28–41 and 6.34–36, supposed by Ganschinietz (1913) 22f. to be drawn from some magician's handbook that Hippolytus had before him. For a Gallic equivalent of Alexander of Abonuteichus, or, perhaps better, of Simon Magus, see Polemo in R. Foerster's Latin translation of the Arabic, *Scriptores physiognomonici graeci et latini* (1893) 1.162.

41. Liebeschuetz (1979) 244 and n.3 on the small Tetrarchic pantheon, compared with the large one, Vesp.-Hadrian. But continue the series: Ant. Pius dropped Bacchus, Castor, the Dioscuri, Mercury, Neptune, Saturn, Sarapis, Sol, Tellus, and Vulcan—from lethargy?

42. Bosch (1935) 170; also above, chap. 1.2 n.71. For the god Men alone, on coins,

Lane (1975-1978) vol. 2 passim has collected the data: 64 cities minting, over 90 percent of their issues datable in the periods A.D. 1-50 (six issues that show Men); 50-100 (12); 100-150 (28); 150-200 (67); 200-250 (184, a great rise); 250-300 (55, largely in the 250s only). But the datable coins of *Brit. Mus.* Lycia, Pamphylia, and Pisidia in the same six half-centuries run 17, 13, 30, 67, 231, 177. Hence the two curves, for Men and for all coins (of one region), differ (i.e., they tell us something about Men) only in the third century, esp. 235 on, since in both curves the Severan rulers account for the identical 28 percent.

43. Geffcken (1920) 15—needing no significant updating; on Vesta, see Latte (1960) 360, the *acta* full until A.D. 241, the last frg. dated to 304, and taurobolia are frequent until 241, thereafter only 2 in the century; Vestal records (ibid.) are full up to ca. 255. On Saturn, see Frend (1952) 76, noting the abrupt falling-off in ex-votos and temple building after 235, and modifications of this picture by LeGlay (1966), accepting the decline, pp. 96f., but insisting (without really very much data, pp. 101f.) on the cult's continued survival; for Jupiter Dolichenus, see Zotovic (1968) 73.

44. Jalabert (1908) 719: pagan to A.D. 250; Christian after 324. On coin distribution across time, cf. n.42 above; on various other categories of silence or lack of evidence—on various élite groups, but also on their fine pottery—see MacMullen (1976) 215 n.1; also 240 n.44, where I report on the dating of 5,000 papyri and ostraca. Their numbers first diminish sharply at the accession of Sept. Severus, fall off a second big step (say, by a half, from the second-cent. average) in A.D. 225, and a third, in 300.

45. Above, chap. 2.4 n.56, on Greece and other impoverished points; on blooming areas even in bad times, see MacMullen (1976) 119 and notes.

46. Above, n.44; below, Epilogue, n.8; Frend (1952) 76; Geffcken (1920) 20f., appealing to nonepigraphic testimonies.

47. Mrozek (1973) 118.

48. The angle of attack chosen by the later, heavier persecutions is obvious. Gagé (1964) 327 draws out some of its chief features.

49. Ox prices, approximate, are based on Frank (1933-1940) 1.189, wages, and 200, oxen, in the second cent. B.C.; Sperber (1966) 184 and 188 in later second-cent. A.D. Egypt and Palestine.

50. MacMullen (1966a) 355f., on eastern native cults, to which add the evidence on Men, above, n.42, and the interesting statistics in Keil (1923) 253-266, esp. 266, on pre-Greek Lydian cults; and MacMullen (1966a) 361f., on northern native cults, to which add Balla (1967) 73, on reviving Illyric-Celtic cults from the later second century.

EPILOGUE

1. Euseb., *Praep. ev.* 4.2 (135c-136a) and *Hist. eccl.* 9.11.6 on the pagan leadership, hierophants, magistrates, and intellectuals of Antioch and Miletus.

2. To A.H.M. Jones (1964) 938-943 and refs. in 1391 nn.7-13, there is little to add from literary sources; but, on Shenute's campaigns, cf. passages in Kaegi (1966) 255f., and, on compulsion of peasants, MacMullen (1980) 28. Among inscriptions, Geffcken notices *Forschungen in Ephesos* i.103.

3. As to the army, its constituents before A.D. 312 of course were pagan, and "its

intake must have remained predominantly pagan" throughout the fourth cent.—so says A. H. M. Jones (1963) 24. *CT* 7.20.2 receives more weight than it deserves (ibid.), since it gives the shouts, *dei te nobis servent,* of only one army unit at one date—both unknown. Jones intends to follow Seeck (who surmises A.D. 326, on the basis of an emendation); but his confused sentence actually indicates 322. The fourth-cent. burial practices of soldiers in the West are abundantly attested, but only show that some were pagan, not how many. The only indications of religion in the ranks of the competing forces in 394 are Christian—in Theodosius's army folded in with Eugenius's, after the Frigidus. Cf. Hoffmann (1963) 24f. and his nos. 11, 14, and 35.

4. Old inscriptions, like *CIL* 6.102, 937 and 50=*IG* 14.1018; new, like *AE* 1969-1970 no. 116 and 1975 no. 54; and neglected details, e.g., Macrob. 1.23.13, Antium, and Maximus of Turin, *Sermo* 72.2.42 (for the date, cf. Mutzenbecher in Corp. Christ. Lat. p. xxxv n.1).

5. E.g., *CIL* 8.6975; 12272; and 24521.

6. Cf. texts like Aug., *Ep.* 16f. and *Civ. dei* 7.26. On the strength of fourth cent. African paganism in general, see Warmington (1954) 35f. and above, chap. 2.5 n.10. On Saturn cult, against Frend (1952) 83f., I would set LeGlay (1966) 101f. and Frend's own picture (pp. 61-64) of the sharp decline of the classes and centers which were most likely to produce records and buildings of any sort. The existence of a church in a town or village, here in Africa or anywhere else, of course does not prove Christian predominance. Christians and pagans everywhere coexisted. That is easily shown to be the rule—with noted exceptions.

7. *ILS* 4197 (A.D. 360s) and *Paneg. vet.* 12(2).37.4 (A.D. 388).

8. Pautalia (in Moesia, later Dacia Mediterranea), in Hoddinott (1975) 182. Mocsy (1974) 324 offers more (but undatable) examples of vandalized shrines and statues; also, p. 323, some interesting speculation on the epigraphic evidence, within which, in the earlier 300s, pagan epitaphs vanish and Christian begin to appear. For the burning and smashing of pagan temples and images in the upper Danube areas, see Alföldy (1974) 210f., A.D. 380 and later, and Stähelin (1948) 580, A.D. 340s and later.

9. Frantz (1965) 191-197; Edelstein and Edelstein (1945) 1.323f. and 423f.; 2.257; and *IG* 4², 1.438. On the rest of the east, cf. A. H. M. Jones, cit. above, n.2, to which I can add only Zos. 1.38 and 4.18; *Expositio tot. mundi* 22, 30, and 34f.; and the interesting circle of pagan speculation revealed in *PHermopolis* 2-4. On pagan cults vigorous specifically in Egypt, see Hanslik (1954) 180f. and Rémondon (1952) 63-78.

10. Petit (1955) 200f.; on state functionaries, p. 202: in A.D. 360, in the east, 8 Christians, 15 pagans (and after Julian, far more paganized).

11. Bell et al. (1962) 20 and papyri nos. 4-8 etc. (Christian) and 36 (pagan oath formula—cf. *POslo* 113 of A.D. 346).

12. Marc. Diac., *Vita Porph.* 41 (Arcadius's speech), and miracles at 19, 31, 61, and 66f., with conversions, 21; for other mass conversions produced by miracles see Theod., *Hist. relig.* 17 (*PG* 82.1421-1423) and Soz. 5.15.14, comparing above, chap. 2.4 n.1.

13. Brown (1964) 109.

14. For example, Scroggs (1980) 170-175 and 177-179 provides recent handy

access to a long tradition of writing, "bourgeois" and Marxist, on the socioeco-
nomic orientation of the Church. But discussion of what life and views the convert
would find in the Church does not seem to me very useful in explaining the growth
of the Church, unless one supposes that many converts (in the sense of persons now
believing that the Christian God really existed and really was supreme) would
promptly have fallen away if they had not found other essential things that held
them unshakably in the faith.

15. A.H.M. Jones (1964) 938-943 collects the legal texts.

16. Adolf von Harnack in his *Mission und Ausbreitung des Christentums* (1902
and later edns.) rightly claimed that his was the first work devoted to the subject of
his title; and so far as I know it is the last—certainly still standard. It is justly admired for its scholarship. Among its thousands of references to sources, however, I
can find not one to a pagan source and hardly a line indicating the least attempt to
find out what non-Christians thought and believed. Thus to ignore the prior views
of converts or to depict the Mission as operating on a clean slate is bound to strike an
historian as very odd indeed.

Bibliography of Secondary Works Cited

Agache (1973)—Agache, R., "Quelques fana repérées par avion en Picardie et en Artois," *Caesarodunum* 8 (1973) 50-55.

Albertini (1931)—Albertini, E., "Inscriptions d'El-Kantara et de la région," *Rev. afr.* 72 (1931) 193-261.

Albertini (1943)—Albertini, E., "Une nouvelle basilique civile à Cuicul (Djemila)," *CRAI* 1943, 376-395.

A. Alföldi (1948)—Alföldi, A., *The Conversion of Constantine and Pagan Rome*, Oxford 1948.

A. Alföldi (1963)—Alföldi, A., *Early Rome and the Latins*, Ann Arbor 1963.

A. Alföldi (1967)—Alföldi, A., *Studien zur Geschichte der Weltkrise des 3. Jahrhunderts nach Christus*, Darmstadt 1967.

M. R. Alföldi (1963)—Alföldi, M. R., *Die Constantinische Goldprägung. Untersuchungen zu ihrer Bedeutung für Kaiserpolitik und Hof-Kunst*, Mainz 1963.

Alföldy (1961)—Alföldy, G., "Geschichte des religiösen Lebens in Aquincum," *Acta arch. acad. sci. Hung.* 13 (1961) 103-124.

Alföldy (1974)—Alföldy, G., *Noricum*, London and Boston 1974.

Amelung (1905)—Amelung, W., "Ex-voto an Asklepios," *Archiv für Religionswissenschaft* 8 (1905) 157-160.

Anderson (1913)—Anderson, J.G.C., "Festivals of Men Askaenos in the Roman colonia at Antioch of Pisidia," *JRS* 3 (1913) 267-300.

Anderson (1937)—Anderson, J.G.C., "An imperial estate in Galatia," *JRS* 27 (1937) 18-21.

Andreae (1963)—Andreae, B., *Studien zur römischen Grabkunst* (Mitt. des Deutschen Arch. Inst., Röm. Abt., Ergänzungsheft 9), Heidelberg 1963.

Andresen (1955)—Andresen, C., *Logos und Nomos. Die Polemik des Kelsos wider das Christentum*, Berlin 1955.

Angyal (1971)—Angyal, K. B., "Epigraphica. Contribution à l'étude historique des religions orientales de Dacie," *Studium* 2 (1971) 17-21.

Archambault (1909)—Archambault, G., ed., *Justin. Dialogue avec Tryphon*, Paris 1909.

Arnheim (1972)—Arnheim, M.T.W., *The Senatorial Aristocracy in the Later Roman Empire*, Oxford 1972.

Arnim (1921)—Arnim, H. von, *Plutarch über Dämonen und Mantik* (Verhandelingen der Koninklijke Akademie van Wetenschappen te Amsterdam, Afdeeling Letterkunde 22, 2), Amsterdam 1921.

Attridge (1978)—Attridge, H. W., "The philosophical critique of religion under the early Empire," *ANRW* II, 16, 1 (Berlin 1978) 45-78.

Audollent (1890)—Audollent, A., "Mission épigraphique en Algérie," *MEFR* 10 (1890) 397-588.

Audollent (1901)—Audollent, A., *Carthage romaine, 146 avant Jésus-Christ-698 après Jésus-Christ* (Bibl. des Ecoles Fr. d'Athènes et de Rome 84), Paris 1901.

Audollent (1904)—Audollent, A., *Defixionum tabellae quotquot innotuerunt tam in Graecis Orientis quam in totius Occidentis partibus praeter Atticas in 'Corpus Inscriptionum Atticarum' editas*, Paris 1904.

Aymard (1951)—Aymard, J., *Essai sur les chasses romaines, des origines à la fin du siècle des Antonins*, Paris 1951.

Balla (1967)—Balla, L., "Zur Geschichte des religiösen Lebens von Savaria," *Acta class. univ. sci. Debrecen.* 3 (1967) 67-76.

Balla (1971)—Balla, L., "Possessores et vicani vici Vindoniani," *Debreceni Déri Múzeum Évkönyve* 1971, 55-63 (Fr. summary, p. 64).

Barb (1963)—Barb, A. A., "The survival of magic arts," in *The Conflict Between Paganism and Christianity in the Fourth Century*, ed. A. Momigliano, Oxford 1963, 100-125.

Bardenhewer (1912-1932)—Bardenhewer, O., *Geschichte der altkirchlichen Literatur*[2], 5 vols., Freiburg im Breisgau 1912-1932.

Bardon (1956)—Bardon, H., *La littérature latine inconnue, 2: L'époque impériale*, Paris 1956.

Bardy (1948)—Bardy, G., *Théophile d'Antioche. Trois livres à Autolycus*, Paris 1948.

Barkóczy et al. (1954-1957)—Barkóczy, L., et al., *Intercisa (Dunapentele-Sztálinváros). Geschichte der Stadt in der Römerzeit*, 2 vols., Darmstadt 1954-1957.

Barr (1974)—Barr, J., "Philo of Byblos and his 'Phoenician History,'" *Bull. John Rylands Lib.* 57 (1974) 17-68.

Bataille (1952)—Bataille, A., *Les Memnonia. Recherches de papyrologie et d'épigraphie grecques sur la nécropole de la Thèbes d'Egypte aux époques hellénistique et romaine*, Le Caire 1952.

Baur (1902)—Baur, P. V. C., *Eileithyia*, Columbia (Missouri) 1902.

Baynes (1931)—Baynes, N. H., *Constantine the Great and the Christian Church*, Oxford 1931.

Beaujeu (1955)—Beaujeu, J., *La religion romaine à l'époque de l'empire, 1: La politique religieuse des Antonins (96-192)*, Paris 1955.

Beaujeu (1966)—Beaujeu, J., "Religion in the second century A.D.," *Bucknell Review* 14, 2 (1966) 1-18.

Becatti (1954)—Becatti, C., *I Mitrei* (Scavi di Ostia 2), Rome 1954.

Behr (1968)—Behr, C. A., *Aelius Aristides and the Sacred Tales*, Amsterdam 1968.

Bell et al. (1962)—Bell, H. I., et al., *The Abinnaeus Archive*, Oxford 1962.

Benabou (1976)—Benabou, M., "Resistance et romanisation en Afrique du Nord sous le Haut-Empire," in *Assimilations et resistance à la culture gréco-romaine dans le monde ancien. Travaux du VI Congrès international de la Fédération Internationale des Associations d'études classiques . . . 1974*, Paris 1976, 367-375.

Bernand (1969)—Bernand, A., *Les inscriptions grecques de Philae* . . . , 2 vols., Paris 1969.

Bernand (1972)—Bernand, A., *Le Paneion d'El Kanais. Les inscriptions grecques,* Leiden 1972.

Beschaouch (1975)—Beschaouch, A., "A propos de récentes découvertes épigraphiques dans le pays de Carthage," *CRAI* 1975, 101-118.

Beskow (1978)—Beskow, P., "The routes of early Mithraism," in *Etudes Mithriaques. Actes du 2e Congrès international* . . . *1975*, Leiden 1978, 7-18.

Besset (1901)—Besset, A., "Inscription d'Asie Mineure," *BCH* 25 (1901) 325-336.

Bessou (1978)—Bessou, M., "Le fanum de Camp-Ferrus à Loubers (Tarn)," *Gallia* 36 (1978) 187-212.

Betz (1961)—Betz, H. D., *Lukian von Samosata und das Neue Testament. Religionsgeschichtliche und paränetische Parallelen* . . . (Texte und Untersuchungen 76), Berlin 1961.

Bickerman (1973)—Bickerman, E., "Consecratio," in *Le culte des souverains dans l'empire romain* (Entretiens sur l'antiquité classique 19, Fondation Hardt), Geneva 1973, 3-25.

Bidez (1913)—Bidez, J., *Vie de Porphyre, le philosophe néo-platonicien, avec les fragments des traités* Περὶ ἀγαλμάτων *et De regressu animae*, Gand and Leipzig 1913.

Bieber (1910)—Bieber, M., "Attische Reliefs in Cassel," *Ath. Mitt.* 35 (1910) 1-16.

Bieler (1935-1936)—Bieler, L., ΘΕΙΟΣ ANHR. *Das Bild des 'göttlichen Menschen' in Spätantike und Frühchristentum*, 2 vols., Vienna 1935-1936.

Binsfeld (1969)—Binsfeld, W., "Das Quellenheiligtum Wallenborn bei Heckenmünster (Kr. Wittlich)," *Trier. Zeitschr.* 32 (1969) 239-268.

Birley (1974)—Birley, E., "Cohors I Tungrorum and the oracle of the Clarian Apollo," *Chiron* 4 (1974) 511-513.

Birley (1978)—Birley, E., "The religion of the Roman army: 1895-1977," *ANRW* II 16, 2 (Berlin 1978) 1506-1541.

Bivar (1975)—Bivar, A.D.H., "Mithra and Mesopotamia," in *Mithraic Studies. Proceedings of the First International Congress of Mithraic Studies*, ed. J. R. Hinnells, Manchester 1975, 275-289.

Blinkenberg (1941)—Blinkenberg, C., *Lindos. Fouilles et recherches 1902-1914*, II: *Inscriptions*, I-II, Copenhagen 1941.

Boehringer (1959)—Boehringer, E., "Pergamon," in *Neue deutsche Ausgrabungen im Mittelmeergebiet und im vorderen Orient*, Berlin 1959, 121-171.

Bogaers (1955)—Bogaers, J.E.A.T., *De gallo-romeinse tempels te Elst in de Over-Betuwe*, The Hague 1955.

Bookidis (1973)—Bookidis, N., "The sanctuary of Demeter and Kore in Corinth. Excavations 1970-1972," *AJA* 77 (1973) 206-207.

Boulanger (1923)—Boulanger, A., *Aelius Aristide et la sophistique dans la province d'Asie au IIe siècle de notre ère*, Paris 1923.

Boyce (1937)—Boyce, G. K., "A corpus of the lararia of Pompeii," *MAAR* 14 (1937) 5-112.

Bosch (1935)—Bosch, C., *Die kleinasiatischen Münzen der römischen Kaiserzeit* (II, *Einzeluntersuchungen*; 1, *Bithynien*), Stuttgart 1935.

Brenk (1973)—Brenk, F. E., "'A most strange doctrine': *Daimon* in Plutarch," *CJ* 69 (1973) 1-11.

Brilliant (1963)—Brilliant, R., *Gesture and Rank in Roman Art. The Use of Gestures to Denote Status in Roman Sculpture and Coinage*, Copenhagen 1963.

Brommer (1973)—Brommer, F., *Der Gott Vulkan auf provinzialrömischen Reliefs*, Cologne and Vienna 1973.

Brown (1964)—Brown, P. R. L., "St. Augustine's attitude to religious coercion," *JRS* 54 (1964) 107-116.

Brown (1971)—Brown, P., "The rise and function of the holy man in Late Antiquity," *JRS* 61 (1971) 80-101.

Brown (1972)—Brown, P., *Religion and Society in the Age of Saint Augustine*, London 1972.

Bruhl (1953)—Bruhl, A., *Liber Pater. Origines et expansion du culte dionysiaque à Rome et dans le monde romain*, Paris 1953.

Buckler (1914-1916)—Buckler, W. H., "Some Lydian propitiatory inscriptions," *BSA* 21 (1914-1916) 169-183.

Buckler (1933)—Buckler, W. H., "A pagan recantation," *CR* 47 (1933) 7-8.

Buckler et al. (1926)—Buckler, W. H., et al., "Monuments from central Phrygia," *JRS* 16 (1926) 53-94.

Buckler and Robinson (1932)—Buckler, W. H., and D. M. Robinson, *Sardis VII: Greek and Latin Inscriptions*, Part I, Leiden 1932.

Bücheler (1865)—Bücheler, F., "Philodemos περὶ εὐσεβείας," *NJbb. für Philologie* 9 (1865) 513-541.

Buecheler (1895-1897)—Buecheler, F., *Carmina latina epigraphica*, 2 vols., Leipzig 1895-1897.

Buffière (1962)—Buffière, F., *Héraclite, Allégories d'Homère, texte et traduction*, Paris 1962.

Bull (1978)—Bull, R. J., "The Mithraeum at Caesarea Maritima," in *Etudes Mithriaques. Actes du 2ᵉ Congrès international . . . 1975*, Leiden 1978, 75-90.

Butler (1915)—Butler, H. C., *Ancient Architecture in Syria* (Publications of the Princeton University Archaeological Expeditions to Syria in 1904-05 and 1909, II A, Part 5), *Haurân Plain and Djebel Haurân*, Leiden 1915.

Cagnat (1898)—Cagnat, R., *Cours d'épigraphie latine³*, Paris 1898.

Calder (1935)—Calder, W. M., "Silius Italicus in Asia," *CR* 49 (1935) 216-217.

Cameron (1939)—Cameron, A., "Inscriptions relating to sacral manumission and confession," *HThR* 32 (1939) 143-179.

Canarache et al. (1963)—Canarache, V., et al., "Le dépôt des monuments sculpturaux récemment découverts à Constanta," in *Acta antiqua philippopolitana. Studia archaeologica*, Sophia 1963, 133-152.

Capello (1941)—Capello, C. F., "Una stipe votiva d'età romana sul Monte Genevris (Alpi Cozie)," *Rivista Ingauna e Intemelia* 7 (1941) 96-137.

Caputo (1977)—Caputo, G., "Sincretismo religioso ed espressione figurativa in Tripolitania," *Quaderni di archeologia della Libia* 9 (1977) 119-124.

Caquot (1954-1957)—Caquot, A., "Quelques nouvelles données palmyréniennes," *Comptes rendus du groupe linguistique d'études chamito-sémitiques* 7 (1954-1957) 77-78.

Cardauns (1958)—Cardauns, B., *Varros Logistoricus über die Götterverehrung (Curio de cultu deorum). Ausgabe und Erklärung der Fragmente,* Würzburg 1958.

Cardauns (1978)—Cardauns, B., "Varro und die römischen Religion. Zur Theologie, Wirkungsgeschichte und Leistung der 'Antiquitates Rerum Divinarum,'" *ANRW* II 16, 1 (Berlin 1978) 80–103.

Carton (1908)—Carton, L., "Le sanctuaire de Tanit à El-Kénissia," *Mémoires de l'Acad. des Inscriptions et Belles-Lettres* 12, 1 (1908) 1–160.

Casson (1974)—Casson, L., *Travel in the Ancient World,* London 1974.

Castren (1975)—Castren, P., *Ordo populusque Pompeianus. Polity and Society in Roman Pompeii,* Rome 1975.

Chadwick (1952)—Chadwick, H., "An Attis from a domestic shrine," *JThStudies*[2] 3 (1952) 90–92.

Chadwick (1965)—Chadwick, H., *Origen: Contra Celsum, translated with an Introduction and Notes,* Cambridge 1965.

Chadwick (1967)—Chadwick, H., "Philo and the beginnings of Christian thought," in *The Cambridge History of Later Greek and Early Medieval Philosophy,* ed. A. H. Armstrong, Cambridge 1967, 137–194.

Charles-Picard (1943-1945)—Charles-Picard, G., "La collection Boglio à Siliana," *BCTH* 1943-1945, 375–381.

Charles-Picard (1954)—Charles-Picard, G., *Les religions de l'Afrique antique,* Paris 1954.

Charpin (1930-1931)—Charpin, L., "Testimonianze cristiane sul Teatro Romano dell'età imperiale," *Atti, Reale Istituto Veneto* 90 (1930-1931) 571–591.

Cherniss (1976)—Cherniss, H., *Plutarch's Moralia* (Loeb Classical Library), vols. 13, 1-2, Cambridge and London 1976.

Chilton (1967)—Chilton, C. W., *Diogenis Oenoandensis fragmenta,* Leipzig 1967.

Chilton (1971)—Chilton, C. W., *Diogenes of Oenoanda. The Fragments. A Translation and Commentary,* London 1971.

Cintas (1947)—Cintas, P., "Le sanctuaire punique de Sousse," *Rev. afr.* 91 (1947) 1–80.

Clauss (1973)—Clauss, M., "Probleme der Lebensalterstatistiken auf Grund römischer Grabinschriften," *Chiron* 3 (1973) 395–417.

Clerc (1885)—Clerc, M., "Inscription de Nysa," *BCH* 9 (1885) 124–131.

Clermont-Ganneau (1920)—Clermont-Ganneau, C., "Découverte à Jérusalem d'une synagogue de l'époque hérodienne," *Syria* 1 (1920) 190–197.

Coarelli (1974)—Coarelli, F., *Guida archeologica di Roma,* Milan 1974.

Collart (1937)—Collart, P., *Philippes, ville de Macédoine, depuis ses origines jusqu'à la fin de l'époque romaine,* Paris 1937.

Collart (1944)—Collart, P., "Rejouissances, divertissements et artistes de province dans l'Egypte romaine," *Rev. de philol.*[3] 18 (1944) 134–152.

Collart and Ducrey (1975)—Collart, P., and P. Ducrey, *Philippes I: Les reliefs rupestres (BCH* Suppl. II), Paris 1975.

Collins-Clinton (1977)—Collins-Clinton, J., *A Late Antique Shrine of Liber Pater at Cosa,* Leiden 1977.

Conze and Schuchhardt (1899)—Conze, A., and C. Schuchhardt, "Die Arbeiten zu Pergamon 1886-1898," *Ath. Mitt.* 24 (1899) 97–240.

Cook (1903)—Cook, A. B., "Zeus, Jupiter and the Oak," *CR* 17 (1903) 174–186, 268–278, 403–421.

Cook (1914-1940)—Cook, A. B., *Zeus. A Study in Ancient Religion*, 3 vols., Cambridge 1914-1940.

Corbett (1970)—Corbett, P. E., "Greek temples and Greek worshippers: the literary and archaeological evidence," *Bull. Inst. Class. Studies* (Univ. London) 17 (1970) 149-158.

Cousin (1904)—Cousin, G., "Inscriptions du sanctuaire de Zeus Panamaros," *BCH* 28 (1904) 20-53, 238-262, 345-352.

Crema (1959)—Crema, L., *L'architettura romana* (Enciclopedia classica VII, xii, 1), Turin 1959.

Cumont (1888)—Cumont, F., "Les dieux éternels des inscriptions latines," *Rev. arch.* 11 (1888) 184-192.

Cumont (1896-1899)—Cumont, F., *Textes et monuments figurés relatifs aux mystères de Mithra* 1 (Brussels 1899) and 2 (Brussels 1896).

Cumont (1902)—Cumont, F., *Les mystères de Mithra*,[2] Paris 1902.

Cumont (1912)—Cumont, F., "J. Toutain—Les cultes paiens . . . .," *Rev. de l'hist. des religions* 66 (1912) 125-129.

Cumont (1913)—Cumont, F., "La théologie solaire du paganisme romain," *Mémoires, Acad. des Inscriptions et Belles-Lettres* 12 (1913) 447-479.

Cumont (1915a)—Cumont, F., "Découvertes nouvelles au mithréum de Saint-Clément à Rome," *CRAI* 1915, 203-211.

Cumont (1915b)—Cumont, F., "Les anges du paganisme," *Rev. de l'hist. des religions* 72 (1915) 159-182.

Cumont (1917)—Cumont, F., "Gainas le δειπνοκρίτης," *CRAI* 1917, 275-284.

Cumont (1920)—Cumont, F., "Groupe de marbre du Zeus Dolichenos," *Syria* 1 (1920) 183-189.

Cumont (1923a)—Cumont, F., "Il sole vindice dei delitti ed il simbolo delle mani alzate," *Memorie* I, 1 (1923), *Atti della Pont. Accad. Romana di Archeologia* (Serie III) 65-80.

Cumont (1923b)—Cumont, F., *After Life in Roman Paganism. Lectures Delivered at Yale University* . . . , New Haven 1923.

Cumont (1926)—Cumont, F., *Fouilles de Doura-Europos (1922-1923)*, Paris 1926.

Cumont (1929)—Cumont, F., *Les religions orientales dans le paganisme romain*[4], Paris 1929.

Cumont (1939)—Cumont, F., "Mithra en Asie Mineure," in *Anatolian Studies Presented to William Hepburn Buckler*, eds. W. M. Calder and J. Keil, Manchester 1939, 67-76.

Cumont (1942)—Cumont, F., *Recherches sur le symbolisme funéraire des Romains*, Paris 1942.

Cumont (1949)—Cumont, F., *Lux perpetua*, Paris 1949.

Cumont (1975)—Cumont, F., "The Dura Mithraeum," in *Mithraic Studies. Proceedings of the First International Congress of Mithraic Studies*, ed. J. R. Hinnells, Manchester 1975, 155-207.

Dain (1933)—Dain, A., *Inscriptions grecques du Musée du Louvre. Les textes inédits*, Paris 1933.

Daniels (1975)—Daniels, C. M., "The role of the Roman army in the spread and practice of Mithraism," in *Mithraic Studies. Proceedings of the First Interna-*

tional Congress of Mithraic Studies, ed. J. R. Hinnells, Manchester 1975, 249-274.

D'Arms (1972)—D'Arms, J. H., "A new inscribed base from fourth century Puteoli," *La parola del passato* 27 (1972) 255-270.

De Blois (1976)—De Blois, L., *The Policy of the Emperor Gallienus* (Studies of the Dutch Archaeological and Historical Soc. 7), Leiden 1976.

Decharme (1904)—Decharme, P., *La critique des traditions religieuses chez les Grecs, des origines au temps de Plutarque*, Paris 1904.

Degrassi (1962)—Degrassi, A., "I culti della Venezia Tridentina," *Scritti vari di antichità* II (Rome 1962) 993-1009.

Dell (1893)—Dell, J., "Ausgrabungen in Carnuntum im Jahre 1891," *AEM* 16 (1893) 156-204.

DenBoeft (1977)—DenBoeft, J., *Calcidius on Demons (Commentarius Ch. 127-136)*, Leiden 1977.

Déonna (1924)—Déonna, W., "Les collections archéologiques et historiques . . . ," *Genava* 2 (1924) 29-57.

DeRicci (1934)—DeRicci, S., "Deux nouvelles inscriptions grecques d'Egypte," *CRAI* 1934, 256-261.

Deschamps and Cousin (1887)—Deschamps, G., and G. Cousin, "Inscriptions du temple de Zeus Panamaros," *BCH* 11 (1887) 373-391.

Deschamps and Cousin (1891)—Deschamps, G., and G. Cousin, "Inscriptions du temple de Zeus Panamaros," *BCH* 15 (1891) 169-209.

DesPlaces (1969)—DesPlaces, E., *La religion grecque. Dieux, cultes, rites, et sentiment religieux dans la Grèce antique*, Paris 1969.

L. Deubner (1932)—Deubner, L., *Attische Feste*, Berlin 1932.

O. Deubner (1977-1978)—Deubner, O., "Das Heiligtum der alexandrinischen Gottheiten in Pergamon gennant 'Kizil Avli' ('Rote Halle')," *Mitt. des Deutschen Arch. Inst., Istanbul* 27/28 (1977-1978) 227-250.

Diehl and Cousin (1887)—Diehl, C., and G. Cousin, "Inscriptions de Lagina," *BCH* 11 (1887) 5-89, 145-163.

Dionigi (1976)—Dionigi, I., "Lucr. 5, 1198-1203 e *P. Oxy.* 215 col. I 7-24," *Studi italiani di filol. class.²* 48 (1976) 118-139.

Dodds (1965)—Dodds, E. R., *Pagan and Christian in an Age of Anxiety: Some Aspects of Religious Experience from Marcus Aurelius to Constantine*, Cambridge 1965.

Dothan (1968)—Dothan, M., "The representation of Helios in the mosaic of Hammath-Tiberias," in *Tardo antico e alto medioevo. La forma artistica nel passaggio dall'antichità al medioevo . . . 1967* (Accad. Naz. dei Lincei. Problemi attuali . . . 105), Rome 1968, 99-104.

Drachmann (1922)—Drachmann, A. B., *Atheism in Pagan Antiquity*, London 1922.

Drew-Bear (1978)—Drew-Bear, T., *Nouvelles inscriptions de Phrygie* (Studia Amstelodamensia 16), Zutphen (Netherlands) 1978.

Drexel (1922)—Drexel, F., "Die Götterverehrung im römischen Germanien," *BRGK* 14 (1922) 1-68.

Dreyer (1970)—Dreyer, O., *Untersuchungen zum Begriff des Gottgeziemenden in der Antike*, Hildesheim 1970.

Dubois (1902)—Dubois, C.-A., "Culte et dieux à Pouzzoles," *MEFR* 22 (1902) 23-68.

Dufournet (1974)—Dufournet, J., "Le dieu Vintius . . . ," in *Mélanges offerts à Roger Dion*, ed. R. Chevallier, Paris 1974, 379-405.

Du Mesnil du Buisson (1943-1944)—Du Mesnil du Buisson, R., "L'offrande de poisson à Ishtar," *BSAF* 1943-1944, 317-327.

F. Dunand (1972-1973)—Dunand, F., *Le culte d'Isis dans le bassin orientale de la Mediterranée*, 3 vols., Leiden 1972-1973.

M. Dunand (1939)—Dunand, M., "Nouvelles inscriptions du Djebel Druze et du Hauran," in *Mélanges syriens offerts à Monsieur René Dussaud . . .* , 2 (Paris 1939) 559-576.

Dupont-Sommer and Robert (1964)—Dupont-Sommer, A., and L. Robert, *La déesse de Hiérapolis Castabala (Cilicie)*, Paris 1964.

Dussaud (1922)—Dussaud, R., "Le temple de Jupiter Damascénien et ses transformations aux époques chrétienne et musulmane," *Syria* 13 (1922) 219-250.

Duthoy (1969)—Duthoy, R., *The Taurobolium. Its Evolution and Terminology*, Leiden 1969.

Edelstein and Edelstein (1945)—Edelstein, E. J. and L., *Asclepius. A Collection and Interpretation of the Testimonies*, 2 vols., Baltimore 1945.

Eitrem (1929)—Eitrem, S., "Philostrats Heroikos," *Symb. Oslo.* 8 (1929) 1-56.

Eitrem (1939)—Eitrem, S., "Die magischen Gemmen und ihre Weihe," *Symb. Oslo.* 19 (1939) 57-85.

Elderkin (1937)—Elderkin, G. W., "Two curse inscriptions," *Hesperia* 6 (1937) 382-395.

Emmett and Pickering (1975)—Emmett, A. M., and S. R. Pickering, "The importance of P. Bodmer XX, the *Apology of Phileas*," *Prudentia* 7 (1975) 95-103.

Engelmann (1976)—Engelmann, H., ed., *Die Inschriften von Kyme*, Bonn 1976.

Erbse (1952)—Erbse, H., "Plutarchs Schrift περὶ δεισιδαιμονίας," *Hermes* 80 (1952) 296-314.

Etienne et al. (1976)—Etienne, R., et al., "Les dimensions sociales de la romanisation dans la Péninsule ibérique des origines à la fin de l'Empire," in *Assimilation et resistance à la culture gréco-romaine dans le monde ancien. Travaux du VIᵉ Congrès international de la Fédération Internationale des Associations d'études classiques . . . 1974*, Bucharest 1976, 95-109.

Evans (1939)—Evans, E. C., *The Cults of the Sabine Territory*, Rome 1939.

Fears (1977)—Fears, J. R., *Princeps a diis electus. The Divine Election of the Emperor, as a Political Concept at Rome*, Rome 1977.

Fentress (1978)—Fentress, E., "Dii Mauri and dii patrii," *Latomus* 37 (1978) 507-516.

Ferguson (1970)—Ferguson, J., *The Religions of the Roman Empire*, London 1970.

Festugière (1935)—Festugière, A.-J., "Les mystères de Dionysos," *Rev. bibl.* 44 (1935) 192-211, 366-396.

Festugière (1945)—Festugière, A.-J., *Traités I-XII (Corpus Hermeticum I*, texte établi par A. D. Nock et traduit par A.-J. Festugière), Paris 1945.

Festugière (1949)—Festugière, A.-J., "A propos des arétalogies d'Isis," *HThR* 42 (1949) 209-234.

Festugière (1959)—Festugière, A.-J., *Antioche paienne et chrétienne. Libanius, Chrysostome, et les moines de Syrie,* Paris 1959.

Février (1977)—Février, P.-A., "A propos du repas funeraire: culte et sociabilité," *Cahiers archéologiques* 26 (1977) 29-45.

Fink et al. (1940)—Fink, R. O., et al., "The Feriale Duranum," *Yale Class. Studies* 7 (1940) 1-222.

Finke (1927)—Finke, H., "Neue Inschriften," *BRGK* 17 (1927) 1-107.

Fishwick (1967)—Fishwick, D., "Hastiferi," *JRS* 57 (1967) 142-160.

Fishwick (1978)—Fishwick, D., "Augustus deus and deus Augustus," in *Hommages à M. J. Vermaseren,* ed. M. B. de Boer and T. A. Edridge, I, Leiden 1978, 375-380.

Fitz (1959)—Fitz, J., "Der Besuch des Septimius Severus in Pannonien im Jahre 202 u.Z.," *Acta arch. acad. sci. Hung.* 11 (1959) 237-263.

Fitz (1968)—Fitz, J., "M. Campanius Marcellus," *Acta ant. acad. sci. Hung.* 16 (1968) 313-323.

Fitz (1972)—Fitz, J., *Les Syriens à Intercisa,* Brussels 1972.

Flusser (1975)—Flusser, D., "The great goddess of Samaria," *Israel Exploration Journ.* 25 (1975) 13-20.

Fontrier (1883)—Fontrier, A., "Inscriptions d'Asie Mineure," *BCH* 7 (1883) 501-506.

Formigé (1944)—Formigé, J., "Le sanctuaire de Sanxay . . . ," *Gallia* 3 (1944) 43-97.

Forrer (1915)—Forrer, R., *Das Mithra-Heiligtum von Königshofen bei Strassburg,* Stuttgart 1915.

Fossey (1897)—Fossey, C., "Inscriptions de Syrie, II. Djôlan et Hauran," *BCH* 21 (1897) 39-65.

Foucher (1964)—Foucher, L., *Hadrumetum,* Tunis 1964.

Franchi de' Cavalieri (1901)—Franchi de' Cavalieri, P., *I martiri di S. Teodoto e di S. Ariadne, con un appendice sul testo originale del martirio* (Studi e testi 6), Rome 1901.

Francis (1975)—Francis, E. D., "Mithraic graffiti from Dura-Europus," in *Mithraic Studies. Proceedings of the First International Congress of Mithraic Studies,* ed. J. R. Hinnells, Manchester 1975, 2.424-445.

Franciscis (1954)—Franciscis, A. de, "Regione I (Latium et Campania) (Campania)," *Not. Scavi* 79 (1954) 269-290.

Frank (1933-1940)—Frank, T., *An Economic Survey of Ancient Rome,* 6 vols., Baltimore 1933-1940.

Franke (1968)—Franke, P. R., *Kleinasien zur Römerzeit. Griechisches Leben im Spiegel der Münzen,* Munich 1968.

Frantz (1965)—Frantz, A., "From paganism to Christianity in the temples of Athens," *Dumbarton Oaks Papers* 19 (1965) 187-205.

Fraser (1960)—Fraser, P. M., *The Inscriptions on Stone* (Samothrace. Excavations Conducted by the Institute of Fine Arts of New York University, ed. K. Lehmann, 2, 1), New York 1960.

Frédouille (1972)—Frédouille, J.-C., *Tertullien et la conversion de la culture antique,* Paris 1972.

Frend (1952)—Frend, W.H.C., *The Donatist Church. A Movement of Protest in Roman North Africa,* Oxford 1952.

Frézouls (1952)—Frézouls, E., "Les théâtres romains de Syrie," *Annales arch. de Syrie* 2 (1952) 46-100.

Friedlaender (1921-1923)—Friedlaender, L., *Darstellungen aus der Sittengeschichte Roms in der Zeit von Augustus bis zum Ausgang der Antonine*,[10] ed. G. Wissowa, vols. 1 (1922), 2 (1922), 3 (1923) and 4 (1921), Leipzig.

Frier (1977)—Frier, B. W., "The rental market in early imperial Rome," *JRS* 67 (1977) 27-37.

Fülep (1954)—Fülep, F., "Epigraphie," in *Intercisa I. (Dunapentele-Sztálinváros). Geschichte der Stadt in der Römerzeit*, eds. L. Barkóczi et al., Budapest 1954, 232-273.

Gaertringen (1935)—Gaertringen, H. von, "Ein Asklepiosorakel aus Athen," *Archiv für Religionswiss.* 32 (1935) 367-370.

Gagé (1955)—Gagé, J., *Apollon romain. Essai sur le culte d'Apollon et le développement du 'ritus Graecus' à Rome des origines à Auguste*, Paris 1955.

Gagé (1964)—Gagé, J., *Les classes sociales dans l'empire romain*, Paris 1964.

Gallavotti (1972)—Gallavotti, C., "Esegesi di due epigrafi latine," *Giornale italiana di filol.* 24 (1972) 354-362.

Ganschinietz (1913)—Ganschinietz, R., *Hippolytos' Capitel gegen die Magier. Refut. Haer. IV 28-32* (Texte und Untersuchungen 39), Leipzig 1913.

Gauckler (1899)—Gauckler, P., "Les fouilles à Carthage," *BCTH* 1899, clix-clxiv.

Gaur (1963)—Gaur, A., "Les danses sacrées en Inde," in *Les danses sacrées . . .* (Sources orientales VI), Paris 1963, 315-342.

Gawlikowski (1973)—Gawlikowski, M., *Palmyre VI. Le temple palmyrénien. Etude d'épigraphie et de topographie historique*, Warsaw 1973.

Geffcken (1907)—Geffcken, J., *Zwei griechische Apologeten*, Leipzig-Berlin 1907.

Geffcken (1920)—Geffcken, J., *Der Ausgang des griechisch-römischen Heidentums*, Heidelberg 1920.

Gilliam (1976)—Gilliam, J. F., "Invitations to the kline of Sarapis," in *Collectanea papyrologica. Texts Published in Honor of H. C. Youtie*, Bonn 1976, 1.315-324.

Girard (1878)—Girard, P., "Ex-votos à Esculape trouvés sur la pente méridionale de l'Acropole," *BCH* 2 (1878) 65-94.

Girard (1881)—Girard, P., *L'Asclépieion d'Athènes d'après de récentes découvertes*, Paris 1881.

Girard and Martha (1878)—Girard, P., and J. Martha, "Inventaires de l'Asclépieion," *BCH* 2 (1878) 419-445.

Glueck (1937)—Glueck, N., "A newly discovered Nabataean temple of Atargatis and Hadad at Khirbet et-Tannûr, Transjordania," *AJA* 41 (1937) 361-376.

Golfetto (1961)—Golfetto, A., *Dougga. Die Geschichte einer Stadt im Schatten Karthagos*, Basel 1961.

Goodhue (1975)—Goodhue, N., *The Lucus Furrinae and the Syrian Sanctuary on the Janiculum*, Amsterdam 1975.

Gordon (1972)—Gordon, R. L., "Mithraism and Roman society: social factors in the explanation of religious change in the Roman Empire," *Religion* 2 (1972) 92-121.

Gordon (1975)—Gordon, R. L., "Franz Cumont and the doctrines of Mithraism," in *Mithraic Studies. Proceedings of the First International Congress of Mithraic Studies*, ed. J. R. Hinnells, Manchester 1975, 215-248.

Gough (1952)—Gough, M., "Anazarbus," *Anatolian Studies* 2 (1952) 85-150.

Graeve (1972)—Graeve, V. von, "Tempel und Kult der syrischen Götter am Janiculum," *Jb. des Deutschen Arch. Inst.* 87 (1972) 314-347.

Graillot (1912)—Graillot, H., *Le culte de Cybèle, mère des dieux, à Rome et dans l'empire*, Paris 1912.

Grandjean (1975)—Grandjean, Y., *Une nouvelle arétalogie d'Isis à Maronée*, Leiden 1975.

Grant (1968)—Grant, M., *The Climax of Rome. The Final Achievements of the Ancient World AD 161-337*, London 1968.

Grégoire (1939)—Grégoire, H., "Les pierres qui crient. Les chrétiens et l'oracle de Didymes," *Byzantion* 14 (1939) 318-321.

Gsell (1931)—Gsell, S., "Autel romain de Zana (Algérie)," *CRAI* 1931, 251-269.

Guarducci (1942-1943)—Guarducci, M., "Le impronte del Quo Vadis e monumenti affini, figurati ed epigrafici," *Rend. Pont. Accad. Romana di Archeologia* 19 (1942-1943) 305-344.

Guey (1953)—Guey, J., "Epigraphica Tripolitana," *REA* 55 (1953) 334-358.

Habicht (1959-1960)—Habicht, C., "Zwei neue Inschriften aus Pergamon," *Mitt. des Deutschen Arch. Inst., Istanbul* 9/10 (1959-1960) 109-127.

Habicht (1969)—Habicht, C., *Die Inschriften des Asklepieions* (Altertümer von Pergamon, ed. E. Boehringer, VIII 3), Berlin 1969.

Hall (1977)—Hall, A., "A sanctuary of Leto at Oenoanda," *Anatolian Studies* 27 (1977) 193-197.

Hanfmann and Waldbaum (1975)—Hanfmann, G.M.A., and J. C. Waldbaum, *A Survey of Sardis and the Major Monuments Outside the City Walls*, Cambridge 1975.

Hanslik (1954)—Hanslik, R., "Apollo Pythius und sein Kult," *Vigiliae Christianae* 8 (1954) 176-181.

Hanson (1959)—Hanson, J. A., *Roman Theater-Temples*, Princeton 1959.

Harder (1944)—Harder, R., *Karpokrates von Chalkis und die memphitische Isispropaganda*, Berlin 1944.

Harnack (1905)—Harnack, A. von, *Der Vorwurf des Atheismus in den drei ersten Jahrhunderten* (Texte und Untersuchungen 28, 4), Leipzig 1905.

Harper (1972)—Harper, R. P., "Tituli Comanorum Cappadociae iterum suppleti," *Anatolian Studies* 22 (1972) 225-239.

Hasluck (1904)—Hasluck, F. W., "Unpublished inscriptions from the Cyzicus neighborhood," *JHS* 24 (1904) 20-40.

Hatt (1965)—Hatt, J.-J., "Essai sur l'évolution de la religion gauloise," *REA* 67 (1965) 80-125.

Hatt (1978)—Hatt, J.-J., "Divinités orientales et dieux gaulois," in *Paganisme, judaisme, christianisme . . . Mélanges offerts à Marcel Simon*, Paris 1978, 277-286.

Hatt (1979)—Hatt, J.-J., "Le culte de Mars indigène dans le Nord-Est de la Gaule," *Rev. arch. de l'Est* 30 (1979) 121-138.

Hatzfeld (1920)—Hatzfeld, J., "Inscriptions de Lagina en Carie," *BCH* 44 (1920) 70-100.

Hatzfeld (1927)—Hatzfeld, J., "Inscriptions de Panamara," *BCH* 51 (1927) 57-122.

Haussoullier (1899)—Haussoullier, B., "Notes d'épigraphie milésienne. θυορία, θεωρία, θεορία," *Rev. de philol.* 23 (1899) 313-320.

Haussoullier (1902)—Haussoullier, B., *Etudes sur l'histoire de Milet et du Didy-meion*, Paris 1902.

Haussoullier and Ingholt (1924)—Haussoullier, B., and H. Ingholt, "Inscriptions grecques de Syrie," *Syria* 5 (1924) 316-341.

Heitsch (1961-1964)—Heitsch, E., *Die griechischen Dichterfragmente der römischen Kaiserzeit*, 1st ed., vol. 1, Göttingen 1961; ed. 2, 2 vols., Göttingen 1963-1964.

Hepding (1903)—Hepding, H., *Attis, seine Mythen und sein Kult*, Giessen 1903.

Herbillon (1929)—Herbillon, J., *Les cultes de Patras . . .* , Baltimore 1929.

Herrmann and Polatkan (1969)—Herrmann, P., and K. Z. Polatkan, *Das Testament des Epikrates und andere neue Inschriften aus dem Museum von Manisa*, Vienna 1969.

Herzog (1931)—Herzog, R., *Die Wunderheilungen von Epidauros. Ein Beitrag zur Geschichte der Medizin und der Religion*, Leipzig 1931.

Heuten (1937)—Heuten, G., "Primus in orbe deos fecit timor," *Latomus* 1 (1937) 3-8.

Heyder and Mallwitz (1978)—Heyder, W., and A. Mallwitz, *Die Bauten im Kabirenheiligtum bei Theben* (Das Kabirenheiligtum bei Theben II), Berlin 1978.

Hicks (1891)—Hicks, E. L., "Inscriptions from western Cilicia," *JHS* 12 (1891) 225-273.

Hill (1897)—Hill, G. F., "Notes on additions to the Greek coins in the British Museum, 1887-1896," *JHS* 17 (1897) 78-91.

Hill (1911)—Hill, G. F., "Some Graeco-Phoenician shrines," *JHS* 31 (1911) 56-64.

Hinnells (1975)—Hinnells, J. R., "Reflections on the bull-slaying scene," in *Mithraic Studies. Proceedings of the First International Congress of Mithraic Studies*, ed. J. R. Hinnells, Manchester 1975, 290-312.

Hinrichs (1970)—Hinrichs, A., "Pagan ritual and the alleged crimes of the early Christians. A reconsideration," in *Kyriakon. Festschrift Johannes Quasten*, Münster 1970, 18-35.

Hoddinott (1975)—Hoddinott, R. F., *Bulgaria in Antiquity . . .* , London 1975.

Hoffiller and Saria (1938)—Hoffiller, V., and B. Saria, *Antike Inschriften aus Jugoslavien*, Heft I: *Noricum und Pannonia Superior*, Zagreb 1938.

Hoffmann (1963)—Hoffmann, D., "Die spätrömischen Soldatengrabschriften von Concordia," *Mus. Helv.* 20 (1963) 22-57.

Hohlwein (1940)—Hohlwein, N., "Déplacement et tourisme dans l'Egypte romaine," *Chron. d'Egypte* 30 (1940) 253-278.

Homo (1904)—Homo, L., *Essai sur le règne de l'empereur Aurélien*, Paris 1904.

Homolle (1882)—Homolle, T., "Comptes des hiéropes du temple d'Apollon délien," *BCH* 6 (1882) 1-167.

Hopfner (1922)—Hopfner, T., *Ueber die Geheimlehren von Jamblichus*, Leipzig 1922.

Hopkins (1978)—Hopkins, K., *Conquerors and Slaves . . .* , Cambridge and New York 1978.

Ianovitz (1972)—Ianovitz, O., *Il culto solare nella 'X Regio,'* Milan 1972.

Imhoof-Blumer (1911)—Imhoof-Blumer, F., "Beiträge zur Erklärung griechischen Münztypen," *Nomisma* 6 (1911) 1-23.

Ivanov (1974)—Ivanov, T., "Die letzten Ausgrabungen des römischen und früh-byzantinschen Donaulimes in der VR Bulgarien," in *Actes du IXᵉ Congrès international d'études sur les frontières romaines . . . 1972*, Bucharest 1974, 55-69.

Jalabert (1908)—Jalabert, L., "Deux missions archéologiques américaines en Syrie," *Mél. de l'Univ. St. Joseph* 3 (1908) 713-752.

James (1924)—James, M. R., *The Apocryphal New Testament, being the Apocryphal Gospels, Acts, Epistles, and Apocalypses*, Oxford 1924.

Jerphanion and Jalabert (1908)—Jerphanion, G. de, and L. Jalabert, "Inscriptions d'Asie Mineure (Pont, Cappadoce, Cilicie)," *Mél. de l'Univ. St. Joseph* 3 (1908) 437-479.

Jobst (1976)—Jobst, W., "Der Pfaffenberg—ein Zentrum römischer Staatsreligion in Carnuntum," *Neue Forschungen in Carnuntum* (Kultur und Natur im Niederösterreich—Studien und Forschungen 1), Vienna 1976, 33-52.

A. H. M. Jones (1940)—Jones, A. H. M., *The Greek City, from Alexander to Justinian*, Oxford 1940.

A. H. M. Jones (1962)—Jones, A. H. M., *Constantine and the Conversion of Europe*, New York 1962.

A. H. M. Jones (1963)—Jones, A. H. M., "The social background of the struggle between pagans and Christians," in *The Conflict Between Paganism and Christianity in the Fourth Century*, ed. A. Momigliano, Oxford 1963, 17-37.

A. H. M. Jones (1964)—Jones, A. H. M., *The Later Roman Empire 284-602. A Social Economic and Administrative Survey*, 2 vols., Norman 1964.

L. W. Jones (1929)—Jones, L. W., *The Cults of Dacia*, Berkeley 1929.

Jouguet (1911)—Jouguet, P., *La vie municipale dans l'Egypte romaine*, Paris 1911.

Jucker (1960)—Jucker, H., "Geküsste Götterbilder," *Antike Kunst* 3 (1960) 91-92.

Jullian (1908-1926)—Jullian, C., *Histoire de la Gaule*, 8 vols., Paris 1908-1926.

Kabbadia (1885)—Kabbadia, P., "'Επιγραφαὶ ἐκ τῶν 'εν 'Επιδαυρία ἀνασκαφῶν," *Ephem. arch.* 1885, 189-199.

Kaegi (1966)—Kaegi, W. E., "The fifth-century twilight of Byzantine paganism," *Classica et mediaevalia* 27 (1966) 243-275.

Kahrstedt (1954)—Kahrstedt, U., *Das wirtschaftliche Gesicht Griechenlands in der Kaiserzeit. Kleinstadt, Villa und Domäne*, Bern 1954.

Kaibel (1878)—Kaibel, G., *Epigrammata graeca ex lapidibus conlecta*, Berlin 1878.

Kalinka (1933)—Kalinka, E., "Aus Bithynien und Umgegend," *JOAI* 28 (1933) Beibl. cols. 45-112.

Kan (1943)—Kan, A. H., *Juppiter Dolichenus. Sammlung der Inschriften und Bildwerke*, Leiden 1943.

Kane (1975)—Kane, J. P., "The Mithraic cult meal in its Greek and Roman environment," in *Mithraic Studies. Proceedings of the First International Congress of Mithraic Studies*, ed. J. R. Hinnells, Manchester 1975, 2.313-351.

Kantorowicz (1961)—Kantorowicz, E. H., "Gods in uniform," *Proc. Am. Philos. Soc.* 105 (1961) 368-396.

Kantorowicz (1963)—Kantorowicz, E. H., "Oriens Augusti—Lever du roi," *Dumbarton Oaks Papers* 17 (1963) 117-177.

Keil (1908)—Keil, J., "Zur Geschichte der Hymnoden in der Provinz Asia," *JOAI* 11 (1908) 101-110.

Keil (1923)—Keil, J., "Die Kulte Lydiens," in *Anatolian Studies Presented to William M. Ramsay*, Manchester 1923, 239-266.

Keil (1939)—Keil, J., "Kulte im Prytaneion von Ephesos," in *Anatolian Studies Presented to W. H. Buckler*, Manchester 1939, 119-128.

Keil and Premerstein (1908)—Keil, J., and A. von Premerstein, *Bericht über eine Reise in Lydien und der südlichen Aiolis ausgeführt 1906* . . . (Denkschriften der kaiserlichen Akad. der Wiss. in Wien, Phil.-hist. Kl. 53, 2), Vienna 1908.

Kerenyi (1955)—Kerenyi, C., "The mysteries of the Kabeiroi," in *The Mysteries* (Papers from the Eranos Yearbooks, 2), New York 1955, 32-63.

Kern (1892)—Kern, O., "Δημήτηρ Σελήνη," *Ephem. arch.* 1892, 113-118.

Kern (1900)—Kern, O., *Die Inschriften von Magnesia am Maeander*, Berlin 1900.

Koethe (1933)—Koethe, H., "Die keltischen Rund- und Vielecktempel der Kaiserzeit," *BRGK* 23 (1933) 10-108.

Koets (1929)—Koets, P. J., Δεισιδαιμονία. *A Contribution to the Knowledge of the Religious Terminology in Greek*, Purmerend (Netherlands) 1929.

Kötting (1950)—Kötting, B., *Peregrinatio Religiosa. Wahllfahrten in der Antike und das Pilgerwesen in der alten Kirche*, Münster 1950.

Krill (1978)—Krill, R. M., "Roman paganism under the Antonines and Severans," *ANRW* II 16, 1 (Berlin 1978) 27-44.

Kroll (1924)—Kroll, W., *Studien zum Verständnis der römischen Literatur*, Stuttgart 1924.

Kunze et al. (1958)—Kunze, E., et al., *VI Bericht über die Ausgrabungen in Olympia* . . . , Berlin 1958.

Labhardt (1960)—Labhardt, A., "Curiositas. Notes sur l'histoire d'un mot et d'une notion," *Mus. Helv.* 17 (1960) 206-224.

Lafaurie (1966)—Lafaurie, J., "Dies imperii Constantini Augusti: 25 décembre 307. Essai sur quelques problèmes de chronologie constantinienne," in *Mélanges d'archéologie et d'histoire offerts à A. Piganiol*, Paris 1966, 795-806.

Lambrechts (1952)—Lambrechts, P., "Les fêtes 'phrygiennes' de Cybèle et d'Attis," *Bull. Inst. Hist. Belge de Rome* 27 (1952) 141-170.

Lambrechts and Noyen (1954)—Lambrechts, P., and P. Noyen, "Recherches sur le culte d'Atargatis dans le monde grec," *Nouvelle Clio* 6 (1954) 258-277.

Lanckoronski (1890-1892)—Lanckoronski, K., *Städte Pamphyliens und Pisidiens*, unter Mitwirkung von G. Niemann und E. Peterson, 2 vols., Vienna 1890-1892.

Lane (1971-1978)—Lane, E. N., *Corpus monumentorum religionis dei Menis*, 4 vols., Leiden 1971-1978.

Lane (1978a)—Lane, E. N., "The temple-type of Prostanna: a query," in *Studien zur Religion und Kultur Kleinasiens. Festschrift für Friedrich Karl Dörner* . . . , Leiden 1978, 2.540-545.

Lassère (1973)—Lassère, J.-M., "Recherches sur la chronologie des épitaphes paiennes de l'Afrique," *Antiquités africaines* 7 (1973) 7-151.

Latte (1931)—Latte, K., "Inscriptiones Graecae . . . ," *Gnomon* 7 (1931) 113-135.

Latte (1960)—Latte, K., *Römische Religionsgeschichte* (Handbuch der kl. Altertumswiss. V, 4), Munich 1960.

Lattimore (1942)—Lattimore, R., *Themes in Greek and Latin Epitaphs*, Urbana 1942.

Laumonier (1934)—Laumonier, A., "Notes sur une inscription de Stratonicée," *REA* 36 (1934) 85-87.

Laumonier (1937)—Laumonier, A., "Recherches sur la chronologie des prêtres de Panamara," *BCH* 61 (1937) 236-298.

Laumonier (1958)—Laumonier, A., *Les cultes indigènes en Carie*, Paris 1958.

Launey (1937)—Launey, M., "Le verger d'Héraclès à Thasos," *BCH* 61 (1937) 380-409.

Laurin (1954)—Laurin, J. R., *Orientations maîtresses des apologistes chrétiens de 270 à 361*, Rome 1954.

Lebreton (1923-1924)—Lebreton, J., "Le désaccord de la théologie savante et de la foi populaire dans l'Eglise chrétienne du IIIᵉ siècle," *Rev. d'hist. ecclésiastique* 19 (1923) 481-506 and 20 (1924) 5-37.

LeGlay (1954)—LeGlay, M., "Le mithraeum de Lambèse," *CRAI* 1954, 269-278.

LeGlay (1966)—LeGlay, M., *Saturne africain, histoire*, Paris 1966.

LeGlay (1971)—LeGlay, M., "La vie religieuse à Lambèse d'après de nouveaux documents," *Ant. afr.* 5 (1971) 125-153.

LeGlay (1972)—LeGlay, M., "Une ville à vocation de capitale: Lugdunum," *Archeologia* 50 (1972) 10-14.

LeGlay (1976)—LeGlay, M., "Hadrien et l'Asklépieion de Pergame," *BCH* 100 (1976) 347-372.

Lehmann (1939)—Lehmann (-Hartleben), K., "Excavations in Samothrace," *AJA* 43 (1939) 133-145.

Lehmann (1954)—Lehmann, K., "The mystery cult of Samothrace," *Archaeology* 7 (1954) 91-95.

Leonhard (1914)—Leonhard, F., *Das Kastell Altstadt bei Miltenberg* (Obergermanisch-Raetische Limes des Römerreiches BIII 38), Heidelberg 1914.

Leschi (1957)—Leschi, L., *Etudes d'epigraphie, d'archéologie et d'histoire africaines*, Paris 1957.

Lesky (1966)—Lesky, A., *A History of Greek Literature*, trans. J. Willis and C. de Heer, London 1966.

Levi (1944)—Levi, D., "Aion," *Hesperia* 13 (1944) 269-314.

E. Lévy (1968)—Lévy, E., "Nouveaux bijoux à Délos," *BCH* 92 (1968) 523-539.

I. Lévy (1895)—Lévy, I., "Etudes sur la vie municipale en Asie Mineure au temps des Antonins," *REG* 8 (1895) 203-250.

Liebeschuetz (1979)—Liebeschuetz, J. H. W. G., *Continuity and Change in Roman Religion*, Oxford 1979.

Lörincz (1978)—Lörincz, B., "Die Besatzungstruppen des Legionslager von Aquincum am Ende des 1.-Anfang des 2. Jahrhunderts," *Acta arch. acad. sci. Hung.* 30 (1978) 299-312.

Longo (1969)—Longo, V., *Aretalogie nel mondo greco*, 2 vols., Genoa 1969.

L'Orange (1935)—L'Orange, H. P., "Sol invictus imperator. Ein Beitrag zur Apotheose," *Symb. Oslo.* 14 (1935) 86-114.

Maas (1933)—Maas, P., *Epidaurische Hymnen* (Schriften der Königsberger Gelehrten Gesellschaft 9, 5), Halle 1933, 125-162.

MacMullen (1962)—MacMullen, R., "Roman bureaucratese," *Traditio* 18 (1962) 364-378.

MacMullen (1966a)—MacMullen, R., *Enemies of the Roman Order* . . . , Cambridge 1966.

MacMullen (1966b)—MacMullen, R., "A note on sermo humilis," *JThStudies* 17 (1966) 108-112.

MacMullen (1968)—MacMullen, R., "Constantine and the miraculous," *GRBS* 9 (1968) 81-96.

MacMullen (1970)—MacMullen, R., "Roman market days," *Phoenix* 24 (1970) 333-341.

MacMullen (1972)—MacMullen, R., "Sfiducia nell'intelletto nel quarto secolo," *Rivista storica italiana* 84 (1972) 5-16.

MacMullen (1974)—MacMullen, R., *Roman Social Relations* . . . , New Haven 1974.

MacMullen (1976)—MacMullen, R., *Roman Government's Response to Crisis . . .* , New Haven 1976.

MacMullen (1980)—MacMullen, R., "The power of bishops outside the Church," in *The Role of the Christian Bishop in Ancient Society*. Thirty-fifth Colloquy . . . 1979 (Center for Hermeneutical Studies, Grad. Theol. Union, Berkeley 1980) 25-29.

Macpherson (1972)—Macpherson, I. W., "Six inscriptions from Galatia," *Anatolian Studies* 22 (1972) 217-223.

Magie (1950)—Magie, D., *Roman Rule in Asia Minor to the End of the Third Century after Christ*, 2 vols., Princeton 1950.

Maguire (1939)—Maguire, J. P., "The sources of Pseudo-Aristotle De Mundo," *Yale Class. Studies* 6 (1939) 111-167.

Malaise (1972)—Malaise, M., *Les conditions de pénétration et de diffusion des cultes égyptiens en Italie*, Leiden 1972.

Marchetti Longhi (1943-1945)—Marchetti Longhi, G., "Gli scavi del largo Argentina," *Bull. comm.* 71 (1943-1945) 57-95.

Marcillet-Jaubert (1974)—Marcillet-Jaubert, J., "A propos de M. Aurelius Decimus," *ZPE* 14 (1974) 249-251.

Martroye (1915)—Martroye, F., "Mesures prises par Constantin contre la superstitio," *BSAF* 1915, 280-292.

Martroye (1916)—Martroye, F., "Du sens du mot superstitio," *BSAF* 1916, 106-107, 111-113.

Mattingly (1928)—Mattingly, H., *Roman Coins from the Earliest Times to the Fall of the Western Empire*, London 1928.

Matz (1940)—Matz, F., "Die griechischen Sarkophage mit bakchischen Darstellungen," in *Bericht über den VI. internationalen Kongress für Archäologie . . . 1939*, Berlin 1940, 502-503.

McCown (1938)—McCown, C. C., "The festival theater at the Birketein," in C. H. Kraeling, *Gerasa, City of the Decapolis* . . . , New Haven 1938, 159-167.

McPhee (1966)—McPhee, C., *Music in Bali*, New Haven 1966.

Meiggs (1960)—Meiggs, R., *Roman Ostia*, Oxford 1960.

Mellor (1975)—Mellor, R., ΘΕΑ ΡΩΜΗ. *The Worship of the Goddess Roma in the Greek World*, Göttingen 1975.

Merkelbach (1962)—Merkelbach, R., *Roman und Mysterium in der Antike*, Munich 1962.

Merkelbach (1973)—Merkelbach, R., "Zwei Texte aus dem Sarapeum zu Thessalonike," *ZPE* 10 (1973) 45-54.

Merlan (1967)—Merlan, P., "Greek philosophy from Plato to Plotinus," in *The Cambridge History of Later Greek and Early Medieval Philosophy*, ed. A. H. Armstrong, Cambridge 1967, 14-136.

Merlat (1951)—Merlat, P., *Répertoire des inscriptions et monuments figurés du culte de Jupiter Dolichenus*, Paris and Rennes 1951.

Merlin (1908)—Merlin, A., *Le temple d'Apollon à Bulla Regia*, Paris 1908.

Merlin (1909)—Merlin, A., "Les dernières découvertes d'antiquités en Tunisie," *BCTH* 1909, ccxxxi-ccxxxviii.

Merlin (1910)—Merlin, A., "Le sanctuaire de Baal et de Tanit près de Siagu," *Notes et documents* 4 (1910) 3-58.

Merlin (1916)—Merlin, A., "Une nouvelle inscription à Thuburbo Majus," *CRAI* 1916, 262-267.

Merlin and Poinssot (1908)—Merlin, A., and L. Poinssot, "Les inscriptions d'Uchi Majus d'après les recherches du Capitaine Gondouin," *Notes et documents* 2 (1908) 3-128.

Meslin (1974)—Meslin, M., "Realités psychiques et valeurs religieuses dans les cultes orientaux (Ier-IVe siècles)," *Rev. hist.* 252 (1974) 289-314.

Meslin (1978)—Meslin, M., "Convivialité ou communion sacramentelle? Repas mithriaque et Euchariste chrétienne," in *Paganisme, judaisme, christianisme . . . Mélanges offerts à Marcel Simon*, Paris 1978, 295-306.

Milik (1972)—Milik, J. T., *Recherches d'épigraphie proche-orientale*, I: *Dédicaces faites par des dieux (Palmyre, Hatra, Tyr) et des thiases sémitiques à l'époque romaine*, Paris 1972.

Milne (1925)—Milne, J. G., "The kline of Sarapis," *JEA* 11 (1925) 6-9.

Mirković and Dusanić (1976)—Mirković, M., and S. Dusanić, *Inscriptions de la Mésie Supérieure*, I: *Singidunum et le Nord-Ouest de la province*, Belgrade 1976.

Mitford (1971)—Mitford, T. B., *The Inscriptions of Kourion*, Philadelphia 1971.

Mocsy (1970)—Mocsy, A., *Gesellschaft und Romanisation in der römischen Provinz Moesia Superior*, Amsterdam 1970.

Mocsy (1974)—Mocsy, A., *Pannonia and Upper Moesia. A History of the Middle Danube Provinces of the Roman Empire*, London 1974.

Momigliano (1977)—Momigliano, A., *Essays in Ancient and Modern Historiography*, Oxford 1977.

Mommsen (1868)—Mommsen, T., "Schauspielerinschrift von Philippi," *Hermes* 3 (1868) 461-465.

Mordtmann (1881a)—Mordtmann, J. H., "Zur Epigraphik von Kyzikos," *Ath. Mitt.* 6 (1881) 121-131.

Mordtmann (1881b)—Mordtmann, J. H., "Inschriften aus Kallipolis," *Ath. Mitt.* 6 (1881) 256-265.

Mouterde (1930-1931)—Mouterde, R., "Le glaive de Dardanos. Objets et inscriptions magiques de Syrie," *Mél. de l'Univ. St. Joseph* 15 (1930-1931) 53-137.

Mrozek (1973)—Mrozek, S., "A propos de la répartition chronologique des inscriptions latines dans le Haut-Empire," *Epigraphica* 35 (1973) 113-118.

Müller (1904)—Müller, A., "Die Parasite Apollinis," *Philologus* 63 (1904) 342-361.

Mundle (1961)—Mundle, I., "Dea Caelestis in der Religionspolitik des Septimius Severus und der Julia Domna," *Historia* 10 (1961) 228-237.

Musurillo (1972)—Musurillo, H., *The Acts of the Christian Martyrs* . . . , Oxford 1972.

Negev (1971)—Negev, A., "The Nabataean necropolis of Mampsis (Kurnub)," *Israel Exploration Journal* 21 (1971) 110-129.

Nestle (1948)—Nestle, W., *Griechische Studien. Untersuchungen zur Religion, Dichtung und Philosophie der Griechen*, Stuttgart 1948.

Neubecker (1977)—Neubecker, A. J., *Altgriechische Musik. Eine Einführung*, Darmstadt 1977.

Nilsson (1941-1955)—Nilsson, M. P., *Geschichte der griechischen Religion* (Handbuch der Altertumswiss. 5, 2), 2 vols., Munich 1941-1955.

Nilsson (1945a)—Nilsson, M. P., "Pagan divine service in late paganism," *HThR* 38 (1945) 63-69.

Nilsson (1945b)—Nilsson, M. P., "The syncretistic relief at Modena," *Symb. Oslo.* 24 (1945) 3-7.

Nilsson (1947-1948)—Nilsson, M. P., "Die Religion in den griechischen Zauberpapyri," *Årsberättelse, Kungl. Humanistiska Vetenskapssamfundet i Lund (Bull. de la Soc. des Lettres de Lund)* 1947-1948, 59-93.

Nilsson (1949)—Nilsson, M. P., "A propos du tombeau de Vincentius," *Rev. arch.* 31-32 (1949) 764-769.

Nilsson (1950)—Nilsson, M. P., "Lampen und Kerzen im Kult der Antike," *Opuscula archaeologica* 6 (1950) 96-111.

Nilsson (1963)—Nilsson, M. P., "The high god and the mediator," *HThR* 56 (1963) 101-120.

Nock (1925)—Nock, A. D., "Studies in the Graeco-Roman beliefs of the empire," *JHS* 45 (1925) 84-101.

Nock (1926)—Nock, A. D., *Sallustius, Concerning the Gods and the Universe*, Cambridge 1926.

Nock (1930)—Nock, A. D., "A diis electa. A chapter in the religious history of the third century," *HThR* 23 (1930) 251-274.

Nock (1933)—Nock, A. D., *Conversion: The Old and the New in Religion from Alexander the Great to Augustine of Hippo*, Oxford 1933.

Nock (1934)—Nock, A. D., "A vision of Mandulis Aion," *HThR* 27 (1934) 53-104.

Nock (1937)—Nock, A. D., "The genius of Mithraism," *JRS* 27 (1937) 108-113.

Nock (1946)—Nock, A. D., "Sarcophagi and symbolism," *AJA* 50 (1946) 140-170.

Nock (1958a)—Nock, A. D., "M. J. Vermaseren, Corpus inscriptionum et monumentorum religionis Mithriacae, vol. 1," *Gnomon* 30 (1958) 291-295.

Nock (1958b)—Nock, A. D., "A cult ordinance in verse," *HSCP* 63 (1958) 415-421.

Nock (1964)—Nock, A. D., *Early Gentile Christianity and its Hellenistic Background*, London 1964.

Ohlemutz (1940)—Ohlemutz, E., *Die Kulte und Heiligtümer der Götter in Pergamon*, Würzburg 1940.

Oliver (1936)—Oliver, J. H., "The Sarapion monument and the Paean of Sophocles," *Hesperia* 5 (1936) 91-122.

Oliver (1963)—Oliver, J. H., "The Athenian archon Thisbianus," *Hesperia* 32 (1963) 318.

Oliver (1978)—Oliver, J. H., "Hartmut Wolff. Die Constitutio Antoniniana...," *AJP* 99 (1978) 403-408.

Onurkan (1969-1970)—Onurkan, S., "Artemis Pergaia," *Mitt. des Deutschen Arch. Inst., Istanbul* 19/20 (1969-1970) 289-298.

Otto (1909)—Otto, W. F., "Religio und Superstitio," *Archiv für Religionswiss.* 12 (1909) 533-554.

Otto (1955)—Otto, W. F., "The meaning of the Eleusinian Mysteries," in *The Mysteries* (Papers from the Eranos Yearbooks 2), New York 1955, 14-31.

Pace (1923)—Pace, B., "Artemis Pergaea," in *Anatolian Studies Presented to William M. Ramsay*, London 1923, 296-314.

Pack (1965)—Pack, R. A., *The Greek and Latin Literary Texts from Greco-Roman Egypt*², Ann Arbor 1965.

Packer (1967)—Packer, J. E., "Housing and population in imperial Ostia and Rome," *JRS* 57 (1967) 80-95.

Page (1962)—Page, D. L., *Literary Papyri. Poetry* (Select Papyri, ed. A. S. Hunt, 3), Cambridge and London 1962.

Palmer (1978)—Palmer, R. E. A., "Severan ruler-cult and the moon in the city of Rome," *ANRW* II 16, 2 (Berlin 1978) 1085-1120.

Parassoglou (1976)—Parassoglou, G. M., "Circular from a prefect: sileat omnibus perpetuo divinandi curiositas," in *Collectanea papyrologica. Texts Published in Honor of H. C. Youtie*, I, Bonn 1976, 261-274.

Paribeni (1919)—Paribeni, R., "Rilievo con scene egizie," *Not. scavi* 1919, 106-112.

Parvan (1913)—Parvan, V., "Rumänien," *Arch. Anz.* 1913, 364-392.

Pekary (1965)—Pekary, T., "Inschriftenfunde aus Milet 1959," *Mitt. des Deutschen Arch. Inst., Istanbul* 15 (1965) 118-134.

Pekary (1978)—Pekary, T., "Statuen in kleinasiatischen Inschriften," in *Studien zur Religion und Kultur Kleinasiens. Festschrift für Friedrich Karl Dörner...*, Leiden 1978, 727-744.

Pepe (1964)—Pepe, L., "Una lectio difficilior in Petronio (71, 10 triclia)," *Giornale italiana di filol.* 17 (1964) 321-328.

Pépin (1966)—Pépin, J., "Porphyre exégète d'Homère," in *Porphyre* (Entretiens sur l'Antiquité classique 12, Fondation Hardt), Geneva 1966, 231-266.

Perdrizet (1900)—Perdrizet, P., "Lettre au R. P. Séjourné sur des inscriptions de Syrie publiées dans la Revue biblique," *Rev. bibl.* 9 (1900) 429-443.

Perret (1949)—Perret, J., "Le polythéisme de Virgile," *Rev. arch.* 32 (1949) (*Mél. d'arch. et d'hist. offerts à Ch. Picard* 4) 793-802.

E. Peterson (1926)—Peterson, E., Εἷς θεός. *Epigraphische, formgeschichtliche und religionsgeschichtliche Untersuchungen*, Göttingen 1926.

R. M. Peterson (1919)—Peterson, R. M., *The Cults of Campania*, Rome 1919.

Petit (1955)—Petit, P., *Libanius et la vie municipale à Antioche au IVe siècle après J.-C.*, Paris 1955.

Pettazzoni (1939)—Pettazzoni, R., "La confession des péchés en Syrie aux époques préchrétiennes," in *Mélanges syriens offerts à M. René Dussaud*, Paris 1939, 197-202.

Pflaum (1960-1961)—Pflaum, H. G., *Les carrières procuratoriennes équestres sous le Haut Empire romain*, 4 vols., Paris 1960-1961.

C. Picard (1922)—Picard, C., *Ephèse et Claros*, Paris 1922.

C. Picard (1955)—Picard, C., "Le théâtre des mystères de Cybèle-Attis à Vienne (Isère) et les théâtres pour représentations sacrées à travers le monde méditerranéen," *CRAI* 1955, 229-247.

G. Picard (1954)—Picard, G., "Un banquet costumé sur une mosaique d'El-Djem," *CRAI* 1954, 418-424.

G. Picard (1970)—Picard, G., "Les théâtres ruraux de Gaule," *Rev. arch.* 1970, 185-192.

G. C. Picard (1972)—Picard, G. C., "Nouvelles images de dieux gallo-romains accroupis," *BSAF* 1972, 48-50.

G. C. Picard (1977)—Picard, G. C., "Imperator caelestium," *Gallia* 35 (1977) 89-113.

Piganiol (1946)—Piganiol, A., "Observations sur le rituel le plus récent des frères Arvales," *CRAI* 1946, 241-251.

Pöhlmann (1960)—Pöhlmann, E., *Griechische Musikfragmente. Ein Weg zur altgriechischen Musik*, Nuremberg 1960.

Poenaru-Bordea (1964)—Poenaru-Bordea, G., "Cîteva inscriptii recent descoperite în Dobrogea," in *Noi monumente epigrafice din Scythia Minor*, ed. C. Daicoviciu (Muzeul de Arheologie Constanta), Constanta 1964, 97-138.

Poland (1909)—Poland, F., *Geschichte des griechischen Vereinswesens*, Leipzig 1909.

Powell (1925)—Powell, J. U., *Collectanea Alexandrina. Reliquiae minores poetarum graecorum aetatis Ptolemaicae (323-146 a. C.)*, Oxford 1925.

Prentice (1908)—Prentice, W. K., *Greek and Latin Inscriptions* (Publications of an American Archaeological Expedition to Syria in 1899-1900, Part III), New York 1908.

Prentice (1922)—Prentice, W. K., *Greek and Latin Inscriptions, Section B. Northern Syria* (Syria. Publications of the Princeton University Archaeological Expeditions to Syria in 1904-5 and 1909, Division III), Leiden 1909-1922.

Price and Trell (1977)—Price, M. J., and B. L. Trell, *Coins and their Cities: Architecture on the Ancient Coins of Greece, Rome and Palestine*, Detroit 1977.

Prieur (1968)—Prieur, J., *La province romaine des Alpes cottiennes*, Villeurbanne 1968.

Quandt (1962)—Quandt, W., *Orphei hymni*[3], Berlin 1962.

Quasten (1930)—Quasten, J., *Musik und Gesang in den Kulten der heidnischen Antike und christlicher Frühzeit*, Münster 1930.

Quasten (1950-1960)—Quasten, J., *Patrology*, 3 vols., Westminster 1950-1960.

Raabe (1892)—Raabe, R., *Die Apologie des Aristides. Aus dem syrischen übersetzt*, Leipzig 1892.

Radet (1890)—Radet, G., "Inscriptions de la region du Méandre," *BCH* 14 (1890) 224-239.

Radnoti (1961)—Radnoti, A., "C. Iulius Avitus Alexianus," *Germania* 39 (1961) 383-412.

Ramsay (1889)—Ramsay, W. M., "Artemis-Leto and Apollo-Lairbenos," *JHS* 10 (1889) 216-230.

Ramsay (1895-1897)—Ramsay, W. M., *The Cities and Bishoprics of Phrygia . . .* , 2 vols., Oxford 1895-1897.

Ramsay (1941)—Ramsay, W. M., *The Social Basis of Roman Power in Asia Minor*, Aberdeen 1941.

Rebuffat (1975)—Rebuffat, R., "Trois nouvelles campagnes dans le sud de la Tripolitaine," *CRAI* 1975, 495-505.

Redo (1973)—Redo, F., *Numismatical Sources of the Illyr Soldier Emperors' Religious Policy*, Budapest 1973.

Rehm (1938)—Rehm, A., "Kaiser Diokletian und das Heiligtum von Didyma," *Philologus* 93 (1938) 74-84.

Rehm (1958)—Rehm, A., *Die Inschriften* (Didyma, ed. T. Wiegand, II), Berlin 1958.

Reinach (1906)—Reinach, T., "Inscriptions d'Aphrodisias," *REG* 19 (1906) 79-150, 205-298.

Reinach (1908)—Reinach, T., "Παρθενών," *BCH* 32 (1908) 499-513.

Rémondon (1952)—Rémondon, R., "L'Egypte et la suprême résistance au christianisme (Vᵉ-VIIᵉ siècles)," *Bull. Inst. Fr. d'arch. orient.* 51 (1952) 63-78.

Renardet (1973)—Renardet, E., "Lieux-saints de la cité des Lingons," *Caesarodunum* 8 (1973) 120-127.

Reuterswärd (1958-1960)—Reuterswärd, P., *Studien zur Polychromie der Plastik*, 2 vols., Stockholm 1958-1960.

Rey-Coquais (1967)—Rey-Coquais, J.-P., *Inscriptions grecques et latines de Syrie, VI: Baalbek et Beqa'*, Paris 1967.

Rey-Coquais (1972)—Rey-Coquais, J.-P., "Une inscription du Liban nord," *Mél. de l'Univ. St. Joseph* 47 (1972) 87-105.

Reynaud et al. (1975)—Reynaud, J. F., et al., "Une nouvelle inscription grecque à Lyon," *Journal des Savants* 1975, 47-75.

Riese (1894)—Riese, A., *Carmina in codicibus scripta*² (*Anthologia Latina sive poesis latinae supplementum*, eds. F. Buecheler and A. Riese, I, 1-2), 2 vols., Leipzig 1894.

Robert and Robert (1946-1947)—Robert, J. and L., "Bulletin épigraphique," *REG* 59/60 (1946-1947) 298-372.

Robert and Robert (1958)—Robert, J. and L., "Bulletin épigraphique," *REG* 71 (1958) 169-363.

Robert (1937)—Robert, L., *Etudes anatoliennes. Recherches sur les inscriptions grecques de l'Asie Mineure*, Paris 1937.

Robert (1939)—Robert, L., "Hellenica," *Rev. de philol.* 13 (1939) 97-217.

Robert (1940a)—Robert, L., *Les gladiateurs dans l'Orient grec*, Paris 1940.

Robert (1940b)—Robert, L., *Hellenica* 1, Limoges 1940.

Robert (1943)—Robert, L., "Voyages épigraphiques en Asie Mineure," *Rev. de philol.* 17 (1943) 170-201.

Robert (1945)—Robert, L., *Le sanctuaire de Sinuri près de Mylasa, 1: Les inscriptions grecques*, Paris 1945.

Robert (1946a)—Robert, L., *Hellenica* 2, Paris 1946.

Robert (1946b)—Robert, L., *Hellenica* 3, Paris 1946.

Robert (1948a)—Robert, L., *Hellenica* 5, Paris 1948.

Robert (1948b)—Robert, L., *Hellenica* 6, Paris 1948.

Robert (1949)—Robert, L., *Hellenica* 7, Paris 1949.

Robert (1950)—Robert, L., *Hellenica* 9, Paris 1950.

Robert (1953a)—Robert, L., *Les fouilles de Claros. Conférence donnée à l'université d'Ankara . . . 1953 . . .* , Limoges 1953.

Robert (1953b)—Robert, L., "Le sanctuaire d'Artemis à Amyzon," *CRAI* 1953, 403-415.

Robert (1955)—Robert, L., *Hellenica* 10, Paris 1955.

Robert (1958a)—Robert, L., "Inscriptions grecques de Side en Pamphylie (époque impériale et Bas-Empire)," *Rev. de philol.* 32 (1958) 15-53.

Robert (1958b)—Robert, L., "Reliefs votifs et cultes d'Anatolie," *Anatolia* (=*Anadolu*) 3 (1958) 103-136.

Robert (1960a)—Robert, L., *Hellenica* 11/12, Paris 1960.

Robert (1960b)—Robert, L., "Recherches épigraphiques, VII: Décret de la Confédération lycienne à Corinthe," *REA* 62 (1960) 324-342.

Robert (1964)—Robert, L., in N. Firatli, *Les stèles funéraires de Byzance gréco-romaine avec l'edition et l'index commente des épitaphes* par L. Robert, Paris 1964.

Robert (1965)—Robert, L., *Hellenica* 13, Paris 1965.

Robert (1966)—Robert, L., *Monnaies antiques en Troade*, Geneva 1966.

Robert (1967)—Robert, L., *Monnaies grecques. Types, Légends. Magistrats monétaires et Géographie*, Geneva and Paris 1967.

Robert (1968)—Robert, L., "Trois oracles de la Théosophie et un prophète d'Apollon," *CRAI* 1968, 568-599.

Robert (1969)—Robert, L., *Laodicée du Lycos. Les inscriptions (Laodicée du Lycos. Campagnes 1961-1968: Le nymphée*, by J. DesGagniers et al.), Quebec and Paris 1969, 247-389.

Robert (1971a)—Robert, L., "Un oracle gravé à Oinoanda," *CRAI* 1971, 597-619.

Robert (1971b)—Robert, L., "Les colombes d'Anastase et autres volatiles," *Journal des Savants* 1971, 81-97.

Robert (1973)—Robert, L., "De Cilicie à Messine et à Plymouth avec deux inscriptions grecques errantes," *Journal des Savants* 1973, 161-211.

Robert (1975)—Robert, L., "Une nouvelle inscription grecque de Sardès; Réglement de l'autorité perse relatif à un culte de Zeus," *CRAI* 1975, 306-330.

Robert and Robert (1954)—Robert, L. and J., *La Carie. Histoire et géographie historique avec le receuil des inscriptions antiques, II: Le plateau de Tabai et ses environs*, Paris 1954.

Robinson (1953)—Robinson, D. M., "A magical inscription from Pisidian Antioch," *Hesperia* 22 (1953) 172-174.

Roebuck (1951)—Roebuck, C. A., *The Asklepieion and Lerna . . .* (Corinth: Results of Excavations Conducted by the Am. School of Class. Studies at Athens 14), Princeton 1951.

Rose (1924)—Rose, H. J., *The Roman Questions of Plutarch . . .* , Oxford 1924.

Rostovtzeff (1937)—Rostovtzeff, M., "Report sur les fouilles de Doura-Europos, campagne de 1936-1937," *CRAI* 1937, 195-204.

Roussel (1916)—Roussel, P., *Délos, colonie athénienne*, Paris 1916.

Roussel (1927)—Roussel, P., "Les mystères de Panamara," *BCH* 51 (1927) 123-137.

Roussel (1931)—Roussel, P., "Le miracle de Zeus Panamaros," *BCH* 55 (1931) 70-116.

Roussel and de Visscher (1942-1943)—Roussel, P., and F. de Visscher, "Les inscriptions du temple de Dmeir," *Syria* 23 (1942-1943) 173-200.

Safrai et al. (1974)—Safrai, S., et al., eds., *The Jewish People in the First Century . . .*, I, Philadelphia 1974.

Sagnard (1948)—Sagnard, F., *Clément d'Alexandrie. Extraits de Théodote* (Sources chrétiennes 23), Paris 1948.

Sahin (1978)—Sahin, S., "Zeus Bennios," in *Studien zur Religion und Kultur Kleinasiens. Festschrift für Friedrich Karl Dörner . . .*, Leiden 1978, 2.771-790.

Salač (1956)—Salač, A., "Zwei vorislamische Gottheiten auf einer römischen Inschrift," in *Carnuntina. Ergebnisse der Forschung über die Grenzprovinzen des römischen Reiches. Vorträge beim internationalen Kongress der Altertumsforscher Carnuntum 1955*, ed. E. Swoboda, Graz 1956, 168-170.

Salviat (1963)—Salviat, F., "Dédicace d'un τρύφακτος par les Hermaistes déliens," *BCH* 87 (1963) 252-264.

Scherer (1960)—Scherer, J., *Entretien d'Origène avec Héraclide* (Sources chrétiennes 67), Paris 1960.

Schermann (1909)—Schermann, T., *Griechische Zauberpapyri und das Gemeinde und Dankgebet im II. Klemensbriefe* (Texte und Untersuchungen 34, 2b), Leipzig 1909.

Schleiermacher (1966)—Schleiermacher, W., "Zu den sogenannten Kulttheatern in Gallien," in *Corolla memoriae E. Swoboda dedicata*, Graz and Cologne 1966, 205-213.

Schmidt (1881)—Schmidt, J., "Aus Constantinopel und Kleinasien," *Ath. Mitt.* 6 (1881) 132-153.

Schuchhardt (1886)—Schuchhardt, C., "Kolophon, Notion und Klaros," *Ath. Mitt.* 11 (1886) 398-434.

Schwertheim (1974)—Schwertheim, E., *Die Denkmäler orientalischer Gottheiten im römischen Deutschland mit Ausnahme der ägyptischen Gottheiten*, Leiden 1974.

Schwertheim (1975)—Schwertheim, E., "Ein neues Weihrelief für Men und seine Mutter aus Lydien im Museum von Izmit," *Mitt. des Deutschen Arch. Inst., Istanbul* 25 (1975) 357-365.

Schwertheim (1978)—Schwertheim, E., "Denkmäler zur Meterverehrung in Bithynien und Mysien," in *Studien zur Religion und Kultur Kleinasiens. Festschrift für Friedrich Karl Dörner . . .*, Leiden 1978, 2.791-837.

Schwertheim (1979)—Schwertheim, E., "Mithras. Seine Denkmäler und sein Kult," *Antike Welt* 10 (1979) 2-76.

Scranton (1944)—Scranton, R. L., "Two temples of Commodus at Corinth," *Hesperia* 13 (1944) 315-348.

Scroggs (1980)—Scroggs, R., "The sociological interpretation of the New Testament: the present state of research," *New Testament Studies* 26 (1980) 164-179.

Seston (1956)—Seston, W., "La conférence de Carnuntum et le 'dies imperii' de

Licinius," in *Carnuntina. Ergebnisse der Forschung über die Grenzprovinzen des römischen Reiches. Vorträge beim internationalen Kongress der Altertumsforscher Carnuntum 1955*, ed. E. Swoboda, Graz 1956, 175-186.

Seyrig (1941)—Seyrig, H., "Antiquités syriennes 38: Inscriptions grecques de l'agora de Palmyre," *Syria* 22 (1941) 223-270.

Seyrig (1970)—Seyrig, H., "Antiquités syriennes 89: Les dieux armés et les Arabes en Syrie," *Syria* 47 (1970) 77-112.

Seyrig (1971a)—Seyrig, H., "Antiquités syriennes 93: Bel de Palmyre; 94: Quatre images sculptées du Musée d'Alep," *Syria* 48 (1971) 85-120.

Seyrig (1971b)—Seyrig, H., "Antiquités syriennes 95: Le culte du soleil en Syrie à l'époque romaine," *Syria* 48 (1971) 337-373.

Simon (1972)—Simon, M., "Theos Hypsistos," in *Ex orbe religionum: Studia Geo Widengren oblata*, Leiden 1972, 1.372-385.

M. Smith (1971)—Smith, M., "Prolegomena to a discussion of aretalogies, divine men, the gospels and Jesus," *Journ. Bibl. Lit.* 90 (1971) 174-199.

M. F. Smith (1978)—Smith, M. F., "Fifty-five new fragments of Diogenes of Oenoanda," *Anatolian Studies* 28 (1978) 39-92.

M. F. Smith (1979)—Smith, M. F., "Eight new fragments of Diogenes of Oenoanda," *Anatolian Studies* 29 (1979) 69-89.

Snyder (1940)—Snyder, W. F., "Public anniversaries in the Roman empire . . . ," *Yale Class. Studies* 7 (1940) 223-317.

Sodano (1958)—Sodano, A. R., *Porfirio, Lettera ad Anebo*, Naples 1958.

Sokolowski (1955)—Sokolowski, F., *Lois sacrées de l'Asie Mineure*, Paris 1955.

Sokolowski (1962)—Sokolowski, F., *Lois sacrées des cités grecques. Supplément*, Paris 1962.

Sokolowski (1969)—Sokolowski, F., *Lois sacrées des cités grecques*, Paris 1969.

Speidel (1978)—Speidel, M. P., *The Religion of Iuppiter Dolichenus in the Roman Army*, Leiden 1978.

Sperber (1966)—Sperber, D., "Costs of living in Roman Palestine," *Journal of Econ. and Soc. Hist. of the Orient* 9 (1966) 182-211.

Spinazzola (1953)—Spinazzola, V., *Pompei alla luce degli scavi nuovi di Via dell'Abbondanza*, 2 vols., Rome 1953.

Stähelin (1948)—Stähelin, F., *Die Schweiz im römischer Zeit*,[3] Basel 1948.

Stambaugh (1978)—Stambaugh, J. E., "The functions of Roman temples," *ANRW* II 16, 2 (Berlin 1978) 554-608.

Starcky (1949)—Starcky, J., "Autour d'une dédicace palmyrénienne à Sadrafa et à Du'anat," *Syria* 26 (1949) 43-85.

Stein (1925)—Stein, A., "Zu Lukians Alexandros," in *Strena Buliciana. Commentationes gratulatoriae in honore F. Bulic*, Zagreb 1925, 257-265.

Steinleitner (1913)—Steinleitner, F., *Die Beicht im Zusammenhange mit der sakralen Rechtspflege in der Antike* . . . , Leipzig 1913.

Stocks (1937)—Stocks, H., "Studien zu Lukians De Syria dea," *Berytus* 4 (1937) 1-40.

Storch (1968)—Storch, R. H., "The 'absolutist' theology of victory: its place in the Late Empire," *Classica et mediaevalia* 29 (1968) 197-206.

Strohm (1952)—Strohm, H., "Studien zur Schrift von der Welt," *Mus. Helv.* 9 (1952) 137-175.

Süss (1972)—Süss, L., "Ein gallo-römischer Achtecktempel in Friedberg," *Germania* 50 (1972) 153-174.

Swoboda (1964)—Swoboda, E., *Carnuntum. Seine Geschichte und seine Denkmäler*[4], Graz and Cologne 1964.

Syme (1972)—Syme, R., "Lawyers in government: the case of Ulpian," *Proc. Am. Philos. Soc.* 116 (1972) 406-409.

Szilágyi (1961)—Szilágyi, J., "Beiträge zur Statistik der Sterblichkeit in den westeuropäischen Provinzen des römischen Imperiums," *Acta arch. acad. sci. Hung.* 13 (1961) 125-156.

Tate (1929)—Tate, J., "Cornutus and the poets," *CQ* 23 (1929) 40-45.

Tate (1930)—Tate, J., "Plato and allegorical interpretation," *CQ* 24 (1930) 1-10.

Taus and Berardi (1972)—Taus, G., and P. Berardi, "Iscrizioni latine inedite di Roma nel Cenobio di S. Paolo," *Epigraphica* 34 (1972) 77-88.

Teixidor (1977)—Teixidor, J., *The Pagan God: Popular Religion in the Greco-Roman Near East*, Princeton 1977.

Ternes (1965)—Ternes, C. M., "Les inscriptions antiques du Luxembourg," *Hémecht. Zeitschrift für Luxemburger Geschichte* 17 (1965) 267-481.

Ternes (1973)—Ternes, C. M., "Les sanctuaires des Trévires," *Caesarodunum* 8 (1973) 6-15.

Themanakis (1893)—Themanakis, "Marbres découvertes à Παλιά," *BCH* 17 (1893) 208-209.

I. Tóth (1971)—Tóth, I., "Sacerdotes Iovis Dolicheni," *Studium* 2 (1971) 23-28.

L. Tóth (1974)—Tóth, L., "Eine Doppelheit der Geschichte des Isis- und Sarapiskultes in Pannonien," in *Studia Aegyptiaca: Recueil d'études . . . à V. Wessetzky*, Budapest 1974, 345-360.

S. Tóth (1967)—Tóth, S., "Zur Frage des Ursprungs und des sozialen Hintergrunds des Silvankultes in Dazien," *Acta class. univ. scient. Debrecen.* 3 (1967) 77-84.

Toutain (1892)—Toutain, J., "Le sanctuaire de Saturnus Balcaranensis au Djebel Bou-Kournein (Tunisie)," *MEFR* 12 (1892) 3-124.

Toutain (1907-1920)—Toutain, J., *Les cultes paiens dans l'empire romain, 1: Les provinces latines*, parts 1-3, Paris 1907-1920.

Toynbee (1944)—Toynbee, J.M.C., *Roman Medallions* (Numismatic Studies 5), New York 1944.

Tran Tam Tinh (1964)—Tran Tam Tinh, V., *Essai sur le culte d'Isis à Pompéi*, Paris 1964.

Tran Tam Tinh (1971)—Tran Tam Tinh, V., *Le culte des divinités orientales à Herculanum*, Leiden 1971.

Tran Tam Tinh (1972)—Tran Tam Tinh, V., *Le culte des divinités orientales en Campanie en dehors de Pompéi, de Stabies et d'Herculanum*, Leiden 1972.

Troiani (1974)—Troiani, L., *L'opera storiografica di Filone da Byblos*, Pisa 1974.

Tudor (1969-1976)—Tudor, D., ed., *Corpus monumentorum religionis equitum Danuvinorum*, 2 vols., Leiden 1969-1976.

Turcan (1975)—Turcan, R., *Mithras Platonicus. Recherches sur l'hellénisation philosophique de Mithra*, Leiden 1975.

Turcan (1978)—Turcan, R., "Note sur la liturgie mithriaque," *Rev. de l'hist. des religions* 194 (1978) 147-157.

VanWinden (1971)—VanWinden, J.C.M., *An Early Christian Philosopher. Justin Martyr's Dialogue with Trypho, Chapters One to Nine* . . . , Leiden 1971.

Velkov (1974)—Velkov, V., "Der kult der Diana Plestrensis in Moesia inferior," in *Actes du IXe Congrès international d'études sur les frontières romaines* . . . *1972*, Bucharest 1974, 151-153.

Vermaseren (1956-1960)—Vermaseren, M. J., *Corpus inscriptionum et monumentorum religionis mithriacae*, 2 vols., The Hague 1956-1960.

Vermaseren (1966)—Vermaseren, M. J., *The Legend of Attis in Greek and Roman Art*, Leiden 1966.

Vermaseren (1969)—Vermaseren, M. J., "Paganism's death struggle. Religions in competition with Christianity," *The Crucible of Christianity* . . . , ed. A. Toynbee, London 1969, 235-260.

Vermaseren (1971)—Vermaseren, M. J., *Mithriaca I: The Mithraeum at S. Maria Capua Vetere*, Leiden 1971.

Vermaseren (1977)—Vermaseren, M. J., *Cybele and Attis, the Myth and the Cult*, trans. A.M.H. Lemmers, London 1977.

Vermaseren and van Essen (1965)—Vermaseren, M. J., and C. C. van Essen, *The Excavations in the Mithraeum of the Church of Santa Prisca in Rome*, Leiden 1965.

Veyne (1967)—Veyne, P., "Autour d'un commentaire de Pline le Jeune," *Latomus* 26 (1967) 723-751.

Vidman (1965)—Vidman, L., "Die Isis- und Sarapisverehrung im 3. Jhdt. u. Z.," in *Neue Beiträge zur Geschichte der alten Welt, II: Römisches Reich*, Berlin 1965, 389-400.

Vidman (1966)—Vidman, L., "Träger des Isis- und Sarapiskultes in der römischen Provinzen," *Eirene* 5 (1966) 107-116.

Vidman (1969)—Vidman, L., *Sylloge inscriptionum religionis Isiacae et Sarapiacae*, Berlin 1969.

Vogliano (1933)—Vogliano, A., "La grande iscrizione bacchica del Metropolitan Museum," *AJA* 37 (1933) 215-231.

Vorbeck and Beckel (1973)—Vorbeck, E., and L. Beckel, *Carnuntum. Rom an der Donau*, Salzburg 1973.

Vučković-Todorović (1964-1965)—Vučković-Todorović, D., "Le sanctuaire de Jupiter Dolichenus à Brza Palanka," *Starinar* 15/16 (1964-1965) 173-182.

Waltzing (1895-1900)—Waltzing, J. P., *Etude historique sur les corporations professionnelles chez les Romains* . . . , 4 vols., Louvain 1895-1900.

Wagenvoort (1966)—Wagenvoort, H., "Auguste et Vesta," in *Mélanges d'archéologie, d'épigraphie et d'histoire offerts à J. Carcopino*, Paris 1966, 965-978.

Warmington (1954)—Warmington, B. H., *The North African Provinces from Diocletian to the Vandal Conquest*, Cambridge 1954.

Weber (1911)—Weber, W., *Drei Untersuchungen zur ägyptisch-griechischen Religion* . . . , Heidelberg 1911.

Weinreich (1909)—Weinreich, O., *Antike Heilungswunder. Untersuchungen zum Wunderglauben der Griechen und Römer*, Giessen 1909.

Weinreich (1912)—Weinreich, O., "θεοὶ ἐπήκοοι," *Ath. Mitt.* 37 (1912) 41-68.

Weisgerber (1975)—Weisgerber, G., *Das Pilgerheiligtum des Apollo und der Sirona von Hochschied im Hunsrück*, Frankfurt 1975.
West (1971)—West, S., "A new reading in PSI XI 1211=Aeschylus, Myrmidons," *ZPE* 7 (1971) 93-96.
Wey (1957)—Wey, H., *Die Funktionen der bösen Geister bei den griechischen Apologeten des 2. Jahrhunderts n. Chr.*, Winterthur 1957.
Wheeler and Wheeler (1932)—Wheeler, R. E. M. and T. V., *Report on the Excavation of the . . . Site of Lydney Park, Gloucestershire*, Oxford 1932.
Wiegand (1932)—Wiegand, T., *Zweiter Bericht über die Ausgrabungen in Pergamon 1928-1932: Das Asklepieion*, Berlin 1932.
Wikander (1950)—Wikander, S., "Etudes sur les mystères de Mithras," *Arsbok, Vetenskaps-Societeten i Lund* 1950, 5-46.
Wilcken (1885)—Wilcken, U., "Arsinoitische Tempelrechnungen aus dem J. 215 n. Chr.," *Hermes* 20 (1885) 430-476.
Wilcken (1912)—Wilcken, U., *Grundzüge und Chrestomathie der Papyruskunde*, 2 vols., Leipzig and Berlin 1912.
Wild (1963)—Wild, H., "Les danses sacrées de l'Egypte ancienne," in *Les danses sacrées . . .* (Sources orientales VI), Paris 1963, 33-118.
Wilhelm (1943a)—Wilhelm, A., "Beschluss zu Ehren des Demetrios ὁ μέγας," *JOAI* 35 (1943) 157-163.
Wilhelm (1943b)—Wilhelm, A., "Zwei Inschriften auf Didyma," *JOAI* 35 (1943) 164-169.
Will (1951)—Will, E., "Le sanctuaire syrien de Délos," *Annales arch. de Syrie* 1 (1951) 59-79.
Will (1975)—Will, E., "Le rituel des Adonies," *Syria* 52 (1975) 93-105.
Williams (1978)—Williams, G., *Change and Decline: Roman Literature in the Early Empire*, Berkeley 1978.
Wilson (1973)—Wilson, D. R., "Temples in Britain. A topographical survey," *Caesarodunum* 8 (1973) 24-44.
Windisch (1920)—Windisch, H., "Der Barnabasbrief," in H. Lietzmann, *Die apostolischen Väter*, Tübingen 1920, 299-413.
Winnett (1957)—Winnett, F. V., *Safaitic Inscriptions from Jordan*, Toronto 1957.
Wiseman (1971)—Wiseman, J., "Excavations at Stobi, 1970," *AJA* 75 (1971) 395-411.
Wiseman (1973)—Wiseman, J., "Gods, war and plague in the time of the Antonines," in *Studies in the Antiquities of Stobi*, ed. J. Wiseman, I, Belgrade 1973, 143-183.
Wissowa (1912)—Wissowa, G., *Religion der Römer*[2] (Handbuch der klass. Altertumswiss. 5, 4), Munich 1912.
Witt (1971)—Witt, R. E., *Isis in the Graeco-Roman World*, London 1971.
Witt (1975)—Witt, R. E., "Some thoughts on Isis in relation to Mithras," in *Mithraic Studies. Proceedings of the First International Congress of Mithraic Studies*, ed. J. R. Hinnells, Manchester 1975, 2.479-493.
Witt (1979)—Witt, R. E., "John Dillon: The Middle Platonists . . . ," *Gnomon* 51 (1979) 382-385.
Wolters (1914)—Wolters, P., "'Ακοαί," *Hermes* 49 (1914) 149-151.

Wortmann (1968)—Wortmann, D., "Neue magische Texte," *BJbb* 168 (1968) 57-111.

Wortmann (1969)—Wortmann, D., "Ein Mithrasstein aus Bonn," *BJbb* 169 (1969) 410-423.

Wright (1895)—Wright, J. H., "A votive tablet to Artemis Anaitis and Men Tiamu . . . ," *HSCP* 6 (1895) 55-74.

Wünsch (1909)—Wünsch, R., "Deisidaimoniaka," *Archiv für Religionswiss.* 12 (1909) 1-45.

Yoyotte (1960)—Yoyotte, J., "Les pèlerinages dans l'Egypte ancienne," in *Les pèlerinages* (Sources orientales 3), Paris 1960, 18-74.

Zotovic (1968)—Zotovic, L., "Les conditions historiques du développement des cultes orientaux dans les provinces romaines du territoire de la Yougoslavie," *Starinar* 19 (1968) 59-74.

Zwicker (1934-1936)—Zwicker, J., *Fontes historiae religionis celticae,* 3 parts in one vol. (paged continuously), Berlin 1934, Bonn 1935, 1936.

Index

DATE DUE

OVERDUE FINES

4-26. 6:00p	
9/30 9:00am	
9.30 2:W	
9/30 8pm	
9/30 11pm	
10/2 3pm	
10/6 8pm	
10/7 8pm	
10/8 9a	
11/15 7:00pm	
11/24 5:00pm	
JUN 01 2006	

DEMCO, INC. 38-2971